Fair Value Accounting

Münsteraner Schriften
zur Internationalen Unternehmensrechnung

Herausgegeben von Peter Kajüter

Band 7

PETER LANG

Frankfurt am Main · Berlin · Bern · Bruxelles · New York · Oxford · Wien

Kristian Bachert

Fair Value Accounting

Implications for Users
of Financial Statements

PETER LANG
Internationaler Verlag der Wissenschaften

Bibliographic Information published by the Deutsche Nationalbibliothek
The Deutsche Nationalbibliothek lists this publication in the Deutsche Nationalbibliografie; detailed bibliographic data is available in the internet at http://dnb.d-nb.de.

Zugl.: Münster (Westfalen), Univ., Diss., 2012

D 6
ISSN 1868-7687
ISBN 978-3-631-63311-3

© Peter Lang GmbH
Internationaler Verlag der Wissenschaften
Frankfurt am Main 2012
All rights reserved.

www.peterlang.de

Preface

Fair values are a major feature of financial accounting under IFRS. Unlike many local GAAP standards, IFRS allows preparers of financial statements to measure assets and liabilities at their market values instead of historical cost. The IASB and many accounting practitioners and academics believe that fair values provide users of financial statements with more timely and more relevant information for making investment decisions. The financial crisis in 2008, however, led to a controversial debate about the usefulness of fair value accounting. It was argued that fair values significantly contributed to the crisis. According to this view, troubled banks sold their assets at fire prices which became relevant also for other banks. The fair value concept was thus blamed of having caused contagion in the financial industry. Additionally, it was postulated that fair values provide no relevant information when these measures are determined "mark-to-model" or when assets are held for a long period of time or until maturity.

Many European and U.S. financial institutions were bailed out or completely nationalized. Nevertheless, fair value accounting is still of great relevance. Today, the European Union is exposed to a significant currency and debt crisis. Some member states face low growth prospects and large financial deficits, resulting in sharp declines of their bond values. These decreases were treated differently by the bondholders, such as banks or financial institutions. Whereas some expected the decreases not to be permanent, others used the lower market values as the new carrying values. This resulted in more significant impairments. These different approaches raised the concerns of auditing firms and standard setters.

The relevance and controversy of fair values made Kristian Bachert to examine the implications of fair value accounting for users of financial statements. Even if fair values are a controversial issue for accounting academics and practioners, their empirical implications for users of IFRS financial statements remained largely unexplored. The work of Kristian Bachert is therefore addressing an important research gap. He analyzes the effects of fair value accounting for two classes of tangible assets, investment properties and assets of PPE, which may voluntarily be measured at fair value instead of historical cost. To provide comprehensive evidence on the fair value issue, both the implications for financial analysts and nonprofessional investors are investigated. In an archival study with financial analysts' forecasts for earnings, the author uses a sample of 2,566 firm-year observations from seven European countries. In addition, various sensitivity analyses and robustness checks are applied to increase the confidence placed into the empirical outcomes. In a second study, Kristian Bachert examines the implications of fair value accounting for nonprofessional investors. As a proxy for nonprofessional investors, third-year bachelor and master students studying at the University of Münster were recruited for a laboratory experiment. In doing so, the author contributes well to empirical literature as experimental-based evidence in this field of research is very scarce.

The empirical results highlight important differences between financial analysts and nonprofessional investors, thus providing a possible explanation for the controversy around fair values. Whereas fair value accounting makes it more challenging for financial analysts to produce accurate forecasts, nonprofessional investors are more confident and more likely to invest larger amounts of capital under a fair value regime. The results imply that fair value accounting demands a sophisticated view. It is necessary to distinguish between different groups of investors and the purpose that financial accounting has to fulfill. As such, the thesis provides both proponents and opponents of fair values with good arguments. However, it is not appropriate, on the basis of the empirical results, to consider fair values as either useful or not.

The results of both studies contribute to prior accounting literature and increase empirical evidence with regard to different kinds of measurement. The findings are of great interest for accounting academics, preparers and users of IFRS financial statements, standard setters, auditors and enforcement institutions.

The thesis provides a comprehensive view about the implications of fair value accounting for users of financial statements. The outcomes of the two studies are relevant both for academics and practioners with an interest in accounting research. Considering the contribution and practical relevance of Kristian Bachert's work, I wish that this thesis will enjoy great popularity in accounting theory and practice.

Münster, March 2012   Prof. Dr. Peter Kajüter

Foreword

I conducted this study on fair value accounting during my time as a PhD student at the Chair of International Accounting at the University of Münster. The thesis was accepted as a dissertation by the Münster School of Business and Economics in January 2012.

In this foreword, I wish to express thanks to everyone who supported me during the process of accomplishing this thesis. First, I want to thank my supervisor Prof. Dr. Peter Kajüter who accepted me as a PhD student and provided me with great support during the time at his chair. The numerous and valuable discussions greatly contributed to the success of this study and motivated me to never give up working on this project. I would also like to thank Prof. Dr. Christoph Watrin who reviewed and evaluated my study as a second referee. My sincere thanks are further given to Prof. em. Dr. Heinz Grossekettler for being the third referee at my disputation. Special thanks go to Markus Titze from FactSet Research Systems Inc. for providing me with empirical data on financial analysts' forecasts. Finally, I would like to thank all students of the University of Münster who participated in the laboratory experiment and thus made my study possible.

I would not have come to a successful end with my thesis without the support and encouragement of my dear colleagues and friends at the Chair of International Accounting. I have very pleasant memories of our annual sailing trips, numerous barbecue sessions at the local lake, frequent visits of several party locations, the Wiwi-Cup, and our doctoral seminars in Cologne and Rothenberge. My colleagues made these events always a great joy. Specifically, I would like to thank my colleague Martin Merschdorf. Our cooperation when doing the laboratory experiments was very fruitful and turned research into something entertaining. Additionally, he became my layout mentor when I started formatting the thesis. I also would like to thank Matthias Moeschler for our numerous nightlife trips in Münster. I have good memories of our hilarious times in local hotspots such as "Destille" or "Schwarzes Schaf". Special thanks go further to Thomas Poplat who shared my passion for the famous German soccer team located in southern Germany, Bayern München, which made him unique in the area of North Rhine-Westphalia. Additionally, I would like to thank Christina Voets and Daniel Blaesing for the wonderful time that we had together when we went for skiing in Ischgl, Marcel Baki for the technical support and our "Wilhelm Busch guys" Max Saucke and Moritz Schröder for providing me with helpful comments in accounting. Last but not least, I would like to thank our student research assistants who supported me with literature research. Their everlasting work at the Chair was a great relief when preparing the thesis.

This thesis would not have been possible without my beloved mother Ilona Bachert. Her continual love and support accompanied me during all of my life and provided me with the freedom to make my own decisions. She always showed great enthusiasm and interest for my projects and I deeply appreciate her permanent encouragement. To her I dedicate this thesis.

Münster, March 2012   Kristian Bachert

Contents summary

Contents

Index of figures

Index of tables

Index of formulas

Index of abbreviations

AG	Aktiengesellschaft
AIG	American International Group
BC	Basis for Conclusions
BLU	Best, Linear and Unbiased
BNP	Banque National de Paris
CAPM	Capital Asset Pricing Model
CFA	Chartered Financial Analyst
CFO	Chief Financial Officer
Col.	Column
DCF	Discounted Cash Flow
Diss.	Dissertation
E.g.	Exempli gratia
EC	European Commission
ECB	European Central Bank
ED	Exposure Draft
Ed.	Edition
EMH	Efficient Market Hypothesis
EPS	Earnings per Share
ESMA	European Securities and Markets Authority
Et al.	Et alii
Etc.	Et cetera
EU	European Union
EUR	Euro
EURIBOR	Euro InterBank Offered Rate
F	Framework
f.	Following (Page)
ff.	Following Pages
FAS	Financial Accounting Standard
FASB	Financial Accounting Standards Board
FREP	(German) Financial Reporting Enforcement Panel
FRS	Financial Reporting Standard
FVM	Fair Value Measurement
GAAP	Generally Accepted Accounting Principles

GB	Great Britain
GICS	Global Industry Classification Standard
GDP	Gross Domestic Product
HGB	Handelsgesetzbuch
HOTS	Heard-on-the Street
HTML	Hypertext Markup Language
I.e.	Id est
IAS	International Accounting Standard(s)
IASB	International Accounting Standards Board
IFRS	International Financial Reporting Standard(s)
IKB	Deutsche Industriebank
IP	Investment Property
IPO	Initial Public Offering
JCF	Jacques Chahine Finance (Company)
LIFO	Last in, First out
MBA	Master of Business Administration
MSCI	Morgan Stanley Capital International
MUA	Measurement Uncertainty Analysis
NAIC	National Association of Investors Corporation
No.	Number
OCI	Other Comprehensive Income
OLS	Ordinary Least Squares
P/E	Price/Earnings
P&L	Profit and Loss Statement
PDF	Portable Document Format
PPE	Property, Plant and Equipment
R&D	Research & Development
SD	Standard Deviation
SEC	Securities and Exchange Commission
SFAC	Statement of Financial Accounting Concepts
SFAS	Statement of Financial Accounting Standards

Index of symbols

β	Regression coefficient
€	Euro
$	Dollar
*	Indicator of significance
ε	Confounding factor
H	Hypothesis
i	Item in the company/participants index
m	Item in the group index
k	Number of variables in regression
N	Number of companies/participants
R^2	R squared
%	Percent
t	Item in the year index
x	Independent variable
y	Dependent variable

1 Introduction

1.1 Groundwork

1.1.1 Background and motivation for the study

"Fair is foul, and foul is fair."
William Shakespeare in Macbeth, Act 1.1.11

This statement is probably the most significant line from the famous William Shakespeare play "Macbeth". It suggests that things are not always as they seem on the first sight and that good things (*fair*) can sometimes turn out to be bad (*foul*) and vice versa. Also centuries later, the statement is still valid when it is transferred to the recent developments in financial accounting. According to this, the basic shift from local GAAP accounting systems to the International Financial Reporting Standards (IFRS) in most European countries[1] provided the preparers of financial statements with an option that was not that common before under local GAAP requirements. To date, **fair value accounting** for certain assets and liabilities is viewed as a major feature of IFRS and several standards either require balance sheet items to be measured at fair value or at least provide an option to fair value measurement instead of applying historical cost accounting. Besides the fact that the fair value approach, since its first appearance, has long been subject of academic research, the recent financial crisis has turned the amplified attention on fair value accounting and led to a considerable policy debate involving among others the U.S. congress, the European Commission, and banking and accounting regulators (*Laux/Leuz* (2009), p. 826). Fair values in financial statements were blamed of being rather *foul* than *fair* and thus, as it stands in contrast to the term by itself, not of great advantage for users of financial statements. The critics argued that fair value accounting has significantly contributed to the financial crisis and exacerbated its severity especially for financial institutions in Europe and around the world (*Bieg et al.* (2008), p. 2549ff.; *Huian* (2010), p. 41; *Laux/Leuz* (2010), p. 93). In a first reaction to this, some standard setters, the International Accounting Standards Board (IASB) among others, have introduced temporary provisions that waived some aspects of fair value accounting for financial institutions (*Magnan* (2009), p. 190).[2]

---

1   Since January 2005, all capital market oriented companies within the European Union must prepare their consolidated accounts in accordance with IFRS (*Watrin et al.* (2006), p. 22).

2   In October 2008, after massive pressure from EU officials, the IASB put aside its normal due process and issued a final amendment to its accounting standard without any prior public consultation. The amendment allowed European banks to revise their bonds and marketable loans from a fair value category to a historical cost category and had an immediate effect on the financial statements of European banks. For example, Deutsche Bank, in the third quarter of 2008, avoided more than € 800 million in losses by shifting assets in a more favorable category. This step enabled Deutsche Bank to report a third quarter profit of € 93 million instead of a loss of more than € 700 million. See *Pozen* (2009), p. 90.

Despite the fact that some specialists found indications already in the year 2007,[3] the whole world became aware of an upcoming massive **financial crisis** in September 2008. During that time, the events on the U.S. markets became of international interest and their consequences became noticeable all over Asia and Europe. The rescue of the two mortgage lenders Freddie Mac and Fannie Mae, which were finally placed under government control, the bankruptcy of the investment bank Lehman Brothers, the sale of Merrill Lynch to Bank of America and the $ 85 billion injection for American International Group (AIG) from the American Treasury were extraordinary events that led the Bush administration to the decision of setting up a bail-out plan of $ 700 billion (*Huian* (2009), p. 2). In October 2008 then, the financial crisis crossed the ocean with Fortis bank partially nationalized and acquired by BNP Paribas, Royal Bank of Scotland and Northern Rock saved from bankruptcy as well as German Hypo Real Estate being bailed out before completely nationalized one year later.

Many blamed fair value accounting for being responsible for one of the biggest crises of the financial system in history. The drop in price of many financial assets measured at fair value led banks to write down the carrying values reported in their balance sheets, thus negatively affecting their capitalization ratios. To consequently improve their capitalization ratios and to comply with regulatory requirements, these banks started to sell securities which even magnified the **downdraft in quoted prices** and additional devaluations of financial assets became necessary (*Magnan* (2009), p. 200). Whereas the application of fair values induces favorable higher earnings and a steady increase of carrying values in good times, the situation is completely reversing during bad times when price declines put pressure on company's earnings situations (*Plantin et al.* (2004), p. 153). During the times of the financial crisis, the application of fair value accounting led to a recognition of losses from increased risk of default expectation at an earlier stage compared to historical cost accounting. Thus, critics often argue that the excessive write-downs due to falling market prices set off a downward spiral when the banks were forced to sell their assets at **fire prices**, which in turn can lead to contagion as prices from asset fire sales from one financial institution become relevant also for other banks (*Laux/Leuz* (2010), p. 93). But, on the other hand and assumed that financial institutions would have applied historical cost measures for some mortgages, the issuance of large amounts of overpriced mortgage securities might have continued for several more years and resulting in an even bigger problem at a later stage (*Wallace* (2009), p. 15).

The turmoil in the financial markets turned the fair value debate, which was before mainly of academic importance, into a debate of public interest. Even if this debate was focused on financial institutions and the valuation of financial instruments, there are further applications of fair value accounting. In this sense, IFRS permits, to a certain degree, tangible assets to be measured at fair value instead of historical cost. Reporting entities may thus voluntarily recognize land or building that is categorized as **investment property** or assets of **property, plant and equipment** (PPE) at fair value. Fair value accounting for investment properties follows a kind of full fair value accounting under the *fair value mod-*

---

3   In July 2007, the German IKB bank was among the first European banks that went into trouble due to liquidity problems stemming from the U.S. subprime mortgage market.

el of IAS 40, which is quite similar to the approach for many financial instruments when they are classified into the trading category. On the other hand, the *revaluation model*, valid for assets of PPE, is in line with some kind of piecemeal fair value accounting that has some similarities with securities that are "available-for-sale" where gains or losses from fair value changes are not always part of the P&L.[4] The opportunity to voluntarily measure such tangible assets at fair value provides a unique setting for academic research. However, discussion in this field of application is manifold. **Proponents** argue that market values better reflect current market conditions, provide more timely information in financial statements, increase transparency and encourage prompt corrective actions (*Laux/Leuz* (2009), p. 827). They point to the fact that tangible assets' historical costs often bear only little relation to their current value (*Pozen* (2009), p. 86). A building or property that is owned by a company for decades, for example, is then likely to appear with a carrying value much lower than it would actually be rated in today's market. On the other hand, **opponents** assume that fair values are potentially misleading and do not provide relevant information, especially for assets that are possessed for a long period of time or even until maturity (*Plantin et al.* (2004), p. 148). In addition, it is argued that fair values which are based on a model instead of available market prices do not provide reliable information and that fair values contribute to the pro-cyclicality of the financial system (*Penman* (2007a), p. 39ff.; *Benston* (2008), p. 104).[5]

Despite of the massive criticisms of fair value accounting that came up with the financial crisis, it is unlikely that the accounting practice returns to the use of a strictly traditional historical cost accounting environment. Both the IASB and its U.S.-based counterpart, the FASB, support the use of fair values and are moving away from historical cost towards fair value in their financial reporting standards (*Foster/Shastri* (2010), p. 20). They both intend to increase the use of fair values in accounting practice (*Horton et al.* (2007), p. 15; *Küting/Kaiser* (2010), p. 376). They argue that fair values in financial statements provide more accurate, comprehensive and timely information which should lead to a more-informed valuation in the equity markets and hence lower the risks for investors (*Ball* (2006), p. 11). On the other hand, academic literature points to the advantages of fair value numbers being more **value relevant** than historical cost numbers, which means that they are more associated with companies' share prices (*Magnan/Thornton* (2010), p. 24).

The application of fair values in financial reporting results from the adoption of IFRS, which caused major changes compared to local GAAP requirements in many European countries. Unlike the national accounting systems in Continental Europe, which are often perceived to be tax driven, law based, creditor oriented and not in particular concerned with the determination of income as a measure of performance, the IFRS have a strict orientation on the **investors' financial information needs** (*Bertoni/de Rosa* (2007), p. 2). Therefore, the required adoption of IFRS did not only represent a major change for the preparers of financial statements, but also implied a radical change for users of financial

---

4   See chapter 2.1.3 for detailed information regarding the measurement of investment properties and PPE.

5   Especially the subjectivity associated with model-based fair values raised many concerns in the public: "Fair value is what you want the value to be. Pick a number" (Charles W. Mulford). See *Craig/Weil* (2004).

statements as well. Whereas for example under many local GAAP regulations, the interests of the firm's stakeholders have been subject to the prudence principle, which forced the company to report earnings only after they are realized, the IFRS follow a different approach. The traditional focus on the prudence principle as an essential principle of Continental European accounting systems is thus replaced by a different concept of income, where also unrealized revenues are recognized in the statement of comprehensive income and constitute an integral part of the financial performance of the firm (*Bertoni/de Rosa* (2007), p. 2). The idea that is behind this concept is the assumption that providing useful and timely information by preparing the accounts in accordance with a set of high-quality standards does best serve the needs of investors.

This focus of IFRS on the informational needs of investors needs further specification. While the main attention of investors is not on the current condition of the company that they intend to buy shares of, they are rather interested in the future prospects of the firm. Therefore, an essential area for investors is the effect of the IFRS on their ability to evaluate the future prospects of the company and, in particular, how IFRS affects their ability to **forecast earnings** (*Ball* (2006), p. 12). The implications in that field might be an ambiguous area. On the one hand, better accounting standards make reported earnings less noisy and more accurate, which would make earnings easier to forecast (*Ashbaugh/Pincus* (2001), p. 418). Whereas on the other hand, when reported earnings in high-quality accounting regimes are more informative and more value relevant, they might also feature a higher degree of volatility and are then more difficult to predict (*Plantin et al.* (2004), p. 148; *Ball* (2006), p. 12). This might be an important issue especially in the case of fair value accounting and needs to be considered when the implications of fair value accounting for users of financial statements are investigated.

As stated above, fair value information is included in IFRS financial statements, which have the main purpose to serve the informational needs of current and possible future investors. Even if the standard setters often use the general term *investor* in order to outline the scope of IFRS, it is expected that the users of financial statements differ largely with regard to their profession and skills in evaluating accounting information. As such, financial statements are used by professional investors, such as funds managers or financial advisors, as well as by nonprofessional investors where every individual only holds a few shares of the regarding company. These heterogeneities among the group of investors require a differentiated view in academic research. However, the information from financial statements is not only interpreted by the investors itself. In fact, as **financial analysts** function as information intermediaries on the capital markets who collect and process available information, they are an important group to be addressed by accounting.[6] Furthermore, as the behavior of investors and their reactions to different properties of financial reporting is not observable in the overall market, the work of financial analysts is perfectly qualified to proxy for professional investors' behavior, because their earnings fore-

---

6   Supporting this view, *Schipper* (1991), p. 105, notes that "given their importance as intermediaries who receive and process financial information for investors, it makes sense to view analysts – sophisticated users – as representatives of the group to whom financial reporting is and should be addressed".

casts are publicly available. Therefore, much research has been carried out on financial analysts in accounting and finance literature.[7]

> *"Financial analysts are an important source of information to stock market partici-pants in the valuation of firms." (Das et al. (1998), p. 277)*

As investors are interested in the future prospects of the company when they intend to generate a significant positive return on their investment in the future, financial analysts are of great support when making investment decisions. Analysts provide, among other services, investors with early **forecasts of earnings**. They collect relevant information about the company that they cover, process the information, and issue research reports with earnings forecasts and a recommendation whether to buy, hold or sell the stock. In-vestors can then take advantage of the comprehensive information contained in research reports rather than evaluating large amounts of information by themselves.

Financial analysts do not only function as important information suppliers for investors. When they make earnings forecasts, they enhance the information contained in stock prices and reduce information asymmetries between the average investor and informed market participants, hence reducing the **agency conflicts** between management and inves-tors (*Kothari et al.* (2009), p. 1640). However, the earnings forecasts of analysts also imply direct advantages for the company. Several empirical findings suggest that when analyst forecasts are more accurate, firm values are higher.[8] Managers should therefore have a strong incentive to support analysts with adequate information to evaluate the future pro-spects of the company when this has a direct implication on firm valuation. Thus, these results support the hypothesis that firm value is a function of estimated risk and the better investors are able to evaluate the prospects of a company, the lower is risk and the greater is the firm value (*Lang et al.* (2003), p. 338). As there is a close correlation between firm valuation and the firm's implied cost of capital, firms with lower forecast errors tend to have a lower implied cost of capital or higher expected cash flows in the future (*Gebhardt et al.* (2001), p. 165ff.). In addition, large companies with a better information environ-ment and greater analyst following are more favored on the capital markets while attract-ing a broader investor base and featuring higher market valuations (*Lang et al.* (2004), p. 612).

The fact that many investors use financial analysts' stock recommendations for trading on securities does not imply that they do not use financial statements when making their in-vestment decisions. Despite of other information sources, such as newspapers, television or the company's website, the annual reports are indeed used especially by **nonprofes-sional investors** when they intend to buy shares of the regarding company.[9] Thus, report-ing entities should be aware that their decision to adopt fair values instead of historical cost is also important for nonprofessional investors. However, their reaction to such in-

---

7 See *Ramnath et al.* (2008) for a review of analyst forecasting research. The authors identify a number of approximately 250 papers that have been published since 1992. Also see *Givoly/Lakonishok* (1984) for a review of papers concerning analysts' forecasting literature prior to 1984.

8 See, among others, the papers by *Gebhardt et al.* (2001) and *Lang et al.* (2003).

9 According to a survey conducted with retail investors of Deutsche Post AG, the annual reports are viewed as second most valuable in making investment decisions. See *Ernst et al.* (2009), p. 29.

formation is likely to differ from the reaction of professional investors. Therefore, the behavior of nonprofessional investors when making investment decisions should not be disregarded in a comprehensive analysis of fair value accounting under IFRS.

After the presentation of some introductory remarks which highlight the motivation for the study, the next chapter presents the research question and the expected contribution of the study in more detail.

1.1.2   Research question and contribution

The implications of fair value accounting for users of financial statements represent the starting point as well as the central research question in the course of this study. Because **financial analysts** are important actors on the capital markets, it is in a first step examined whether and how they can benefit from fair values in financial statements. As the overview of empirical literature reveals, evidence on the implications of fair values for financial analysts when making earnings recommendations is foremost limited to certain industries and the implied studies are mainly based on U.S. GAAP.[10] In addition, financial analysts' forecast accuracy has not yet been examined for tangible assets which are measured at fair value under IFRS. However, the study conducted with financial analysts provides evidence on the fair value implications for professional investors. Because financial statements are also of importance for **nonprofessional investors**, it is in a second step necessary to investigate the association of tangible assets measured at fair value with the investment behavior of nonprofessional investors. This is a necessary step due to some significant differences between professional and nonprofessional investors, for example regarding profession, skill or time constraints for reading the annual reports. Additionally, the group of nonprofessional investors as important users of financial statements should not be ignored when a comprehensive picture regarding the implications of fair value accounting is demanded.

While prior studies dealing with the usefulness of fair values for investors did mainly use value relevance approaches for financial assets held by U.S. banks and financial institutions,[11] there is still no recent study that deals with the implications of fair value accounting for IFRS-based financial statements. However, the results of these U.S.-based studies may not easily be transferred to fair value accounting for investment properties and PPE under IFRS as these studies did solely focus on financial instruments held by financial institutions. As such, the design of the present study allows for a broader sample selection in order to gain results that are easily generalizable. As such, the study aims to make a significant contribution to prior literature.

The increasing importance of fair value accounting within financial statements and the lack of empirical evidence for fair value measurement of non-financial assets under IFRS represent the foundation for the central **research question**. The implications of fair value accounting for users of financial statements are examined empirically by conducting two comprehensive studies:

---

10   See for example *Hirst et al.* (2004), *Fan et al.* (2006), and the literature overview in chapter 3.3.

11   See for example *Petroni/Wahlen* (1995), *Nelson* (1996), and *Khurana/Kim* (2003).

- First, it is examined whether fair values provide more relevant and reliable information in a way that financial analysts can produce **more precise and less dispersed forecasts** and are more likely to **cover** these firms.

- Second, it is examined whether the concrete behavior of nonprofessional investors in making **judgments and investment decisions** changes when they are confronted with a fair value environment instead of historical cost.

The research question demands two different **research methods**. The first study employs an **archival-based research** design and uses a large sample of listed firms from several European countries preparing their financial statements under IFRS. Given their importance as information intermediaries, financial analysts are used to proxy for professional investors as their earnings forecasts are publicly available and may easily be compared to realized earnings. Based on the data contained in companies' annual reports, it is possible to distinguish between fair value or historical cost firms and subsequently measure the implications of fair value accounting on three properties of analysts' forecasts, namely forecast accuracy, forecast dispersion, and analyst following. The sample period of four years from 2005-2008 ensures a constant accounting environment for all companies included in the sample as consolidated statements must be prepared in accordance with IFRS from 2005 on. Because two classes of assets are examined, the results should provide evidence on the implications of some kind of **full** fair value and **piecemeal** fair value accounting for tangible assets. The term "full fair value accounting" in this context refers to the fair value model for investment property (IAS 40), whereas "piecemeal fair value accounting" refers to the revaluation model for property, plant and equipment (IAS 16).[12] The study focuses on the fair value approach applied in IAS 40 and IAS 16 for basically **two reasons**. First, as IAS 40 and IAS 16 use different concepts for the treatment of fair value gains and losses when investment property and property, plant and equipment (PPE) are measured at fair value, the different implications of both concepts can be examined. Since it is expected that the fair value model with gains and losses realized directly in the profit or loss of the period has a greater influence on financial statement users, the magnitude of this difference is of large interest in this study. Second, both IAS 40 and IAS 16 allow a direct and clear comparison between fair value and historical cost accounting. Since the two approaches do coexist in both standards and fair values may be applied on a voluntary basis, it is possible to obtain archival data where the implications of the two approaches can be compared. Finally, several sensitivity analyses are conducted to test for the robustness of the results.

An **experimental-based approach** is used to address the second question of investor's judgments and investment decisions as a response to fair value accounting. The experiment is conducted with master and third-year bachelor students which are used to proxy for nonprofessional investors. The participants of the experiment are provided with extracts from annual accounts of hypothetical firms and are told to provide indications with regard to their share price judgment, the confidence that they put into their judgment, and whether or not they are willing to invest in the given firm. The treatment effect involves the manipulation of the accounting method for a certain tangible asset, which is

---

12   For more details see chapter 2.1.3.

either measured at fair value or historical cost. It is expected that the experiment manipulation causes significant differences in participants' judgments and investment behavior. The experimental design also enables making assumptions about the differences of whether fair values are recognized or only disclosed in the notes[13] and whether the fair values are determined mark-to-market or mark-to-model. The research fields which are addressed within this study and the regarding research approaches are summarized in Figure 1-1.

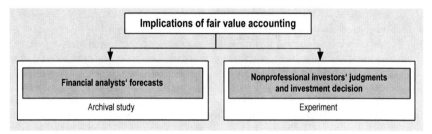

Figure 1-1: Research fields of the study

Taken together, the study aims to investigate the implications of fair value accounting for users of financial statements by examining properties of analysts' earnings forecasts and monitoring nonprofessional investors' judgments and investment decisions when they are provided with fair value information. Thus, the main objective of the study is to provide evidence for implications of fair value accounting. In order to achieve the main objective of the study, **four sub-objectives** are derived based on the main research question:

- In a first step, it is of interest to outline the implications of fair value accounting on the forecasting ability of financial analysts and whether fair values in financial statements are more or less beneficial for users of financial statements in a way to produce precise forecasts.

- In the course of the second sub-objective, the implications of fair value accounting on the behavior of nonprofessional investors are examined. It is expected that fair values significantly affect the way in which nonprofessional investors make judgments and investment decisions on the capital markets. Due to differences in profession, skill and the way in which financial statements are interpreted, the reaction of nonprofessional investors could be significantly different from the reaction of financial analysts.

- The third sub-objective covers differences in the way in which assets can be measured at fair value. It is expected that full fair value accounting (i.e. fair value model for investment properties) has significantly different impacts than piecemeal fair value accounting (i.e. revaluation model for PPE).

---

13 Although, the question of recognition and disclosure is viewed as alternative accounting treatments from a standard-setting perspective (*Ahmed et al.* (2006), p. 568), evidence shows that recognition and disclosure have different impacts. See for example *Belzile et al.* (2006) and *Frederickson et al.* (2006).

- In a last step, it is examined whether investors' perception of fair values is significantly associated with financial statement presentation (recognition vs. disclosure) and the way in which fair values are determined (mark-to-market vs. mark-to-model).

Finally, **implications** for users and preparers of financial statements as well as for standard setters can be derived on the basis of the empirical findings. First of all, the results provide assistance for **investors** when interpreting the research reports of financial analysts. Investors should be aware that fair value accounting can possibly influence the accuracy of analysts' forecasts. In the case that fair values cause a higher bias in earnings forecasts, estimates for companies that rely more on fair value accounting than other firms would have to be interpreted with more caution. Besides analyst reports, it is also of great importance for the single investor to gain knowledge about the general assessment of the investment society with regard to fair values. In the case that fair values would cause a greater willingness to invest, investors could benefit from increasing share prices when investing in fair value firms.

The results may also be of great interest for **corporate managers** and company officials who are responsible of choosing to either apply fair values or not, especially when they receive share-based payments. If managers have the possibility to choose among fair value or historical cost accounting, they are most likely to apply the model that causes earnings forecasts to be more closely to realized earnings when they expect higher valuations due to more accurate analysts' forecasts. The same holds for the outcomes of the study with non-professional investors: When investors are more likely to invest in fair value firms, the share price increases and managers receive greater payout from their stock options.

Standard setters are provided with helpful empirical evidence concerning the influence of fair value accounting on users of financial statements. Whereas previous publications to the role of fair value accounting were to a large extent of conceptual nature, the results of this research may either support or constrain the standard setters' view that fair values provide valuable information in evaluating the future prospects of a company. However, it has to be noted that the research does to a limited extent also provide implications for **auditors** and the **enforcement institutions**. In the case that for example recognized fair values are viewed significantly more important than disclosed fair values, these institutions should put more time and effort on the supervision of recognized fair values rather than disclosed ones.

The next chapter is concerned with the research work's outline. Finally, the methodological grounding of the study is presented in chapter 1.2.

1.1.3 Outline of the study

The study consists of seven chapters. Figure 1-2 presents the outline of the study.

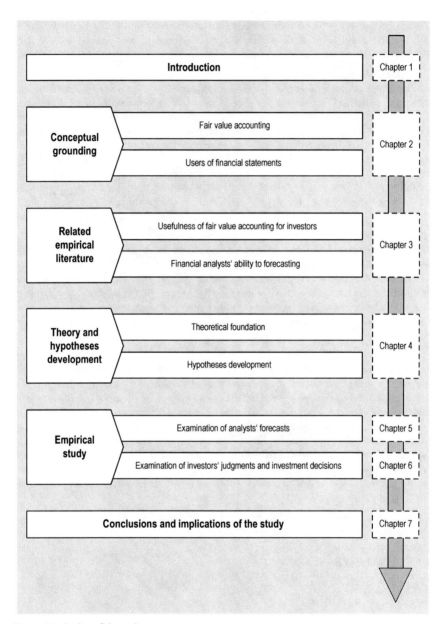

Figure 1-2: Outline of the study

After the motivation and research question is outlined, the methodological grounding of the work is developed and concludes **chapter 1**. The step of developing the methodological grounding is necessary to describe various scientific methods that may be chosen by the researcher in the field of empirical accounting or finance research. This section, among a presentation of different research methods, gives reasons for the application of a certain research method in this study.

Chapter 2 is concerned with the conceptual grounding of the study. In a first step, the chapter describes the fair value approach under IFRS. Because fair value accounting for tangible assets (i.e. investment properties and PPE) provides a unique setting which is used for the empirical analysis in this study, specific regulations for the fair value measurement for these groups of assets are furthermore depicted. The second part of the chapter is concerned with users of financial statements. It deals with financial analysts' information environment and the process of producing a forecast as an in-depth understanding of financial analysts is necessary to interpret and understand the results of the first empirical study.

Chapter 3 reviews related empirical literature and presents the state of research. As the study addresses the implications of fair value accounting for financial analysts and non-professional investors, the chapter presents three streams of related empirical literature, which include the association of fair value accounting with relevance, reliability and the potential to accurately predicting accounting numbers. At the end of the chapter, the findings and limitations of the presented literature are summarized and a research gap for this study is identified.

The theory and hypothesis development is conducted in **chapter 4**. Based on the theoretical foundation of agency theory and the efficient market hypothesis, the hypotheses necessary for the empirical part of the study are then developed in a second step. The sequence of hypotheses development conforms to the research questions raised in the groundwork of the study.

Chapter 5 deals with the first empirical study on properties of analysts' forecasts when confronted with fair value measures for tangible assets. During the study, it is examined whether fair value accounting does significantly influence forecast accuracy, forecast dispersion, and analyst following for a broad sample of companies from the European Union. Before the results can be presented, the section refers to the methodology, the sample, and the dependent and independent variables that are used within this study. Additionally, the results of several sensitivity analyses are reported to demonstrate the strength and reliability of the findings.

The second empirical study does immediately follow and is presented in **chapter 6**. In this chapter, the implications of fair value accounting on investors' judgments and investment decisions are examined experimentally. Similar to the first empirical study, the section presents the methodology for experimental-based research, the participants of the study as well as the dependent and independent variables (treatment effect) of the experiment. It is examined whether the fair value treatment effect, which represents different measures for tangible assets, has a significant influence on participants' judgments, the confidence that participants place into their judgments, and their investment decisions.

Chapter 7 concludes with a summary of the main results of the study. Implications are derived for users and preparers of financial statements as well as for standard setters. The chapter outlines possible limitations of the study and presents directions for further research. Finally, perspectives for the future of fair value accounting are discussed.

The following chapter centers on the research strategy and the conceptualization of this study. Because the study analyzes the behavior of individuals under reality (i.e. the forecasting abilities of financial analysts and the investment behavior of nonprofessional investors) in a way to gain new knowledge, the research methods are based on the academic discipline of the **philosophy of science**. This step is therefore a necessary condition for the research conducted in this study especially with regard to the choice of the research design and the research methods applied.

1.2 Scientific research strategy and conceptualization

1.2.1 Philosophy of science

The *philosophy of science* (or alternatively: *science of science*) is mainly concerned with the question of how science operates and what association it is expected to reveal with the rest of humanity. It does therefore deal with the assumptions, foundations, methods and implications of science that apply to science in general but do also affect particular sciences such as physics, chemistry, or economics. The philosophy of science as a **meta-scientific discipline** is seen as a part of the cognitive science as it views the purpose of science in gaining new knowledge and cognition and marks a necessary starting point for every scientific project (*Poser* (2006), p. 16). Knowledge in this context can be defined as rational cognition that differs from intuition or belief by the condition to be justified. Taken together, science cannot only be seen as the result of the process of systematically gaining cognition and knowledge because science refers also to the process itself and science is also viewed as a system consisting of individuals and objects that is geared to accumulate cognition (*Kornmeier* (2007), p. 4f.). These statements make sufficiently clear that science is not an analytically definable phenomenon but a social occurrence in a certain sociocultural context (*Ulrich/Hill* (1976a), p. 305).

When referring to science in general, one must distinguish between two different classes of sciences: the formal sciences (i.e. philosophy, math) and the empirical sciences such as physics or biology (*Ulrich/Hill* (1976a), p. 305). Whereas, on the one hand, formal sciences only see logical truth and aim at perception, empirical sciences are concerned with the explanation of reality excerpts and the analysis of different action alternatives. It has to be noted that both classes, even though they follow different approaches, are not completely independent from each other as formal sciences serve as supporting sciences which provide the empirical sciences with methodological means and mathematical procedures to solve empirical problems in order to finally enable the generation of cognition (*Bartel* (1990), p. 54). Furthermore, empirical sciences can be categorized into purely theoretical science (natural sciences) and applied science (social science), where the feature which distinguishes between the two is whether newly gained insights help solving practical problems or not (*Ulrich/Hill* (1976a), p. 305).

The social disciplines of economics as well as business economics are both concerned with human activity and do therefore belong to the group of social sciences as a sub-group of humanities (*Bartel* (1990), p. 54). Referring to the sub-objectives presented above, business economics are generally classified as applied sciences, because this discipline intends to give advice on how to modify and improve business reality, taking **cognition** that has been achieved scientifically for granted, as a basis for improvement (*Kornmeier* (2007), p. 22). Dealing with human activity, business economics have to address issues like subjectivity (subjective perception) as well as communication (precise language) which are inherent in every empirical research and have to be solved at all three stages of a typical research process, namely the context of discovery, the context of justification, and the context of application.[14]

From the perspective of the philosophy of science, cognition may in today's research be created by using two different scientific concepts, which are the critical rationalism and the constructivism. A classification of the study into one of the two streams is necessary as the concrete procedure of the study largely depends on the scientific concept applied. Thus, the next chapter presents these two theoretical scientific concepts in more detail. Additionally, several research strategies are presented.

1.2.2   Theoretical scientific concepts and research strategy

The discipline of modern business economics as we know it today is mainly influenced by two different research programs: The critical rationalism on the one hand and the constructivism on the other hand (*Fülbier* (2005), p. 22; *Frank* (2007), col. 2012). The concept of the **critical rationalism** is closely connected with the name *Karl Popper* and combines elements of the classical rationalism and the neo-positivism (*Kornmeier* (2007), p. 39). The basic idea behind this concept is that human knowledge is fallible and that knowledge may be assumed to be right for a certain period of time but can never be seen as true as it can be falsified at any time (*Raffée/Abel* (1979), p. 3). Following the opinion of critical rationalists, scientific theories, and any other claim of knowledge, can and must be rationally criticized and should be subject to tests which may falsify them (*Popper* (1935), p. 40ff.; *Kretschmann* (1990), p. 14f.). The total amount of knowledge available in a society on a specific topic must therefore be treated as temporary, because it can be subject to falsification and a certain verification of knowledge is not possible. The cognition gain based on the theory of critical rationalism can be described as a three step scheme (*Fülbier* (2005), p. 22; *Kornmeier* (2007), p. 42). First, the process starts with an observable problem in reality with a need for explanation. During this step, a kind of explanatory research helps to understand the relationships within that section of reality that needs to be scientifically examined (*Möller/Hüfner* (2002), 351f.). Second, hypotheses are developed to provide proposed solutions to that problem. In a final step, these hypotheses become subject to empirical testing and are possibly falsified and eliminated.

During the process of developing hypotheses to observable problems and hypothesis testing, truth is being approximated. This process may evolve to a so-called "trial-and-error

---

14   For further information to this topic refer to *Ulrich/Hill* (1976a), p. 306f.

process" when hypotheses are permanently set up, tested and rejected. Therefore, the necessary condition during this process is the criterion of **falsification**, which means that hypotheses must be developed in a way that they can be rejected and falsified (*Lingnau* (1995), p. 124). The idea of falsification goes back to *Popper*'s view of science since he argued that the central feature of science is that science aims at falsifiable claims, which he referred to claims that can, at least in principle, be proven false (*Albert* (2000), p. 3; *Schurz* (2006), p. 15).[15] Hypotheses and theories which are developed on the basis of theory are viewed as temporarily valid if they cannot be rejected or falsified after confrontation with reality (*Ulrich/Hill* (1976b), p. 346; *Bartel* (1990), p. 58; *Lingnau* (1995), p. 124). On the other hand, when reality does not conform to the hypothesis, it has to be modified or ultimately rejected.

Although the school of critical rationalism is today dominating the research process in most areas of business economics (*Ulrich/Hill* (1976b), p. 345), the discipline is also influenced by a scientific program of the Erlangen School which is called **constructivism**. While there are several parallels between the concepts of critical rationalism and constructivism (i.e. the fact that human ratio in principle is fallible), the process of creating new knowledge differs fundamentally. Unlike critical rationalisms, supporters of constructivism believe that it is possible to come to methodologically correct decisions based on **deductive argumentation** (*Raffée/Abel* (1979), p. 6). In contrast to empirically tested hypotheses, constructivists create argumentative statements which are a product of deductive reasoning and can be challenged by different perspectives (*Ameln* (2004), p. 3ff.). The basic difference to the concept of critical rationalism, where truth can only approximately be reached through an ongoing process of falsification, is that constructivism refers to a model of pragmatic truth, which involves truth that is defined and decided in a qualified consensus of experts (*Raffée/Abel* (1979), p. 6f.).

Despite of the fact that the critical rationalism is more influencing in today's research in business economics, the constructivism can function as an important part in the process of cognition (*Fülbier* (2005), p. 24). On the one hand, according to the critical rationalism, the researcher may develop hypotheses which can later be tested. One may think here of new accounting standards and its implications on investors after these standards are first applied in companies' balance sheets. The constructivism, on the other hand, may contribute to cognition as it would enable the development of completely new accounting standards or may evaluate how new accounting standards may be applied in accounting practice. The concept of constructivism may therefore complement the thinking of critical rationalism in the regarding field of empirical accounting research (*Fülbier* (2005), p. 24).

The study examining the implications of fair value accounting for users of financial statements is based on the scientific concept of the **critical rationalism.** The study does not provide evidence on this topic based on deductive argumentation as it is the case under the constructivism. Moreover, hypotheses are used to test real existing problems such as the implications of fair value accounting. However, the question of what scientific concept to apply is only the first step in doing research. In a next step, it is necessary to clarify the concrete procedure of the research. Accordingly, every research project should start

---

15   For further information to the criterion of falsifiability in science refer to *Popper* (2002), p. 57ff.

with the decision about the research strategy that should be used. In business economics, the researcher has to choose among three basic research strategies (*Grochla* (1978), p. 71):

- The factual-analytical research strategy,
- the formal-analytical research strategy,
- and the empirical research strategy.

The **factual-analytical** research strategy investigates complex cause-and-effect relationships and develops recommendations for actions that are headmost based on plausibility (*Grochla* (1978), p. 72ff.). It can be described as a theoretical simulation of reality and the outcome of this strategy depends largely on the skills of the researcher. The statements derived cannot be empirically verified and hypothesis testing is not provided within this research strategy. A concrete example for a field of application of the factual-analytical research strategy would be the design of a risk management system.

The **formal-analytical** research strategy develops and examines models, which can be described as a simplified and abstract description of a theoretical problem, to solve them on the basis of theoretical thinking (*Al-Laham* (1997), p. 10). This strategy has no aim to describe reality as a whole but is more intended to deal with a concrete real problem (which differentiates this strategy from the factual-analytical and empirical approach). However, the formal-analytical research strategy is often based on the empirical or factual-analytical research strategy. This strategy would not develop a framework for the organizational design as a whole but would rather focus on concrete problems or situations within that framework.

The **empirical** research strategy is concerned with the search for scientific statements which apply to a majority of cases and which support theory building. It seeks confrontation with reality and systematically tests theoretical statements against reality to either support or confute these statements (*Grochla* (1978), p. 78ff.). This may take the form of real-descriptive statements which enable a pure description of reality or, alternatively, empirical-cognitive statements are used with a stronger pursue of the explanatory and causal direction, whereas the latter focuses more on the relationships between the variables examined.

As stated above, this study focuses on implications of fair value accounting for users of financial statements. It does therefore employ an **empirical research strategy** as it is not intended to give recommendations regarding the use of fair value accounting in IFRS. Moreover, it is the aim of this study to empirically examine the implications of fair value regulations in given accounting standards. While the standards are already available, empirical data may easily be derived. The next chapter presents the scientific position of the research in this study in more detail.

2 Conceptual grounding

2.1 Fair value accounting

This section presents the fair value approach under IFRS and gives an overview of the recent developments which finally resulted in the fair value standard IFRS 13. It reviews the regulations included in the standard and presents the three-step process of fair value determination. The specific regulations for the fair value accounting of investment properties (IAS 40) and PPE (IAS 16) are also presented.

2.1.1 Recent developments of fair value accounting under IFRS

The introduction of IFRS is viewed as a large step to bring about **international convergence** (*Peng/Bewley* (2010), p. 983). In the European Union, the release of Regulation (EC) 1606/2002 required all publicly traded firms to prepare their consolidated financial statements in accordance with IFRS from 2005 onwards (*Aharony et al.* (2010), p. 536). This change induced a big push as it increased the number of enterprises applying the new standards from several hundred to several thousand and ensured the application of IFRS by companies that varied considerably in different aspects such as size, ownership structure, capital structure, political jurisdiction, and financial reporting sophistication (*Schipper* (2005), p. 102). In addition, this decision did not only constitute a large step for the current member states of the EU but also for future member states and for the standard setter as well (*Larson/Street* (2004), p. 90).

Even though the introduction of the new accounting system brought many changes for preparers, auditors and users of financial statements, the feature of the IFRS to measure some assets and liabilities at **fair value** is seen as one major difference to many local GAAP regulations (*Kumarasiri/Fisher* (2011), p. 67). Several standards either require balance sheet items to be measured at fair value or at least provide an option to fair value measurement instead of applying historical cost accounting. In this context, fair values in the financial statement analysis are viewed as more relevant for investors, because a decision of whether to buy, sell or hold an investment is generally based on its fair value and expectations about future changes in its fair value compared to alternative investment opportunities (*McConnell* (2010), p. 211). Although the concept of measuring several items in the balance sheet at fair value is best known, especially after the financial crisis, when dealing with financial instruments, further IFRS standards are today imbued with the fair value idea.[16]

Even if fair value accounting is viewed as one of the most important features of the new accounting system, the concept by itself was not brought into financial reporting through IFRS for the first time. Moreover, there are **local GAAP regulations** that also enable reporting entities to measure assets at fair value. The most prominent example in this context is the United Kingdom (UK), where the British FRS 15 allows a revaluation of tangible fixed assets to market values, which is quite similar to the approach of IAS 16 for

---

16 For an overview of standards that currently feature the fair value conception see chapter 2.1.2.1.

PPE.[17] The same holds in the case of the Netherlands as its accounting practices are much influenced by the UK.[18] Thus, the Dutch local GAAP permits current values for tangible assets such as inventory or depreciable assets.[19] However, this affection towards fair values is not given in other Continental European countries, such as for example France[20] or Germany[21], where the local GAAP regulations are more focused on historical cost accounting. Thus, the adoption of IFRS provides a consistent basis for the fair value accounting not only in a European, but in a worldwide context.

When fair values are applied under IFRS, each standard includes **guidance** to the measurement and determination of fair values (*Fischer* (2009), p. 341). The fair value measurement guidance is dispersed among the IFRS standards with a reference to fair value and many of those standards do not even articulate a clear measurement objective (*IASB* (2010), p. 5). Furthermore, the IASB views the current guidance as incomplete, as it provides neither a clear measurement objective nor a robust measurement framework (*IASB* (2009), p. 5). This results in some IFRS standards containing lots of guidance whereas others only provide limited guidance to the accountant. In addition, the guidance which is provided is not always consistent and the IASB believes that inconsistencies in that guidance have contributed both to the complexity of financial reporting and to the diversity in practice (*IASB* (2010), p. 5).

To address the issues just mentioned, the IASB initiated the project "Fair Value Measurement". After the Exposure Draft (ED FVM) was published in May 2009, the IASB issued the new standard **IFRS 13 Fair Value Measurement** two years later in May 2011. However, the project was firstly initiated with the release of a discussion paper at the end of 2006. This discussion paper conformed almost completely to the SFAS 157 issued by the FASB which provides guidance on fair value measurement under U.S. GAAP (*Fischer* (2010), p. 82). Based on the comment letters that the IASB received in response to the discussion paper, the standard setter then developed ED FVM with an additional comment phase (*Berndt/Eberli* (2009), p. 897). In addition and as a reaction to the fair value determination in the course of the advent of the financial crisis, the IASB published the Exposure Draft "Measurement Uncertainty Analysis Disclosure for Fair Value Measurements" (ED MUA) as an "add-on" to the ED FVM. As a final step, the IASB and the FASB jointly issued common fair value measurement and disclosure requirements in a

---

17   For further information regarding the revaluation model of IAS 16 refer to chapter 2.1.3.2.2.

18   Even if the Netherlands is considered a code law country, accounting is oriented more in the direction of fair presentation than protection of creditors. In addition, financial reporting and tax accounting are two completely separate activities. See *Choi/Meek* (2005), p. 85.

19   Although it is possible in Dutch local GAAP to apply fair value accounting, surveys suggest that historical cost by far dominates fair values in accounting practice (*Nobes/Parker* (2004), p. 211). There are even companies that switched from current cost accounting to historical cost accounting for the sake of international comparability. See *Brink* (1992).

20   Market values were the basis for recognition in France during the 19th century. However, this conception was replaced by historical costs with the appearance of tax regulations in the 20th century. See *Richard* (2004), p. 102.

21   While an earlier version of the German "Handelsgesetzbuch" (HGB) contained a requirement that assets should be recognized with their market values, creditor protection concerns later led to an abandonment of fair value accounting. See *Blaufus* (2005), p. 87.

single standard, resulting in IFRS 13. It must be applied for fiscal years beginning on or after January 1st, 2013.

The standard defines fair value, provides guidance on how to measure fair value, and specifies the disclosure requirements relating to fair value measurements (*Spector* (2009), p. 52f.). It has the purpose to increase the consistency of guidance within IFRS (*Berndt/Eberli* (2009), p. 896). It offers a single source of fair value measurement guidance which clarifies the **definition** of fair value and provides a **framework** for determining fair value (*IASB* (2010), p. 5). With the issuance of IFRS 13, the fair value measurement and disclosure requirements under IFRS and U.S. GAAP are almost identical and bring about further convergence between IFRS and U.S. GAAP. However, the regulations of the standard do only apply when existing IFRS require assets or liabilities to be measured at fair value (*Spector* (2009), p. 52f.). This means that IFRS 13 does not increase the imbuement of IFRS standards with fair values or defines which positions need to be measured at fair value (*Berndt/Eberli* (2009), p. 896f.).

After recent developments of fair value accounting have been described, the fair value approach under IFRS is presented in more detail in the next chapter.

2.1.2 Fair value approach under IFRS

2.1.2.1 Definition of fair value according to IFRS

The IASB defines fair value as a basis for the fair value measurement framework. The following definition is included in IFRS 13.9:

> *"This IFRS defines fair value as the price that would be received to sell an asset or paid to transfer a liability in an orderly transaction between market participants at the measurement date."*

The definition changes the former fair value term.[22] The IASB believes that the new definition fixes some of the remedies of the old version which were for example seen in a missing specification whether an entity is buying or selling an asset or the missing information that an exchange or a settlement takes place at the measurement date (*IASB* (2010), p. 6). The guidance included in the IFRS 13 refers to the fair value measurement for a particular asset or liability (IFRS 13.11). As the fair value for an asset or liability should be determined by using the assumptions which market participants would use in pricing the item, the valuation has not to be performed stereotypically but on the basis of the regarding assets or liabilities instead (IFRS 13.12). Therefore, an assessment is needed with regard to which **characteristics** are relevant for the valuation (*Fischer* (2009), p. 341).

---

22 Before the issuance of IFRS 13, the term fair value was not explicitly defined in the framework. Its definition could be found in the IFRS Glossary or in single IFRS, such as for example IAS 40.5 or IAS 16.6. According to this, the fair value was defined as "*the amount for which an asset could be exchanged, or a liability settled, between knowledgeable, willing parties in an arm's length transaction.*"

The IASB furthermore requires the assumption that the asset or liability is exchanged in an **orderly transaction** between market participants. It is assumed that the resulting market price constitutes the basis for valuation (IFRS 13.15). Although the principal or most advantageous markets (i.e. the markets which anticipate the highest sales price in the case of an asset valuation) have to be chosen (*Große* (2011), p. 288), there is the constraint that the entity should also be able to act on this market as a market participant (IFRS 13.19-20). The market participants, between whom the hypothetical transaction is concluded, should from the IASB's view both act in their best economic interest (IFRS 13.22).

The main task in fair value accounting is the determination of the transaction price between market participants which represents the fair value of an asset or liability. Concerning the determination of the transaction price, the standard distinguishes between the following (*Große* (2011), p. 288):

- Non-financial assets,
- liabilities and an entity's own equity instruments, and
- financial assets and financial liabilities with offsetting positions in market risks or counterparty credit risk.

Whereas the valuation premise for **non-financial assets** is their highest and best use from the perspective of the acquiring market participant (IFRS 13.27-29), this principle does not apply to financial assets or liabilities.[23] The valuation concept of the highest and best use is developed to value many non-financial assets, such as real estate (IFRS 13 BC 68). The highest and best use of an asset should be physically possible, legally permissible and financially feasible, and can be twofold (IFRS 13.28-31): First, the valuation premise assumes that an asset can be used in combination with other assets or with other assets and liabilities. Second, the asset may provide value solely on a stand-alone basis and independently from other assets or liabilities. In the case of a price determination for **liabilities and an entity's own equity instruments**, the IASB assumes that the item is transferred to a market participant at the measurement date (IFRS 13.34). The standard requires that the entity maximizes the amount of observable inputs for the fair value measurement and suggests the usage of observable market prices for such items held as assets by other parties when there is no observable market available for the pricing (IFRS 13.35-36). Finally, the price determination for **financial assets and financial liabilities with offsetting positions in market risks or counterparty credit risks** constitutes an exception for measuring fair value. The standard permits this exception to the requirements in IFRS 13 when an entity manages its financial assets and financial liabilities on the basis of its net exposure to market risks or to the credit risk of a particular counterparty (IFRS 13.49). The exception permits an entity to measure the fair value of a group of fi-

---

23 As a reason for this difference, the IASB states in IFRS 13 BC 63 that "financial assets do not have alternative uses because a financial asset has specific contractual terms and can have different use only if the characteristics of the financial asset (i.e. the contractual terms) are changed."

nancial assets or financial liabilities on the basis of the price that would be received to sell a net long position in an orderly transaction between market participants (IFRS 13.48).[24]

The standard has broad implications for other IAS or IFRS when these standards allow or mandate fair value measures for assets or liabilities. Currently, the fair value is used in the following standards:

- IAS 16.5 (Property, Plant and Equipment),
- IAS 17.3 (Leases),
- IAS 18.7 (Revenue),
- IAS 19.7 (Employee Benefits),
- IAS 20.3 (Accounting for Government Grants and Disclosure of Government As-sistance),
- IAS 21.7 (The Effects of Changes in Foreign Exchange Rates),
- IAS 33.9 (Earnings per Share),
- IAS 38.7 (Intangible Assets),
- IAS 39.9 (Financial Instruments: Recognition and Measurement),
- IAS 40.5 (Investment Property),
- IAS 41.8 (Agriculture),
- IFRS 2.4 (Share-based Payment),
- IFRS 3.2 (Business Combinations),
- IFRS 5.1 (Non-current Assets Held for Sale and Discontinued Operations),
- IFRS 7.8 (Financial Instruments: Disclosures),
- IFRS 9.-3.2.7 (Financial Instruments),[25] and
- IFRS 13.1 (Fair Value Measurement).

This listing of several standards with an appearance of the fair value term highlights the importance of this value under IFRS. To get further insights into the properties of fair values, it is in a next step necessary to examine alternative fair value constructs.

2.1.2.2 Alternative fair value constructs

It is no problem to determine the fair value of an asset or a liability in a world with perfect and competitive markets. When there are buyers and sellers available for an asset or liabil-ity, an **orderly transaction** might always be assumed and a fair value for these items can

---

24 This exception accounts for the fact that entities do typically not manage their exposure to market risks and credit risk by selling a financial asset or transferring a financial liability. They do instead manage their risk exposure by entering into a transaction for another financial instrument, resulting in an offsetting position in the same risk. See IFRS 13 BC 117.

25 IFRS 9 replaces IAS 39. It must be applied for fiscal years beginning on or after January 2013.

be estimated reliably. However, problems arise when an orderly transaction cannot be assumed due to a non-availability of buyers or sellers for an item. To address this concern, the accounting literature basically discusses three different fair value constructs:[26]

- The **entry value** which represents an assets acquisition price or the face value of a liability,

- the **exit value** which is the price for which an asset could be sold or liquidated or a liability could be settled, or

- the **value in use** which is the incremental firm value that is attributable to an asset or the incremental amount of a loan attributable to a liability.

The **entry value** represents the value of an asset which is measured based on the cost of replacing the asset with a similar new or used asset or with an asset having the same productive capacity or service potential (*Shim/Larkin* (1998), p. 38). The determination of the entry value is performed on the basis of prices derived from the supply markets with respect of the principle of individual evaluation and should be consistent with the going concern tenet of the IASB (*Dohrn* (2004), p. 118). Applying entry values in financial reporting comes close to the theory of replacement values which is proposed by *Edwards/Bell* (1995). The authors based income concepts on market values and assumed that the replacement value of a firm does not materially differ from its market value or capitalized value when no one would be willing to pay more for a firm than it is worth according to its capitalized value (*Flesher/Marquette* (1998), p. 239). However, the fact that economies of scope or intangibles, such as unique skills of employees, cannot be considered under this theory makes it impossible to reproduce the capitalized value of a firm through a balance sheet that has been prepared by using replacement values (*Moxter* (1982), p. 107f.).

Applying the **exit value** of an asset or a liability is also possible when determining the fair value. The exit value is based on the amount that would be received in a sale of an item between a willing buyer and a willing seller in the open market in an orderly disposal (*Shim/Larkin* (1998), p. 38). Its determination is therefore sales market oriented and is performed, similar to the entry value, by considering the principle of individual evaluation (*Zülch* (2003), p. 9). As the exit value does not focus on the liquidation value of the firm, the going concern tenet must also be considered when applying the exit value. What exit and entry value have in common is that they both rely only on market information where firm-specific or potentially private information is not considered (*Dohrn* (2004), p. 119). Furthermore, both values are derived from a market at the reporting date.

The **value in use** is based on the assumption that the value of an asset is related to the net cash flow attributable to the use of that asset and measured by using for example DCF models (*Shim/Larkin* (1998), p. 38). In the course of the determination of the value in use, the focus is on the company-specific utility of an asset or liability which means that private company information is considered (*Dohrn* (2004), p. 119). The fact that the val-

---

26 See for example *Barth/Landsman* (1995), p. 99, *Schroeder/Clark* (1998), p. 91, *Shim/Larkin* (1998), p. 38, *Barth* (2000), p. 22, or *Barlev/Haddad* (2003), p. 405f.

ue in use is based on company-specific and private information is also one major difference to entry and exit value.

Although the three values may differ in principle, the most important differences are those between value in use and the remaining two because only value in use always reflects differential management skill including exploiting synergies among assets (*Barth/Landsman* (1995), p. 101). Therefore, the differences between value in use and entry and exit values can be seen as measures of management skill. The choice of one of the three constructs does largely depend on the valuation objective and on the estimation error. Whereas the value in use is the most suitable concept where the objective is the firm's total value, entry or exit values may provide more reliable information when estimation error of the value in use is high (*Barlev/Haddad* (2003), p. 406). However, fair value accounting, which is based on the value in use, will likely be the most difficult to implement because estimating the value in use involves incorporating firm-specific and potentially private information (*Barth/Landsman* (1995), p. 101).

While there are several interpretations of fair value in accounting literature, the IASB requires an orientation on **exit values**. As IFRS 13.9 points to the perspective of a hypothetical seller of an asset or transferor of a liability on the sales market, the fair value is then derived based on the market processes of supply and demand. After presenting the alternative fair value constructs, the different measures of fair value will be illustrated in the following section.

2.1.2.3 Measures of fair value

The definition of fair value in IFRS 13 refers to the transaction price, which is the price that would be received in an orderly transaction between market participants at a certain measurement date. However, there are several measures of fair value that may represent the transaction price and thus have the potential to determine the carrying values of assets or liabilities. The following measures of fair value can be distinguished:

- The **market value**,
- the **realizable value**,
- the **current cost** or **replacement cost**, or
- the **present value**.

The **market value** is the amount that is necessary for the purchase or disposal of an asset or the settlement of a liability on an active market.[27] Market values are based on the assumption that such measures best reflect the consensus expectations of market participants with regard to the economic perspectives of an asset or a liability (*Dohrn* (2004), p. 122). More precisely, they are viewed as the present-based consensus among market participants with regard to future cash flows or risk and rewards which are connected with

---

27   According to IAS 36.6 or IAS 38.8, an active market has the following characteristics:
- "The items traded within the market are homogeneous,
- willing buyers and sellers can normally be found at any time, and
- prices are available to the public."

the ownership of assets or liabilities (*Jones/Stanwick* (1999), p. 104). Concerning the alternative fair value constructs, the market value may be determined as either an exit or entry price, whereas the exit price then represents a realizable value on the sales market and the entry price represents current or replacement costs (*Cairns* (2003), p. 96). It should be noted that transaction costs must not be accounted for when determining the market value (*Mujkanovic* (2002), p. 117).

The term **realizable value** refers to the amount of cash or cash equivalents which is due in the course of the disposal of an asset to a potential acquirer (*Cairns* (2003), p. 96). It is therefore viewed as the realizable amount for an asset if it would be disposed at the balance sheet date in the ordinary course of business (*Mujkanovic* (2002), p. 119). The realizable value has to be determined under the going concern premise and, similar to the market value, transaction costs must also not be accounted for (*Cairns* (2003), p. 96).

The terms **current cost** and **replacement cost** are defined as the amount that an entity would have to pay in form of cash or cash equivalents to replace an asset at the present time (*Dohrn* (2004), p. 123). As this definition holds in the case of assets, current or replacement cost for of liabilities are viewed as the undiscounted amount of cash or cash equivalents which is necessary to settle the liability (*Cairns* (2003), p. 98). The differing definitions of this fair value construct for assets and liabilities constitute a major difference as the current or replacement cost for assets are determined on the supply market, whereas the amount for liabilities is identified on the sales market (*Mujkanovic* (2002), p. 122).

As stated in the IFRS framework, the **present value** of an asset refers to the present discounted value of the future net cash inflows that the item is expected to generate in the normal course of business (F 100 (d)). On the other hand, the present value of a liability is defined as the present discounted value of the future net cash outflows that are expected to be required to settle the liability in the normal course of business. Although the present value is in accordance with IAS 36.5 viewed as a value in use with the focus on future cash flows, this design is widely rejected for the definition of fair value (*Dohrn* (2004), p. 124). However, discounted cash flows are indeed used to the determination of a fair value which is then viewed as the near market value (*Mujkanovic* (2002), p. 124).

When it is referred to the definition in IFRS 13.9, it becomes clear that the fair value is based on market values which have the ability to capture the consensus view of all market participants about an asset's or liability's economic characteristics, such as assumptions about cash flows, profit margins, and risk, and should therefore result in a better portrayal of economic reality (*Jones/Stanwick* (1999), p. 104). Whereas fair values should provide investors with more useful information, this argument only holds for subsequent measurement of assets or liabilities as historical cost and fair value are equal at initial measurement. Fair values provide more useful information in a way that for example management skill is also incorporated in the fair value when changes of the market values of investments are included in the balance sheet (*Barth/Landsman* (1995), p. 100).

2.1.2.4 Determination of fair value

Besides an examination of the several fair value constructs and the definition of fair value in IFRS, the way of how to practically determine the fair value of assets and liabilities is most important. IFRS 13 basically differentiates between three approaches to determine the fair value. Whereas the market approach (mark-to-market) uses prices and other relevant information generated by market transactions, the income approach and the cost approach (mark-to-model) reflect conversions of future amounts or are based on current replacement cost (IFRS 13.62). The entity should apply the valuation technique for which more sufficient data is available to measure the fair value (IFRS 13.67). The new standard adopts the **three-level hierarchy** of input factors embodied in SFAS 157 which are used for the valuation techniques and as inputs to the fair value measurement process (*Spector* (2009), p. 52f.). The fair value hierarchy gives the highest priority to quoted prices in active markets and the lowest priority to unobservable inputs (IFRS 13.72). The way in which fair value is determined is highly dependent on data quality and data availability as the three level hierarchy basically distinguishes between mark-to-market and mark-to-model valuation, where the mark-to-market valuation includes the first two levels of the approach (*Zülch* (2003), p. 184f.). The three input levels are as follows (*Große* (2011), p. 291):

- **Level 1 inputs** are quoted prices (unadjusted) in active markets for identical assets or liabilities that the entity can access at the measurement date (IFRS 13.76). The IASB believes that Level 1 inputs will be available for many financial assets and financial liabilities (IFRS 13.78).

- **Level 2 inputs** are inputs other than quoted prices included within Level 1 that are observable for the asset or liability, either directly (prices) or indirectly (derived from prices) (IFRS 13.81). These include for example quoted prices for similar assets. If the asset or liability has a specified (contractual) term, a Level 2 input must be observable for substantially the full term of the asset or liability (IFRS 13.82).

- **Level 3 inputs** are inputs for the asset or liability that are not based on observable market data (unobservable inputs) (IFRS 13.86). The unobservable inputs must reflect the assumptions (including assumptions about risk) that market participants would use when pricing the asset or liability (IFRS 13.87).

When the inputs used to measure the fair value of an asset or a liability fall into different levels of the hierarchy, the IASB proposes the fair value measurement to be categorized at the lowest level input which is significant to the fair value measurement (IFRS 13.75). The fair value hierarchy gives the highest priority to quoted prices (which are unadjusted) in active markets for identical assets or liabilities (Level 1 inputs) and the lowest priority to Level 3 inputs which are unobservable (*Spector* (2009), p. 52f.). The availability of market data does therefore determine which valuation method has to be applied (*Lüdenbach/Freiberg* (2006), p. 440). Since Level 1 inputs are quoted prices in an active market which makes it not necessary to make adjustments to these prices, Level 1 inputs are viewed as fair values itself, which means fair values in a pure form (*Fischer* (2009), p. 342). The objectivity of the fair values determined decreases significantly when Level 2 or Level 3 inputs are applied. Figure 2-1 presents an overview about the procedure of fair value determination including the differing input levels for valuation.

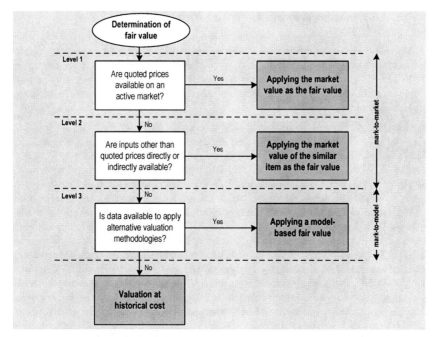

Figure 2-1: Determination of fair value
(Following *Baetge/Zülch* (2001), p. 547; *Zülch* (2003), p. 187; *Dohrn* (2004), p. 131)

In the case of an inability to determine a reliable fair value on any of the levels just presented, the asset or liability has to be measured at historical cost. It has to be noted here that, except for level one inputs, the determination of fair values offers the entity a considerable amount of managerial discretion (*Dohrn* (2004), p. 130). However, the new three-level hierarchy can be viewed more as a **further specification** for fair value determination rather than a change to the previous approach (*Castedello* (2009), p. 917). The market approaches are also rated as being prior to the other approaches in the regulations that are currently valid. Concerning tangible items such as investment property or PPE, the input factors necessary for fair value determination, such as cash flows, will cause as before a classification as Level 3 inputs. Despite the fact that the new standard clarifies the general principle that observable data is superior to unobservable data, the approach by itself remains largely unchanged (*Löw et al.* (2007), p. 733; *Zülch/Gebhardt* (2007), p. 150).

Taken together, it can be stated that the fair value should primarily be derived from an active market with supply and demand dictating the prices for assets and liabilities. In the case of no existing active markets for the regarding item (or similar items in nature), the accountant has to rely on the mark-to-model approach with a relatively high degree of subjectivity when determining the fair value. Finally, valuation can be performed by applying historical cost.

2.1.2.5   Disclosure requirements for level 3 fair value measures

The disclosure requirements for fair value measures are defined in IFRS 13.91-99. They should enable the users of financial statements to assess the valuation approaches (mark-to-market or mark-to-model) and the input factors used for determining the fair values (IFRS 13.91). Whereas these disclosures are required in any case when fair values are determined, additional disclosures are necessary when Level 3 fair values are included in the financial statements.

In a response to the comments received on the questions set out in the ED FVM issued in May 2009, the IASB published further enhancements to the disclosure proposal on Level 3 fair value measurements. As mentioned in chapter 2.1.1, the ED MUA, as an add-on to the ED FVM, was published in June 2010 and comments have been requested to be received by September 2010. For fair value measurements using significant unobservable inputs, the effect of the measurements on profit or loss or other comprehensive income for the period should be disclosed (*Spector* (2009), p. 53). By requiring additional disclosures for Level 3 inputs, the IASB addresses concerns that model-based fair values (and its implications) cannot be traced back by investors. The suggested disclosure requirements for Level 3 inputs are also included in the final standard IFRS 13. This standard requires a so-called **measurement uncertainty analysis** when Level 3 inputs are used for determining fair values in the form of a sensitivity analysis. According to this, it is clarified that the analysis should focus on unobservable inputs when these inputs are used for fair value measurement. The standard states that if changing unobservable inputs to a different amount that could have reasonably been used in the circumstances would have resulted in a significantly higher or lower fair value, this effect must be disclosed by using those different amounts (IFRS 13.93 (h)). In addition, it must be disclosed how the effect has been calculated. Whereas remote scenarios do not have to be taken into account, correlations have to be considered if such a correlation is relevant when estimating the effect on the fair value measurement of using those different amounts.

2.1.2.6   Relevance and reliability of fair values

Although the determination of fair value is in some cases based on market values, it is obvious that there is no active market for a broad number of assets or liabilities such as certain derivatives or intangibles where a market value cannot be determined reliably (*Küting/Kaiser* (2010), p. 377). But it is argued that the existence of a fully competitive market is a necessary condition to derive a reliable market value which can be the basis for the fair value (*Schildbach* (1998), p. 581; 587). As it is expected that the ideal form of a fully competitive market is not available for most assets and liabilities, the fair values need then to be determined based on level three inputs which may lack reliability (*Küting/Kaiser* (2010), p. 383). However, it has to be noted that there is always a relevance and reliability **trade-off** of information contained in financial statements (*Lüßmann* (2004), p. 67).[28] For example, historical cost are viewed as being reliable but less relevant,

---

28   The IASB is aware of this conflict between relevance and reliability, especially with regard to fair values. To overcome potential conflicts, the IASB substitutes the term "reliability" through "faithful presentation" in the conceptual framework of the IFRS. See *Whittington* (2008), p. 146.

fair values carry a higher degree of relevance but are to some extent less reliable. On the one hand, a market price that is derived from an active market is easy to determine and also meets the principles of reliability, verifiability, and objectivity (*Mirza et al.* (2006), p. 308). Whereas on the other hand, the reliability of a fair value for assets or liabilities, which cannot be derived from an active market, is not clear as the verifiability of such values is questionable (*Böcking/Benecke* (2000), p. 193, 200f.).

Besides the problem of the non-existence of an active market for many intangibles, a value for these kind of assets can reasonably be determined for example in the course of a company takeover where assets and liabilities must be valued in a way that both the buyer and the seller of the entity can agree into the deal. This approach does not materially differ from the determination of fair value and it is argued that especially for the case of intangibles, which have been generated internally, a fair value is more easily to determine than historical cost (*Lüßmann* (2004), p. 67). In addition, it is stated that for financial instruments, which are still in the center of the fair value discussion, reliable valuation models do indeed exist nowadays.[29] Furthermore, the accounting literature has examined and confirmed a sufficient degree of objectivity and verifiability of fair values in recent years.[30]

Even if it constitutes a big issue, the uncertainty in the course of determination of fair values is not the basic problem as the increased utilization of market values in financial reporting highlights an upcoming paradigm change in accounting: Whereas the focus of former local GAAP regulations, especially from Continental Europe, was on reliability of the data, the IFRS view **information relevance** at the cost of reliability most important (*Naumann* (2006), p. 75). The fact that the IASB favors the term "fair value" instead of "market value" is a further indication for the standard setter's intention to transfer the fair value idea to non-marketable items instead of assuming the existence of fully competitive markets for all assets and liabilities (*Lüßmann* (2004), p. 68). From this perspective, the standard setter accepted a lack of reliability and assessed an increased portion of relevance in IFRS as more useful for the investors and users of financial statements. It is of importance that investors should be aware of this difference to former local GAAP regulations and it is recommended that they always keep in mind the relevance and reliability conflict not solely, but especially in the case of fair value accounting.[31]

2.1.2.7 Summary and critical analysis

The fair value is of great importance under IFRS with the term included in several standards. Compared to local GAAP requirements, the fair value approach under IFRS requires a major change both for the management and for the relationship that the company maintains with its brokers, the analysts following the company and other advisors (*Scott* (2005), p. 4). Guidance to fair value measurement is included in the new standard IFRS 13 Fair Value Measurement. It clarifies the regulations to fair value measurement

---

29 In addition to the discounted cash flow model which is proposed by the IASB, the Black-Scholes model is widely used for the pricing of European-style options. See *Black/Scholes* (1973).

30 To see a list of literature refer to *Lüßmann* (2004), p. 68.

31 The question of how investors can cope with fair values in financial reporting is the central research question of this study and will be examined empirically in the further chapters.

which were before piecemeal and distributed over several IFRS standards. The process of fair value measurement is clearly exit price oriented (*Fischer* (2009), p. 342). Although the standard does not explicitly specify methods for fair value determination, it includes a design for a hierarchy of input factors with a priority for observable rather than unobservable market data. The **guidance** to valuation is complemented by extensive disclosure requirements, especially when Level 3 inputs are applied (*Fischer* (2010), p. 84). The requirement to disclose additional sensitivity analyses can be seen not solely as a response to comment letters but also to address the concerns which have been raised during the financial crisis when active markets were in short supply and an increased portion of fair value determination was model-based. As the FASB recently initiated a similar project and issued a U.S. GAAP standard of similar wording, both standards are a further step to bring about convergence between IFRS and U.S. GAAP and, as an advantage for investors, make financial statements more comparable (*Castedello* (2009), p. 914; *Große* (2011), p. 296).

Despite of these advantages, a critical analysis of the IASB's fair value measurement project has also to address possible disadvantages and substantive criticism which has been raised after the publication of the ED FVM. To give an example, the restriction of the fair value concept solely on exit prices is considered critical, because it is argued that their relevance in practice may not yet be assessed reliably (*Castedello* (2009), p. 917). In addition, it is argued that an exit price can only be relevant when it is derived from an active market on the basis of conducted transactions, whereas hypothetical or model-based values are viewed as not relevant and enabling **managerial discretion** (*Berndt/Eberli* (2009), p. 898). Although the IASB's orientation on the fair value measurement project of the FASB is assessed as being advantageous to bring about convergence between IFRS and U.S. GAAP, it has to be kept in mind that U.S. GAAP is considered more rule-based while IFRS is considered more principle-based (*Berndt/Eberli* (2009), p. 897).[32]

Due to the fact that the fair value determination based on Level 3 inputs was subject to frequent criticism in the comments that the IASB received in response to the ED FVM, IFRS 13 does also include the disclosure requirements suggested by the ED MUA. Although it is without any doubt true that Level 3 inputs are less reliable than Level 1 or 2 inputs, the additional **disclosure requirements** may lower the criticism raised by unobservable inputs. However, firms may be even more likely to apply historical cost accounting when observable inputs are not available, because of the extensive disclosure requirements in the case of Level 3 inputs. Another issue is the following: While IFRS 13 does formally not increase the scope of fair values, there is the concern that the standard may function as a basis for the IASB to increase fair value application for future projects (*Berndt/Eberli* (2009), p. 897).

Even if this is not part of the research in this study, one of the biggest problems is seen in the fair value accounting for **liabilities**. It is apprehended that a fair value measurement for liabilities provides a counterintuitive view on the performance of a company when liabilities are measured at fair value. This is especially the case when a decreasing credit

---

32   The convergence efforts between IFRS and U.S. GAAP and the implications of SOX introduced
     more principle-based aspects into the U.S. GAAP. See *Watrin/Strohm* (2006), p.127.

rating leads to contrary profits caused by the devaluation of the liabilities (*Castedello* (2009), p. 916). A fair value accounting for liabilities does therefore provide the view that a lower-graded borrower needs less money to settle the debt when compared to a higher graded borrower, while both market participants need the same amount of money at the settlement date (*Berndt/Eberli* (2009), p. 897f.).[33] Even if the IASB received many comments in response to the ED FVM that raised the same concern, the Board concluded that addressing them was beyond the scope of the fair value measurement project.[34]

Fair value accounting causes a conflict between the two principles relevance and reliability when fair values are seen as more relevant but less reliable compared to historical cost. As this conflict constitutes a major point in the recent fair value discussion, the study addresses this issue by examining the usefulness of fair values in financial statements also with regard to their relevance and reliability by performing two empirical studies. As already mentioned in chapter 1.1.1, the two standards whose fair value approach is examined in the course of the two studies are IAS 40 "Investment Property" and IAS 16 "Property, Plant and Equipment". Since it is helpful in a first step to understand the regulations and the valuation models which are postulated in the two standards, both IAS 40 and IAS 16 are presented in detail in the next chapter.

2.1.3   Accounting for fair value according to IAS 40 and IAS 16

After the general fair value approach has been presented in detail in the previous chapters, the **application** of fair value accounting is now illustrated by using concrete examples. As aforementioned, this study examines fair value accounting for investment properties (IAS 40) and assets of PPE (IAS 16). By centering on these two standards, the study focuses on the fair value for tangible assets and does deliberately exclude the fair value approach for financial instruments included in IAS 39. The reason for this is the fact that financial instruments are usually important for financial institutions, such as banks or insurance companies, which are excluded from the study.[35] In addition, IAS 40 and IAS 16 provide a unique environment with regard to fair value accounting when doing research.[36]

Even if accounting for investment properties in IAS 40 represents a special case for asset recognition that is to a large extent based on IAS 16, the chapter deals with the regulations of IAS 40 first. This sequence has been chosen mainly for two reasons: First, the fair value model included in IAS 40 provides fair value accounting in a more unrestrained way with changes in fair value recognized in the profit or loss for the period. Second, investment properties are more important for the two empirical studies. They are not only used

---

33 See also the empirical analyses conducted by *Barth et al.* (2008) and *Lachmann et al.* (2010) who both provide evidence of the confounding effects of liabilities measured at fair value.

34 However, the IASB notes that the issue of an entity's non-performance risk is addressed in developing IFRS 9, which has been issued in October 2010. See IFRS 13 BC 95.

35 Financial firms are excluded due to their substantially different financial reporting environment. This procedure is consistent with prior research in this field. See for example *Acker et al.* (2002), p. 202 or *Athanasakou et al.* (2009), p. 13.

36 See chapter 1.1.2.

for the archival study. Moreover, the regulations of IAS 40 do more conform to the experiment design of the second study than IAS 16.

2.1.3.1 Fair value accounting for investment properties

2.1.3.1.1 Introduction to the standard

The accounting for investment properties is codified in IAS 40 Investment Property. Whereas the standard in its current form must be applied for fiscal years beginning after 1 January 2009, the effective date of a first version of IAS 40 was in 2001. Before IAS 40 became firstly effective in 2001, investment properties were treated similar to property, plant and equipment according to IAS 16.[37] Since 2001 it must be **distinguished** between property and investment property with regard to accounting measures that resulted in differences in fair value accounting. Thus, the valuation measures have been extended in a way that investment properties can be measured at fair value, which means that they can be measured at a carrying value that may increase their acquisition cost (*Dohrn* (2004), p. 168).

Investment properties need to be distinguished from other property or real estate. Assets are either classified as investment property or owner-occupied property, which is used in the production or supply of goods or services or for administrative purposes (*Berkau* (2009), p. 134). Therefore, the **classification** of property in one of the two categories depends on the way the property is used by the company that has the ownership of the property (*Böckem/Schurbohm* (2002), p. 39). According to IAS 40.5, the definition of investment property is as follows:

> *"Investment property is property (land or a building – or part of a building – or both) held (by the owner or by the lessee under a finance lease) to earn rentals or for capital appreciation or both, rather than for:*
>
> *(a) use in the production or supply of goods or services or for administrative purposes; or*
>
> *(b) sale in the ordinary course of business."*

As investment properties are not held in the ordinary course of business and are not used for administrative purposes, they can be viewed more as an asset held for investment (*Hoffmann/Lüdenbach* (2003), p. 565). The most recent amendment of IAS 40, which was published in the course of the "Annual Improvements to IFRSs 2007" project, affected the way to account for property under construction or development. While such property was accounted for under IAS 16 before, it is now under the scope of IAS 40 if it is intended to be used as an investment property after the end of construction (*Zaugg et al.* (2009), p. 531). However, when property is intended for sale after construction or purchase, the property is then accounted for under IAS 2 (Inventories). This is especially expected to be the case when the company's day-to-day business is the steady buying and

---

37   For a detailed description for the accounting treatment of property, plant and equipment see chapter 2.1.3.2.

selling of property (*Küting/Dawo* (2003), p. 234). Figure 2-2 presents an overview of the classification process of property.

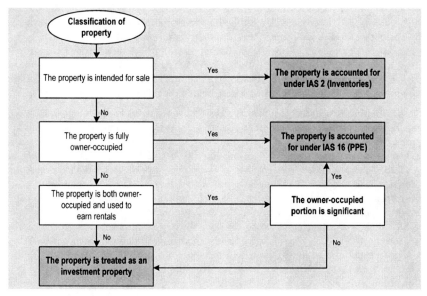

Figure 2-2: Classification process of property
(Following *Zülch* (2003), p. 83)

The definition in IAS 40 implies that property, which is used within the normal course of business, is not treated as investment property. As aforementioned, such property is then **owner-occupied**, which is accounted for under IAS 16 as PPE (*Baetge/Zülch* (2001), p. 554). A further classification issue is given when the property is both owner-occupied and used to earn rentals. The different parts of the building are accounted for separately when they can be sold or leased out separately (*Pellens et al.* (2011), p. 369f.). The part that is rented out is investment property and it is possible to realize gains and losses based on the investment property without a need to dispose the owner-occupied part of the property (*Dohrn* (2004), p. 170). When it is possible to separately dispose the different portions of the property, the fair value is expected to be determined reliably (*Böckem/Schurbohm* (2002), p. 40). If the portions cannot be sold or leased out separately, the property is treated as investment property only when the owner-occupied portion is not significant (IAS 40.10).

Summarizing the classification process, a property is classified as an investment property when it has the purpose to earn rentals or for capital appreciation or both. The next chapter deals with the measurement of investment properties under the fair value model.

2.1.3.1.2 Measurement of investment properties under the fair value model

According to IAS 40.16, assets of investment property can only be recognized when the cost of investment property can be measured reliably and when it is probable that the future economic benefits associated with the investment property will flow to the entity. If this is the case, investment property must initially be measured at **cost** which may be acquisition cost or production cost. While the approach for both measurement bases is not stated in detail in IAS 40, the regulations of IAS 16 are used instead as the initial measurement of investment properties is not materially different from that for PPE.[38] Both acquisition cost and production cost are described in the following.

The **acquisition cost** must be applied as a basis for measurement when the item has been acquired from a third party (*Pellens et al.* (2011), p. 343). Assets are then viewed as acquired when the company obtains economic ownership of the asset either by purchase, exchange or any other form of transmission (*Dohrn* (2004), p. 172). According to IAS 16.16, the acquisition costs consist of the purchase price (less trade discounts and rebates), the transaction costs and any subsequent expenditure. The transaction costs comprise any costs which are directly attributable to bringing the asset to the location and condition necessary for its operation in the manner intended by management. Examples of such directly attributable costs are costs for delivery or installation and costs of site preparation (IAS 16.17), whereas other costs such as administration or other general overhead costs cannot be attributed directly to the item and are explicitly not part of acquisition cost (IAS 16.19). Whereas subsequent expenditure refers to the estimated cost of dismantling and removing the asset and restoring the site at the time of initial measurement, repair and maintenance costs are not part of subsequent expenditure as they are recognized in the profit or loss for the period (*Dohrn* (2004), p. 173). Figure 2-3 presents the procedure for the determination of acquisition cost.

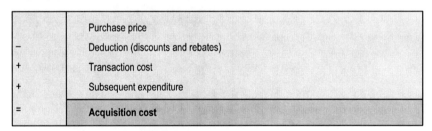

Figure 2-3: Determination of acquisition cost
(Following *Wohlgemuth/Radde* (2000), p. 907)

The **production costs** are the relevant measurement base when the asset has been self-constructed (*Pellens et al.* (2011), p. 343). The production costs correspond to the total amount of costs which incurred during the process of construction until the completion of the production process (*Dohrn* (2004), p. 173). As the standard which needs to be ap-

---

38 Before IAS 40 became effective, the regulations in IAS 16 served as the basement for initial measurement for IAS 25 which was the predecessor of IAS 40. See *Zülch* (2003), p. 164.

plied for the determination of production costs states that "the cost of the asset is usually the same as the cost of constructing an asset for sale" (IAS 16.22), the production cost is determined in accordance with IAS 2. Because IAS 2 obliges companies to include all costs that incurred during the production process of an asset, this approach is also referred to as a "production-based full cost accounting" (*Zülch* (2003), p. 169). In this sense, costs for administrative overheads or selling costs are not part of the production costs (IAS 2.16). On the other hand, borrowing costs which are directly attributable to the production process must be capitalized in the case of the production of a qualifying asset (IAS 2.17 in conjunction with IAS 23.11).

After initial measurement, investment property may subsequently be measured either at fair value or historical cost (IAS 40.30).[39] Therefore, this study focuses on the subsequent measurement as fair value accounting may only be applied when investment property is subsequently measured. Whereas the measurement of investment property at fair value refers to the **fair value model**, measurement at historical cost is described as the cost model. Although the owners of investment property may choose among the two valuation models, the IASB seems to implicitly prefer the fair value model because the standard requires all entities to determine the fair value of investment property either for measurement or disclosure. Thus, the fair values need to be disclosed in the notes section even if an entity chooses the cost model for valuation (IAS 40.79 (e)). This view is also supported by the fact that the IASB does not allow later changes from fair value model to cost model as such a change would not result in a more appropriate presentation in the financial statements (IAS 40.31).

When an entity applies the **cost model**, the subsequent measurement for investment property is not different from the subsequent measurement for PPE (IAS 40.56). Therefore, the standard IAS 40 refers to IAS 16 when dealing with the cost model. The cost model is codified in IAS 16.30. It requires assets to be measured at acquisition or production costs less accumulated depreciation and any accumulated impairment losses. If the entity is reasonably certain of a residual value after the useful life of the asset, the depreciable amount is decreased by that value (IAS 16.53). The depreciation of an asset begins when it is available for use and in the position necessary for operation in the manner intended by management (IAS 16.55), and is performed on a systematic basis over its useful life (IAS 16.50). When determining the useful life of an asset, the expected intensity of use, the expected physical wear and tear with respect to the repair and maintenance program, the technical obsolescence, and legal or similar limits need to be considered (IAS 16.56). The depreciation method has to correspond on how an asset's future economic benefits are expected to be consumed by the entity (IAS 16.61). However, an entity applying the cost model is facing extensive disclosure requirements, such as the depreciation method, the useful live, the accumulated depreciation, and the fair value (IAS 40.31).

When applying the fair value model for investment properties, any changes in the investment property's value become part of the **operating income** of the entity and the regard-

---

39   IAS 40 is viewed as important as it marks the first time the IASB introduced the fair value model for non-financial assets. See *Muller et al.* (2011), p. 1141.

ing assets are not subject to depreciation (*Christensen/Nikolaev* (2009), p. 6). This is a major difference to the accounting for PPE as fair value changes of PPE are not part of the profit or loss for the period.[40] Contrariwise, the fair value model in IAS 40 for investment properties has a greater impact on the entity's earnings. In this sense, fair value changes of investment property may result from varying market conditions or other factors that may have an influence on the utility of the property. The fact that fair value changes are directly recognized in the entity's profit or loss for the period is based on the assumption that investment property, similar to most financial instruments, may easily be sold at any time (*Dohrn* (2004), p. 183). Because it is stated in IAS 40.38 that the "fair value of investment property shall reflect market conditions at the balance sheet date", it is concluded that investment property needs to be revalued at every balance sheet date (*Böckem/Schurbohm* (2002), p. 42). When the revaluation model is applied, investment properties are not subject to periodic depreciation and fair value changes might cause carrying values that are above the regarding assets' acquisition or production costs. This would give rise to **deferred taxes** due to differences between IFRS and tax accounts.

The following chapter deals with the characteristics of the fair value model for investment property, in particular with the fair value-determination of investment property.

2.1.3.1.3   Fair value determination of investment property

When an entity chooses the fair value model for subsequent measurement, the major task is the determination of fair value. From 2013 on, the relevant guidance for fair value determination of investment properties is included in IFRS 13, which then replaces the guidance for fair value determination in IAS 40. Since the market value is the preferred fair value, it is attempted to locate a market value for the investment property as a **Level 1 input** (*Dohrn* (2004), p. 177; *Huschke* (2008), p. 35). However, this constitutes a significant problem as it is not expected that, in contrast to many financial instruments, there is an active market for the regarding investment property. The real estate market may rather be characterized as a highly imperfect market when single properties are not comparable and are to a large extent unique (*Zülch* (2003), p. 31). Quoted and unadjusted prices in active markets for identical assets are not available at the measurement date (IFRS 13.76). The fair value determination based on a Level 1 input as the first-best solution of a fair value is therefore viewed as an exception in the case of investment properties. Level 2 and Level 3 inputs are therefore more relevant for fair value determination.

According to IFRS 13.81, **Level 2 inputs** are inputs other than quoted prices that are observable for the asset. In the case of investment properties, these inputs correspond to current prices in an active market for property in the same location and condition and which are subject to similar lease and other contracts. Insofar, an approximated fair value of the investment property that is derived from an active market needs to be identified. In the absence of such information, current prices for properties of a different nature or which are subject to different conditions or recent prices on active markets could be considered (IFRS 13.83). Such information must be adjusted to reflect changes in economic condi-

---

40   Moreover, these changes are recognized as a revaluation surplus of the OCI. For a detailed description of the revaluation model for PPE see chapter 2.1.3.2.2.

tions when compared to the investment property which needs to be valued.[41] But as properties are highly unique and their economic conditions are likely to differ to a large extent, the approach based on Level 2 inputs remains notional (*Zülch* (2003), p. 182). While the heterogeneity of property makes it difficult to determine Level 2 inputs, the fair value determination will in most cases be based on Level 3 inputs (*Dohrn* (2004), p. 178).

In this sense, **Level 3 inputs** as are not based on observable market data and do thus refer to mark-to-model fair values (IFRS 13.86). They refer to widely accepted methods of real estate valuation. Whereas Level 1 and Level 2 inputs are based on market values or adjustments to market values, Level 3 inputs correspond to comparison values (for which a premium or a discount needs eventually to be estimated) or discounted cash flows which are estimated under market conditions (*Dohrn* (2004), p. 178). Level 3 inputs simulate a value that is based on market conditions and is determined hypothetically (*Zülch* (2003), p. 184). According to IAS 40.46, both the sales comparison approach and the discounted cash flow method may be applied for the valuation of investment property. The two models are presented in the following.[42]

The **sales comparison approach** is a common technique in real estate valuation. Real estate appraisers are often required to perform a sales comparison approach as part of the process to prepare a market value for a particular property (*Healy/Bergquist* (1994), p. 587). The approach compares a subject property's characteristic with those of comparable properties which have recently been sold in similar transactions.[43] The technique is based on the principle of substitution as a knowledgeable and prudent purchaser will not pay more for a particular property without delay (*Williams* (2004), p. 155). It uses one of several techniques to adjust the prices of the comparable transactions according to the presence, absence, or degree of characteristics which influence value, whereas the prices can be adjusted in basically two ways:[44] First, object-related adjustments need to be conducted when there are timely transactions of properties that cannot be compared to the property which needs to be valued. Second, temporal adjustments need to be arranged when there are comparable transactions available in the past. The sales comparison approach does therefore use transactions between buyers and sellers to provide a direct indication of value perceptions in order to establish asset value that reflects current market conditions and motivations within a particular market (*Healy/Bergquist* (1994), p. 588). It is highly dependent on the appraiser's ability to identify transactions involving comparable assets to obtain adequate specific information concerning the asset (*Ellsworth* (2001), p. 266). The method can be applied to almost all kind of property as long as there is sufficient market information available (*Williams* (2004), p. 155). However, it is argued that in real estate valuation, locating a comparable sale is only the starting point in valuation and that every single sale must be verified with sources that are both informative and reliable (*Crookham* (1995), p. 181).

---

41 See *Zülch* (2003), p. 107ff., for a detailed description of economic conditions with the potential to influence the value of property.
42 Although the sales comparison approach is not explicitly stated in IAS 40.46, the wording of the standard indicates the application of this model implicitly. See *Dohrn* (2004), p. 178.
43 See IAS 40.46 (a) and IAS 40.46 (b).
44 For a detailed presentation of the two kinds of adjustments see *Olbrich* (2003), p. 347.

The **discounted cash flow** (DCF) model which is often referred to as the **income capitalization approach** in real estate valuation (*Zülch* (2003), p. 159). It can be assigned to level three inputs because the property value is determined mark-to-model. The DCF model is widely used to value larger and more expensive income-producing properties and applies market-supported yields to future cash flows (such as annual income figures and typically a lump reversion from the sale of the property) to arrive at a present value (*Dohrn* (2004), p. 180). The basic idea behind the income capitalization approach is that of a simple rental:[45] Property can either be owner-occupied or the owner can choose to pass the right of occupation to a third party by letting the property. When the level of rent is determined by the supply and demand for such property in the market, this rent is simply a cash flow and, as such, the basis for valuation. Besides the fact that the appraiser needs sufficient data, such as annual cash flows, the residual value of the property, and the discount rate to come to a valuation, the utilization of complex numerical techniques, which attempt to take into account the mathematical probability of future events, is also necessary (*Blackledge* (2009), p. 287). There may be additional factors with the potential to increase or decrease the value of property. However, these factors affecting the fair value of investment properties cannot be considered.[46] Examples for such factors are (IAS 40.49):

- Additional value derived from the creation of a portfolio of properties in different locations,
- synergies between investment property and other assets,
- legal rights or legal restrictions that are specific only to the current owner, and
- tax benefits or tax burdens that are specific to the current owner.

The DCF model is based on the net income (or investment return) that a potential buyer expects from the property (*Ventolo/Williams* (2001), p. 69). Therefore, it is not allowed to consider subjective estimates that may reflect company-specific value increases as well as possible future capital expenditure potentially improving or enhancing the value of the property (IAS 40.51).

The two approaches to real estate appraisal require different kinds of information which include data on comparable nearby property sales (sales comparison approach) and investment return (income capitalization approach). The information available will help to determine which of the methods should be applied and will be given the most validity in the appraiser's final estimate of the value of the investment property (*Ventolo/Williams* (2001), p. 71). The sales comparison approach and the DCF method are likely to result in differing values for investment property as different kind of information is expected to yield different valuation results (*Zülch* (2003), p. 184). Before arriving at a final value, the value arrived at by the sales comparison approach should thus be compared to the value based on the DCF model and vice versa (*Menorca* (1993), p. 216). However, a compari-

---

45 For a detailed description see *Pagourtzi et al.* (2003), p. 388f.
46 This requirement is due to the fact that fair value should reflect the knowledge of willing buyers and sellers. Such factors would otherwise reflect knowledge specific only for the owner. See *Dohrn* (2004), p. 180.

son can only be accomplished when there is **sufficient information** available to compute the values of both approaches. In addition, firms are encouraged, but not required, to enlist independent evaluators with relevant qualification and experience when determining investment property fair values (*Muller et al.* (2011), p. 1141). To determine the final value, the appraiser must then (according to IAS 40.47) choose the most reliable estimate of fair value that is within a range of reasonable results. In the case that the fair value cannot be determined reasonably with appraisal methods, the entity has to apply the cost model for subsequent measurement (IAS 40.53).

2.1.3.1.4 Disclosure requirements of investment properties

The accounting for investment properties is different from the accounting for PPE. Therefore, the classification into the category of PPE in the balance sheet is not viewed reasonable as it is preferred to disclose investment property separately (*Zülch* (2003), p. 339). When an entity applies the fair value model, all fair value changes are recognized in the profit or loss and a gain or loss arising from a change in the fair value is recognized for the period in which it arises (IAS 40.35). Concerning the kind of disclosure in the comprehensive income statement, it has to be investigated whether the holding of investment property constitutes a part of the core business or just additional business of the entity (*Dohrn* (2004), p. 184f.): When the holding of investment property is part of the core business of the entity, income from rental or leasehold contracts have to be recognized as **operating result** and fair value changes have to be recognized in other operating income and expenses. Otherwise, if the holding of investment property is an entity's additional business, all income and expense is accounted for as **financing costs**.[47]

The companies that are holding investment properties are obliged to make extensive disclosures in the notes section. According to this, an entity has to disclose information no matter whether it applies the cost model or the fair value model for its investment properties.[48] When an entity chooses to subsequently measure investment property at fair value, **reconciliations** between the carrying amounts of investment property at the beginning and the end of the period need to be disclosed additionally.[49] Otherwise, when the fair value of an investment property cannot be determined reliably by using any of the approaches, the entity has to apply the cost model. In this case, the entity must disclose information such as a description of the investment property, an explanation of why the fair value cannot be determined reliably, or (if possible) the range of estimates within which the fair value is highly likely to fall between (IAS 40.78). Additionally, an entity must also

---

47 See IAS 1.82 and *Zülch* (2003), p. 342f.
48 According to IAS 40.75 such disclosures for example include the methods and assumptions applied in determining the fair value, the extent to which the fair value is based on a valuation by an independent valuer, or substantial gains and losses that are associated with the holding of investment property.
49 The reconciliation has for example to show net gains or losses from fair value adjustments or transfers to and from inventories and owner-occupied property (IAS 40.76).

comply with the disclosure requirements stated in IFRS 13, especially when the fair values are determined mark-to-model.[50]

2.1.3.1.5   Critical analysis of fair value accounting for investment properties

It has been shown that fair values for investment properties which are derived from an active market represent the exception rather than the rule. The same applies to the case when the fair value is attempted to be determined on the basis of comparable transactions of similar property, the so-called Level 2 inputs (IFRS 13.81-85). Due to the high degree of **uniqueness**, investment property is in most cases valued on the basis of Level 3 inputs. To determine the fair value of investment property, IAS 40 allows both the sales comparison approach and the DCF model. The sales comparison approach enables the determination of a marketable value which is based on transactions of other property with adjustments to the property subject to valuation. When the sales comparison approach is not applicable (for example due to a lack of information), the fair value must be determined mark-to-model. Then, the DCF model or income capitalization approach is applied. Whereas the fair value determination on an active market constitutes the first-best solution, the Level 2 and especially Level 3 inputs have to be interpreted with caution. Because Level 2 inputs represent data that is derived from other property, the selection of the comparable transaction or property is up to the management of the entity. The election of the comparable transaction is therefore highly subjective (*Dohrn* (2004), p. 188).

When the DCF model is used to determine the fair value, certain parameters necessary for valuation, such as cash flows, discount rate, or residual value, which are also expected to yield a significant degree of **subjectivity**, have to be identified (*Engel-Ciric* (2002), p. 782f.). However, as the cash flows are usually contract-based and fix, the discount rate and the residual value based on market data and external information must be defined. Here, it is up to the reporting entity to choose among the available information to come up with a valuation which also results in subjectivity. Compared to this, an even larger extent of subjectivity is imbued into the valuation when there are no sufficient market data at all and when the definition of the parameters depends completely upon the management (*Dohrn* (2004), p. 188). If fair values are determined in such a way, the verifiability of the data can be described as highly questionable (*Olbrich* (2003), p. 348).

On the one hand, the application of fair value measurement is generally preferred due to the fact that financial statements reveal a higher level of information, even if its adoption requires specific conditions such as liquid markets or a large data base of available prices (*Ball* (2006), p. 12ff.). On the other hand, the reliability of fair value estimates is viewed as the most critical point with a potential to damage the stewardship function of financial reporting (*Whittington* (2008), p. 164; *Quagli/Avallone* (2010), p. 463). It is also argued that a fair value which is estimated by managers could never reach the information level of the whole financial market due to the enormous number of market participants and information contributing to determine prices (*Watts* (2006), p. 57). But it should not be expected that managers will always prefer fair values instead of historical cost, because they

---

50   See chapter 2.1.2.5.

may influence the determined fair value. As the changes of fair value of investment property are directly recognized in the profit or loss for the period, managers are conscious that the fair value choice implies **substantial variations** in accounting results that may not always be desirable (*Quagli/Avallone* (2010), p. 465). Thus, the fair value model leads to earnings that are more volatile but can be influenced to a certain degree.

In summary, especially Level 2 and Level 3 inputs provide the entity with a significant amount of managerial discretion. The determination of fair value enables management with the ability to manage earnings without the fear of detecting this manipulation. However, the IASB seems to be aware of this risk because it recommends determining the fair value of investment property on the basis of a valuation by an independent valuer who has sufficient experience of the item that is being valued (IAS 40.32). This would decrease management's ability to influence fair value determination.

2.1.3.2   Fair value accounting for property, plant and equipment

2.1.3.2.1   Introduction to the standard

Accounting for property, plant and equipment (PPE) is codified in IAS 16. In addition to this standard, the measurement of PPE is also to a large extent affected by IAS 36 which deals with the impairment of assets (*Schmidt/Seidel* (2006), p. 596). Whereas IAS 16 covers a wide range of PPE in IFRS financial statements, the standard makes clear that agriculture (IAS 41), exploration for and evaluation of mineral assets (IFRS 6) and investment property (IAS 40) are not accounted for under IAS 16. Although, the first version of IAS 16 became effective in 1983, the standard has passed through several changes and faced several amendments during the time it was effective. The most recent amendment to IAS 16 was brought through the "Annual Improvements to IFRSs 2007" project. It affected the way to account for routine sales of assets that are held for rental (IAS 16.68).

The scope of IAS 16 includes tangible assets which are in a company's ownership and are used in the **ordinary course of business**. According to IAS 16.6, PPE is defined as follows:

"*Property, plant and equipment are tangible items that:*

(a) are held for use in the production or supply of goods or services, for rental to others, or for administrative purposes; and

(b) are expected to be used during more than one period."

Typical examples of PPE in the understanding of IFRS are machinery, motor vehicles, or land and buildings which are used in the ordinary course of business (IAS 16.37). Real estate which is not used in the ordinary course of business (investment property) is not subject of IAS 16 but rather accounted for under IAS 40.[51]

Although, the basis for recognition of PPE does conform to the general recognition criteria which is included in the IFRS framework, the recognition criteria can also be found in

---

51   See chapter 2.1.3.1 for a detailed presentation of IAS 40 Investment Property.

IAS 16 (*Buschhüter/Striegel* (2009), p. 128). Therefore, PPE can only be recognized when it is probable that future economic benefits associated with the item will flow to the entity and when the cost of the item can be measured reliably (IAS 16.7). If items fulfill the recognition criteria and are treated as PPE, each item is treated and accounted for separately (*Vollmer* (2008), p. 181). However, items which are individually insignificant, such as tools and dies, may be aggregated according to IAS 16.9 when they have a multi-period useful life (*Pellens et al.* (2011), p. 342). The so-called **component approach** needs to be applied when items of PPE are subject to depreciation (*Hagemeister* (2004), p. 9ff.). According to this approach, each part of an item of PPE with a cost significant in relation to the total cost of the item has to be depreciated separately (IAS 16.43). The depreciation of the total asset value is then calculated as the sum of the depreciation amounts of its components (*Mujkanovic/Raatz* (2008), p. 246). This component approach obligates the companies to disperse PPE even when the single parts are only used together and cannot operate separately.[52]

2.1.3.2.2   Measurement of PPE under the revaluation model

After an item has been classified as PPE, it must initially be recognized in the balance sheet of the entity. Basically, assets of PPE are measured at cost (IAS 16.15). The cost of an asset may be determined by either its **acquisition cost** or **production cost**. However, both value measures have been described already in chapter 2.1.3.1.2 in conjunction with the initial measurement of investment properties.

After initial measurement, assets of PPE may subsequently be measured at cost less accumulated depreciation and impairment losses or at a revalued amount, which is its fair value less subsequent depreciation and impairment losses (*Pellens et al.* (2011), p. 347). Whereas the first measurement option refers to the cost model, the second possibility is the revaluation model. The decision between the cost model and the revaluation model should be made with caution because the option to choose among the two models is only available once at the beginning of subsequent measurement (*Wobbe* (2008), p. 45). A later change may only be applied when this **enhances** an investor's view on the financial position of the firm or when another standard explicitly demands a change (*Pellens et al.* (2011), p. 348).[53] Assets of PPE must be classified into groups and the valuation model must be consistently applied to all assets within one group, which means that if an asset is revalued, then the entire class of assets must also be revalued (IAS 16.36). The fact that IAS 16.36 demands that only entire classes of assets may be subject to revaluation prevents the management from *cherry-picking*, which refers to the procedure when only assets with an increased fair value are revalued and assets with a decreased fair value are not (*Mujkanovic* (2002), p. 136; *Tanski* (2005), p. 90). In addition, a selective revaluation of certain assets of PPE is avoided to prevent reporting a mixture of historical cost and fair values for the same asset class in the financial statements (*Herrmann et al.* (2006), p. 45).

---

52   An example for such a case is seen in the depreciation of an aircraft when the cabin and engine are depreciated separately. See *Hoffmann/Lüdenbach* (2004), p. 375.

53   Such an enhancement is regularly expected from a change of the cost model to the revaluation model. See *Wobbe* (2008), p. 45f.

Under der cost model, PPE is measured at acquisition or production costs less accumulated depreciation and impairment losses (IAS 16.30). The cost model for PPE is not different from the cost model for investment properties.[54] However, when assets of PPE are subsequently measured on the basis of the **revaluation model**, assets are revalued to their fair value less depreciation and impairment losses (*Wobbe* (2008), p. 47). Because this approach focuses on the fair value of assets, a necessary condition for the application of the revaluation model is that the fair value of the PPE can be determined reliably (*Vollmer* (2008), p. 183). Basically, it is sufficient for items of PPE to perform revaluations every three to five years in the case of only insignificant changes in fair value (IAS 16.34). However, the frequency of revaluations depends upon the changes of fair value of the regarding asset. Thus, it could be the case that revaluations must be performed annually in the case of high volatility of fair values (*Mujkanovic* (2002), p. 136f.).

If an asset of PPE is revalued, the fair value of this asset represents the carrying amount in the balance sheet of the entity which has ownership of the PPE (*Vollmer* (2008), p. 183). If a revaluation results in an increase above the former carrying value, it is recognized as a revaluation surplus in the **other comprehensive income** (OCI) unless it represents the reversal of a revaluation decrease of the same asset which was previously recognized as an expense, in which case it has to be recognized as profit or loss for the period (IAS 16.39). On the other hand, a decrease arising as a result of a revaluation must be recognized as an expense to the extent that it exceeds any amount which has previously been credited to the revaluation surplus relating to the same asset (IAS 16.40). After an asset of PPE has been revalued to fair value, the new carrying value represents the measurement base for regular depreciation which is performed in accordance to the cost model (*Vollmer* (2008), p. 183). Whereas it is usually not expected that the revaluation changes the depreciation method and the useful life of an asset, the total depreciation amount does materially differ when assets are revalued with a change of the carrying value (*Mujkanovic* (2002), p. 142). The fact that items of PPE are, in addition to revaluations to fair value, subject to regular depreciation is viewed as a major difference to the fair value model applied for investment properties which are not depreciated.[55]

IAS 16 permits the revaluation surplus to be treated in two ways: First, it may be transferred directly to retained earnings (and not through the profit or loss for the period) when the asset is disposed (IAS 16.41). Second, the entity may also transfer the difference between the depreciation on the revalued amount and the depreciation on historical cost to retained earnings in every period.[56] It has to be mentioned that the revaluation model gives rise to **deferred taxes** when there are differences in the carrying amounts of PPE in the financial and tax accounts (*Mujkanovic* (2002), p. 146ff.). Deferred taxes resulting from asset revaluations should be treated similar to the revaluation surplus. Assets of PPE are derecognized on disposal or when no future economic benefit is expected from its use or disposal (IAS 16.67). Although any gains or losses which result from asset derecogni-

---

54   Refer to chapter 2.1.3.1.2 for a detailed description of the cost model.
55   For a description of the fair value model for the measurement of investment properties see chapter 2.1.3.1.2.
56   See *Pellens et al.* (2011), p. 350ff., who also provide some illustrative examples.

tion must be recognized in the profit or loss for the period, it is not allowed to classify such gains as revenue (IAS 16.68). In the case of asset impairment, the IAS for PPE refers to IAS 36 Impairment of Assets (IAS 16.63).

2.1.3.2.3   Fair value determination of property, plant and equipment

When an entity chooses the revaluation model for subsequent measurement, the fair value for assets of PPE needs to be determined. However, PPE may be of specialized nature and it is thus not probable that market values can be derived from an active market. Therefore, IAS 16 enables the entity to make use of market price estimates (*Wobbe* (2008), p. 48f.). IAS 16.32 states that the measurement base for land and buildings is **market-based evidence** by appraisal which is normally undertaken by professionally qualified valuers, whereas the fair value of plant and equipment should usually represent their market value determined by appraisal. Although these specifications are close to Level 2 inputs in the fair value hierarchy (IFRS 13.81-85) and these market values are viewed as more reliable and value relevant than level three inputs,[57] the IASB recognized the problems with the fair value determination of PPE and provides alternative measurement procedures in IAS 16.33. Indeed, an entity may also apply an income approach or a depreciated replacement cost approach to determine the fair value of PPE.

When an entity chooses to apply the **income approach**, the fair value is determined on the basis of DCF models. Therefore, assumptions regarding the useful life, the interest rate and the cash flows which are likely to be generated by the asset in the future have to be made (*Wobbe* (2008), p. 49). The income approach for the DCF computation of assets of PPE does not materially differ from that approach employed in commercial real estate valuation. Thus, a detailed presentation of the DCF model can be found in chapter 2.1.3.1.3 which is concerned with the valuation of investment properties.

The **replacement cost approach** focuses on the amount that an entity would have to pay to replace an asset at the present time. Therefore, when the value of any PPE needs to be determined, it is necessary to determine the market price of a similar item of PPE and adjust this market price to depreciation corresponding to the maturity and wear and tear of the asset of which the fair value needs to be determined (*Thomas/Wilson* (2005), p. 5). Items are viewed as similar and applicable for this procedure when the asset that needs to be valued and the object of comparison are substantially similar with regard to their potential use.[58]

2.1.3.2.4   Disclosure requirements of property, plant and equipment

When items of PPE are recognized in the financial statements of an entity, extensive disclosures are required in the notes section for each class of assets. As the amount of disclosure basically depends on the valuation model chosen for the asset class, the revaluation

---

57   See chapter 2.1.2.4.

58   According to this, a top-class performance personal computer which has been purchased years ago may only be compared with a personal computer of the same performance class (which would today likely be the lowest performance class). See *Wobbe* (2008), p. 49.

model demands an additional amount of disclosure to the disclosure necessary under the cost model (*Oppermann et al.* (2008), p. 69). For **each class of assets**, an entity has to disclose information such as the depreciation model employed, the useful lives or annual depreciation rates, accumulated depreciation and impairment, and a reconciliation of the carrying amount of PPE at the beginning and at the end of the period (IAS 16.73). Further information must be included in the notes, for example if the entity has any restrictions on title or receives compensation from third parties for the PPE (IAS 16.74).

Additional disclosure is required when an entity applies the revaluation model for items of PPE. According to IAS 16.77, the disclosure requirements include the following:

- The effective **date** of the revaluation;
- whether an **independent valuer** was involved;
- the methods and significant **assumptions** used in estimating fair values;
- the extent to which fair values were determined directly by reference to **observable prices** in an active market or recent market transactions on arm's length terms or were estimated using other valuation techniques;
- for each revalued class of property, the carrying amount that would have been recognized had the assets been carried under the **cost model**; and
- the **revaluation surplus**, including changes during the period and any restrictions on the distribution of the balance to shareholders.

By requiring these disclosures, the standard mainly focuses on the procedure of fair value determination and the origin of fair values as this information is assessed of being relevant for investors. First, the information should enable investors to understand the value changes of assets of PPE and the implications of the revaluation model on carrying values, especially in comparison to the cost model. Second, the requirement to disclose information regarding the process of determination allows users of financial statements to assess the reliability of the revalued amounts. In addition to the requirements in IAS 16, a reporting entity must also disclose the information required in IFRS 13, especially when mark-to-model fair values are applied.[59]

2.1.3.2.5 Critical analysis of fair value accounting for property, plant and equipment

Even if the IASB enables the entity to measure items of PPE at fair value, it is often claimed that the revaluation model may cause several problems. As it is not expected to derive the fair value for PPE from an active market, alternative measurement procedures are usually applied for determining the fair value (*Küting/Kaiser* (2010), p. 382). The fair value is then largely influenced by management which introduces a degree of **subjectivity** and leaves significant room for managerial discretion (*Küting et al.* (2007), p. 1714). This problem is even increased by the fact that IAS 16 does not include detailed instructions for the determination of fair value, because it is only stated that income approaches or the

---

59   For further information see chapter 2.1.2.5.

replacement cost approach should be applied when there are no market values available (*Hüning* (2007), p. 178). However, IFRS 13 attenuates this concern as the new standard provides detailed guidance on fair value measurement. While the income approach does largely depend on subjective factors such as the expected cash flows, the interest rate and the terminal value, the replacement cost approach has also raised some concern. Even if a fair value based on this approach can usually be determined reliably, it does not necessarily reflect the market consensus (*Ranker* (2006), p. 316f.).

The critics on IAS 16 are not exclusively on the determination of the fair value. Moreover, the component approach for the valuation of PPE has raised many concerns. It is argued that the **decomposition** of assets in single parts, which are depreciated separately, also provides management with discretion (*Hüning* (2007), p. 165). Additionally, it is mentioned that the revaluation model mixes gains and losses that are recognized in the profit or loss with gains and losses which are recognized in the OCI, thus inducing a bias in the financial position of the entity. While transfers to or from the revaluation surplus are recognized in the OCI, the regular depreciation is recognized in the profit or loss for the period (*Schmidt/Seidel* (2006), p. 599). Thus, this approach causes the effect that the increased depreciation expenses on the basis of the revaluation are included in the profit or loss, the transfers from the revaluation surplus are not recognized in the profit or loss but in the OCI instead. It is therefore assumed that asset revaluations under IAS 16 violate the **clean surplus principle** (*Küting/Reuter* (2008), p. 660f.; *Küting/Reuter* (2009), p. 173).

2.1.4 Summary

This chapter presents the accounting for investment property and PPE in IFRS financial statements. The explicit option to apply fair values for both types of assets is uncommon for IFRS as the accounting system intends to reduce accounting options to make financial statements more comparable (*Wobbe* (2008), p. 46). While investment properties and assets of PPE are initially measured at cost, the subsequent measurement may also, in addition to the measurement at historical cost, be performed at fair values. Fair values may therefore only be applied for **subsequent measurement**. When fair values are applied, investment properties are measured in accordance with the fair value model whereas assets of PPE are accounted for under the revaluation model. Although both models focus on fair values, their application results in significant differences. Whereas gains and losses resulting from fair value changes under the fair value model are recognized in the profit or loss for the period, the revaluation model causes fair value changes to be recognized in the OCI.

One of the major tasks in fair value accounting is the process of **fair value determination**. In short, the method of how the fair value is determined is specified by the information available. Whereas a fair value based on level one or level two inputs may easily be determined and apparent as market value, a fair value based on level three inputs becomes more technical. However, as it is expected that market values are not available for most tangible assets, the fair value does largely depend on model-based estimates and the parameters which are used for the computation of such models (*Küting/Kaiser* (2010), p. 382). In this case, the determination of fair value provides the potential for managerial discretion. But then the question remains whether historical cost accounting causes significantly less discretion. One may think here of depreciation methods or decisions whether an asset is impaired or not which are also to a large extent subjective.

Technical issues concerning the fair value determination are not the key issues that need to be examined in this study. Moreover, it is of interest to examine the implications of fair value accounting under IFRS for users of financial statements. After the fair value approach under IFRS has been outlined, it is thus in a next step necessary to identify users of financial statements.

2.2 Users of financial statements

This section deals with possible users of IFRS financial statements. This is a necessary step as the implications of fair value accounting for users of financial statements need to be examined. After a presentation of nonprofessional investors and their informational needs, this chapter deals with financial analysts as they are among the most important financial statement users. Furthermore, their earnings forecasts are used for the first empirical study.

2.2.1 Nonprofessional investors

The IFRS serve the informational needs of financial statement users. Although the IFRS framework for the preparation and presentation mentions seven categories of users of financial statements,[60] the IASB recognizes that not all users can be satisfied by financial statements (F 10). Even if it is not stated, **investors** are privileged users and satisfying their informational needs will also meet the needs of most other types of users (*Mihaela* (2008), p. 50). One group of investors addressed by the IASB is the group of nonprofessional investors (or: *private investors*).

Private investors differ in many respects from professional investors. Compared to institutional investors, they hold only a small number of shares in the regarding company. Thus, they have lower capital available for making an investment (*Kirchhoff/Piwinger* (2007), p. 729). Due to their lower capital investment, they are generally less diversified investors when they possess shares of only a few different firms (*Klein/Zur* (2009), p. 191). Whereas many institutional investors need to generate stock returns in the short term, private investors are usually **long-term oriented** (*Porák et al.* (2007), p. 268) and are more concerned about dividends and future earnings (*de Mesa Graziano* (2006), p. 44). Even if the company gets into trouble, private investors are more likely to remain loyal shareholders, which may have a positive influence on the share price (*Kirchhoff/Piwinger* (2007), p. 730). That is because their investment decisions are usually not based on complex analytical models, but on a personal connection with the company instead (*Porák et al.* (2007), p. 268).

---

60 The framework identifies investors, employees and groups that represent them, lenders and suppliers, customers, governments and their agencies, and the general public as possible users of financial statements (F 9).

Even if there are significant differences between professional and nonprofessional investors, there is no difference regarding their main interest. The investors are interested in the company's ability to achieve future earnings and to increase its wealth (*Mihaela* (2008), p. 51). Investors are interested in the future of the company they invest in rather than the current state. A central question also focuses on the upside potential of the company's shares (*Hocker* (2009), p. 473). Therefore, it is necessary for investors to obtain information in order to make an assessment about the future potential of the company. The financial statements are an instrument for the provision of information. Thus, this section presents some empirical evidence regarding nonprofessional investors' use of financial statement information.

Conducting a survey with UK private shareholders, *Bartlett/Chandler* (1997) examine the readership and understanding of different parts of the annual report. The results suggest on the one hand that financial press reports are most widely read by UK private shareholders (*Bartlett/Chandler* (1997), p. 255f.). On the other hand, the study provides evidence that much of the annual report is largely ignored by shareholders, or at best, is read only briefly. The authors suggest that this relatively low readership of much of the annual report may be a reflection of the **passive nature** of many private shareholders (*Bartlett/Chandler* (1997), p. 254). Instead of the detailed disclosure in the annual reports, it is expected that they are more interested in summary financial data, which do not feature the degree of complexity of primary financial data. However, when private shareholders read annual reports, they view the profit or loss statement as most important compared to other parts of the financial statements (*Bartlett/Chandler* (1997), p. 253).

In a further study, *Hodge* (2003) surveys U.S. private investors who are members of the "National Association of Investors Corporation" (NAIC) with regard to their perception of the degree of earnings management of listed companies. Moreover, the participants should indicate their perception of auditor independence and the relevance and reliability of audited financial statements. The results show that NAIC members, on average, believe that managers manage earnings approximately 50 percent of the time (*Hodge* (2003), p. 42). The majority of the respondents believe that auditor independence has decreased (34%) than increased (11%) over the last five years (*Hodge* (2003), p. 44). In addition, more respondents indicate that the **reliability** of audited financial information has decreased than increased (27% vs. 18%). However, concerning the relevance of audited financial statements, more respondents believe that the relevance has increased than decreased over the last five years. The author attributes this contrary finding to the decrease in perceived reliability, what causes investors to examine a firm's audited financial statements more thoroughly in order to validate the disclosed information (*Hodge* (2003), p. 46). As a result, this behavior may lead to an increase in the perceived relevance of audited financial statements.

In a further study, *Hodge/Pronk* (2006) examine whether professional and nonprofessional investors use different online quarterly financial information and whether the online information they use depends on whether they intend to make a new investment or evaluating a current investment. To provide evidence on these research questions, the authors use the website of the Dutch Philips company. Their results show that investors who are visiting the website to evaluate a current investment retrieve the data earlier than investors who are researching for a new investment. Professional investors evaluating a current investment tend to visit the website earlier than nonprofessional investors evaluating a current investment (*Hodge/Pronk* (2006), p. 280). Concerning the presentation format of the quarterly reports, professional investors prefer the less structured PDF file format, whereas nonprofessional investors tend to use the HTML version more often. In interesting finding of the study is that **investor expertise** influences the types of information investors focus on within the quarterly reports. While professional investors use financial statements more often, nonprofessional investors focus more on the management's discussion and analysis (MD&A), which summarizes the company's position from the management's view (*Hodge/Pronk* (2006), p. 283ff.).

The study of *Elliott et al.* (2008) refers to the prior finding that nonprofessional investors tend to rely more on filtered (MD&A) than unfiltered (financial statements) information when making investment decisions. Thus, the authors examine the relationship between nonprofessional investors' financial information choices, their investing expertise and their portfolio returns. The results provide evidence that less experienced investors generate higher portfolio returns when their use of filtered information increases (*Elliott et al.* (2008), p. 485ff.). However, this relationship depends upon investors' experience as more experienced investors are less likely to generate higher returns when they rely on filtered information. Moreover, experienced nonprofessional investors generate higher portfolio returns when they make their investment decisions on the basis of **unfiltered information**. *Elliott et al.* (2008) hypothesize that, one the one hand, experienced investors are better able to understand the quantitative information that is provided in the financial statements (*Elliott et al.* (2008), p. 491). On the other hand, the group of less experienced investors would benefit from information intermediaries who evaluate the information before passing the transformed information to the investors.[61]

Ernst et al. (2009) examine the informational needs and investment behavior for a sample of shareholders of Deutsche Post AG. The results of the survey-based research show that the annual report is the second most important **information source** for German private investors (*Ernst et al.* (2009), p. 29). However, investors seem to rely more on information provided in newspapers or the television instead of quantitative financial statement data. Given these results, the study confirms the findings of *Elliott et al.* (2008) regarding less experienced investors' use of unfiltered information. Within the annual report, the P&L and the balance sheet are most frequently used, whereas the notes are only used very rarely. As a reason for this finding, the authors mention the large comprehensiveness and the lack of understandability of mainly technical issues included in the notes (*Ernst et al.* (2009), p. 54). The authors conclude that private investors use mainly secondary sources instead of the financial statements when making investment decisions and that they rely to a large extent on information intermediaries (*Ernst et al.* (2009), p. 13f.).

Taken together, the empirical studies examining the behavior and use of company reports of nonprofessional investors provide mixed evidence. Nonprofessional investors use information contained in annual and quarterly reports. However, professional investors seem to use that kind of information more frequently. Even if nonprofessional investors

---

61   See chapter 2.2.2.3.

use financial statement information, they may find it challenging to understand the **quantitative information** disclosed. Therefore, they are more likely to use filtered information, such as for example from the MD&A. As a result, *Elliott et al.* (2008) and *Ernst et al.* (2009) point to the importance of information intermediaries for nonprofessional investors. Because financial analysts can function as information intermediaries on the capital markets, this group of professional investors is presented in the following chapter.

2.2.2 Professional investors

Since investors are interested in the future prospects of a company, they have an interest in the publication of forecasted information (*Mihaela* (2008), p. 51). Financial analysts as a specific kind of professional investor can provide investors with forecasts. Furthermore, financial analysts are among the most important users of financial statements (*Schipper* (1991), p. 105). Thus, this chapter presents the different types of financial analysts, describes their role as information intermediaries and deals with their research process. Finally, the chapter depicts the decision context and the incentives that analysts are exposed to, which may cause biased forecasts.

2.2.2.1 Financial analysts as professional investors

Investors are exposed to a large portion of information relevant to making an investment decision. Since nonprofessional investors would face problems to process this large amount of complex information in an appropriate way, financial analysts function as filters and transformers of available information (*de Bondt/Thaler* (1990), p. 56f.; *Bittner* (1996), p. 24; *Wichels* (2002), p. 30; *Weber* (2006), p. 18). Financial analysts obtain information from different public and private sources to generate **forecasts** on companies' earnings and future prospects that finally lead to recommendations about the buying or selling of the companies' stock (*Pietzsch* (2004), p. 11; *Cheng et al.* (2006), p. 51). They mainly use external information to create analysts' reports and forecasts on capital markets (securities and bonds), industry sectors, and single companies to prepare an investment (*Eberts* (1986), p. 255). The fact that analysts receive, process and deliver information to investors constitutes them as important users of financial information and as representatives of the group to whom financial reporting is and should be addressed by listed companies (*Schipper* (1991), p. 105).

Basically, the financial analysts' range of responsibilities can be divided into three different steps: information gathering, information processing, and information distribution.[62] During the process of **information gathering**, analysts use different information channels which may both involve primary sources of information (e.g., direct contact with managers) as well as information from public sources (e.g., newspapers, databases, or reports by other financial analysts). This information is in a next step used to analyze and prepare the data (**information processing**) for making investment decisions (*Hax* (1998), p. 15). Finally, the last step in financial analysts' work involves the **distribution of information** as recommendations to the public (*Wichels* (2002), p. 28f.). As financial analysts may obtain

---

62   See chapter 2.2.2.4 for more details on these three tasks that are performed by financial analysts.

their information through different channels, they gather and process firm-specific, industry, as well as macroeconomic information where most of which is obtained from public sources such as disclosure by firms or analyst conferences. By issuing earnings forecasts of the companies that they cover, they reduce information asymmetries between management and investors and embody therefore the role of **information intermediaries**[63] on the capital markets (*Chung/Jo* (1996), p. 493; *Benston* (2008), p. 216ff.).

The output of financial analysts, namely analysts' reports, provide information content to investors and are likely to influence not only investors when making their investment decisions but may also affect the risk of the firm, proxied by stock return volatility (*Kothari et al.* (2009), p. 1639)[64]. According to *Chen et al.* (2002), the two most important functions of financial analysts are the release of information to investors and the monitoring activity of firm management. First, by **transforming** a large amount of publicly available data into buy or sell recommendations, analysts provide information to the investment community and add value to the single investor. Second, by **monitoring** and assessing firms, analysts are able to reduce agency problems between investors and management (also see *Chung/Jo* (1996), p. 511 and *Doukas et al.* (2000), p. 54). As professional financial analysts are among the most important users of financial reports, the focus of researchers shifted to learning about their use of accounting information (*Schipper* (1991), p. 105).

2.2.2.2 Focus on sell side financial analysts

Financial analysts can be classified into three different groups: Buy side, sell side, and independent analysts. On the one hand, **buy side** financial analysts work for money management firms such as mutual funds, pension funds, trusts, or hedge funds (*Callsen-Bracker* (2007), p. 19). They are required to identify investment opportunities that will improve the net worth of the portfolio of the money managers that they work for (*Stubenrath* (2001), p. 22; *Wichels* (2002), p. 33; *Henze* (2004), p. 5f.). However, the research of buy side analysts is not publicly available as they forecast solely for their employers (*Cheng et al.* (2006), p. 52). On the other hand, **sell side** analysts are employees of investment banks. Their recommendations are publicly available (*Groysberg et al.* (2008), p. 25). Finally, **independent analysts** work for independent research firms and are not employed at investment banks or money management firms. They are usually working project-based for institutional investors to support buy side analysts which are employed there in a way to lower their workload and to provide fund managers with additional know how (*Weber* (2006), p. 25f.).

The recommendations of sell side financial analysts are the only recommendations produced by analysts available to the public. Thus, sell side analysts are important for accounting research. Their recommendations are also used for the first empirical study in

---

63 See chapter 2.2.2.3 for more details on financial analysts as information intermediaries.

64 Through a content analysis of several news sources, e.g. business reports, analysts' reports and the business press, the authors document a significant decline in the risk of the firm when the model indicates favorable disclosures in the news reports.

chapter 5. Therefore, sell side financial analysts are described in more detail in the following.

Sell side financial analysts are employed at broker firms like big investment banks and are viewed as the **primary producers** of earnings recommendations or recommendations about what stocks to buy, sell, or hold (*Schipper* (1991), p. 106). They develop recommendations for the stocks that they cover, based on their forecasts of companies' earnings, revenues, or cash flows for a certain period of time in the future (*Nix* (2000), p. 36). They usually cover a certain number of companies within one industry and may become well-known experts for this single industry (*v. Düsterlho* (2000), p. 74).[65] Their research may significantly improve through interactions with sales representatives and traders who also work within their firm (*Groysberg et al.* (2008), p. 26). Their earnings forecasts and stock recommendations are provided to the firm's clients and to the public as well (*Cheng et al.* (2006), p. 51).

Due to the fact that stock recommendations of sell side analysts are usually distributed at no cost, their individual earnings depend heavily on the trading activities of the investment banks' clients that are triggered by the analysts' stock recommendations (*Wichels* (2002), p. 33; *Callsen-Bracker* (2007), p. 19). Therefore, sell side analysts have to reconcile a steady flow of revenues for their employers with an objective and independent investment research, serving both the investment banks for which they work and the clients of these institutions with high-quality analysis of stocks (*Beyer/Guttman* (2011), p. 451). The clients of the investment bank are then expected to create **trading volume** for the investment bank by redeploying their capital. However, this can only be achieved when the analysts that are employed at the investment bank have gained a high reputation through appropriate investment research in the past (*Weber* (2006), p. 24). Thus, if analysts of sell side firms provided high-quality research in the past, clients would reward these institutions for providing these services by directing trading activity to their firms (*Winchel* (2008), p. 23).

The trading activity that is based on the stock recommendations of sell side analysts refers to the term **soft dollars** and describes the commissions that are generated from a trade or another financial transaction between a client and an investment manager (*Eccles et al.* (2001), p. 314). Brokerage commissions that include soft dollar arrangements are therefore higher than they would be if the buy or sell order would be execution only. In addition to these soft dollar commissions, analysts create value for the firms that they cover by lowering the information costs of potential investors that are considering an investment in the stock and increase the liquidity of this stock in the market, whereas these costs are recovered indirectly through investment banking fees (*Groysberg et al.* (2008), p. 26).

Taken together, four different tasks of sell side analysts have to be distinguished (*Nix* (2000), p. 36):

- To **mediate** between the investor and the company,

---

65 According to *Schipper* (1991), p. 112, financial analysts tend to follow between 10 and 20 stocks in a certain industry or economic industry.

- to **improve** the information supply in order to increase transparency and efficiency of the capital markets,

- to **advice** investors in a way to give a broad view over the company that an investor is interested in, and

- to **sell** stock recommendations to institutional investors.

The fact that sell side analysts' recommendations are available to the public and that their recommendations can have a significant influence on stock prices when investors trade on analysts' forecasts makes them highly relevant for the investor relations departments of listed companies (*Tiemann* (1997), p. 67; *v. Düsterlho* (2000), p. 73; *Henze* (2004), p. 6). Compared to the total number of investors in the market, there are only a small number of analysts available. Thus, an orientation of the investor relations efforts on the needs of financial analysts makes sense for listed companies due to analysts' **multiplier effects** (*v. Düsterlho* (2000), p. 73). In addition, analysts can be addressed directly and at low cost (*Achleitner/Wichels* (2003), p. 51ff.). Although it is important for companies to supply analysts with the information needed to make appropriate recommendations regarding the share, direct contact with the covering analyst can also lead to problems. This might be the case when analysts prefer to talk straight to the top management of the firm, thus providing managers with less time for the day-to-day business (*Michalkiewicz* (2003), p. 120f.).

After a presentation of sell side financial analysts, the next chapter deals with one of the reasons for analysts being of advantage for investors. Therefore, the chapter examines analysts purpose to serve as information intermediaries on the capital markets.

2.2.2.3 Analysts as information intermediaries

The information available on capital markets that is relevant to make an investment in a stock is not only interpreted by the investors itself. Financial analysts function as **information intermediaries** on the capital markets and evaluate the existing information before passing the transformed information to the investors (*Michaelsen* (2001), p. 70). The purpose of financial analysts is therefore to support investors with useful information and to reduce information asymmetries (*Hax* (1998), p. 46). The question that still remains is why investors do not evaluate the information solely on their own which would leave no room for a specialized group of information intermediaries. Skilled private investors or fund managers may indeed know how to transform the existing information in an appropriate way by themselves which would make financial analysts' work redundant. On the other hand, the existence of financial analysts could be explained with several competitive advantages that the investor with a diversified portfolio, in contrast, does not have.

Following this argumentation, *Benston/Smith, JR.* (1976) refer to aspects of **financial intermediation**[66] and identify three possible sources of comparative advantages of financial

---

66   The authors refer to the role of financial intermediaries, such as banks, financial brokers, or pension funds, whose main purpose is to channel funds between lenders and borrowers. They should not be confused with information intermediaries, as they serve different tasks on the capital markets. For a definition of financial intermediation see *Scholtens* (1993), p. 114ff.

intermediaries, which also hold for the group of information intermediaries (*Benston/Smith, JR.* (1976), p. 222f.). If the aspects that have been delineated in this paper are assigned to this group, the three arguments would be like the following: First, the intermediary may be able to achieve economies of scale through **specialization**. Thus, the intermediary could specialize in a certain industry and could only do research in this industry which would lower its own costs to process the available information. He could also develop or design **unique techniques** for a timely information processing, which would make information intermediation highly cost-effective. Second, some information, such as details about a company's financial constitution or the expected sales of a forthcoming all-new product, could be shared more likely with an intermediary than with the direct investor. This may be the case when the company can expect the intermediary to treat this sensitive information with caution. The intermediary has an intention to do so when reputation gains help to share similar information in the future. Finally, an individual who wants to invest in a company can reduce the **transaction costs** that are associated with the search for the appropriate investment. In fact, identifying a promising investment on the capital market can be costly and time-consuming. On the other hand, stock recommendations of financial analysts should normally contain the comprehensive information that is available on the capital markets.

But why should investors rely on information intermediaries when they cannot be sure about the quality of the information that is contained in stock recommendations? Thus, the problem that might arise between financial analysts and investors is the **reliability problem** (*DiPiazza/Eccles* (2002), p. 170). When financial analysts possess exclusive information about the future returns of securities, it may be challenging for them to show credibly of the information.[67] As a result, investors may not use stock recommendations at all. Especially in the case of informed professional investors, the importance of analysts in the market can then be mitigated. However, the literature reveals differing approaches to overcome this problem. *Leland/Pyle* (1977) propose to solve this problem as follows: An informed individual could **signal** his or her informed status and the quality of the information by investing in the recommended stocks. So, the willingness to invest may serve as a signal to the market of the true quality of the information (*Leland/Pyle* (1977), p. 371). Uninformed individuals would not find it advisable to spend money on their recommended stocks because of the risk, which would enable the market to distinguish between the uninformed and the informed. *Ramakrishnan/Thakor* (1984) mention the fact that information intermediaries are less likely to produce non-reliable information when their group size increases. Due to the **competition** among the information intermediaries, they have an increased incentive to produce reliable information (*Ramakrishnan/Thakor* (1984), p. 416).

---

67 It is assumed that "…it may not be easy for an informed individual to authenticate possession of valuable foreknowledge for resale purposes. After all, anyone could claim to have such knowledge." See *Hirshleifer* (1971), p. 565.

2.2.2.4 Research process of financial analysts

When financial analysts make recommendations, the process of converting available information into a stock recommendation can basically be divided into three steps (*Eberts* (1986), p. 98). First of all, analysts have to look for publicly available information about the company that they cover and for which they intend to make a stock recommendation (**search for information**). In a second step, analysts have to evaluate the available information and transform it into a recommendation which includes appraising the future prospects of a company and making a judgment whether to sell, hold, or buy a stock (**processing of information**). In principle, two techniques are used for the stock analysis. That is the technical analysis and the fundamental analysis. However, the fundamental analysis is far more widely used by security analysts (*Arnold/Moizer* (1984), p. 200; *Pike et al.* (1993), p. 498; *Vergoossen* (1993), p. 225). Finally, the stock recommendation has to be made public to enable the investors to use the recommendation for their investing decision (**distribution of information**). Figure 2-4 depicts the three steps of analysts' research process.

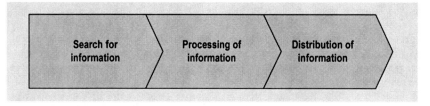

Figure 2-4: Research process of financial analysts
(Following *Stanzel* (2007), p. 94)

The different steps in the research process of financial analysts are described in the following chapters. This is necessary in the course of this study. It helps to understand how financial analysts use information from financial statements to finally transform this information into a forecast.

2.2.2.4.1 Search for information

The first step in the process of making a stock recommendation is the search for information. Financial analysts may use different sources of information. Given the evidence from several surveys and interviews that have been conducted on the methods of appraisal, security analysts agree to a large extent in their answers concerning possible sources of information. They view financial statement data as well as talks with the management of the company as the most influential sources in the process of appraisal. Analysts rely here both on the **annual financial statements** which are audited by an auditing firm as well as, to a lesser extent, on quarterly reports (*Michalkiewicz* (2003), p. 118).

The importance of financial statement data is well-documented in empirical accounting literature. *Chugh/Meador* (1984) conclude that financial statement data is of greatest interest when making stock valuations in the long run, whereas in the short run, environmental, economic, and industry conditions are relatively more important than information from the company accounts (*Chugh/Meador* (1984), p. 42). In a further study, it is reported that the most influential sources are the company's annual profit and loss account, its balance sheet, and, to a lesser extent, its interim results (*Arnold/Moizer* (1984)). The results of *Vergoossen* (1993) point to the recent annual report as the most important source of information. Even if *Bouwman et al.* (1995) confirm the importance of financial data, they also note that financial analysts demand more information from the reports, especially segment and future-oriented information. The findings of *Graham et al.* (2002) highlight the financial report as information source for financial analysts. The balance sheet is viewed as most important, followed by the income statement and the cash flow statements. The results of a more recent study corroborate the *Graham et al.* (2002) findings. *Ernst et al.* (2009) provide evidence for financial reports being second most important for financial analysts.[68] In addition, analysts use the income statement and the balance sheet most frequently when making a stock recommendation.

However, one would expect financial statement data to be of lower importance for analysts as financial statement data is primarily past-oriented and security analysts aim to assess the future prospects of the company (*Hax* (1998), p. 12). But the research results also confirm that information from the company's financial reporting is seen by security analysts as only one possible source of information and functions as an objective **reference document** or starting point for further research (*Day* (1986), p. 295).[69] As a first step in the research process, analysts may gain a general overview over the company by reading the annual accounts (*Vergoossen* (1993), p. 226). In fact, financial statements are checked by an auditor which makes the information more reliable for the analysts compared to information from other sources. In addition, analysts tend to use financial statements as a source for further information about the company, as a reference for certain definitions or methods of calculation of financial ratios or to verify some kind of information (*Kajüter et al.* (2010), p. 459).[70]

Despite of the company's accounts, **direct communication** with management of the company has been proven to be of great importance for financial analysts in evaluating the future prospects of a company.[71] Many analysts maintain good relations with the company's top-management or to the investor relations department. Maintaining a good relationship with the covering analysts is also important for the company which is the reason for companies to hold regularly analyst conferences where analysts may establish contact

68   However, analysts view direct communication with management as most important. See *Ernst et al.* (2009), p. 48.
69   See *Day* (1986), p. 301, who states that the report and the accounts are „very much seen as a basepoint or a point of reference".
70   However, the authors refer to the usage of management reports in Germany and state that management reports by financial analysts are not read in full but rather selective due to time constraints. See *Kajüter et al.* (2010), p. 459.
71   *Arnold/Moizer* (1984), p. 203, note that the importance of close contact to management may be even higher than reported in their survey: "Respondents might have understated their importance for fear that disclosure of the true importance could result in suspicions of 'inside information' being used with a consequence increase in the probability of such use being effectively controlled."

with company officials (*Hax* (1998), p. 12). In addition to analyst conferences, most analysts discuss a company's financial performance with its management at least once or twice a year and some analysts have direct contact to management at least three times a year (*Arnold/Moizer* (1984), p. 203). In addition to maintaining good relations to the management, analysts give attention to major changes in management as such changes could be the trigger for operational shifts of the company (*Previts et al.* (1994), p. 65).

The importance of direct contact to company officials seems surprising at first glance. Compared to the information from annual accounts, the information from management is more costly, because company's officials may not readily be available in explaining the financial results to security analysts (*Arnold/Moizer* (1984), p. 203). Especially in the case of the top management, individuals may not always find the time for responding to analyst questions in a timely manner. However, the high influence of direct contact to management when producing a stock recommendation may be due to the fact that analysts expect to get an **informational advantage** over other analysts covering the same firm (*Park/Stice* (2000), p. 261). There may also be suggestions that all public information is impounded in the share price very quickly.[72] Thus, the desire to close company contact can be interpreted as a search for non-publicly available information (*Day* (1986), p. 305). Although analysts tend to gain an informational advantage through the contact to a company's officials, it does not mean that they attempt to make their stock recommendations more valuable for investors through insider information. In fact, analysts may also gain an informational advantage by evaluating data that is close to insider information (*Hax* (1998), p. 13).

Analyst conferences are a second possible source which enables face to face interaction between company representatives and analysts. Analyst conferences play a key role in the process of getting input for making stock recommendations, because new information about the company is presented (*Henze* (2004), p. 15). Companies usually hold between one and two analyst conferences per year and normally schedule the conferences in combination with the press conference to the annual accounts or when the interim reports are made public (*v. Düsterlho* (2000), p. 77f.). In contrast to the annual general meeting, where most of the disclosed information is past-oriented, the top management focuses on information about future prospects of the firm or answers questions of analysts (*Tiemann* (1997), p. 40). Because analyst conferences are restricted to a small professional guild, namely financial analysts, and the private investor may not attend such a meeting, the release of insider information is not allowed (*Verse* (2006), p. 533). Anyhow, there is evidence that such analyst conferences may have significant effects on share prices and carry information content. *Regan* (1980) reports abnormal returns not only during the day of the analyst conference but also during a period of several weeks prior to the presentation (*Regan* (1980), p. 15). This would support the argument that, as analyst conferences are held voluntarily, companies hold conferences when they have favorable information to disclose. This results in significant abnormal returns prior to the date of the analyst con-

---

72   Here, it is referred to capital market efficiency in its semi-strong form. See chapter 4.1.2.1.

ference (*Hax* (1998), p. 14). *Sundaram et al.* (1993) find significant abnormal returns for two trading days, that is the day of the presentation and the day after the presentation.[73]

As the empirical research shows, annual report data and face to face interaction with company's management are most important when making stock recommendations. Nevertheless, analysts use further information sources in evaluating the future prospects of a company. Analysts gain further data for their recommendations from **press releases** to the company or from company releases that go well beyond the information contained in the annual reports (*Michalkiewicz* (2003), p. 118). Despite of primary sources of information (i.e. information directly released by the company), financial analysts use secondary information as well. As empirical evidence shows, analysts tend to obtain information from journals, magazines, or newspapers but also incorporate the reports of other investment analysts into their own evaluation of the company (*Pike et al.* (1993), p. 496; *Vergoossen* (1993), p. 229).[74] As there can be significant implications from industry developments on single companies within that industry, information about industry developments like for example industry statistics or price indices are also used by financial analysts (*Day* (1986), p. 304).

The search for information represents the first step in the research process of financial analysts. After this step and possible information sources has been presented in this chapter, the next chapter deals with the processing of information. This is important as the chapter reports the models that analysts may use when examining financial statement data.

2.2.2.4.2 Processing of information

The most important point during the step of information processing is the bottom line: An analyst evaluates the available information from different sources and transforms the information into a stock recommendation (*Steiner/Uhlir* (2001), p. 2). Although, financial analyst may use different methods and models in doing security analysis, there are two approaches which are used most commonly in practice, which are the technical and the fundamental analysis. **Technical analysts** do not rely on company's earnings or other information available but focus solely on the price history of a share. The idea behind the technical approach in stock analysis is that the stock market moves in trends which are determined by changing attitudes of investors to a variety of economic, monetary, political and psychological forces (*Pring* (1980), p. 2). Technicians seek to identify price patterns and trends in financial markets from past stock movements and attempt to predict the price movements in the future (*Laser* (1995), p. 10). In contrast to this, **fundamental**

---

73 However, the authors note that relaying of insider information at analyst conferences is not likely to happen. A more plausible explanation for the abnormal returns during the presentation is that "managements confirm financial analysts' positive expectations or allay concerns in the case of negative expectations. Rather than new information becoming available, previously available information may be interpreted in a more positive light after a presentation." See *Sundaram et al.* (1993), p. 89.

74 Based on the surveys, the importance of recommendations from other analysts may well be undervalued, because analysts are not likely to admit that they rely on other analysts when making their forecasts. See *Hax* (1998), p. 15.

analysts believe that there is still publicly available information not yet reflected in the share price (*Henze* (2004), p. 13; *Chen* (2010), p. 3).

Information from the financial statements can only be used within the fundamental stock analysis. Such information is not needed when doing technical analysis. However, this study examines the implications of fair values within financial statements. Therefore, only the fundamental analysis is presented in more detail in the following.[75]

The fundamental analysis includes both economic, industry, and company analysis. Financial analysts may perform the fundamental analysis either as a top-down or a bottom-up approach. On the one hand, the **top-down** analyst starts the analysis with indicators of global economics (e.g., growth rates, inflation, interest rates) and then narrows the search down to regional or industry analysis while searching for a recommendable stock in this area (*Steiner/Bruns* (2002), p. 230). On the other hand, the **bottom-up** approach is based on company-specific data. Thus, the analyst starts with specific businesses, regardless of their geographic or industrial origin and uses regional or industry data only in a second step (*Wichels* (2002), p. 67).[76]

The main purpose of the fundamental analysis is to determine the **intrinsic value** of a share (*Penman* (2007b), p. 5). The intrinsic value of a share refers to the true value of a company, including all aspects of business, which means both tangible and intangible aspects and factors (*Röckemann* (1995), p. 5f.). As this value is expected to change overtime and fluctuates in certain ranges, the intrinsic value does not always equal the current market value on a stock exchange (*Steiner/Bruns* (2002), p. 228f.). The fundamental analysis is therefore based on the assumption that the market may misprice shares in the short run but that the correct price (the intrinsic value) will eventually be reached (*Graham/Le Dodd* (2008), p. 64). Finally, in the long run, shares' market prices should equal their intrinsic values. Earnings can be realized by trading on the mispriced securities and waiting for the market to realize its mistake and bring the mispriced security closer to its intrinsic value. To calculate the intrinsic value, analysts have to evaluate the constitution of the business, which means they have to look at ratios and have to determine future growth rates that can later be used as inputs for different valuation models (*Dinauer* (1977), p. 10f.). The valuation model that is most frequently used is the DCF model, which calculates the company's value as the present value of the discounted cash flows of the company.[77] However, the general approach of the DCF may also be applied to further performance figures, such as for example future dividends received by the investor or company's earnings (*Achleitner et al.* (2001), p. 73). After the intrinsic value is determined on the basis of one of the valuation models, the value is compared to the market value. If the intrinsic value is higher than the market price, the analyst recommends buying the share. If the intrinsic value is equal to market price the analyst recommends holding the share and if it

---

75 In addition, empirical evidence shows that the fundamental analysis is by far dominating the other techniques of equity analysis. See for example *Arnold/Moizer* (1984), *Pike et al.* (1993) or *Vergoossen* (1993).

76 For a detailed comparison of the top-down and the bottom-up approaches see *Hooke* (1998), p. 73ff.

77 For a detailed description of the DCF model see chapter 2.1.3.1.3.

is lower than the market price, the analyst issues a sell recommendation, respectively (*Kames* (2000), p. 50; *Weber* (2006), p. 41).

When financial analysts use the **DCF model**, the company's earnings, dividends, or cash flows of the future periods are forecasted and have to be discounted for time periods (*Steiner/Uhlir* (2001), p. 105ff.). In addition, a terminal value as the present value at a future point in time of all future inflows may be added to calculation when a stable growth rate is expected forever until infinity (*Damodaran* (2002), p. 303f.). However, there are no fixed rules for the determination of the terminal value. Therefore, the value remains largely subjective and depends on the valuation model applied. The discount factor, which is used for adjusting cash flows for the different future periods, does also influence the outcomes of the DCF model. Foremost, the discount factor is determined by using the **CAPM**[78] that is mainly based on three measures: The risk free interest rate, the market risk premium, and the beta factor, which is a measurement of how a company's share price reacts to a change in the market (*Bittner* (1996), p. 40).[79] Although the model is widely used in practice, the CAPM has several shortcomings and the validity of the model is questionable.[80] In addition, it has to be mentioned that the fundamental analysis can only be fruitful in a capital market that is informationally efficient in the weak-form, because stock prices then do not reflect all publicly available information (*Friedrich* (2007), p. 67).[81] Furthermore, as there are no fixed rules for the determination of the intrinsic value and the choice for the computation method is up to the single evaluator, the intrinsic value remains largely subjective (*Laser* (1995), p. 29).

2.2.2.4.3   Distribution of information

After the information necessary for making a stock recommendation has been obtained and evaluated, the information needs to be distributed to the investors. Getting an in-depth understanding about the way in which recommendations are distributed to the investors is important, because it represents the last step in financial analysts' research process. However, the distribution of information is only relevant for sell siders. As aforementioned, buy side analysts are employed at money management firms like mutual funds. Thus, they do not have to take care for the distribution of their recommendations when their research work is only used within the regarding money management firms they work for.

Sell side financial analysts are not independent as they work for banks and investment companies. The clients of these investment banks, usually investors who manage their shares in a custody account at this financial institution, receive the stock recommenda-

---

78   The term CAPM refers to the „Capital Asset Pricing Model". For further information see *Sharpe* (1964) and *Lintner* (1965).

79   The different values for the beta denote the following: A beta higher than one states that a change in share price is exaggerated compared to the remaining shares in the market. A beta less than one means that the share is relatively stable and not very responsive to changes in the market and a negative beta means that a share is moving in the opposite direction of the market. See *Mullins, JR.* (1982), p. 108.

80   There are studies that have tested the validity of the CAPM. See, among others, *Black et al.* (1972), *Fama/MacBeth* (1973) and *Gibbons* (1982).

81   For further information concerning the efficient market hypothesis see chapter 4.1.2.

tions at **no cost**. The investment bank does not charge a fee for each analyst recommendation made available to their customers. However, the investment bank expects their customers to make the trades that are based on the buy or sell recommendations from their in-house sell side analysts with its own trading division (*Hax* (1998), p. 19). The fees that investment banks charge their clients for the trading of shares can be divided into two parts: First, a part that consists of the remuneration for the trading of the share, which is for example a fee for the stock exchange, and as a second part the remuneration for the trading advice and the stock recommendation (*Henze* (2004), p. 19). Although sell side financial analysts do not receive a direct compensation for their research work as they are not able to sell their recommendations straight to the investors, they generate revenue for their employers when investors trade on their recommendations (*Michalkiewicz* (2003), p. 125).

The deregulation of the brokerage industry, which started in 1975 in the U.S. and abolished high fixed fees for trading stocks and allowed market competition to dictate commissions, gave rise to the discount brokerage industry and introduced the cheap online-trading of stocks (*Hax* (1998), p. 20). In addition to the U.S., **discount brokers** became also existent in recent years in other countries, especially in Europe. The distinction between full service providers, like investment banks who provide investors with investment information, and discount brokers who charge lower commissions and provide only transaction services enables traders to choose between these two institutions. The problem for the investment banks is the fact that they cannot force their clients to do the trading activities within their own investment departments as there is an obvious incentive for investors to receive information from the full-service brokers and then doing their trades at discount brokers (*Brennan/Chordia* (1993), p. 1380).

Because **timing** is an important factor in a successful trading strategy, the point in time when investors gain notice of the new stock recommendation is essential. But the recommendations are not available at the same time for all investors (*Henze* (2004), p. 19). First of all, the investment banks provide electronic databases with up to date stock recommendations. These services make the information available immediately to their subscribers who are often also customers of the investment banks (*Womack* (1996), p. 140). These investors, who are often institutional investors such as investment funds, then belong to the first group which is able to trade on the new information. For the further distribution of the recommendations, the sell side analysts create written reports which are then made available to the clients of the investment banks (*Hax* (1998), p. 21). These written reports are often distributed sometime after the date when the information is made available in specific databases (*Womack* (1996), p. 140). Finally, the information is released to the public through different channels, which may include newspapers, the internet or TV stations.

An example for an announcement of stock recommendations in publicly available media is the "Heard-on-the-Street" (HOTS) column of *The Wall Street Journal*.[82] The HOTS

---

82 The daily HOTS column of The Wall Street Journal includes macroeconomic conditions as well as information about a firm or a group of firms. The articles present the opinions of one or more securi-

column and the stock recommendations included have been in the focus of academic researchers and evidence suggests that even the lowest degree of information channels has substantial information content and is useful for investors. Thus, the two empirical studies by *Liu et al.* (1990) and *Beneish* (1991) provide similar results and both report that the publication of buy or sell recommendations in the HOTS column is associated with significant **abnormal returns** on the publication day (*Liu et al.* (1990), p. 399; *Beneish* (1991), p. 394). However, the joint finding of the two papers, that significant abnormal returns are also present two days prior to the publication date, leads to the suggestion that several investors possess the information prior to the public disclosure and take advantage by trading on that information.

After the different types of financial analysts, their function on the capital markets and the way in which they produce forecasts have been presented in the previous chapters, the next chapter focuses on the decision context in which analysts make their recommendations. In addition, several incentives, which may hinder analysts from producing reliable forecasts, are presented.

2.2.2.5   Decision context and incentives facing financial analysts

Not only financial statement information may significantly affect financial analysts' behavior when producing a forecast. Moreover, the decision context and incentives facing financial analysts should also be taken into account. It is important to get an in-depth understanding regarding possible influences on accurate and unbiased forecasts. This chapter is necessary for the first empirical study as it helps to understand possible reasons for financial analysts not producing accurate forecasts. While it is intended to examine the implications of fair value accounting, there could be further influences on financial analysts' forecasting ability.

The environment of analysts contains a wide variety of tasks when analysts select stocks, collect information, forecast earnings, and write reports. They have an incentive to maintain good relations with management of the company that they cover and face incentives associated with their employer's brokerage, underwriting, and investment banking activities. Thus, analysts face many **competing incentives:** They do not only want to be accurate to signal their skill and build their reputation. They also want to issue optimistic long-term forecasts to please the firms they follow or to generate trading volume for their brokerage houses (*Feng/McVay* (2010), p. 1617). These competing incentives are presented in more detail in the following.

The accuracy of financial analysts' earnings forecasts does not solely depend on the skills and abilities that analysts have in transforming available information into a forecast. In addition, the work of analysts largely depends on the information that they possess when making a forecast. Insofar, analysts need to have reliable and high-quality information sources in their day-to-day work. One source of such information is the company's management. Thus, a possible bias in forecasting may result from the **analyst-manager**

---

ty analysts, report revisions in analysts' recommendations and cite analysts' reasons for their revisions. See *Beneish* (1991), p. 397, and *Liu et al.* (1990), p. 400, for further information.

relationship (*Schipper* (1991), p. 114f.). When analysts intend to gain an informational advantage when making their forecast, it is highly recommended that they maintain a stable and intensive communication with management. An interruption of this relationship would cause significant problems for the analysts, because the information from management must then be obtained from other sources at probably higher costs and increased effort (*Hax* (1998), p. 22). If the worst comes to the worst, the information normally obtained from management cannot be received from other sources and the forecast has to be made with insufficient data.

Managers of a company may use these circumstances and the dependency of analysts for their own purpose. Specifically, some managers can make it difficult for unfavorable analysts to maintain any reasonable kind of contact (*Stanzel* (2007), p. 144). It is possible that analysts who issued pessimistic forecasts in the past are being **cut off** from information, because the forecasts have been too pessimistic from a managements' point of view. Because it is assumed that management has a strong interest in the sense that investors and the public have a positive image of their company, they have an interest in rather optimistic than pessimistic comments of financial analysts (*Achleitner et al.* (2001), p. 53). In this sense, it is possible that management intends to reach a better performance on the own company's stock due to possible share-based payments and equity options which only can be executed when the stock price reaches a certain level. In addition, a higher stock price enables management to have more freedom of action. This could be beneficial in the case of takeovers and acquisitions of other companies, when the purchase price is paid in shares and a higher stock price enables management to exchange less own shares to gain control over the assets of the company purchased (*Göres* (2004), p. 54).

If this influence on analysts does exist and if it has the given widespread effects, this may help to account for the tendency that analysts in general tend to issue optimistic earnings forecasts, especially in the face of negative share returns and earnings forecasts (*Schipper* (1991), p. 115). Following this notion, analysts have an incentive to issue **optimistic** forecasts that are not based on rational behavior but follow from a wish by analysts to cultivate management relations (*Francis/Philbrick* (1993), p. 217). The assumption that analysts tend to publish rather optimistic than pessimistic forecasts can be supported by empirical evidence. Thus, many descriptive studies in the field of international forecasting literature report a significantly higher number of buy recommendations than sell recommendations.[83] In addition to descriptive evidence, the optimism bias can also be reported by comparing the forecasted earnings and the realized earnings, thus resulting in average forecast errors that are significantly positive.[84] This leads to the assumption that financial analysts systematically overestimate companies' earnings.

Besides analysts' intention to remain in a good relationship with the management of a company, there may be further influences resulting in biased forecasts, resulting from the **brokerage and investment banking activities** of analysts' employers. Hence, sell side analysts are employed at broker firms like big investment banks. As financial intermediaries, the banks that analysts work for provide various services for their clients and custom-

---

83   See, among others, *DeBondt/Thaler* (1990), *Beneish* (1991), *Stickel* (1995), and *Womack* (1996).
84   See for example *Francis/Philbrick* (1993), *Dreman/Berry* (1995) or *Mande/Kwak* (1996).

ers, including merger and acquisition advice, brokerage services, underwriting services, and their own trading activities as well (*Schipper* (1991), p. 113). Therefore, the research reports and recommendations of sell side analysts are usually part of a group of bundled services offered by these full-service investment banking firms (*Beyer/Guttman* (2011), p. 451). The different services that investment banks provide to their clients have the potential to influence analysts' behavior. This may lead to a bias in the stock recommendations made by financial analysts. The investment bank can take advantage of favorable stock recommendations to make more revenue in other departments which puts significant pressure on analysts not to report truthfully but making recommendations that are in the interest of the investment banking firm (*Lin/McNichols* (1998), p. 105ff.). This leads to the assumption that analysts or the research departments of investment banks are not independent at all, even when these departments are outsourced into a subsidiary firm (*Hax* (1998), p. 26). Otherwise, companies could reduce or even cancel any business with the investment bank when one of their analysts issued a recommendation that has not been to favorable in the eyes of management.[85]

Another instance which induces sell side analysts to issue optimistic forecasts is the fact that their **compensation** is partly based on the sales commissions that they generate. Optimistic forecasts that are accompanied by buy recommendations result in a greater number of trades than do pessimistic forecasts which are accompanied by either hold or sell recommendations. Thus, analysts are more likely to be overly optimistic (*Trueman* (1994), p. 114). However, it is much easier to convince clients to invest in new stocks rather than to sell them or to short-sell stocks that the clients do not own. Therefore, the investment bank's research departments is usually required to have a greater number of buy recommendations than hold or sell recommendations outstanding (*Brown* (1993), p. 303).

Despite of the interests of the companies that analysts cover and the investment banks that analysts work for, there is a third possible explanation for the existence of biased research reports. To lower the risk of making imprecise earnings forecasts, analysts may more rely on the consensus forecast than their own ability and skill to process the available information (*Callsen-Bracker* (2007), p. 57). The social background for this behavior is seen in analysts' effort to gain reputation, which may improve their position in the financial analysts' labor market.[86] Thus, analysts own considerations for reputation or career concerns can sometimes lead them to ignore their private information and valuation opinion about a stock and copy the recommendations of other analysts (*Hong et al.* (2000), p. 121). The likelihood that the analyst issues a forecast that is similar to previously by other analysts announced forecasts is to a large extent greater than could be justified by his own information (*Trueman* (1994), p. 98). Such action of analysts which leads to a potential bias in forecasts is a manifestation of **herding behavior** and is mainly undertaken in order

---

85   See *Regan* (1993) who documents several cases in the U.S. where brokerage firms came under pressure by clients after their analysts issued less favorable recommendations.

86   In academic research, the degree of analyst reputation is often proxied by analyst rankings, such as the Institutional Investor Ranking. The resulting rankings are powerful determinants of analyst reputation. See *Leone/Wu* (2007), p. 1.

to favorably affect individual investor's assessment of the analyst's ability to forecast earnings.[87]

Furthermore, as investors require analysts do make forecasts that are both accurate and timely after new information is released to the public, it may be that analysts mimic forecasts that have been announced by informed analysts (*O'Brien* (1990), p. 303). The basic problem that might arise due to herding behavior is when a large number of analysts orientate their earnings forecasts at the consensus which is already imprecise and wrong to a large extent. A single wrong forecast of earnings that is already in the market then is being repeated and consequently confirmed at some point in time (*Callsen-Bracker* (2007), p. 57). Although this behavior is inefficient from a social standpoint, it can be rational from the perspective of individual equity analysts who are concerned about their **reputations** in the capital market as information intermediaries (*Scharfstein/Stein* (1990), p. 465).

Taken together, investors should interpret financial analysts' recommendations with caution. There may be a bias in their forecasts due to the analyst-manager relationship and their integration into the brokerage and investment banking activities of their employer. Finally, analysts may adopt some kind of herding behavior.

2.2.3 Summary

Financial analysts are important actors on the capital markets. They provide information to the investment community and add value to the single investor by transforming publicly available data into buy or sell recommendations for companies' shares. In addition, they monitor the management and assess the prospects of the firm in a way to mitigate possible agency conflicts between investors and management. Although, the stock analysis is performed by buy side, sell side, and independent analysts, the fact that the recommendations of sell siders are publicly available constitutes them as **adequate research object** in accounting literature. This does also apply to this study. Financial analysts use different sources of information when evaluating a company's shares in order to produce a recommendation. Despite of other information sources such as conference calls or direct communication with management, accounting data has proven to be of significant importance for financial analysts. This fact is seen in connection with the importance of the fundamental analysis which is most often applied in the course of stock analysis. However, investors should interpret research of financial analysts with caution as there are many **incentives** which may lead to a possible bias in stock recommendations. Whereas on the one hand, financial analysts may have an intention to maintain good relations with the management in order to gain an informational advantage, the brokerage activities of their employers represent a further explanation for biased forecasts. Finally, analysts' own career concerns may result in a herding behavior.

---

87 Empirical evidence confirms analysts' tendency to herd. See for example *Hong et al.* (2000), *Doukas et al.* (2000) or *Clement/Tse* (2005). For an explanation of herding behavior from a theoretical viewpoint see *Graham* (1999).

The next chapter presents and reviews several streams of empirical literature, which relate to the two empirical studies performed in this research. This step is necessary for positioning the two studies. Moreover, the research gap is identified and presented.

3 Related empirical literature

Based on the research questions identified in the first chapter, this chapter reviews related empirical literature and highlights the research gap of the study. The research investigates several characteristics of fair value accounting and has, as such, broad implications for several streams of literature. The first study provides evidence on the forecasting ability of financial analysts when they are either confronted with assets measured at historical cost or fair value. In the course of the second study, implications of fair value accounting on the judgments and investment decisions of nonprofessional investors are examined. Figure 3-1 presents a classification of the related empirical literature which is reviewed in this chapter.

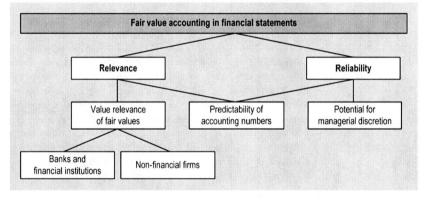

Figure 3-1: Classification of related empirical literature

While fair value accounting has already been examined in manifold ways, the empirical accounting literature reviewed is selected to best apply to the objects of this study. As Figure 3-1 demonstrates, the related literature can basically be divided into literature examining the relevance and the reliability of fair value accounting in financial statements. As aforementioned in chapter 2.1.2.6, there is a trade-off between **relevance and reliability** when dealing with fair values. However, both requirements are qualitative characteristics of financial statements in the IFRS framework and determine the usefulness of financial reporting. Whereas the characteristic of relevance is operationalized by value relevance of fair value measures in this chapter,[88] reliability is represented by the potential for managerial discretion provided by fair value accounting. Because a great number of value relevance studies have been conducted for banks and financial institutions, fair value relevance is investigated separately for banks and non-financial firms. The extent of reliability and relevance impacts the predictability of accounting numbers, which are mainly annual earnings, turnover or cash flow measures. Referring to the study regarding financial ana-

---

88 An accounting amount will be value relevant in the way that it has a predicted significant relation with share prices only if the amount reflects information relevant to investors in valuing the firm (*Barth et al.* (2001), p. 80). See chapter 3.1.

lysts' ability to forecasting, the studies presented in the following deal with the predictability of accounting numbers and fair value accounting. Additionally, the effect of additional disclosure is investigated.

The majority of the studies reviewed use archival-based approaches. However, the studies use to some extent experimental-based approaches. Survey-based methods and the event study methodology are only applied rarely. Whereas the literature regarding the value relevance of fair value accounting is reviewed in chapter 3.1, its reliability and potential for managerial discretion is discussed in chapter 3.2. Finally, the predictability of accounting numbers is outlined in chapter 3.3.

3.1 Relevance of fair value accounting

A common way to assess the relevance of a recognized or disclosed accounting amount is to assess its incremental association with share prices or share returns after controlling for other accounting or market information (*Landsman* (2007), p. 22).[89] **Incremental association studies** in this sense investigate whether the accounting number of interest is helpful in explaining value or returns, that is, when its estimated regression coefficient is significantly different from zero (*Holthausen/Watts* (2001), p. 6). According to this, accounting information is considered to be value relevant when it has the expected association with the market value of equity, which is the share price (*Barth et al.* (2001), p. 79f.). If a significant association can be verified, then it is assumed that the accounting information is relevant to investors and is considered important enough to be reflected in share prices (*Chang Joon Song et al.* (2010), p. 1379). The **value relevance accounting literature** does therefore provide direct evidence of the importance of recognized fair values in financial statements or its disclosure in the accompanying notes section.

3.1.1 Value relevance of fair value accounting for banks and financial institutions

Much of the value relevance research assessing the relevance of fair value information focuses on banks and financial institutions since these entities hold a significant amount of financial assets and liabilities in their portfolio (*Landsman* (2007), p. 22). Several studies compare the value relevance of disclosed and recognized fair values for banks' investment securities as **SFAS 115** made the recognition of fair values mandatory. In general, SFAS 115 deals with the measurement of financial instruments under U.S. GAAP and determines which kind of assets or liabilities have to be recognized at historical cost or fair value (*Wallace* (2006), p. 17). All studies concerning the value relevance of fair values for banks and financial institutions have been conducted in the United States. A summary of the results from empirical studies for banks and other financial institutions is presented in Table 3-1.

---

89   For a comprehensive overview of the value relevance literature in financial accounting, see *Holthausen/Watts* (2001).

Reference	Method	Key results
Barth (1994)	Archival, 1971-1990, U.S.	Fair value estimates of investment securities provide significant explanatory power beyond that provided by historical cost.
Barth et al. (1995)	Archival, 1971-1990, U.S.	The increased volatility of earnings due to fair value accounting is not reflected in stock prices. Under fair value accounting, banks do more frequently violate regulatory capital requirements.
Petroni/Wahlen (1995)	Archival, 1985-1992, U.S.	Share prices of property-liability insurers can be explained by fair values of equity investments and U.S. treasury investments.
Barth et al. (1996)	Archival, 1992-1993, U.S.	Fair value estimates of loans, securities and long-term debt disclosures under SFAS 107 provide significant explanatory power for bank share prices which is greater than the explanatory power provided by book values.
Cornett et al. (1996)	Event study, 1989-1993, U.S.	Announcements which signal an increased (decreased) probability of issuance of fair value accounting standards produce negative (positive) abnormal returns.
Eccher et al. (1996)	Archival, 1992-1993, U.S.	Whereas differences between fair values and book values of financial instruments are associated with market-to-book ratios, fair value disclosures for financial instruments other than securities are value relevant only in limited settings.
Nelson (1996)	Archival, 1992-1993, U.S.	Reported fair values of investment securities have incremental power relative to book value.
Venkatachalam (1996)	Archival, 1993-1994, U.S.	Fair value estimates for derivatives explain cross-sectional variation in bank share prices and have explanatory power above notional amounts of derivatives.
Mozes (2002)	Archival, 1996, U.S.	Fair value disclosures within a residual-income valuation model are value relevant.
Carroll et al. (2003)	Archival, 1982-1997, U.S.	For closed-end mutual funds, fair values are significantly associated with stock prices and fair value security gains and losses are significantly associated with stock returns.
Khurana/Kim (2003)	Archival, 1995-1998, U.S.	Mark-to-market fair values are more value relevant than mark-to-model fair values.
Ahmed et al. (2006)	Archival, 1995-2000, U.S.	Fair values of derivatives are only value relevant when the amount is recognized, whereas disclosed amounts are not value relevant.
Song et al. (2010)	Archival, 2008, U.S.	Level 1 and Level 2 fair value estimates are significantly more value relevant than Level 3 fair value estimates.

Table 3-1: Value relevance of fair value accounting for banks and financial institutions

For a sample of U.S. banks with data from 1971-1990, *Barth* (1994) finds that the fair values of investment securities are **incrementally associated** with share prices of banks after controlling for investment securities' book values (*Barth* (1994), p. 2). However, the study produces mixed results for whether unrecognized securities' gains and losses provide incremental power relative to other components of income when examined in an annual returns context (*Barth* (1994), p. 12). A possible explanation for this ambiguous finding provided in the paper is that estimates for gains and losses may contain too much measurement error relative to the true underlying changes in the market values. Additionally, it is mentioned that securities' gains and losses might be offset by unrecognized gains and losses of other assets or liabilities, thus suggesting that the findings are due to omitted variables (*Barth* (1994), p. 23). Despite of these clear implications for users of financial statements, it has to be noted as a limitation of the study that the power of the research design may be an issue when securities' gains and losses are measured with error, thus making it difficult to detect the fair value effect (*Barth* (1994), p. 12).

Barth et al. (1995) use essentially the same database and confirm the key results of the *Barth* (1994) findings. The authors lend support to the measurement error explanation and provide evidence that fair value-based measures of net income are **more volatile** than measures based on historical cost, but that incremental volatility is not reflected in share prices (*Barth et al.* (1995), p. 602). The study also finds that banks tend to violate regulatory capital requirements more frequently under fair value than under historical cost accounting, and fair value regulatory capital violations help predict future historical cost regulatory capital violations, but share prices fail to reflect this increased regulatory risk (*Barth et al.* (1995), p. 577). Thus, the authors suggest that possible concerns to use fair values are not supported by their findings. Even if fair values cause earnings to be more volatile, the increased volatility does not represent an increased economic risk (*Barth et al.* (1995), p. 603).

The association of fair values for equity/debt securities and share prices of property-liability insurers for 1985-1992 is examined by *Petroni/Wahlen* (1995).[90] The authors find that share prices can be explained by fair values of equity instruments and U.S. **treasury investments** (*Petroni/Wahlen* (1995), p. 719). However, the authors find no evidence of other types of investment securities' fair value disclosures explaining share prices beyond historical cost. The authors hypothesize that other types of investment, such as municipal or corporate bonds, may be less actively traded and have longer terms to maturity than treasury securities, thus resulting in a lack of value relevance (*Petroni/Wahlen* (1995), p. 735). However, this conclusion needs to be interpreted with caution as the lack of value relevance may also be due to the research design which is not sensitive enough to detect this relation.

Barth et al. (1996), *Eccher et al.* (1996), and *Nelson* (1996) employ similar approaches to assess the incremental value relevance of fair values in 1992-1993. Confirming the findings of *Barth* (1994), all three studies document investment securities' fair values are in-

---

90   The authors restrict their sample to property-liability insurers, because they state that "investment securities comprise over 60 percent of the total assets of a typical property-liability insurer" (*Petroni/Wahlen* (1995), p. 720).

crementally informative compared to their book values in explaining bank share prices. By using a more powerful research design which also controls for the effect of potential omitted variables and in contrast to the other two studies, *Barth et al.* (1996) find evidence that fair values for loans provide more **explanatory power** than their book values (*Barth et al.* (1996), p. 513). The authors also provide additional evidence that the fair values of loans adequately reflect information regarding the default and interest rate risk of those loans.[91] Based on their findings, the authors conclude that the fair value disclosure requirements have made GAAP financial statements a more comprehensive source of value relevant information (*Eccher et al.* (1996), p. 114). However, it is also pointed to the fact that it is necessary to control for variables, such as future profitability, that have been omitted in earlier studies (*Nelson* (1996), p. 181). A limitation of the studies is that the authors use sample years which are characterized by decreasing interest rates, thus resulting in fair value estimates exceeding book values. Proponents of fair value accounting are more concerned about the opposite scenario when decreases of fair value serve as an early signal of solvency problems (*Eccher et al.* (1996), p. 115). Fair values may then have different implications under such a setting compared to the setting used in the studies.

A different approach to measure the relevance of fair value accounting is applied by *Cornett et al.* (1996). The authors use the **event study methodology** in order to document movements in financial institutions' share prices after announcements which do either increase or decrease the probability of a new fair value standard under U.S. GAAP.[92] During 1989-1993, fair value announcements seem to be of relevance, but investors tend to take a more **critical position** with regard to fair values. Whereas announcements signaling an increased probability of an upcoming fair value standard result in negative abnormal returns, a decrease results in the opposite and positive abnormal returns (*Cornett et al.* (1996), p. 119). Based on these findings, the authors suggest that investors view the new costs imposed on banks by accounting pronouncements as greater than the benefits resulting from fair value accounting (*Cornett et al.* (1996), p. 152). Despite of the general problems associated with the event study methodology,[93] another limitation of the study is that the authors base their findings on a sample of 23 events relating to fair value accounting. Even if it is therefore ensured that the events do not overlap (resulting in correlated estimates), the database is relatively small, thus making it difficult to draw reliable conclusion.

Venkatachalam (1996) examines the value relevance of banks' derivatives disclosures for a sample of U.S. banks in 1993 and 1994. The findings from the study suggest that derivatives' fair value estimates explain **cross-sectional variation** in bank share prices incremental to fair values of the primary on-balance accounts, which are cash, investments, loans,

---

91 It is also interesting to note that the studies' findings suggest that investors tend to discount the fair value estimates of financially less healthy banks, which is consistent with investors being able to see through attempts by managers to make their banks appear healthier by exercising discretion. See *Barth et al.* (1996), p. 530.

92 The authors use announcements referring to SFAS 105, SFAS 107, and SFAS 115. See *Cornett et al.* (1996), p. 125.

93 Among others, there are problems with event-date uncertainty and nonsynchronous trading. Additionally, it is not certain which model to use to determine a normal level of security returns. See *May* (1991) or *MacKinlay* (1997).

deposits, and debt (*Venkatachalam* (1996), p. 347). The author notes that his findings are in contrast to prior research that documented only inconclusive evidence on the value relevance of off-balance sheet instruments (*Venkatachalam* (1996), p. 354). However, the difference in the findings may also be due to the inherent limitations of performing tests on cross-sectional data.

The empirical studies of *Mozes* (2002), *Carroll et al.* (2003), and *Khurana/Kim* (2003) correspondingly document a value relevance of fair values. Whereas *Mozes* (2002) provides evidence of fair values being relevant within a **residual-income valuation model**, *Carroll et al.* (2003) examine fair value information for **closed-end mutual funds** and find a significant association of fair values with stock prices and fair value security gains or losses with stock returns. *Mozes* (2002) also indicates that the results are highly sensitive to the valuation model applied. This makes it difficult to interpret evidence either for or against increased disclosures of financial instrument fair values (*Mozes* (2002), p. 14). Additionally, it is suggested that reliability problems of fair values did not cause the contrary findings concerning the value relevance of fair values in prior literature,[94] because quoted market prices are often available (*Carroll et al.* (2003), p. 21). *Khurana/Kim* (2003) provide evidence regarding the **different types of fair value inputs**. While especially fair value disclosures of available-for-sale securities are more relevant than historical cost, the authors find that fair values are more relevant when objective market-determined fair value measures are available (*Khurana/Kim* (2003), p. 19). However, their findings also indicate that historical cost measures are more value relevant when objective fair value measures are not available (*Khurana/Kim* (2003), p. 40), suggesting that market participants clearly differentiate between mark-to-market and mark-to-model fair values.

The empirical study conducted by *Ahmed et al.* (2006) contributes to the related literature about the recognition vs. disclosure issue. Using a sample of bank holding companies between 1995 and 2000 in the U.S., the authors provide evidence on how investor valuation of derivative financial instruments differs depending upon whether the fair value of these instruments is recognized or disclosed. Similar to the findings of *Petroni/Wahlen* (1995) and *Eccher et al.* (1996), they find that while the valuation coefficients on recognized derivatives are significant, the valuation coefficients on disclosed derivatives are not significant (*Ahmed et al.* (2006), p. 585). Based on their findings, the authors suggest that recognition and disclosure cannot be viewed as alternative accounting treatments because they are not substitutes and result in **different reactions** on the capital market (*Ahmed et al.* (2006), p. 567). Even if the authors run several sensitivity analyses to strengthen their results, they are not able to completely rule out the role of reliability that is placed by market participants in recognized and disclosed amounts. When it is assumed that market participants expect higher standards for recognized than for disclosed amounts, the reliability criterion could serve as another explanation for the findings.[95]

Finally, the empirical study conducted by *Song et al.* (2010) provides evidence on the value relevance of different levels of fair value measurement. Using recent banking firm data

---

94   See for example *Eccher et al.* (1996).
95   It has also been shown that auditors impose higher standards for recognized information than for disclosed information (*Libby et al.* (2006), p. 556).

from the first three quarters of 2008, the authors compare the value relevance of Level 1 and Level 2 fair values to the value relevance of Level 3 fair values. Despite of the finding that all fair values are value relevant to some degree and that the value relevance is greater for firms with strong corporate governance, the authors report that Level 3 measures are **less value relevant** than Level 1 and Level 2 fair values (*Song et al.* (2010), p. 1404). While market participants may discount less reliable Level 3 fair values due to information asymmetry and moral hazard problems, a strong corporate governance is likely to lessen that problem (*Song et al.* (2010), p. 1404). The basic caveat of the study is the fact that the sample period is quite short and that it is in the middle of the financial crisis from 2008. Thus, the results may not be generalizable as they may only hold during times of decreased market liquidity with less market values available compared to times prior to the financial crisis. Empirical evidence after the end of the financial crisis in this field of research is thus still missing.

As the literature review demonstrates, much of the literature examining the value relevance of fair values has been conducted between 1994 and 2003 with banks and financial institutions based in the U.S. It addresses the FASB's intention during that time to require measuring all financial instruments at fair value (*Carroll et al.* (2003), p. 20; *Khurana/Kim* (2003), p. 40). Although early evidence on the value relevance of fair values is to some extent mixed, the different findings are caused by differences in the research designs, such as omitted variables or other factors that need to be controlled for (*Barth et al.* (1996), p. 514f.; *Nelson* (1996), p. 181). Taken together the findings of the papers reviewed in this chapter, fair values are value relevant in a way that fair value changes **reflect share price movements**. This finding applies for most of the financial assets and liabilities that U.S. banks and financial institutions hold in their portfolio. Whereas, on average, recognized fair values are more value relevant than disclosed amounts, market participants expect Level 1 and Level 2 fair values to be significantly more reliable than Level 3 fair values, thus resulting in greater association of mark-to-market fair values with share prices. Additional evidence on the reliability of fair value measures is provided in the literature review in chapter 3.2.

3.1.2 Value relevance of fair value accounting for non-financial firms

Table 3-2 provides an overview of empirical findings of the value relevance of fair values for **non-financial firms**.

Whereas studies in the U.S. focus mainly on the impact of current cost accounting compared to historical cost accounting,[96] studies that have been conducted in Australia and the UK focus on asset revaluations. Because Australian and UK GAAP to some extent permit upward revaluations of tangible assets but require downward revaluations in the case of impairment, several studies examine the value relevance in these countries. Studies which focus on revaluations of tangible assets are of potential interest to standard setters because revaluations to fair value are likely to fall into the Level 3 category of the fair value measurement hierarchy (*Landsman* (2007), p. 23).

---

96 Current cost accounting measures assets at current replacement costs rather than historical costs. For further details see *Skogsvik* (1990), p. 139.

Reference	Method	Key results
Sharpe/Walker (1975)	Archival, 1960-1970, Australia	Asset revaluations to market value are associated with stock price movements.
Beaver/Ryan (1985)	Archival, 1979-1982, U.S.	Current cost earnings provide no incremental information beyond that provided by historical cost earnings.
Bernard/Ruland (1987)	Archival, 1961-1980, U.S.	Incremental information content of current cost income is evident only for a small subset of industries.
Hopwood/Schaefer (1989)	Archival, 1967-1980, U.S.	Current cost income is value relevant in a way that cost changes are associated with equity returns.
Lobo/Song (1989)	Archival, 1980-1982, U.S.	Current cost and constant dollar operating income measures have incremental information over historical cost income and its cash and accrual components.
Easton et al. (1993)	Archival/survey, 1981-1990, Australia	Book values including asset revaluation reserves are more value relevant than book values excluding revaluations.
Barth/Clinch (1998)	Archival, 1991-1995, Australia	Revaluations to fair value of financial, tangible, and intangible assets are value relevant.
Aboody et al. (1999)	Archival, 1983-1995, UK	Upward revaluations of fixed assets are significantly positively related to changes in future performance.
Simko (1999)	Archival, 1992-1995, U.S.	Fair values of liabilities are value relevant when fair value and book value differences are substantial.
Cotter/Zimmer (2003)	Archival, 1987-1997, Australia	Market reactions for recognized asset revaluations are significantly stronger than market reactions for revaluations that are only disclosed.
Robinson/Burton (2004)	Event study, 2001-2002, U.S.	The decision to adopt the fair value method in SFAS 123 causes positive and significant abnormal returns.
Deng/Lev (2006)	Archival, 1993-2000, U.S.	Values of acquired in-process R&D and acquiring firm's future cash flows are significantly associated.
Hann et al. (2007)	Archival, 1991-2002, U.S.	Whereas fair value pension accounting improves the credit relevance of the balance sheet, it impairs both the value and credit relevance of the income statement.
Danbolt/Rees (2008)	Archival, 1993-2002, UK	Fair value income in the UK real estate industry is considerably more value relevant than historic cost income.
Wier (2009)	Archival, 1996-2003, Canada	When inventory and income in the gold industry do mainly consist of fair value measures, the value relevance is significantly increased compared to historical cost.
Deaconu et al. (2010)	Archival, 2003-2007, Romania	Revaluations of tangible fixed assets are in general value relevant.

Table 3-2: Value relevance of fair value accounting for non-financial firms

Early evidence on the value relevance of current cost accounting in the U.S. provides mixed results. *Beaver/Ryan* (1985) and *Bernard/Ruland* (1987) employ U.S. archival data for 1979-1982 and 1961-1980 and find no clear evidence of **current cost accounting** having a stronger association with stock prices. Even if *Beaver/Ryan* (1985) note that their findings are consistent with some prior work, they refer to the risk that their results might be influenced by some flaw in their research design, which failed to detect an incremental explanatory power of current cost accounting (*Beaver/Ryan* (1985), p. 69). *Bernard/Ruland* (1987) report that the incremental information content of current cost income is evident at least for a small subset of industries where the correlation between historical and current cost income is low (*Bernard/Ruland* (1987), p. 706). The authors therefore conclude that their results must be interpreted with caution as they may apply to only a limited number of industries (*Bernard/Ruland* (1987), p. 719). This implies that the results of the study may not easily be generalized.

Contrary findings are provided by *Hopwood/Schaefer* (1989) and *Lobo/Song* (1989). The authors examine the association of risk-adjusted security returns with current cost income (*Hopwood/Schaefer* (1989)), and investigate whether measures of current cost and constant dollar income[97] convey incremental information beyond that provided by historical cost (*Lobo/Song* (1989)). The authors report that **current cost income** is not only value relevant in a way that cost changes are associated with equity returns in general (*Hopwood/Schaefer* (1989), p. 313), but that current cost and constant dollar operating income measures have incremental information over historical cost income and its cash and accrual components (*Lobo/Song* (1989), p. 342). The issue of generalizability applies also for the studies of *Hopwood/Schaefer* (1989) and *Lobo/Song* (1989). Since data availability and the focuses on a single accounting standard significantly reduce the industries contained in the sample, the results may not be transferred to firms from other industries.

Using a sample of Australian firms with data from 1960-1970, *Sharpe/Walker* (1975) find that asset revaluations to market value are significantly associated with **stock price movements**. The shifts in stock prices are generally sustained in the post-announcement months (*Sharpe/Walker* (1975), p. 293). However, the authors note that their results need to be interpreted with caution in view of the small sample, the market model applied and the association of asset revaluations with an increase in reported earnings (*Sharpe/Walker* (1975), p. 293ff.). Also for Australian firms with data from 1981-1990, *Easton et al.* (1993) estimate **annual return regressions** and find that asset revaluations of tangible and long-lived assets have incremental explanatory power relative to earnings and changes in earnings (*Easton et al.* (1993), p. 3). While the results suggest that book values including asset revaluation reserves are more aligned with the market value of the firm than book values excluding these reserves, it is concluded that asset revaluations provide a better summary of the current state of the firm (*Easton et al.* (1993), p. 36).

For a later period and based on an Australian sample from 1991-1995, *Barth/Clinch* (1998) estimate annual stock price regressions to determine whether financial, tangible, and intangible asset revaluations have incremental explanatory power relative to operating earnings and to equity book value less the book value of revalued assets. The authors find

---

97   Constant dollar income refers to price-adjusted income variables. See *Lobo/Song* (1989), p. 332.

that revalued investments are **incrementally priced** (*Barth/Clinch* (1998), p. 230). Contrary to the view that intangible asset revaluations are expected to be biased and uninformative, the study documents a positive association between such revaluations and share prices (*Barth/Clinch* (1998), p. 230). However, the study does not find, with the exception of mining firms, a value relevance of revaluations of PPE (*Barth/Clinch* (1998), p. 218f.). Perhaps surprisingly, the authors do only provide little evidence to indicate that director- and independent appraiser-based revaluations are viewed differently by market participants. Because especially this finding is against intuition, the results should be interpreted with caution. Additionally, the sample contains 100 firms from the Australian stock exchange. Despite of the low degree of generalizability to other countries due to the unique Australian setting, the number of firms in the sample is rather small.

Aboody et al. (1999) analyze the performance prediction and pricing implications of fixed asset revaluations for a sample of UK firms from 1983-1995. The authors find that **upward revaluations** are significantly positively related to changes in future performance that is measured by operating income and cash from operations over three years subsequent to the revaluation (*Aboody et al.* (1999), p. 149). Regarding pricing effects, the study uses annual regressions similar to those employed by *Easton et al.* (1993) and *Barth/Clinch* (1998) and reports current year revaluations being significantly positively related to annual stock returns, and current year asset revaluation balances are significantly positively related to annual stock prices (*Aboody et al.* (1999), p. 176). Based on their findings, the authors conclude that revaluations of fixed assets reflect changes in management expectations about future firm performance (*Aboody et al.* (1999), p. 176f.).

The papers by *Simko* (1999), *Deng/Lev* (2006), and *Hann et al.* (2007) focus on the U.S. and are concerned with fair value accounting for liabilities, in-process research and development, and pension accounting. By using a sample with data from 1992-1995, *Simko* (1999) provides evidence of fair values of liabilities of non-financial firms being value relevant when the amounts of fair values and book values do substantially differ and are on average loss positions (*Simko* (1999), p. 247). Because *Simko* (1999) examines the implications of fair value accounting for financial instruments possessed by non-financial firms, his results complement and extend financial institutions' fair value research.[98] *Deng/Lev* (2006) employ data from 1993-2000 and examine whether in-process R&D is an asset worthy of capitalization or expense. They find a significant association between the values of in-process R&D and acquiring firms' cash flows during the three years subsequent to an acquisition (*Deng/Lev* (2006), p. 18). Regarding pension accounting, *Hann et al.* (2007) report that fair value models for pension accounting improve both the **credit relevance**[99] of the balance sheet as well as the value and credit relevance of the income statement (*Hann et al.* (2007), p. 328). These results arise mainly because of aggregating the highly transitory unrealized gains and losses on net pension assets with more persistent income components (*Hann et al.* (2007), p. 351).

---

98 See for example *Barth et al.* (1996), *Eccher et al.* (1996), *Nelson* (1996) and the literature review provided in chapter 3.1.1.

99 The authors define credit relevance as the association between financial statement measures and creditors' future cash flow expectations, proxied by credit ratings. See *Hann et al.* (2007), p. 329.

Similar to *Ahmed et al.* (2006) who analyze the different effects of recognition and disclosure for banking firms, *Cotter/Zimmer* (2003) use a sample of Australian real estate firms between 1987 and 1997 and examine the effects of asset revaluations which are either recognized or disclosed. In accordance with the findings of *Ahmed et al.* (2006), the authors report that investors react more to Australian asset revaluations that are **recognized** than to those that are only disclosed (*Cotter/Zimmer* (2003), p. 82). Additionally, firms are more likely to recognize asset revaluations when asset value estimates are more reliable, such that investors appear to be correctly viewing recognition as a signal of greater information reliability (*Cotter/Zimmer* (2003), p. 85). However, the same caveats as for the study by *Ahmed et al.* (2006) do also apply here. With a sample of Australian real estate firms, the focus on the study is on a single industry within one country which strongly limits the generalizability of the findings.

Robinson/Burton (2004) use an approach similar to the study of *Cornett et al.* (1996) in documenting the value relevance of fair values through performing an event study. The authors base their findings on a sample of firms which announce their decision to adopt a new fair value standard (fair value accounting for employee stock options) in the years 2001 and 2002. In contrast to the findings of *Cornett et al.* (1996), *Robinson/Burton* (2004) find significant and **positive abnormal returns** in the three days around the adoption announcement caused by the decision to adopt the fair value method of SFAS 123 (*Robinson/Burton* (2004), p. 97). Based on their findings, the authors suggest that investors consider the recognition of employee stock options at fair value to be value relevant (*Robinson/Burton* (2004), p. 107).[100] Because the study uses a similar research design and dataset as the paper of *Cornett et al.* (1996), the same limitations do also apply here.

Even if the title of their paper suggests a different research approach,[101] *Danbolt/Rees* (2008) use archival data of the UK real estate industry for 1993-2002. Firms from the real estate industry are chosen for the analysis due to the fact that most assets are stated in the accounts at fair value (*Danbolt/Rees* (2008), p. 297). While the authors find that fair value income is considerably **more value relevant** than historical cost income, it becomes less relevant when fair values are included in the balance sheet. This leads to the conclusion that fair values in the income statement provide no additional information to investors if fair values are reflected in the balance sheet (*Danbolt/Rees* (2008), p. 298). *Wier* (2009) uses a sample of firms from the Canadian gold industry for 1996-2003 and examines the value relevance of inventory and income figures. The paper provides evidence of increased value relevance when inventory and income are measured at fair value instead of historical cost (*Wier* (2009), p. 1208). The author mentions that this finding conforms well with intuition, because for commodities, such as gold, with prices available in well-established markets, firm value should be more related with selling prices than to its cost (*Wier* (2009), p. 1227). However, the results of the two studies need to be interpreted with caution, because they do only hold for two specific industries. Finally, in a very recent study

---

100 Although it would be interesting to examine the differences to the findings of *Cornett et al.* (1996), the authors do not mention the alternative findings and do not refer to these differences in their paper.

101 The title of the paper is "An Experiment in Fair Value Accounting: UK Investment Vehicles".

Deaconu et al. (2010) employ data from Romania from 2003-2007 and investigate the value relevance of revalued tangible assets and its variation depending on industry, firm size, and age of the revalued amounts. Besides the general finding that revaluations are value relevant, the authors find differences of the degree of value relevance with regard to industry and the age of revalued amounts, whereas results for firm size are not significant (*Deaconu et al.* (2010), p. 151). Even if the paper provides helpful insights into the value relevance of revalued tangible assets in a certain country such as Romania, the results may not be generalized to other countries.

Taken together, the empirical literature concerning the value relevance of fair values can be divided into U.S.-based research investigating current cost accounting and research conducted for Australian and UK firms examining the effect of asset revaluations. Whereas contrary findings are provided for current cost accounting, revaluations of tangible assets conducted by non-financial firms are generally value relevant. Even if this finding conforms to the finding for banks and financial institutions mostly in the case of financial assets and liabilities, it seems surprising at the first sight. Assuming that upward revaluations of tangible assets are almost exclusively revaluations to Level 3 fair values, the results suggest that **market participants do not discount model-based fair values**, even when they are subject to managerial discretion. Moreover, market participants seem to put significant weight into Level 3 fair values as they expect that revaluations reflect management's expectation about the future performance of the firm (*Aboody et al.* (1999), p. 176f.). Therefore, the value relevance literature does, to some extent, also provide empirical evidence regarding the reliability of fair value measures. However, the reliability of fair value accounting is addressed on its own right in the next chapter.

Even if the literature review provides evidence on the value relevance of fair value accounting, there is still a need for further research. While it is reported that Level 3 fair values might also be helpful for investors when they reflect management's expectations, it has not been examined to what extent Level 1 and Level 3 estimates have different implications for market participants. Additionally, it would be of interest to investigate the implications of fair value accounting for a broad sample of firms from different countries in a way to provide country-based evidence. Since most of the accounting literature is concerned with asset revaluations in Australia and the UK, cross-country evidence is still scarce.

3.2   Reliability of fair value accounting

Value relevance studies examine the incremental value of accounting numbers. The criterion of value relevance captures the reaction of market participants who trade on the new information included in financial statements. Another criterion that denotes the usefulness of fair value accounting for investors is the qualitative characteristic of **reliability**.[102]

---

102 Even if reliability as a qualitative characteristic of financial reporting is no longer included in the conceptual framework of the IASB (it is replaced by the criterion of "faithful presentation"), it is used as a criterion that denotes the usefulness of accounting for investors in this study. See *Whittington* (2008), p. 146, who views this replacement mainly as a "change of language".

Reliability is already addressed by the value relevance literature as accounting numbers can only be associated with share prices when they are viewed both relevant and reliable. Nevertheless, the reliability of fair value accounting needs further consideration. Therefore, the literature reviewed in this chapter surrounds the question whether fair values are more likely to become subject of managerial discretion. It is also of interest whether fair values cause higher or lower earnings volatility through income smoothing activities, because this issue is of great relevance for users of financial statements. The papers presented in this chapter apply empirical approaches that are different from the value relevance literature. Besides archival-based evidence, results are also based on experiments or questionnaires. An overview of empirical findings concerning the reliability of fair values is presented in Table 3-3.

In an early work from 1975, *Parker* (1975) examines the comparability and objectivity of exit values (market selling price) compared to historical cost accounting. Based on a questionnaire conducted in the U.S., he finds that exit values exhibit **greater comparability** and are more objective than historical cost (*Parker* (1975), p. 523). However, he also mentions that the lack of objectivity of historical cost numbers is caused by the dispersion of accounting estimates and not due to the accounting methods by itself (*Parker* (1975), p. 523). Since this study is one of the first survey-based studies on fair value accounting, the findings provide initial evidence on the topic but may not be generalized. Due to the unique setting with only one restricted class of assets, the results should be interpreted with caution.

Brown et al. (1992) employ a sample of Australian firms from 1974-1977 and 1984-1986 and analyze why firms make asset revaluations. The authors find evidence that firms are more likely to revalue their fixed assets to market values when they are more highly levered, closer to violating their debt covenant constraints, have lower tax-free reserves, and are closer to face a takeover bid (*Brown et al.* (1992), p. 56). The authors do therefore hypothesize that voluntary asset revaluations are viewed as an instrument to prevent **wealth transfer** and are applicable to send a signal to users of financial statements (*Brown et al.* (1992), p. 36). To give an example, the authors view the fact that firms close to facing a takeover bid are more likely to make revaluations as a signal to frustrate the bidder, thus preventing him to make the takeover bid (*Brown et al.* (1992), p. 56). However, the regression models applied in the research suffer from low R squared values,[103] thus suggesting possible misspecifications. Even if the paper provides statistical significance for the relationship between firm characteristics and the tendency to make asset revaluations, this limitation should be kept in mind.

---

103 The adjusted R squared is between 10.20% and 12.00%. The authors note that the model "is far short of providing a complete explanation of the revaluation decision". See *Brown et al.* (1992), p. 56.

Reference	Method	Key results
Parker (1975)	Questionnaire, U.S.	Exit values exhibit greater comparability and are more objective than book values.
Brown et al. (1992)	Archival, 1974-1977 and 1984-1986, Australia	Firms which revalue their fixed assets to market values are more highly levered, closer to violating debt covenant constraints and have lower tax-free reserves.
Bernard et al. (1995)	Archival, 1976-1989, Denmark	Price adjustments to fair value are not manipulated. Earnings volatility is increased after fair value adjustments.
Black et al. (1998)	Archival, 1985-1995, Australia, NZL, UK	The possibility to revalue assets to fair value leads to a decrease in income smoothing.
Dietrich et al. (2001)	Archival, 1988-1996, UK	Appraisal estimates of fair value for investment property understate actual selling prices and are considerably less biased and more accurate measures than historical cost.
Cotter/Richardson (2002)	Archival, 1981-1990 and 1994-1999, Australia	Revaluations made by independent appraisers are considered more reliable than those by directors.
Muller/Riedl (2002)	Archival, 1990-1999, UK	Market makers set lower bid-ask spreads for firms employing external appraisers relative to firms employing internal appraisers for the determination of fair value.
Nissim (2003)	Archival, 1994-1995, U.S.	The estimated extent of a disclosed fair value overstatement of loans is negatively related to regulatory capital, asset growth, liquidity and the gross book value of loans.
Beatty/Weber (2006)	Archival, 2001, U.S.	The inclusion of unverifiable fair values in SFAS 142 increases incidence of fraudulent financial reporting.
Ramanna/Watts (2007)	Archival, 2003-2006, U.S.	Unverifiable fair values for goodwill under SFAS 142 are used for managerial discretion.
Ramanna (2008)	Archival, 1999-2000, U.S.	The use of unverifiable fair values for goodwill accounting retains discretion potential for management.
Ding et al. (2009)	Experiment with MBA students, U.S.	When a range is disclosed for the fair value, participants bid prices lower than the fair value and earn a lower return on their investment compared to a point estimate.
Muller et al. (2011)	Archival, 2005, Europe	The mandatory provision of investment property fair values mitigates information asymmetry differences.
Gassen/Schwedler (2010)	Questionnaire, Germany	Respondents consistently rank mark-to-market fair values as most decision-useful.
Lachmann et al. (2010)	Experiment with MBA students, Germany	Investors can be misled by liabilities measured at fair value.

Table 3-3: Reliability of fair value accounting

In a study conducted with a sample of Danish banks, *Bernard et al.* (1995) focus on the impact of fair value accounting on bank regulatory capital. While the study finds that there is evidence of earnings management, there is no reliable evidence that mark-to-market numbers are managed to avoid regulatory capital constraints (*Bernard et al.* (1995), p. 29). Despite of the fact that price adjustments to fair value are not manipulated, the authors find that earnings for Danish banks are three times more **variable** after mark-to-market adjustments than before (*Bernard et al.* (1995), p. 30). The authors conclude that their findings lend support to a mark-to-market accounting for banks and financial institutions. However, the narrow focus on a sample of Danish banks causes the generalizability of the results to be limited.

Supporting the argument that fair values are not manipulated for earnings management, *Black et al.* (1998) use a broader sample and provide similar findings. For a sample of Australian, New Zealand, and UK firms in 1985-1995, the study finds no difference in **earnings management behavior** for asset revaluing and non-asset revaluing firms (*Black et al.* (1998), p. 1314f.). In a way to strengthen the results of their study, the authors apply a pre- and a post-period for UK firms and investigate the implications for the sample firms in both periods. During the pre-period before 1993, UK firms were allowed to calculate their gains and losses from asset disposals on the basis of historical cost even if these assets have been revalued in the past (*Black et al.* (1998), p. 1288). After 1993 and with the implementation of FRS 3, gains and losses from such disposals had to be calculated on the basis of the revalued amounts. The authors find a significant increase in earnings management behavior in the pre- compared to the post-period. Thus, further evidence is provided that mandating fair value measurement for gains and losses is likely to reduce the practice of timing asset sales for earnings management purposes (*Black et al.* (1998), p. 1308).

Dietrich et al. (2001) and *Cotter/Richardson* (2002) provide similar results concerning the reliability of fair value estimates. Both papers focus on investment properties and PPE. Although appraisal estimates of fair value for investment property understate actual selling prices, they are considerably less biased and more accurate measures of the selling price than historical cost for a sample of UK firms in 1988-1996 (*Dietrich et al.* (2001), p. 125). The authors expect that the underestimation of investment properties' fair values reflects managers' incentives to undervalue property, which is expected to be sold, in order to increase earnings at the time of the disposal (*Dietrich et al.* (2001), p. 156). Based on a sample of companies from Australia in 1981-1990 and 1994-1999, *Cotter/Richardson* (2002) find that when plant and equipment is subject to revaluation, revaluations made by independent appraisers are considered to be more **reliable** than those revaluations that are made internally by management (*Cotter/Richardson* (2002), p. 435). However, the authors do not report a statistically significant difference of the reliability for other asset classes. Based on their findings, the authors conclude that mandating revaluations made by independent appraisers is only necessary in cases when market values (as input factors for the revaluation) are not readily available (*Cotter/Richardson* (2002), p. 454f.). Similar to previous studies in this field, the authors focus on Australia and the UK due to the unique setting regarding asset revaluations in these countries. Due to this focus and unique setting, the results may not be generalizable to other countries.

A similar contribution is provided by *Muller/Riedl* (2002) who also report evidence that the market finds asset revaluation estimates made by external appraisers as more informative than those made by internal appraisers. Using a sample of UK investment property firms for the period 1990-1999, the study shows that **information asymmetry** (as measured by the adverse-selection component of the firms' average stock price bid-ask spread in the seven months subsequent to fiscal year-end) is greater for firms employing internal appraisers (*Muller/Riedl* (2002), p. 877). Although the authors interpret this result as evidence that the market finds asset revaluation estimates based on external appraisals to be more reliable (*Muller/Riedl* (2002)), the conclusion should be made with caution as the regarding sample is limited to a specialized industry where external appraisals are viewed as an institutional feature (*Landsman* (2007), p. 24).

For a sample of U.S. banks during the period 1994-1995, *Nissim* (2003) examines whether the sample firms manage the disclosed fair value of their major asset and provides evidence of banks managing the fair value of loans (*Nissim* (2003), p. 355). Whereas the author documents a **negative association** of the estimated extent of a disclosed fair value overstatement of loans with regulatory capital, asset growth, liquidity, and the gross book value of loans, the change in the rate of credit losses is positively associated with the overstatement of loans (*Nissim* (2003), p. 374). The results suggest that the disclosed fair value estimates may not be reliable and that specific guidance on how to determine the fair values should be provided. Alternatively, the author recommends that the standard setter should require companies to disclose the methods and assumptions used in estimating the fair values (*Nissim* (2003), p. 374).

Several empirical studies on fair value accounting deal with the FASB's SFAS 142 which addresses financial accounting and reporting for acquired goodwill and other intangible assets. For an U.S.-based sample, *Beatty/Weber* (2006), *Ramanna/Watts* (2007), and *Ramanna* (2008) provide similar results with regard to the accounting treatment of goodwill and unverifiable fair values under this statement. Although it is mentioned that the SFAS 142 eliminated the pooling of interest method as one possible source of discretion when accounting for goodwill, it is expected that the use of unverifiable fair values retains **discretion potential** for management (*Ramanna* (2008), p. 253). Furthermore, results suggest that both contracting and market incentives affect firms' accounting choices relating to the trade-off between the timing and the presentation of expense recognition in the income statement (*Beatty/Weber* (2006), p. 284). Consistent with this finding, *Ramanna/Watts* (2007) report that non-impairment is more common and increases financial characteristics predicted to be associated with greater unverifiable fair value-based discretion, even if non-impairment is not associated with managers producing better estimates of goodwill than the market (*Ramanna/Watts* (2007), p. 42f.). The results are important when it is expected that, under the agency theory, discretion potential may be used opportunistically and thus significantly reducing the reliability of fair values (*Ramanna* (2008), p. 276).

Using an **experimental approach**, *Ding et al.* (2009) investigate the economic consequences of additional disclosure about Level 3 fair value measurements as a response to the IFRS 7 requirement to disclose sensitivity tests for assets with no active market. The authors compare situations with limited (i.e. when only a point estimate is given for the fair value) and full disclosure (i.e. when a range is given for the fair value in addition to a point estimate). Their study provides evidence that the full disclosure case is associated with a change in investors' market participation, their perception of information reliability, and their ability to earn returns on their investments (*Ding et al.* (2009), p. 22). More precisely, participants make offers more frequently, bid prices lower than the fair value and earn a lower return on their investment in the full disclosure case compared to the disclosure of just a point estimate (*Ding et al.* (2009), p. 1). However, the results need to be interpreted with caution as the research design remains largely abstract.[104] This makes it difficult to address the research question of whether the disclosure requirements of IFRS 7 are useful for investors or not.

For a 2005 sample, an archival study of firms within the European real estate industry examines the consequences of the adoption of IAS 40, which mandated the provision of fair values for investment properties. *Muller et al.* (2011) find that the adoption of IAS 40 resulted in reduced information asymmetry across market participants with information asymmetry proxied by bid-ask spreads. Additionally, the authors report a larger decline for firms not providing fair values prior to 2005 when compared to firms that voluntarily disclosed these values before the adoption of IAS 40 (*Muller et al.* (2011), p. 1138). However, mandatory adoption firms continue to have significantly higher information asymmetry than voluntary adopters. The results provide evidence on the implications of mandated fair values. Thus, mandatory fair values for long-lived tangible assets may reduce, but not necessarily eliminate, information asymmetry across firms.

Based on a **questionnaire**, *Gassen/Schwedler* (2010) provide evidence on the decision usefulness of different measurement concepts of fair values. While the respondents, namely professional investors and their advisors, consider fair value accounting as being **advantageous**, they clearly differentiate between measurement concepts and consistently rank mark-to-market fair values as most decision-useful and rank mark-to-model fair values as least decision-useful (*Gassen/Schwedler* (2010), p. 495). Additionally, respondents do even assess historical cost measures as more decision-useful than mark-to-model fair values. However, this finding may be due to the fact that investors seem reasonably familiar only with historical cost accounting and mark-to-market fair value accounting (*Gassen/Schwedler* (2010), p. 506). Based on the findings, the authors suggest that investors do not view fair value as a homogeneous measurement concept (*Gassen/Schwedler* (2010), p. 506). Even if the authors base their findings on a total number of responses of 383, they only realize a response rate of roughly 1.9%, which is a quite low response rate when compared to other questionnaires in this field of research.

Finally, another experiment contributes to the ongoing debate of fair value accounting for **liabilities**. Consistent with prior research in this field, a recent study conducted by *Lachmann et al.* (2010) with German MBA students confirms concerns about liabilities measured at fair value as the authors report that investors can be misled by liabilities measured at fair value (*Lachmann et al.* (2010), p. 1179). The authors also document that under some circumstances the participants learn to interpret the financial data correctly (*Lach-*

---

104 Even if the authors employ a so-called double-auction design, they use rather ordinary proxies to simulate a market and to determine market values.

mann et al. (2010), p. 1206). However, the authors mention that this learning effect does not fully compensate for the counter-inductive effects of liabilities measured at fair value. They conclude that fair value accounting for liabilities makes higher demands on the users of financial statements in evaluating the financial position of the firm (*Lachmann et al.* (2010), p. 1195).

The results of the papers reviewed in this chapter are twofold. While it is on the one hand likely that fair value measures are used for managerial discretion, market participants do on the other hand respond to this potential bias in fair value determination, especially in the case of Level 3 revaluations by management. Firm characteristics, such as leverage or the earnings situation, have been proven to be significantly associated with the tendency to revaluations or how these revaluations are carried out (*Brown et al.* (1992); *Nissim* (2003)). Another potential bias resulting from managerial discretion is consistent with the **signaling theory**, when managers perform or neglect asset revaluations prior to a potential takeover or to signal an improved earnings situation. While the survey-based empirical evidence provides the view that the respondents clearly differentiate between the fair value hierarchy and do even rank historical cost as being more useful than mark-to-model fair values (*Gassen/Schwedler* (2010)), archival-based research supports these findings as it is reported that unverifiable fair values may be subject to discretion (*Beatty/Weber* (2006); *Ramanna/Watts* (2007); *Ramanna* (2008)). However, the expectation that market participants account for the discretionary potential of fair value estimates is supported by the fact that revaluations made by independent appraisers are considered to be more reliable than those made by management (*Cotter/Richardson* (2002); *Muller/Riedl* (2002)).

Although the papers reviewed in this chapter provide evidence on the reliability of fair values in financial statements, there are still issues not covered by the existing work. With the majority of archival-based studies concerned with different types of proxies measuring the potential for discretion, only two experimental-based approaches examine the concrete investors' behavior under a fair value regime (*Ding et al.* (2009); *Lachmann et al.* (2010)). However, the approach of *Ding et al.* (2009) is a very general one with results that may only be transferred piecemeal to issues of fair value accounting in financial reporting. Additionally, *Lachmann et al.* (2010) focuses solely on the special case of fair value accounting for liabilities. However, fair values for liabilities remain different from fair values for assets, because liabilities measured at fair value are likely to confuse financial statement users. According to this, troubled firms could report net income from decreases in their own debt value under a fair value accounting regime for liabilities.

3.3 Predictability of accounting numbers

Much research has been conducted on financial analysts and the properties of their earnings forecasts.[105] Financial analysts are viewed as important users of financial statements and earnings forecasts are probably their most notable output (*Schipper* (1991), p. 40). If earnings forecasts are important and frequently used by investors (*Das et al.* (1998), p.

---

105 For a review of the financial analyst forecasting literature prior to 1993 see *Schipper* (1991) and *Brown* (1993). For a review of research examining the role of financial analysts in capital markets after that date refer to *Ramnath et al.* (2008).

277), it makes sense to examine properties of earnings forecasts with regard to accounting measures, especially the recognition or disclosure of fair values or other disclosure requirements. More specifically, this chapter reviews literature that is concerned with the **predictive value** of accounting numbers as represented by earnings forecasts of financial analysts.

Empirical evidence on the association of analysts' forecasts and fair value accounting is scarce. Thus, the section also reviews literature which is concerned with the implications of additional disclosure not specifically related to fair value measures. This makes sense when fair values are not only viewed as a method for measurement, but also as a specific type of **disclosure**. Therefore, it makes sense to investigate whether specific types of disclosures are related with financial analysts' ability to forecasting and in what way these disclosures affect the forecasts. However, the results of the studies reviewed in this chapter may not be transferred to the fair value case as they address different aspects of financial reporting. It is important to choose among the financial analyst literature with caution, because the number of papers in this stream of research is very large. Thus, the papers in this review have research questions and use approaches that are closest to the ones applied in the fair value study. An overview of the empirical literature presented can be found in Table 3-4.

Early studies dealing with financial analysts are concerned with the implications of disclosure on properties of analysts' earnings forecasts. For a sample of U.S.-based firms from 1974-1979, *Brown* (1983) investigates the relationship between certain **accounting principle changes** and the ability of security analysts to project the affected firms' earnings numbers. The author bases his findings on several accounting changes caused by new U.S. standards such as SFAS 8, SFAS 13, and SFAS 34 and reports significant improved earnings predictions (*Brown* (1983), p. 442). Although changes to LIFO and actuarial changes for pensions indicate some impairment of predictive earnings accuracy, the author suggests that financial statement users can benefit from additional disclosures, when firms change their accounting principles and provide more disclosure (*Brown* (1983), p. 439ff.). Similar results are provided by *Lang/Lundholm* (1996) who examine the relations between the disclosure practices of firms, the number of analysts following each firm and properties of analysts' earnings forecasts on the basis of an empirical study conducted from 1985-1989 in the U.S. The study provides evidence that companies with more disclosure exhibit higher forecast accuracy, lower forecast dispersion, and less volatility in forecast revisions (*Lang/Lundholm* (1996), p. 467). In addition, the authors also find that the firm's **disclosure quality** is the most important factor which drives the analyst following and that the amount of disclosure is positively related to analyst following.

Das et al. (1998) investigate analysts' incentives to seek non-public information and find that analysts have a higher demand of non-public or private information for firms whose earnings are difficult to **predict accurately** than for firms whose earnings can be accurately forecasted using public information (*Das et al.* (1998), p. 277). Furthermore, analysts are more likely to issue more optimistic forecasts for low predictability firms than for high predictability firms, which leads to the suggestion that analysts intend to maintain a good relationship with a company's management (*Das et al.* (1998), p. 291). The results of the study therefore support the concerns raised in chapter 2.2.2.5.

Reference	Method	Key results
Brown (1983)	Archival, 1974-1979, U.S.	Financial analysts benefit from additional disclosures, including pro forma adjustments, when firms change their accounting principles.
Lang/Lundholm (1996)	Archival, 1985-1989, U.S.	Firms with more informative disclosure policies have a larger analyst following, more accurate and less dispersed forecasts and less volatility in forecast revisions.
Das et al. (1998)	Archival, 1989-1993, U.S.	Analysts have a higher demand of non-public information for firms whose earnings are difficult to predict. Analysts issue more optimistic forecasts for low predictability firms.
Hirst/Hopkins (1998)	Experiment with financial analysts, U.S.	Analysts can more completely distinguish differences in firm risk and value when firms report more complete and transparent income measures.
Eng/Teo (2000)	Archival, 1995-1996, Singapore	The level of annual report disclosure is positively (negatively) related to forecast accuracy (forecast dispersion).
Acker et al. (2002)	Archival, 1987-1996, UK	Whereas in the first year of FRS 3, analysts' forecast errors increased, the additional information provided by FRS 3 increased the accuracy of analysts' forecasts.
Hope (2003)	Archival, cross-country sample	The level of accounting policy disclosure is significantly negatively related to forecast dispersion and forecast error.
Vanstraelen et al. (2003)	Archival, cross-country sample	Higher levels of forward looking non-financial disclosures are associated with lower dispersion and higher accuracy in financial analysts' earnings forecasts.
Hirst et al. (2004)	Experiment with financial analysts, U.S.	Bank analysts' risk and value judgments distinguish banks' exposure to interest-rate risk only under full fair value income measurement.
Peek (2005)	Archival, 1988-1999, Netherlands	Changes in accounting procedures can significantly affect analysts' forecast accuracy and forecasting advantage.
Fan et al. (2006)	Archival, 1989-1998, U.S.	The fair value reporting requirement of SFAS 115 enhances the accuracy of analysts' forecasts for publicly traded insurance companies.
McEwen et al. (2008)	Experiment with financial analysts, U.S.	Financial analysts expect firm managers to take advantage of discretionary valuation judgments when assessing the fair value of non-financial assets and liabilities.

Table 3-4: Predictability of accounting numbers

Mainly due to the limitations of archival research, a growing body of empirical literature uses **experimental approaches** to assess implications of accounting information for analysts' earnings predictability. Conducting an experiment within the U.S. banking industry, *Hirst/Hopkins* (1998) vary the comprehensive income format and analyze the judgments of non-specialist analysts (i.e. analysts who did not specialize in banking, insurance, or other financial industries). They find that when firms report more complete and transparent income measurements, analysts make judgments that distinguish more completely differences in **firm risk and value** (*Hirst/Hopkins* (1998), p. 64f.). The clear display of comprehensive income and its components in a separate statement made earnings management more transparent and resulted in almost equal stock price judgments for earnings management and non-earnings management firms (*Hirst/Hopkins* (1998), p. 68). Following up the earlier work, specific experimental-based evidence with regard to fair value accounting is provided by *Hirst et al.* (2004). The authors examine how fair values affect U.S. commercial bank equity analysts' risk and value judgments by providing either full fair value (will all fair value changes recognized in the net income) or piecemeal fair value materials where some fair value changes are disclosed only in the notes. They find that analysts' risk and value judgments distinguish banks' exposure to interest-rate risk only in the case of full fair values but not under piecemeal fair value accounting (*Hirst et al.* (2004), p. 453). Based on their findings, the authors suggest that a more complete measurement of fair value gains and losses in the net income can be useful for analysts in a way that they can assess risk and link those assessments to valuation judgments (*Hirst et al.* (2004), p. 470). However, a limitation of the study is that the authors base their results solely on univariate comparisons of mean values and analyses of variance and do not perform multivariate analyses.

Eng/Teo (2000) and *Acker et al.* (2002) conduct archival studies and provide evidence of a positive relationship between additional disclosure and forecast accuracy. For a sample of companies listed on the stock exchange in Singapore in the years 1995 and 1996, *Eng/Teo* (2000) examine the impact of annual report disclosures on analysts' forecasts. The authors report a **positive relation** of the quantity of annual report disclosure and analyst forecast accuracy, whereas forecast dispersion is negatively related to disclosure quantity (*Eng/Teo* (2000), p. 219). *Acker et al.* (2002) investigate the impact of the FRS 3 on the ability of analysts to predict companies' future EPS for a sample of UK firms for 1987-1996. Consistent with this assumption, the paper documents increased forecast accuracy after the adoption of FRS 3. The fact that the forecast accuracy is significantly decreased in the first year of FRS 3 can be traced back to differences in predictability of pre- and post FRS 3 EPS figures (*Acker et al.* (2002), p. 214).

Whereas earlier studies focused on single countries, the studies of *Hope* (2003) and *Vanstraelen et al.* (2003) employ cross-country samples. Using an archival design with a sample consisting of firms from 18 countries from different continents, *Hope* (2003) finds that the quantity of accounting policy disclosures is significantly negatively related to forecast dispersion and forecast error (*Hope* (2003), p. 295). *Vanstraelen et al.* (2003) employ a multi-country sample consisting of three countries from the European Union (Belgium, Germany and the Netherlands) and examine forward looking non-financial disclosures in the three countries. Their results support the findings of *Hope* (2003) in a way that more **forward looking disclosures** are associated with lower dispersion and higher accuracy in financial analysts' earnings forecasts (*Vanstraelen et al.* (2003), p. 249). However, both authors note the small sample size of the country-samples included in their study as a limitation and mention that this is due to the time-consuming process of data collection.[106]

Peek (2005) focuses on the implications of **discretionary accounting changes** on analysts' earnings forecasting in change years and the years after the change. The results indicate that changes in accounting procedures significantly affect analysts' forecast accuracy and forecasting advantage, whereas this is specifically the case when the changes have not been disclosed previously (*Peek* (2005), p. 261). To increase the strength of his results, the author also tests for potential increases in forecasting quality (i.e. changes from current cost to historical cost accounting and changes from expensing to capitalization) and finds that forecast accuracy is significantly improved (*Peek* (2005), p. 284f.). Even if the author mentions that "legislation and guidelines concerning the adoption of accounting changes in the Netherlands are fairly similar to those of other industrialized countries" (*Peek* (2005), p. 271), there remains the question whether the results may easily be transferred to other countries. Therefore, this fact represents a limitation of the study.

While the two studies by *Fan et al.* (2006) and *McEwen et al.* (2008) use different approaches, they both estimate the effect of fair value accounting on financial analysts. For a sample of U.S. insurance companies during the period 1989-1998, *Fan et al.* (2006) examine the impact of the fair value reporting requirement in SFAS 115 for earnings predictions. Consistent with the findings on the value relevance of SFAS 115 requirements presented in chapter 3.1.1, the results suggest that fair values in financial statements are **useful** for financial analysts and significantly enhance the accuracy of their forecasts (*Fan et al.* (2006), p. 105). However, the results of the study may not be generalized as the authors focus solely on the impact of fair value accounting in the life insurance industry. Another limitation is the fact that the study only examines forecast accuracy and forecast dispersion, but does not investigate the effect of fair value accounting on analyst following. Because analyst following proxies for the richness of a firm's information environment (*Yu* (2010), p. 2), these effects are important and should also be investigated.

McEwen et al. (2008) perform an experiment with financial analysts in the U.S. and investigate the extent to which analysts expect firms to manage their earnings when accounting rules allow for discretionary choice and low level of transparency. Their findings suggest that financial analysts expect firm managers to take advantage from discretionary accounting choices when assessing the fair value of non-financial assets and liabilities, and that analysts do in particular expect **earnings management** when fair values are not derived from an active market (*McEwen et al.* (2008), p. 241). The authors use a 2x2 between-subjects design for their experiment, thus resulting in four different treatments. Because only 44 analysts took part in the experiment and this number was divided upon the four different treatments, the research design has the basic caveat of a very small number of

---

106 Because *Hope* (2003) employs a total sample size of only 1,205 observations in all countries, this results in small numbers of observations in each of the 18 countries. *Vanstraelen et al.* (2003) uses a sample consisting of only 120 observations in three countries.

participants in each treatment.[107] This makes it almost impossible to perform statistical tests as well as to draw reliable conclusions on the basis of the results.

Summarizing this chapter, studies on the association of financial analysts' forecasting ability and fair value accounting are scarce. More specifically, the papers of *Hirst et al.* (2004), *Fan et al.* (2006) and *McEwen et al.* (2008) are the only ones that provide direct empirical evidence on the association of analysts' forecasting abilities and fair values. However, these studies do not use a sophisticated research design (*Hirst et al.* (2004)), do not take into account important aspects of analysts' behavior (*Fan et al.* (2006)), or attempt to draw conclusions on the basis of a very small sample (*McEwen et al.* (2008)). If it is accepted that disclosure studies can function as proxies for fair value accounting, the literature review reports that fair values (as a specific type of "additional disclosures") may be **positively related to analysts' ability to make forecasts**.[108] On the other hand, the results of some disclosure studies may not easily be transferred to firms based in other countries (*Engl/Teo* (2000); *Acker et al.* (2002)), and it has to be kept in mind that some disclosure studies also base their findings on very small sample sizes (*Hope* (2003); *Vanstraelen et al.* (2003); *McEwen et al.* (2008)).

3.4 Summary and research gap

This section summarizes the basic contributions and limitations of prior empirical research reviewed in this chapter. Furthermore, it presents the research gap for the two empirical studies conducted in this research work. The discussed studies on the value relevance of fair value accounting for banks and financial institutions make **contributions** in a way that fair value changes are reflected in share price movements (*Barth* (1994); *Nelson* (1996); *Mozes* (2002)). This finding applies for most of the financial assets and liabilities that U.S. banks and financial institutions hold in their portfolio (*Petroni/Wahlen* (1995); *Carroll et al.* (2003)). Additionally, recognized fair values reveal a greater association with stock prices than disclosed fair values (*Ahmed et al.* (2006)). The value relevance literature does in addition provide first evidence on the reliability of fair value measures, as it is reported that Level 1 and Level 2 fair values are more related with share prices than Level 3 fair values (*Khurana/Kim* (2003); *Song et al.* (2010)).

Referring to non-financial firms, prior literature can be divided into research examining the value relevance of current cost accounting in the U.S. and research concerning the value relevance of asset revaluations conducted by Australian and U.K. firms. For current cost accounting, prior literature provides both evidence for (*Hopwood/Schaefer* (1989); *Lobo/Song* (1989)) and against (*Beaver/Ryan* (1985); *Bernard/Ruland* (1987)) an **increased degree of value relevance** compared to historical cost. Thus, results in this field are ambiguous. However, revaluations of tangible assets conducted by non-financial firms are generally value relevant (*Easton et al.* (1993); *Barth/Clinch* (1998); *Aboody et al.* (1999);

---

107 The number of participants in each of the four treatments ranges from 10 to 12 (*McEwen et al.* (2008), p. 246).

108 This view is also supported by a survey conducted by *Thinggaard* (1996) with financial analysts. He finds that financial analysts prefer an accounting system based on market value accounting for both speculative and non-speculative financial instruments. See *Thinggaard* (1996), p. 72.

Danbolt/Rees (2008)). Even if the results for non-financial firms are basically limited to firms located in Australia and the U.K., the evidence provided conforms to the findings for banks and financial institutions.

The findings of the papers reviewed on the reliability issue provide the following results: While it is on the one hand likely that fair value measures are used for managerial discretion (*Brown et al.* (1992); *Black et al.* (1998); *Nissim* (2003)), users of financial statements **respond to this potential bias**, especially in the case of Level 3 revaluations (*Cotter/Richardson* (2002); *Muller/Riedl* (2002)). While it is reported that unverifiable fair value estimates are responsible for the discretionary potential included in financial statements (*Beatty/Weber* (2006); *Ramanna/Watts* (2007); *Ramanna* (2008)), the results of a survey conducted with professional investors and their advisers reveal that respondents consistently rank mark-to-market fair values as most decision-useful (*Gassen/Schwedler* (2010)).

When turning to fair value accounting and its association with the predictability of earnings, the literature review shows that the papers of *Hirst et al.* (2004), *Fan et al.* (2006) and *McEwen et al.* (2008) are the only papers that are concerned with fair values. They provide evidence that, in very limited settings, financial analysts can benefit from fair value accounting (*Hirst et al.* (2004); *Fan et al.* (2006)), while they also expect that managers take advantage of **discretionary** fair value judgments (*McEwen et al.* (2008)). Even if the other literature reviewed is not directly concerned with fair value accounting, it centers on the question of whether additional disclosures affect analysts' forecasts. According to the results, additional disclosures are positively related to analysts' ability to make forecasts (*Eng/Teo* (2000); *Hope* (2003)) and higher levels of forward looking disclosures lead to significantly higher forecast precision (*Vanstraelen et al.* (2003)). If these results are transferred to fair value accounting and when it is accepted that fair values function as an instrument to provide an increased information environment for earnings prediction, the findings suggest that fair values could significantly be associated with better earnings forecasts.

The prior empirical literature reviewed above also reveals certain **limitations** which leave room for further research. Most of the results obtained from the value relevance literature **lack generalizability**. Since the value relevance literature for banks and financial institutions focuses on U.S. banks and centers around the question of whether certain SFASs are more or less value relevant, the findings for these entities may not be transferred to other countries or even accounting systems such as IFRS. The U.S. GAAP and IAS/IFRS regulations were different during that time, even if the FASB and the IASB intend to bring about convergence between U.S. GAAP and IFRS. Additionally, financial institutions outside of the U.S. face different regulatory environments and they are not under the supervision of the SEC.

Turning to non-financial firms, much of the research concentrates on the implications of asset revaluations in certain countries or industries. A vast majority of the studies are conducted for real estate firms in Australia and the U.K. These two countries provided a unique setting as they allowed asset revaluations for tangible assets. However, the situation significantly changed with the adoption of IFRS. The IFRS provide a single financial reporting system in many countries around the world and enables researchers to investigate the implications of uniform financial reporting standards. Therefore, and from today's perspective, a restriction to two countries is no longer recommendable. Moreover, empirical evidence on the implications of asset revaluations could also be maintained in a broad cross-country setting.

The empirical literature on fair value accounting and the predictability of earnings is very **scarce**. The study conducted by *Fan et al.* (2006) is the only study that relates characteristics of analysts' forecasts to fair value accounting. The authors document a positive (negative) relation between analysts' forecast accuracy (dispersion) and the fair value reporting requirement of SFAS 115. However, the results should be interpreted with caution as the findings may not be generalized due to a restriction on the U.S. life insurance industry. Additionally, it is not examined whether fair value measures influence the number of analysts following the company. While analysts' forecast accuracy and dispersion are used in existing research as a proxy for the quality of firms' information environment, the level of analyst following is used as an indicator for the richness of firms' information environment (*Yu* (2010), p. 2). As a large analyst following is expected to cause several advantages for the firm,[109] it is a basic caveat to exclude analyst following when investigating characteristics of financial analysts' forecasts.

The vast majority of the studies reviewed in this chapter use **archival-based approaches**. Even if it is possible to investigate the market's response (e.g., through the value relevance literature) to fair value or historical cost accounting, it is not possible to examine investors' behavior and the confidence that investors place into their actions undertaken on the basis of fair value or historical cost information. Although experimental-based approaches are more adequate than archival studies to provide that evidence, the experiments reviewed in this chapter are either concerned with very limited settings (*Hirst et al.* (2004); *Lachmann et al.* (2010)), suffer from very small sample sizes (*McEwen et al.* (2008)) or use very general approaches with little connection to concrete accounting standards and thus might not be transferrable to financial accounting reality (*Ding et al.* (2009)).

Based on the limitations outlined above, the identified **research gap** is defined as follows:

- The analysis of fair values in financial statements is limited to **certain industries**: On the one hand, studies examining the implications of fair value accounting for financial instruments focus on banks and financial institutions. On the other hand, empirical evidence concerning fair value accounting for tangible assets is limited to the real estate industry. However, assets measured at fair value may not only be possessed by financial or real estate firms. Thus, a comprehensive analysis is necessary as there is no study that analyzes the implications of fair value accounting for a broad sample of firms from different industries.

- There is only limited **multi-country** evidence of fair value accounting: The empirical literature mainly focuses on fair value accounting for U.S. financial institutions or real estate firms from Australia or the UK. The studies are therefore limited to one single country or make comparisons between two country samples. The results of these studies may not easily be transferred to other countries due to differences

---

109 See chapter 4.2.2.3.

in the regulatory environment. Additionally, multi-country analyses provide larger sample sizes and allow testing for differences between the country samples.

- There is only limited evidence on the implications of **asset revaluations** under IFRS: Empirical literature provides evidence on revaluations for tangible assets for Australian and UK country samples. However, these revaluations are performed under local GAAP regulations, but not under IFRS. Thus, the results of these studies may not be generalized to the IFRS environment. As the IFRS allow the revaluation for tangible assets, it makes sense to investigate the implications of such revaluations for a broad sample of firms preparing their financial statements under IFRS.

- Fair value accounting and **analyst following** has not been examined, even if accounting literature points to the importance of analyst following (see chapter 4.2.2.3). There is only one study that deals with the implications of fair value accounting for financial analysts (*Fan et al.* (2006)). However, the study only deals with forecast accuracy and forecast dispersion without taking into account the number of analysts following the firm. Moreover, the study is limited to the life insurance industry. Results may thus not easily be generalized.

- Studies on fair value accounting are mainly **archival-based**. Archival-based approaches have several advantages. When empirical data is available, financial statement data may easily be compared to market measures. As such, it makes sense that the value relevance literature uses archival-based approaches. However, archival designs also have limitations (*Hirst et al.* (2004), p. 455). Since these approaches are dependent on empirical data, it is only possible to examine the implications of existing data for investors, such as for example the effects of managements' decisions to measure assets. The design cannot vary how firms measure their assets to test whether (or how) investors would react on these variations. Moreover, it is contingent upon the data available. Thus, it would be more recommendable to use alternative approaches besides archival studies.

These limitations are addressed by conducting two empirical studies. After the hypothesis development in chapter 4, the first study with financial analysts as professional investors is conducted in chapter 5. The study uses a broad sample of European listed firms from several industries and is not only focusing on the real estate industry.[110] In contrast to related empirical literature, the study is **not limited to certain industries** and provides **multi-country** evidence. It examines the implications of **asset revaluations** for investment property and PPE. In order to provide a comprehensive analysis of the implications of fair value accounting for financial analysts, **analyst following** is also considered. The second study is conducted in chapter 6. It provides evidence on nonprofessional investors' judgments and investment decisions under fair value accounting when compared to historical cost. The first study with financial analysts is archival-based. The second study uses an

---

110 Banks and financial institutions are excluded from the sample due to their special regulatory environment.

experimental-based approach. Thus, the second study addresses the limitation of **archival-based research** and allows a direct control of the research setting.

4 Theory and hypotheses development

4.1 Theoretical foundation

This study is classified into the theoretical scientific concept of the critical rationalism. Under this approach, an empirical research strategy is used in a way to develop hypotheses based on theory and prior research to either confirm or reject the hypotheses against empirical data. As related literature has already been reviewed, this chapter presents the relevant **theory** for the development of the hypotheses necessary for the two empirical studies. First, the theoretical approach of the agency theory is presented. Second, the chapter presents the theory of efficient markets as this approach is necessary to explain why financial analysts' forecasts may be beneficial for investors.

4.1.1 Agency theory

4.1.1.1 Agency theory as a part of the new institutionalism

The **new institutionalism** is based on neoclassical economics but does not require the simplified and easy-to refute assumptions.[111] Therefore, the new institutionalism appears to be closer to transactions as they are likely to occur in reality. The new institutionalism does not assume a perfectly competitive capital market with complete information available to every trader and free access to the financial market with trading at no cost and in particular accounts for asymmetric information in the market and transaction costs. However, when the assumptions of the neoclassical economics do no longer hold under the new institutionalism, the results of perfectly functioning markets that result from neoclassical economics cannot longer be valid (*Schmidt/Terberger* (2006), p. 399ff.). It is then more likely to think of certain friction losses, which makes it more difficult to achieve a state of cross-social welfare (*Vollmer* (2008), p. 12).

In view of these losses of welfare, the theories of new institutionalism focus on developing a sociological view of **institutions** and describe the way how these institutions interact and how they affect society. Basically, new institutionalists believe that institutions matter and that in examining how they matter, the assumption of methodological individualism and individual rationality must be rejected (*Carruthers* (1995), p. 314f.). The purpose of these institutions is then to work against the limited efficiency of imperfect markets in order to create positive welfare effects (*Schmidt/Terberger* (2006), p. 395). Thus, the term "institution" in this context refers both to systems or arrangements under which individuals act in society as well as to organizations within which individuals may jointly operate (*Schneider* (1995), p. 20ff.). Taken together, the new institutionalism contains several scientific approaches, which include the concept of property rights, the theory of transaction cost, and the agency theory.

---

111 Neoclassical economics are based on the assumption of a perfectly competitive financial market. It is characterized by certain conditions such as costless trading and access to financial markets, freely available information about borrowing and lending opportunities, and many traders available with no single trader having a significant impact on market prices (*Süchting* (1995), p. 370; *Perridon/Steiner* (2009), p. 81f.).

The **concept of property rights** is concerned with rights of ownership in an asset, which generally include the rights to use and consume the asset, to omit others from the use of the asset, to modify its form and substance, to obtain income from it, and to transfer these rights either completely through sale or in parts/for a certain time, for example through rental (*Furubotn/Pejovich* (1974), p. 4). While property rights may usually be exclusive to the owner, they are generally not unrestricted, since for example governments often impose regulations limiting the owners' options in terms of how they are able to use their resource (*Fuchs* (2003), p. 44). The property rights should be conceived as bundles of rights (*Kasper/Streit* (2001), p. 175f.). They consequently represent future claims on services, property or other property rights, with each property right or bundle of property rights to be offset by a commitment to another person (*Schneider* (1995), p. 3f.). Therefore, the concept of property rights and the object that is subject to exchange can be interpreted in a way that property rights encompass binding social relations among individuals (*Furubotn/Pejovich* (1974), p. 3f.). The property rights and the contracts that assign the market participants with the corresponding rights and obligations represent institutional arrangements within the scope of the theory of the new institutionalism (*Schmidt/Terberger* (2006), p. 397).

The **transaction cost theory** addresses the fundamental question of why firms exist at all in the form of a hierarchical organization structure (*Funke* (2006), p. 35). Based on neoclassical arguments that resources are efficiently allocated only through the price system, the existence of companies with individuals who coordinate the production cannot be explained (*Coase* (1937), p. 388). The main reason for the foundation of enterprises is seen in the fact that using the price system is not possible without cost which removes a key premise of neoclassical economics (*Vollmer* (2008), p. 14). Instead of that, costs do usually incur during the search for relevant prices and by the negotiation of a separate contract for each transaction. Such costs cannot be eliminated completely by the foundation of a company, but significantly reduced compared to using the price system (*Franken* (2001), p. 19). Thus, the decision of whether establishing a company or using the market depends on the following: Although the costs of using the market can significantly be reduced in an enterprise, companies do also cause costs which are increasing with company size (*Funke* (2006), p. 35). In transaction cost theory, an optimum is reached when the sum of both costs is minimal (*Coase* (1937), p. 392ff.).

Finally, the **agency theory** is a part of the new institutionalism that is viewed as an appropriate research approach to examine accounting practices due to agency conflicts (*Schroeder et al.* (2008), p. 127). As the agency theory constitutes a major part necessary for hypotheses development in this study, the approach is presented in detail in the following chapter.

4.1.1.2 Conception of the agency theory

Agency theory (or: principal-agent theory) focuses on the relationship between the agent and the principal. Especially in the fields of political science and economics, it deals with the difficulties that arise when a principal hires an agent for performing certain tasks that are beneficial to the principal and costly to the agent (*Franke* (1993), p. 38). *Jen-*

sen/Meckling (1976) define an agency relationship as "a contract under which one or more persons (the principal(s)) engage another person (the agent) to perform some service on their behalf which involves delegating some decision making authority to the agent" (*Jensen/Meckling* (1976), p. 308). As the agent receives a compensation for his service which depends on certain pre-agreed criteria and the principal receives the residual amount, the decisions that are taken by the agent after the contractual relationship has been formed do both influence his own welfare as well as the welfare situation of the principal (*Arrow* (1985), p. 37).

Agency relationships are omnipresent in economic life because there are numerous situations with gains to specialization in which an individual acts on behalf of a principal due to some comparative advantage (*Hart/Holmström* (1987), p. 75). However, there is a problem with **information asymmetry**, uncertainty, and risk if the agent possesses an information advantage and if the principal cannot efficiently monitor the actions of the agent at no cost (*Franke* (1993), p. 39). The principal is not able to observe the actions of the agent and sees only the results which may not solely depend on the actions of the agent but also on other circumstances. Thus, the principal cannot conclude anything certain about the actions of the agent by only relying on the outcomes (*Richter/Furubotn* (2003), p. 173f.). The problems that arise from the separation of ownership and control are targeted by the agency theory which explicitly distinguishes between difficulties that arise before (hidden characteristics and hidden information) and after (hidden action) entering into such an agreement (*Hart/Holmström* (1987), p. 76):

- It is difficult for the principal to assess the characteristics of the agent before entering into an agreement (**hidden characteristics**) (*Göbel* (2002), p. 101). Due to information asymmetries concerning the characteristics of the agent, the principal expects an average quality of the service offered. He therefore only pays an average price (*Horsch* (2005), p. 86). This means that agents with an above average quality are not able to receive a price high enough to offer their services worthwhile. Such agents will thus not offer their services on the market. The withdrawal of high-quality agents reduces the average quality of the remaining agents, causing principals to revise their expectations downward for any remaining agent on the market. Finally, there is a risk of adverse selection.[112]

- After entering into an agreement, the problem of **hidden action** arises when the principal cannot observe the actions undertaken by the agent without cost. Additionally, the results of the agent's activities may also depend on other circumstances that cannot be influenced by the agent, such as the normal business cycle (*Arrow* (1985), p. 38f.). As a consequence, the principal is not able to measure the labor input of the agent based on an observable result which provides the agent with discretion (*Decker* (1994), p. 20f.). The agent may take advantage of the information asymmetry if he reduces his work input (shirking) or if he demands company resources for his own purposes, such as using company cars for private purposes (consumption on the job).

---

112 The problem of adverse selection was first demonstrated by *Akerlof* (1970) who used the market for used cars as an example for the problem of quality uncertainty (market for lemons).

- In situations with **hidden information**, the agent has superior information and uses this information to make decisions. However, the principal cannot assess whether these decisions are beneficial for him or not (*Arrow* (1985), p. 38f.). These information problems do increase with the degree of specification because it is not expected that a regular shareholder can assess whether a manager has made an investment decision in order to increase shareholder value or just on the basis of selfish acting (fringe benefits) (*Friedl* (2003), p. 513). While the problems that arise from hidden action and hidden information allow an agent to use discretionary potential, the principal on the other hand faces a moral hazard (*Arrow* (1985), p. 38ff.).

The agency theory constitutes the basis for a series of other scientific approaches which are intended to characterize the relationship between principal and agent. The next chapters present the theories which are necessary for developing the hypotheses. While the **agency cost theory** deals with the costs that arise from the contractual relationship between principal and agent (chapter 4.1.1.3), the **signaling theory** presents possible solutions to the agency problems just elaborated (chapter 4.1.1.4). Finally, the implications of the agency theory for the monitoring function of financial analysts are discussed (chapter 4.1.1.5).

4.1.1.3 Agency cost theory

The principals face several limitations when they form contracts with agents. However, when the principals are aware of the problems that may arise due to the separation of ownership and control, they are likely to implement certain contractual controls. In this sense, they have the following opportunities (*Schmidt* (1981), p. 147f.):

- The principal may establish certain **monitoring and bonding** activities which enable him to assess the performance of the agent.

- The principal may limit the agent's room for **discretion** without preventing him of developing his abilities.

- **Penalties** may be implemented which become effective in the case of the agent's failure and induce a behavior that is in the sense of the principal.

The problem that becomes evident is that such contracts cannot be implemented at no cost. Therefore, the costs that are occurring in the agency cost theory are called agency costs and consist of the following three components (*Jensen/Meckling* (1976), p. 308):

- The **monitoring costs** of the principal to observe the activities of the agent. These may also include costs that arise when the principal controls the behavior of the agent for example through budget restrictions or compensation policies.

- The **bonding costs** occur when the agent acts on behalf of the principal. Such costs also include costs that arise for the agent when he intends to reduce information asymmetries through signaling or reporting activities.

- The **residual loss** refers to the divergence between the agent's decisions (based on an optimal monitoring and bonding environment) and those decisions which would hypothetically maximize the welfare of the principal. When this is the case, the residual loss represents the dollar equivalent of the reduction in welfare that is experienced by the principal due to this divergence.

Taken together, the sum of these three components represents agency costs for contracts between agents and principals, which are likely to differ for firm size and firm complexity. It is expected that bigger firms and firms with a higher organizational complexity face an increasing degree of information asymmetry and more agency costs (*Jensen/Meckling* (1976), p. 305ff.). The signaling theory, which is presented in the next chapter, involves ways to cope with agency costs.

4.1.1.4 Signaling theory

The main problem addressed by the agency theory is the fact that the two contractual parties have different amounts of information. A possible approach to solve the agency conflicts mentioned in the previous chapters does therefore involve a reduction of the information asymmetries between principals and agents (*Göbel* (2002), p. 110ff.). On the one hand, the principal may carefully observe the activities of the agent (**screening**) prior to the signing of the contract (*Stiglitz* (1975), p. 283ff.). After the agreement into a contract, the principal may on the other hand monitor and supervise (**monitoring**) the activities of the agent in a way to reduce information asymmetries (*Arrow* (1985), p. 45–46; *Göbel* (2002), p. 112). Such monitoring activities do not have to be conducted by the principal itself but may be performed by other bodies, such as supervisory boards or auditors.

From the view of the agent, agency theory problems may be reduced by signaling or reporting. If an agent has an interest to reduce the information asymmetries before entering into a contract, he is likely to credibly signal (**signaling**) his characteristics to the principal (*Spence* (1973), p. 357). After the contract has been signed and the principal-agent relationship is established, the agent has, under certain conditions, an incentive to make his acting transparent to the principal (*Barth* (2009), p. 91f.). According to this, the agent could perform activities of **reporting**, which includes for example the regular generation of reports or the submission of controls on a voluntary basis (*Barth* (2009), p. 92). Table 4-1 presents an overview of the agency problems and possible solutions.

Appearance	Problem	Issue	Possible solutions	
			Principal	Agent
Before contract	Hidden characteristics	Adverse selection	Screening	Signaling
After contract	Hidden action	Shirking, consumption on the job	Monitoring	Reporting
	Hidden information	Fringe benefits		

Table 4-1: Agency problems and possible solutions
          (Following *Göbel* (2002), p. 100, 110)

Taken together, the signaling theory is concerned with solutions to solve possible conflicts arising in the course of agency relationships to decrease information asymmetry. Such information asymmetry can be reduced through information distribution of the better-informed party. Because financial analysts function as information intermediaries on the capital markets, it is important to investigate the implications of the agency cost theory on their role to monitor management.

4.1.1.5 Agency theory and the monitoring function of financial analysts

As outlined in chapter 2.2.2.3, financial analysts function as information intermediaries on the capital markets and reduce information asymmetries between management and investors. However, there is another fact which highlights the importance of financial analysts on the capital markets. Financial analysts are gaining in importance to mitigate the agency conflict between management and investors through their ability to efficiently monitor the management of a company. Thus, investors may delegate their own **monitoring** to financial analysts and benefit from several advantages instead of monitoring on their own.

Jensen/Meckling (1976) and *Chung/Jo* (1996) argue that the activities of financial analysts help reduce agency costs associated with the separation of ownership and control. Analysts help to discipline corporate managers by closely monitoring and publicizing their decisions. Analyst following has a significant and positive impact on the **market value** of the firm, thus suggesting that security analysis activity affect firm value through its monitoring function (*Chung/Jo* (1996), p. 493f.). Additionally, the Tobin's q ratio is significantly and positively associated with the number of analysts following the firm (*Chung/Jo* (1996), p. 495). It is therefore suggested that security analysis has a positive impact on the market value of the firm as the monitoring of financial analysts prevents managers from non-value maximizing behavior (*Chung/Jo* (1996), p. 511; *Doukas et al.* (2000), p. 54). However, the effect of monitoring depends on certain company characteristics, such as the degree of diversification of a firm and its number of segments. Security analysts exert substantially greater influence on reducing agency costs for single-segment companies than for multi-segment companies. This means that the monitoring role of security analysts is more pronounced for focused than for more diversified companies.[113]

Besides of external monitoring by financial analysts, investors may also benefit from **internal monitoring** through managerial ownership. It is assumed that managers act more in the investors' interest when they are holders of their own company's shares. According to this, there is a significant and positive association between the Tobin's q ratio of the firm and the degree of managerial ownership (*Morck et al.* (1988), p. 311f.). Even if investors benefit from internal monitoring through managerial ownership, internal monitoring and external monitoring are not perfect substitutes. Whereas a higher level of external monitoring in the form of security analysis significantly reduces the need for internal monitoring, this cannot be reported for the inverse relation (*Chen* (2005), p. 15). It is thus suggested that external monitoring reduces agency costs more efficiently than internal monitoring. Additionally, internal monitoring may not compensate for a lack of external monitoring. Financial analysts serve an external monitoring function by reducing agency costs that are associated with the separation of ownership and control. Through the decreased agency costs, their effort significantly enhances firm value.

---

113 This is viewed as one possible explanation for the fact that diversified companies trade at a discount compared to their more focused counterparts. See *Doukas et al.* (2000), p. 59.

Despite of an increase in firm valuation and Tobin's q ratio, there is a further effect that makes delegation of monitoring profitable for investors. Investors may benefit from third-party supervision through incentives (*Strausz* (1997), p. 347f.). Investors who employ an external monitor have an extra contract and can better regulate incentives for monitoring and the effort of the agent. The monitoring function of financial analysts can also be explained on the basis of **financial intermediation**. The introduction of a financial intermediator is useful for solving incentive problems between borrowers and lenders of money due to its monitoring function. However, aspects of financial intermediation can be transferred to explain the existence of information intermediaries like financial analysts as well. According to this, financial analysts have a monitoring function for the companies' management in terms of making decisions in the interest of the investors to resolve moral hazard problems (*Diamond* (1984), p. 394). It is assumed that monitoring causes costs that make the existence of financial analysts even more necessary, because the investors want to delegate their own monitoring to an agent who undertakes this task of monitoring (*Diamond* (1984), p. 409f.).

Summarizing this chapter, financial analysts play an important role as information providers for investors and act as a monitoring mechanism to reduce agency costs. Such agency costs arise with the separation of ownership and control between investors and management. Financial analysts' coverage of firms is likely to cause greater confidence into an investment by the investors, which is thus represented by higher market values. Greater analyst following and therefore a greater extent of expected monitoring is positively associated with firm value.

After the agency theory has been presented in this chapter, the efficient market hypothesis is outlined in the next chapter. This step is necessary to explain the existence of financial analysts on the capital markets. A certain degree of market efficiency should not be exceeded. Otherwise, the research of financial analysts may not generate value for investors.

4.1.2 Efficient market hypothesis

4.1.2.1 Conception of the efficient market hypothesis

The **efficient market hypothesis** (EMH) describes market prices on stock exchanges with the amount of information available (*Damodaran* (2002), p. 113). As the primary role of capital markets is the efficient allocation of capital and investors trade on the information available in the market, it is important that there is a close link between companies' direct activities and the market price of its stock. The definition of EMH is based on the work of *Fama* (1970) which is important for understanding and doing empirical research in finance and is viewed as one of the most important ideas in economics (*Ball* (2009), p. 10). He formally describes an efficient market as

> "*a market in which prices always 'fully reflect' available information.*"
> *(Fama (1970), p. 383)*

Following this definition, security prices will always be in equilibrium when the information level remains constant and no new information reaches the market. Prices will remain unchanged until new information is released to the investors who will then trade on this information causing a new equilibrium of prices. There are **three sufficient market conditions** that have to be fulfilled for market efficiency (*Fama* (1970), p. 387):

- The trading of securities causes no transaction costs,
- all market participants have the same information available at no cost, and
- all market participants have identical thoughts and beliefs about information that is currently available in the market.

As these three conditions are necessary for a market that fully reflects available information and it is hard to believe that a completely frictionless market does exist in reality, the concept of the EMH is likely to remain a theoretical concept (*Vorstius* (2004), p. 16). All three conditions might to some extent not occur in **real existing markets**. That is, trading of securities is likely to cause a certain amount of transaction costs, information is not freely available to all market participants and they might also disagree about the information that is currently available in the market. Therefore, the term *fully reflect* is categorized in three different subsets of efficient markets, which are the weak form efficiency, the semi-strong form efficiency, and the strong form efficiency (*Fama* (1970), p. 388; *Sapusek* (1998), p. 16ff.; *Henze* (2004), p. 8; *Franke/Hax* (2009), p. 436):[114]

Weak form efficiency

In markets featuring the weak form efficiency, share prices do not have any serial dependence, which means that they follow a **random walk**. Future prices of stocks can therefore not be predicted by analyzing prices from the past or by using investment strategies based on historical data already included in the share prices. In markets that are efficient in the weak form, the technical stock analysis would not consistently produce excess returns, in contrast to some sort of fundamental analysis which would still enable the investor to gain abnormal returns on his investment.[115]

Semi-strong form efficiency

When markets are efficient in the semi-strong form, stock prices include all information that is obviously **publicly available** to the market participants. The semi-strong market efficiency implies that share prices immediately adjust to new information that becomes publicly available. Thus, investors can earn no excess returns by trading on this information. Are markets semi-strong efficient, neither the technical nor the fundamental analyses provide the investor with abnormal returns. Only trading on some sort of private or insider information would be worthwhile.

Strong form efficiency

In markets that are efficient in the strong form of the EMH, no investor may earn excess returns by using public or private information (e.g. that information received from insid-

---

114 *Fama* formally changed the names of his categories in one of his papers later. He substituted weak, semi-strong, and strong forms of market efficiency into the terms of *return predictability, event studies,* and *private information*. See *Fama* (1991).

115 For more information about the different sorts of stock analysis, like the technical and fundamental analysis, refer to chapter 2.2.2.4.2.

ers and individuals with monopolistic access to information like members of the management) as all available information is already reflected in share prices. This means that not even individual investors or groups with exclusive access to **monopolistic information** may earn any abnormal return when they trade on this information before the information is made public. The strong form of market efficiency is likely to remain a theoretical concept with little relevance to reality as there is a broad consensus about insider trading being rewarding for individuals with exclusive access. This is also mentioned by *Fama* (1970), p. 414: "One would not expect such an extreme model to be an exact description of the world, and it is probably best viewed as a benchmark against which the importance of deviations from market efficiency can be judged."

It has to be noted that the strong form of market efficiency also includes the characteristics of the other two weaker forms and the semi-strong form of market efficiency also includes the characteristics of the weak form of market efficiency. The different forms of information efficiency are depicted in Figure 4-1.

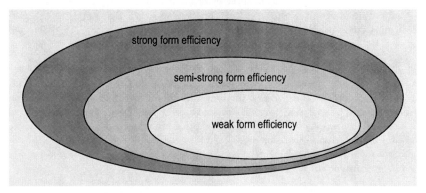

Figure 4-1: Forms of information efficiency
      (*Mühlbradt* (1978), p. 37; *Steiner/Bruns* (2002), p. 42)

Since its first definition and categorization into three groups, the EMH has gained much attention in capital market research (*Beaver* (1983), p. 346; *v. Heyl* (1995), p. 36). On the one hand, researchers support the theoretical concept of *Fama* which is easy to understand and gave research in this area a big push. For example, the concept of the semi-strong form of market efficiency that promoted the **event study methodology** became an important part of finance, especially corporate finance (*Fama* (1991), p. 1599f.). Further researchers highlight the empirical evidence of the EMH as the concept has been tested and found consistent with the data in a wide variety of markets, including the U.S., Australian, English, and German stock markets.[116] On the other hand, opponents refer to movements in stock prices which are, according to the EMH, caused by the information in the market and describe this as "one of the most remarkable errors in the history of

---

116 *Jensen*, in this sense, states that "there is no other proposition in economics which has more solid empirical evidence supporting it than the Efficient Market Hypothesis" (*Jensen* (1978), p. 95).

economic thought" (*Shiller* (1984), p. 459).[117] Others mainly focus on the market conditions for efficient markets and argue that only in rare cases investors would have homogeneous information and beliefs about stocks and that it is a basic error of not considering transaction costs and costs for processing new information (*Ball* (2009), p. 13).

The theory of the EMH and the different forms of market efficiency more or less lead to a kind of **information paradox** which refers to the so-called *Grossman-Stiglitz paradox*. It postulates that if the stock markets were informationally efficient, that is, all relevant information is already reflected in stock prices, then no single investor would have a sufficient incentive to acquire the information on which share prices are based (*Grossman/Stiglitz* (1980), p. 404). If prices are already in equilibrium, based on the information available, no investor would spend time and energy researching securities because he would not achieve any advantage compared to investors not doing any research on securities (*Damodaran* (2002), p. 115). Well-informed traders would not be able to earn a return on their information what would cause these investors not continuing costly information gathering and processing. But, however, if no one spends time and energy researching securities and trading on his information, prices cannot be in equilibrium and the market can never become informationally efficient (*Franke/Hax* (2009), p. 436f.). This interesting paradox is actually a caveat of the EMH, especially in its strong and semi-strong form and when information gathering and processing is possible at no cost. But since this would not likely be the case (i.e. information gathering and processing is costly for individuals),[118] new information does not immediately lead to a new equilibrium of prices which enables investors to gain advantages by doing costly stock research (*Franke/Hax* (2009), p. 437). The next chapter highlights the implications of the EMH for the work of financial analysts.

4.1.2.2   Implications for financial analysts

The form of the EMH denotes the right to exist and role of financial analysts on the capital markets. In markets that are informationally efficient in the **strong form**, the work of financial analysts would be of no use for investors as all information is already contained in stock prices (*Henze* (2004), p. 9). An important requirement for the research of financial analysts being helpful for investors is therefore the non-existence of a capital market in the strong form. As already mentioned in chapter 4.1.2.1, the strong form market efficiency is likely to remain a theoretical concept. This is supported by empirical evidence which negates the existence of capital markets being strongly efficient.[119] Corresponding

---

117 The author, among others, points to the phenomenon of mass psychology which plays an important role in how stock prices change over time. The stock market is likely to overreact because of investors' mentality and other herd-like behavior (*Shiller* (1984), p. 64).

118 See *Grossman/Stiglitz* (1980), p. 404, who mention that "price systems and competitive markets are important only when information is costly." For the importance of price systems in society see also *Hayek* (1945), p. 528f.

119 See *Jaffe* (1974) and *Laffont/Maskin* (1990) who provide evidence of insiders earning excessive returns when trading on private information.

to empirical evidence, also *Fama* (1991) expresses his doubts about the strong form of the EMH.[120]

It is not the purpose of analysts to use private information from company insiders as this behavior is restricted by law in most countries. Thus, the EMH in its **semi-strong form** does also cause problems for the work of financial analysts. It is therefore essential for the existence of financial analysts to neglect the semi-strong market efficiency in its "pure" form (*Wichels* (2002), p. 55; *Henze* (2004), p. 9). In addition, the semi-strong EMH has implications for the needs of corporate disclosure, as financial reporting and disclosure would no longer be necessary in markets that are informationally efficient (*Schmidt* (1982), p. 728). While the empirical literature provides clear evidence against the strong form of the EMH, results for the testing of the semi-strong form are mixed. The concept in its semi-strong form can easily be tested by using the event study methodology.[121] There are both studies providing support for the existence and rejecting the semi-strong form of the EMH.[122]

While there is no clear evidence for the semi-strong form of market efficiency, there is empirical support for the EMH in its **weak form**.[123] According to this, it is not possible for investors to gain abnormal returns by relying only on security prices from the past (*v. Heyl* (1995), p. 36f.). Financial analysts would find it therefore not helpful to rely solely on some sort of technical analysis. However, financial analysts may use the fundamental analysis when doing equity research as there is no clear evidence for the semi-strong form of the EMH (*Henze* (2004), p. 10). And since there are information costs, financial analysts may gain a competitive advantage in evaluating the future prospects of a company through specialization on specific industries.

4.2   Hypotheses development

4.2.1   Preliminary considerations

Hypotheses are proposed explanations for observable phenomena and represent relationships on the basis of a certain theory that can be tested empirically (*Wagenhofer* (1990), p. 222). Because hypotheses are developed based on a certain theory, they do not only predict the results of an empirical analysis but do in addition provide an explanation of the effect which is examined (*Bortz et al.* (2006), p. 23). Scientific hypotheses are generally based on previous observations which cannot sufficiently be explained with the available theories. When hypotheses are statistically tested, two kinds of hypotheses are generally compared which are called the null hypothesis and the alternative hypothesis (*Smith*

---

120 *Fama* notes that "since there are surely positive information and trading costs, the extreme version of the market efficiency hypothesis is surely false". See *Fama* (1991), p. 1575.

121 An event study uses financial market data and measures the impact of a specific event on the market value of the firm. Refer to *MacKinlay* (1997) for more information.

122 For studies doubting the existence of the EMH in its semi-strong form, see *Jensen* (1978) or *May* (1991). For empirical evidence supporting the semi-strong form of the EMH refer to *Ball* (1978) or *Roll* (1984).

123 See for example *Fama* (1970), p. 389ff. or *May* (1991), p. 327.

(2003), p. 52f.). Whereas the **null hypothesis** is the hypothesis which states that there is no relation between the phenomena whose relation is under investigation, the **alternative hypothesis** (as the name suggests) is the alternative to the null hypotheses which states that there is some kind of relation. Depending on the nature of the assumed relation, the alternative hypothesis may take several forms. On the one hand, when it is hypothesized that there is some kind of effect with the direction unclear, the hypothesis is two-sided (*Bolstad* (2007), p. 173). On the other hand, when the direction of the relation is clear, the hypothesis takes the form of a one-sided hypothesis (*Siegel* (2012), p. 262).

The next section is concerned with hypotheses development. Basically, the hypotheses are derived from the theoretical foundation presented in the previous chapter. However, the hypotheses are also developed on the basis of certain related empirical literature which has been presented in chapter 3. The order of hypotheses development conforms to the order of the questions raised in the introduction: First, implications of fair value accounting for financial analysts' forecasts (chapter 4.2.2) and second, implications of fair value accounting for investors' judgments and investment decisions (chapter 4.2.3).

4.2.2   Fair value accounting and financial analysts' forecasts

4.2.2.1   Fair value accounting and forecast accuracy

Under the assumption of a capital market that is **informationally efficient in the weak form**, analysts' recommendations provide additional utility for investors when new information is not immediately reflected in stock prices. In addition, the work of financial analysts is helpful for investors because they monitor a company's management in a way that management acts and makes decisions which do best serve the needs of investors. Taken together, the relevance of financial analysts' forecasts can be explained on the basis of the **agency cost theory**. When there are information asymmetries between management and investor, investors are likely to rely on a third party which has special abilities in **monitoring** in a way to reduce these information asymmetries more significantly compared to monitoring activities performed by the investors themselves.

When fair value measures in accounting provide more relevant and reliable information to users of financial statements, it is expected that financial analysts can produce more precise forecasts in a way that forecasts for earnings are good predictions for realized earnings. The empirical literature presents evidence on fair value accounting providing significantly more relevant information than historical costs.[124] Fair values are also viewed as more reliable compared to historical cost when they are derived from active markets or when fair value estimates are determined from independent appraisers rather than the management.[125] Therefore, a choice to apply value accounting can be justified on the basis of the **signaling theory**. If management believes that fair values provide more relevant and reliable information for investors, they are likely to adopt fair value measures instead of historical cost. Additionally, management may benefit from fair value disclosures because more

---

124 See for example *Easton et al.* (1993), *Barth/Clinch* (1998), *Danbolt/Rees* (2008), and the overview in chapter 3.1.

125 See for example *Cotter/Richardson* (2002), *Muller/Riedl* (2002), and the overview in chapter 3.2.

accurate forecasts are viewed as an instrument to lower the firm's implied cost of capital (*Gebhardt et al.* (2001), p. 165ff.).

Proponents of fair value accounting argue that measuring assets and liabilities at fair value provide more valuable and reliable information to investors (*Ball* (2006), p. 13; *CFA Institute Centre* (2008)) and do therefore broaden the investors view over the **firm's constitution**.[126] As historical cost accounting involves several disadvantages including past orientation and numbers that are not updated from the transaction day onwards, market prices should reduce information asymmetry and should force companies to apply the fair value method instead of the cost method (*Quagli/Avallone* (2010), p. 489). On the other hand, opponents argue that some fair value measures might also reduce **reliability** and usefulness of financial statements to investors. Due to illiquid markets, the prices for assets may not always be available. The accountant then has to rely on estimates or valuation models which lead to highly subjective and less reliable financial statements (*Watts* (2006), p. 57; *Whittington* (2008), p. 164). Since single estimates of fair values made by individuals based on valuation models can never reach the effectiveness of the whole financial market with its numerous market participants' decisions to determine the prices, reliable prices for assets that are close to the market can hardly be reached.

With fair value accounting, changes of market values do have a direct impact on the company's income. Therefore a higher amount of assets measured at fair value may lead to a higher **volatility** of earnings that are subject of analysts' forecasts. Historical costs are easier to assess in the profit or loss for the period. As financial analysts' normally cover not just one firm but usually a few companies in the same business, fair value accounting makes companies more difficult to compare. This would lead to less precise earnings forecasts. In addition, the use of fair value accounting makes earnings predictions more difficult. As changes in fair value are usually reported at the end of a fiscal year, financial analysts have to predict changes in fair value before the fiscal year-end as well. This additional challenge does not exist in a historical cost accounting environment and makes forecasting easier. This could improve the quality of earnings predictions (*Peek* (2005), p. 283).

Evidence on empirical forecasting literature reveals that financial analysts make extensive use of financial statement information and benefit from high quality disclosures in a way that these disclosures result in more accurate forecasts.[127] In addition, evidence shows that financial analysts tend to prefer fair value accounting when making forecasts, at least for certain industries (*Fan et al.* (2006), p. 128). Thus, when fair values are viewed as high quality disclosures in financial statements, it is expected that forecast accuracy significantly increases compared to historical cost accounting. However, the increased volatility resulting from fair value changes may also cause a greater bias in analysts' forecasts for firms which are applying fair value accounting. Taken together, it is expected that there is a significant association of fair value accounting with financial analysts' forecast accuracy. As the direction of the fair value implications on analysts' ability to forecast earnings precisely

---

126 This view is also supported by the community of financial analysts itself: *Thinggaard* (1996) conducted a questionnaire with financial analysts and found evidence that financial analysts prefer an accounting system based on fair values rather than historical cost.

127 See *Hope* (2003), *Vanstraelen et al.* (2003), *Yu* (2010), and the overview in chapter 3.3.

remains initially uncertain, the following **non-directional hypothesis** (stated in the null form) is subject to testing:

> H_1: *Financial analysts' forecast accuracy of earnings for firms that measure their tangible assets at fair value does not significantly differ from analysts' forecast accuracy of earnings for firms that measure their tangible assets at historical cost.*

4.2.2.2 Fair value accounting and forecast dispersion

The dispersion among analysts' earnings forecasts refers to the difference between the earnings forecasts provided by individual analysts. Because the hypothesis which concerns forecast accuracy only investigates consensus forecasts for a given firm share, forecast dispersion is examined as an additional measure for the quality of analysts' forecasts. Similar to the case of forecast accuracy, the hypothesis can be developed on the basis of the **signaling theory** that financial analysts monitor management and serve informational needs of investors since there are information asymmetries between management and investor. Based on the **efficient market hypothesis**, it can be argued that when new information, such as company disclosure or accounting choices, reaches the market, it is reflected in share prices until the new market equilibrium is reached. However, when information is processed by individuals, it is likely that these individuals have heterogeneous beliefs with regard to the information (*Patton/Timmermann* (2010), p. 803). In addition, individual analysts may also use heterogeneous information sets so that dispersion in beliefs reflects differences in information sets (*Capistrán/Timmermann* (2009), p. 366).

It is noted in accounting literature that analysts' dispersion of forecasts exists primarily due to two reasons (*Lang/Lundholm* (1996), p. 471f.; *Eng/Teo* (2000), p. 223). First, dispersion may be caused by **differences in information** when each analyst has the same public information but different access to private information. This difference in information is likely to cause the dispersion in their forecasts. Second, dispersion may be due to **differences in forecasting models** when, despite of having the same information, each analyst uses unique forecasting models which also causes forecasts to be dispersed. If individual analysts have asymmetric information available, an increase of corporate disclosure (such as the application of fair values) should reduce forecast dispersion because individual analysts then have more similar information. On the other hand, when forecast dispersion is due to different forecasting models, an increase in disclosure should result in an increase of dispersion because the larger amount of information is now used as input for the different forecasting models.

Both *Harris/Raviv* (1993) and *Kandel/Pearson* (1995) support this argument as they present models in which investors differ in their interpretation of publicly available data. Their models show that traders in speculative markets hold different opinions about the same information that is released to the market. According to this, *Barron et al.* (2002) provide evidence that information asymmetry may increase when new information reaches the market and consequently the amount of liquidity decreases. They show that the commonality of the information contained in individual analysts' forecasts of earnings is significantly lower after earnings announcements which lead to a higher level of dispersion of forecasts. While additional data through the disclosure and measurement of fair values in financial statements can result in **divergence of beliefs** of investors or financial analysts, the degree of dispersion is expected to vary with respect to the characteristics of the information. When a company's disclosure of information can be interpreted by analysts in a common way, which is quantifiable and directed, one could expect earnings forecasts to be more similar and accurate, that means, less dispersed (*Bozzolan et al.* (2009), p. 439).

Assuming that fair value measures are important for financial analysts, it is expected that fair values reduce the uncertainty of analysts and thus reduce dispersion of forecasts. According to this, fair values help analysts to make better judgments with regard to a firm's performance. However, analysts may also have different time constraints in analyzing financial statement information with some analysts performing a more comprehensive stock analysis with the available data than others. This would result in a larger degree of dispersion. Taken together, the association of fair value accounting with forecast dispersion remains an empirical question. Therefore, the hypothesis is stated in the **null form**:

H₂: *The dispersion of financial analysts' forecasts for firms that measure their tangible assets at fair value does not significantly differ from the dispersion of financial analysts' forecasts for firms that measure their tangible assets at historical cost.*

4.2.2.3 Fair value accounting and analyst following

Beside analysts' forecast accuracy and dispersion, the number of analysts following a firm is also viewed as an important measure of analyst behavior. While financial analysts' forecast accuracy and dispersion are commonly used in existing research to indicate the quality of firms' information environment, the level of analyst following is used as a proxy for the **richness** of the firms' information environment (*Yu* (2010), p. 2). The positive economic consequences of having a large analyst following have been extensively documented in empirical accounting literature. While *Lang et al.* (2004) find that increased analyst following is associated with higher firm valuations, *Bowen et al.* (2008) provide evidence that analyst following is negatively associated with a firm's cost of equity capital. In addition, *Roulstone* (2003) find that analyst following is positively related to market liquidity for the regarding stock.

When the management of a firm is aware of these positive economic consequences of analyst following, the hypothesis development can be conducted on the basis of the **signaling theory**. In an attempt to attract a greater number of analysts following the company, the management may apply fair value accounting instead of historical cost to signal a better information environment for financial analysts. As fair values are predicted of being helpful for financial analysts in providing better information for forecasting (*CFA Institute Centre* (2008)), analysts are more likely to follow fair value firms because they find it easier to forecast earnings for these firms.

The model-based approach of *Bhushan* (1989) demonstrates that the number of analysts following a firm depends on both the supply and the demand of analyst services (*Bhushan* (1989), p. 257ff.). It is assumed that fair values provide more useful information for financial analysts in a way that they can better assess the future prospects of the company compared to historical cost. Then, the application of fair value accounting may reduce the time analysts must spend on scrutinizing the accounting numbers and reduce the cost of collecting information on their own (i.e. the additional time for the determination of market values for assets which are measured at historical cost), which in turn increases the **supply** of analyst forecasting service. When demand remains unchanged, the increase in supply will cause higher analyst following (*Yu* (2010), p. 5). On the other hand, fair value accounting may also have an impact on the **demand** for analyst service. The demand for analyst service depends on whether analysts are viewed as information intermediaries or information providers. In the case of information intermediaries, fair values will provide more information to analysts and make their reports more valuable for investors which results in higher demand for analyst services. However, when analysts are mainly information providers, the more information made available to investors through fair value accounting will reduce the demand for analyst services and analyst following will subsequently decrease (*Lang/Lundholm* (1996), p. 471).

The impact of fair value accounting on the level of analyst following is uncertain and remains an empirical question. The hypothesis is therefore stated in a **non-directional form**:

H₃: *The number of analysts following a firm is unrelated to whether the firm applies fair value or historical cost accounting for tangible assets.*

It has to be noted that the direction of **causality** between firms either applying fair value or historical cost accounting and analyst following is debatable. An observed positive relation could reflect either the fact that analysts are attracted by firms applying fair values or that analysts are able to exercise pressure on firms which they follow for other reasons to apply fair values (*Lang/Lundholm* (1996), p. 471). Although the hypothesis is based on theory and is therefore formulated in a non-directional form, both U.S. and international studies find a positive relation between analyst following and the extent or quality of corporate disclosure.[128] Taken together, analysts tend to follow firms with a tendency to disclose more information.

4.2.3 Fair value accounting and investors' judgments and investment decisions

4.2.3.1 Fair value accounting and dispersion of investors' judgments

The relationship between management and investors can be characterized as a typical principal agent problem with management possessing information that is not available to the investors. Contrary to the hypotheses development conducted in chapter 4.2.2, investors do not have the possibility to rely on information intermediaries and have to interpret financial statement information by themselves. The resulting information asymmetries cause different investors' judgments and expectations about a company's future prospects, because it is expected that financial statement information is interpreted differently by different investors. It is examined whether recognized or disclosed fair values affect non-professional investors' behavior which corresponds to the accounting procedure of in-

---

128 See *Lang/Lundholm* (1996) and *Eng/Teo* (2000).

vestment property. In addition, it is of interest whether investors make a difference between Level 1 fair values (mark-to-market) and Level 3 fair values (mark-to-model). Therefore, the hypotheses development in this chapter is both concerned with the question of how fair value information is **presented** in the financial statements and how fair value measures are **determined**. As these two questions do largely correspond to the valuation practice of IAS 40 with fair values either recognized or disclosed (with assets measured at historical cost), it is expected that the information which is derived on the basis of these hypotheses complement the findings of the archival study on financial analysts. Because accounting is viewed as useful when it provides information in such a way that investors end up with similar judgments, the first hypothesis in this chapter is concerned with the dispersion of investors' judgments.

The **efficient market hypothesis** (EMH) postulates that information, when it becomes available, is immediately used by investors to trade on this information.[129] As a result, new information is incorporated in stock prices no matter where to find that information. This means that in the case of fair value accounting, the question of whether fair values are recognized in the profit or loss for the period or disclosed in the notes should make no difference (*Belzile et al.* (2006), p. 150). However, the assumption that financial statement users view recognized and disclosed items similarly may not hold as empirical literature reveals that recognition and disclosure can influence users' judgments differently.[130] Moreover, and contrary to the assumption of the EMH, the differences between recognition and disclosure are due to the investors' limited capacity to perceive and process available information (*Libby et al.* (2002), p. 779), or result from investors not adjusting their judgments when information is solely disclosed in the notes section (*Sami/Schwartz* (1992), p. 61).

Contrary to financial analysts, who are expected to adopt a special valuation model in assessing firm value and non-sequentially search the annual reports for information that is relevant for their valuation model, nonprofessional investors are likely to acquire information in a relatively non-structured manner (*Belzile et al.* (2006), p. 151). As research shows that investors often read financial statements in the order in which it is presented and the notes are usually the last part of the annual reports, investors who read information sequentially may reach an **overload cognitive state** before reaching the notes section (*Hodge et al.* (2004), p. 688). However, even if investors read the notes section carefully, they may discount or adjust the information stated there when they assess the disclosed information as being less relevant than recognized information due to its placement in the notes (*Maines/McDaniel* (2000), p. 185). Providing additional information or changing the format of information helps users to overcome information-processing deficiencies, perhaps by making key components of the decision environment more clear (*Fiske/Taylor* (2008), p. 130). Clearer presentation of information increases the likelihood that the information will be used in a way that judgments will be unbiased (*Johnson et al.* (1988), p. 18f.; *Sanbonmatsu et al.* (1997), p. 251). Taken together, investors' judgments for disclosed information may be more dispersed than investors' judgments for recognized

---

129 See chapter 4.1.2.
130 See, for example, *Maines/McDaniel* (2000) or *Anandarajan et al.* (2002).

information when it is assumed that not all investors do carefully take into account the information given in the notes section. In addition, it could be hypothesized that not all investors even read the notes section at all.

An important issue when examining recognition and disclosure questions is the **functional fixation hypothesis** (*Tinic* (1990), p. 783). This concept from the psychology literature postulates that individuals are likely to attach a certain meaning to an object and are unable to perceive other acceptable meanings or uses (*Hirshleifer/Teoh* (2003), p. 353). When the concept is applied in an accounting context, it refers to decision makers who are concentrating on a certain number in the financial statements which is used without any adjustments.[131] According to this view, the choice of reporting information through recognition or disclosure is expected to cause different investors' judgments. Information disclosed in the notes is ignored when investors keep interpreting the reported net income in the same way as they did before the disclosed information was provided (*Viger et al.* (2008), p. 97). For the case of fair value recognition and disclosure, the group of investors that is affected by functional fixation would not consider disclosed fair value information, whereas the other group of investors would account for this information in assessing the future performance of the company. Functional fixation is not a problem in the case of recognized fair values. However, the functional fixation hypothesis causes judgments for firms that disclose fair values to be more dispersed than for firms with recognized fair values.

According to aspects of functional fixation and considering the risk of investors reaching an overload cognitive state, the hypothesis is stated in a **directional form**:

H_{4a}: *The dispersion of investors' judgments for firms only disclosing fair values is greater than the dispersion of investors' judgments for firms recognizing fair values.*

The hypothesis is consistent with prior experimental literature. *Maines/McDaniel* (2000) report that nonprofessional investors' judgments incorporate information to evaluate the performance of the company only when it is included in the statement of comprehensive income rather than in the notes (*Maines/McDaniel* (2000), p. 179). *Belzile et al.* (2006) examine two different reporting methods for stock option compensation plans and provide evidence **consistent** with the functional fixation hypothesis. The authors find a significant influence of the reporting format for stock compensation plans on investors' judgments only when the expense is recognized in the profit or loss for the period (*Belzile et al.* (2006), p. 147).

Empirical literature indicates that investors clearly differentiate fair value estimates with regard to the determination process: Whereas Level 1 or Level 2 based fair values are assessed as reliable estimates, model-based fair values are viewed as being less reliable.[132] In addition, investors tend to make a **difference** between fair value estimates that are made by independent appraisers and managers (*Cotter/Richardson* (2002), p. 23). Consistent with empirical literature, it is expected that investors make different judgments when they

---

131 The bottom line accounting numbers are usually the main items of functional fixation (*Tinic* (1990), p. 783).

132 See for example the results of the survey of *Gassen/Schwedler* (2010) and the overview in chapter 3.2.

are confronted with either mark-to-market or mark-to-model fair value estimates. It is assumed that investors face a higher degree of uncertainty in the case of mark-to-model fair values, whereas mark-to-market fair values should be assessed as reliable measures.

Mark-to-model measures, such as discounted cash flow values, integrate a potential for **managerial discretion** into a firm's financial statements. It could be the case that the higher degree of uncertainty of mark-to-model fair values is addressed differently by the investors. Some investors could make certain downward adjustments in the case of a fair value increase whereas others do not. Mark-to-market fair values are on the other hand adopted without any change into valuation. This would result in greater dispersion in the case of mark-to-model fair values. Therefore, the hypothesis is stated in a **directional form**:

H_{4b}: *The dispersion of investors' judgments for firms applying mark-to-model fair values is greater than the dispersion of investors' judgments for firms applying mark-to-market fair values.*

4.2.3.2 Fair value accounting and investors' confidence

This chapter deals with the degree of investors' confidence when they make decisions under different information environments. More precisely, it is of interest whether the question of recognition and disclosure of different fair value measures has a significant influence on the confidence that investors place into their judgment with regard to the performance of a certain firm. In general, investors should be confident and satisfied with their judgment if they believe that they can base their judgment on a considerable amount of **high quality information** that is both reliable and relevant for making that decision. Thus, the level of information is expected to increase the confidence that investor's place into their judgments (*Gill et al.* (1998), p. 1101). Because investors estimate the parameters needed in order to make their decisions on available information, their confidence levels depend on the characteristics of their information sets (*Botosan* (2006), p. 33). Taken together, an examination of investors' confidence with their valuation judgment enables an investigation of both the relevance and reliability criteria.

The association of recognized or disclosed fair values and investors' confidence can be explained on the basis of the **signaling theory**. If managers decide to recognize fair values on a voluntary basis rather than disclosing them, nonprofessional investors may interpret this choice as a signal for the reliability of the information (*Frederickson et al.* (2006), p. 1077). Thus, recognized information may signal a higher reliability of the data compared to information that is disclosed. It is assumed that investors are then more satisfied, because they made their investment decision on the basis of reliable data. However, nonprofessional investors are still aware of principal agent conflicts because they may view such choices by management as motivated by management's incentive to report strategically (*Hodge* (2003), p. 43ff.).

Nonprofessional investors may also interpret the choice of management to recognize fair values rather than disclosing them as a signal about the degree of **management bias** (*Frederickson et al.* (2006), p. 1079). According to attribution and persuasion theory, the degree of bias users of financial statements perceive in information reported by management depends on the consistency between the reported information and users' beliefs about management's reporting incentives (*Eagly/Chaiken* (1975), p. 142). If, for example, it is believed that management has an incentive to report optimistic and management reports incentive-consistent, such information is viewed as more strategic and biased than if management had reported not incentive-consistent. Whereas incentive-consistent information is viewed as self-serving and intended to promote management's position, incentive-inconsistent information is viewed as less biased and less self-serving (*Frederickson et al.* (2006), p. 1079).[133] In the case of fair value accounting, choosing to recognize fair value decreases in the profit or loss for the period reduces reported net income while disclosing these decreases does not. Given that nonprofessional investors will view recognized fair values as a less biased reporting choice than disclosure as managers are more interested in reporting higher net income. However, managers may also benefit from a higher net income in the case of increasing fair values. Nevertheless, investors may reward the risk taking of managers when they choose to recognize these amounts due to a significant increase in earnings volatility with recognized fair value changes.[134] Therefore, a higher degree of reliability should then increase the confidence that investors place into their judgments.

Auditor behavior is another possible source leading to a significant difference between the degrees of reliability of disclosed and recognized items (*Schipper* (2007), p. 314). According to the findings of *Libby et al.* (2006), auditors are more likely to accept a certain degree of misstatement in a disclosed item (here: the fair value of share-based payments) than in an item that is recognized in the balance sheet (the amount of a balance sheet lease). The authors conclude that this difference is caused at least in parts of an auditor's perception that errors in disclosed amounts are less material (*Libby et al.* (2006), p. 535). If investors do conform with the auditors' view that recognized amounts are more material than disclosed amounts (*Libby et al.* (2006), p. 533), they could conclude that disclosed information is less reliable due to the fact that recognition and disclosure are treated differently during the auditing process. If investors expect a significantly greater bias in disclosed items compared to recognized items, they consequently should view disclosed information as being less reliable than recognized amounts.

Taken together, recognized accounting information should increase investors' confidence when making judgments concerning the future performance of a company. Both the signaling theory and the empirical findings concerning auditors' behavior suggest that investors may be more confident when they make judgments on the basis of recognized information. Therefore, the hypothesis is stated in a **directional form**. It is as follows:

> *H5a:* *Investors' confidence is greater when they make their judgments on the basis of recognized fair values rather than on disclosed fair value information.*

The overview of empirical literature in chapter 3.2 provides evidence concerning the reliability of different fair value estimates. It is reported that unverifiable fair values is viewed

---

133 Empirical evidence supporting this view is provided by *Hirst et al.* (1995) and *Hodge et al.* (2006).
134 See also *Bernard et al.* (1995) who report a three times higher earnings volatility after firms perform fair value adjustments.

by the investors as an incidence for possible managerial discretion and fraudulent financial reporting (*Beatty/Weber* (2006); *Ramanna/Watts* (2007); *Ramanna* (2008)). Similar to the dispersion of investors' judgments, it is therefore expected that investors view some fair value measures as being more **reliable** than others. As mark-to-market fair value measures are derived from an active market, investors would associate these measures with a greater degree of reliability than mark-to-model fair values which are for example based on DCF models.[135] When investors expect a significant bias in model-based fair values, they may place a significantly smaller degree of confidence into judgments that are based on such measures. Therefore, the **directional hypothesis** has the following form:

> *H5b:* *Investors' confidence is greater when they make their judgments on the basis of mark-to-market fair values rather than on mark-to-model fair values.*

4.2.3.3 Fair value accounting and investors' willingness to invest

The first two hypotheses for the experimental approach concern investors' judgments and the confidence that investors place into these judgments. The hypotheses developed in this section deal with investors' willingness to invest and with their investment decisions. The hypothesis does not only capture investors' behavior as investment decisions are likely to influence certain **market characteristics** such as market liquidity or bid-ask spreads. In general, it is examined whether the recognition or disclosure of different fair value measures is associated with investors' willingness to invest, which is important because an investors' willingness to invest has further implications for the market characteristics of companies' shares.

Investors' willingness to invest is significantly associated with the level of **information asymmetry**. In the case of a high level of information asymmetry in the market, investors do not expect to have sufficient information for making adequate investment decisions and are likely to stop or withdraw from trading. However, the amount of disclosure and the manner in which that information is presented in financial statements may influence the level of information asymmetry in the market (*Ding et al.* (2009), p. 9). According to an economic point of view, an increased level of disclosure is associated with lower information asymmetry and a greater investors' willingness to invest (*Akerlof* (1970), p. 489; *Diamond/Verrecchia* (1991), p. 1348). Consistent with this view, *Bailey et al.* (2006) examine the implications of increased disclosure that non-U.S. firms face after a cross listing in the U.S. and find that volume reactions to earnings announcements typically increase significantly after the cross listing (*Bailey et al.* (2006), p. 208). According to this, if investors find that recognized fair value amounts provide a richer supply of information, they may adjust their willingness to invest and are more likely to make investment decisions when provided with recognized rather than disclosed fair value measures.

Differences in investors' willingness to invest can also be explained by the **signaling theory**. Whereas in the previous section it was argued that investors may interpret the choice between recognition and disclosure as a signal about the reliability of the recognized or disclosed amount, it is now argued that investors may also view the management's choice

---

135 For a critical analysis of the determination process of mark-to-model fair values see chapter 2.1.2.6.

as a signal for the future prospects of the firm (*Frederickson et al.* (2006), p. 1080). Users of financial statements may interpret accounting choices as signals about a firm's future prospects. Especially **income-reducing accounting choices**, for example through recognized expenses, are viewed as a signal that the company has more favorable future prospects compared to firms only disclosing such information (*Levine/Hughes* (2005), p. 846f.). It is suggested that investors view a choice of management to voluntarily report lower earnings as a signal that the company has more favorable future prospects (*Belzile et al.* (2006), p. 154). In the case of fair value accounting, it could be argued that recognized fair values are associated with a greater willingness to invest only during times of price decreases. This could be interpreted as a signal of more favorable earnings in the future, when fair values are recognized during price decreases, thus causing lower earnings in the short-term. In general, nonprofessional investors would expect managers to disclose fair value information during price decreases with no effect on the profit or loss for the period. However, financial statement users are expected to exhibit a significantly lower willingness to invest in the case of fair value price increases. The choice of management to report higher income is interpreted as a negative signal about the firm's future prospects (*Frederickson et al.* (2006), p. 1080).[136] Nonprofessional investors would then expect management to be more self-seeking in a way to realize earnings in the short-term rather than ensuring long-term company performance.

Therefore, in view of the relationship between the quality of disclosure and information asymmetries in the market, it is expected that recognized fair values are significantly associated with investors' willingness to invest. However, the signaling theory highlights the fact that investors may interpret recognized amounts with regard to the performance of fair values. In the case of increasing fair values, recognized amounts may be interpreted in a way that investors expect negative earnings in the future. Because the experimental study models a situation of increasing fair values for an asset, the hypothesis has the following **directional form**:

> *H_{6a}: During times of increasing fair values, investors' willingness to invest is smaller for firms recognizing fair values than for firms only disclosing fair value information.*

In addition to a general investigation the willingness to invest, the association of fair values and the amount to be invested by nonprofessional investors' should also be examined. It could be the case that investors are, in general, willing to invest in a company. This means that they are willing to buy shares of the regarding company. However, the amount that they would invest in a company could be different depending on the information provided in the financial statements. This would refer to either recognized or disclosed fair value information. Thus, this measure could be viewed as an **add-on** to the general willingness to invest, because investors' behavior is then examined in more detail. Taken together, the hypothesis largely conforms to the prior one. It is therefore stated in the **directional form**:

---

136 Archival research provides support for this view as it links more conservative accounting with higher stock prices. See for example *Wahlen* (1994), p. 456, or *Aboody et al.* (2004), p. 149.

H₆ᵦ: *During times of increasing fair values, the amount that is invested in a firm recognizing fair values is smaller than the amount invested in a firm only disclosing fair value information.*

The willingness to invest of users of financial statements is likely to be affected by the determination process of fair value measures. Compared to mark-to-market fair values, modeled fair values are by nature uncertain as they aggregate a distribution of probabilities to one single estimate (*Ding et al.* (2009), p. 7). It is then of interest whether and how investors react on financial statement information of similar nature but which is different with regard to its incremental degree of vagueness. Literature shows that investors respond in a way that they adopt a **vagueness avoidance** behavior when they are confronted with vague or uncertain information (*Du/Budescu* (2005), p. 1799).[137] If investors view the amount of vagueness or uncertainty that is associated with mark-to-model fair values to be significantly higher compared to mark-to-market fair values, their willingness to invest should be significantly lower in the case of model-based fair values. The hypothesis is therefore stated in the **directional form**:

H₆ᵧ: *Investors' willingness to invest is greater for firms that use mark-to-market fair values rather than for firms that use mark-to-model fair values.*

Similar to the hypothesis investigating financial statement presentation, it is also of interest whether investors adjust the amount that they are ready to invest in a company. Even if nonprofessional investors would be willing to invest in a company, they are likely to adjust the amount of money that they spend for buying the shares. Model-based fair values are viewed as less reliable compared to market-based fair values. As aforementioned, nonprofessional investors are expected to adopt a greater degree of vagueness avoidance in the case of mark-to-model fair values. It could thus be assumed that investors spend a significantly higher amount into firms which are determining their fair values of tangible assets mark-to-market instead of mark-to-model. The **directional hypothesis** is therefore as follows:

H₆ᵈ: *The amount invested into firms with mark-to-market fair values is greater than the amount invested into firms with mark-to-model fair values.*

Figure 4-2 summarizes and depicts the hypotheses with their regarding theoretical foundation.

---

137 This behavior is demonstrated in the context of a lottery setting where participants overwhelmingly favored a lottery with known probabilities rather than unknown probabilities and with participants that are even willing to pay to avoid an uncertain lottery (*Ellsberg* (1961), p. 669).

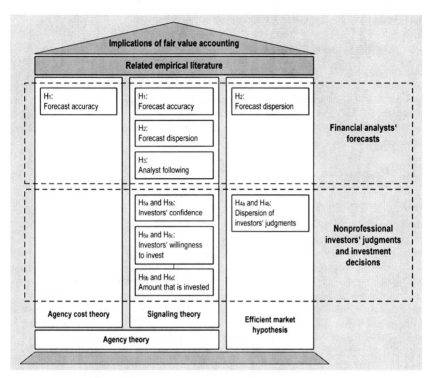

Figure 4-2: Theory and hypotheses
        (Following *Barth* (2009), p. 111)

After the theoretical foundation and the hypotheses development, all necessary steps are performed to prepare for the empirical analysis. Thus, the next two chapters present the results of the two fair value studies, which are providing empirical evidence on the implications of fair value accounting for users of financial statements.

5 Analysis of financial analysts' forecasts

5.1 Methodological approach

This chapter describes the methodological approach used to investigate financial analysts' forecasts. It presents the research design and the variables that are used within the regression analyses. The chapter also presents some procedures for additional analyses which are intended to both support the main results and strengthen the confidence that is placed into the main findings. The additional analyses refer to a matched sample design and to a difference in differences analysis.

5.1.1 Research design

5.1.1.1 Regression analysis and assumptions

Similar to the majority of the studies which are presented in the state of the research section (chapter 3) the study presented in this chapter uses an archival-based approach. To provide evidence on the association between fair value accounting and financial analysts' ability to forecasting (i.e. forecast accuracy and forecast dispersion) and analyst following, and to address the hypotheses, the method of **multiple regression analysis** is used. Representing a statistical method, regression analyses help to understand the changes of a certain dependent variable when any one of the independent variables (explanatory variables) is modified in some way.[138] In general, the multiple regression model with the number of k independent variables is stated as follows (*Eckstein* (2010), p. 337):

$$(5.1) \qquad y_i = \beta_0 + \beta_1 x_{1,i} + \beta_2 x_{2,i} + \ldots + \beta_k x_{k,t} + \varepsilon_t,$$

where i indicates the number of observations (i = 1,2,…,N) and y represents the dependent variable and x the independent variables. β_0 indicates the constant and $\beta_1 - \beta_k$ represent the coefficients for the regarding values of the independent variables. The factor ε_t is the confounding factor of the regression estimation. It captures the influencing effects of the realized values which are not included in the regression estimation. The values of the confounding factors are also referred to as "residuals" (*Greene* (2003), p. 21).

The regression coefficients are estimated by using the method of **ordinary least squares** (OLS). The OLS method minimizes the sum of squared vertical distances between the observed expressions of the variables and the responses as they are predicted by the linear regression model (*Greene* (2003), p. 20f.). The OLS method only provides best, linear, and unbiased (BLU) estimators (or predictors), if several assumptions of the linear regression model are fulfilled. The assumptions are as follows:[139]

- The econometric model is not **misspecified** in a functional way. This implies that the model includes all relevant independent variables and that the variables used within the model are all relevant and important with regard to the research.

---

138 For a detailed description regarding regression analyses see *Eckstein* (2010), p. 336ff.
139 For a detailed description of the assumptions see *v. Auer* (2011), p. 146ff.

- The confounding factor of the regression estimation is a **random variable** with a mean of zero on the independent variables. This implies that the positive and negative deviations between the observed and estimated values are fully compensated. This implies that $E(\varepsilon_t) = 0$.

- The confounding factors feature a constant variance across observations (**homoscedasticity**): $\text{var}(\varepsilon_t) = 0$.

- The independent variables are not correlated with the confounding factors (**endogeneity**): $\text{cov}(\varepsilon_t, x_{k,t}) = 0$.

- The confounding factors are not correlated (**autocorrelation**): $\text{cov}(\varepsilon_t, \varepsilon_s) = 0$.[140]

- The confounding factors are **normally distributed**.

- The predicators are linearly independent, which means that it is not possible to express any independent variable as a linear combination of the others (**multicollinearity**).

Several tests are suggested to test the available dataset for the assumptions of the OLS model and are performed with the sample of firm-year observations. The **Durbin-Watson statistic** (*Greene* (2003), p. 270) for autocorrelation of the confounding factors indicates that autocorrelation is not present in the dataset and does not need any further consideration. The values obtained for the **variance inflation factors** (VIF) suggest that multicollinearity is not present in the dataset.[141] Additionally, the correlation analysis reveals a significant correlation between two explanatory variables. Thus, several regression models are used where single variables are omitted from the equations in addition to the full model with all variables included.[142] A caveat in the dataset is heteroscedasticity as the **White test** (*Greene* (2003), p. 222) indicates that the confounding factors are not homoscedastic.[143] Because heteroscedasticity is likely to cause biased estimates for the variables, the coefficients are also estimated on the basis of the method of **weighted least squares** (WLS).[144] The WLS results are consistent with the OLS results, suggesting that the OLS results are robust to the alternative approaches and do not produce biased estimates.[145] Because the variables are not always normally distributed across the sample even when the OLS meth-

---

140 This applies for all cases when t≠s.
141 The VIFs for the OLS regression results are all below the value of 10, which rules out multicollinearity.
142 See chapter 5.2.2 for further details.
143 The p-values that test for homoscedasticity in the case of forecast accuracy, forecast dispersion and analyst following are all below 0.05 so the hypothesis that there is no heteroscedasticity in the data must be rejected.
144 The regression analysis with WLS estimators is more efficient than OLS in the case of heteroscedasticity of the confounding factors. See *Wooldridge* (2009), p. 276.
145 As it has been found that the three variables market capitalization, analyst following and leverage are responsible for the heteroscedasticity in the dataset, the WLS regressions are performed with these three variables as weighting factors. The WLS results for the basic regression analysis are provided in appendix A, Table A-5 – Table A-7.

od assumes a normal distribution of the dataset to produce BLU estimators,[146] the results of non-parametric **rank regressions** are provided as well.

In the empirical study, the **dependent variables** represent measures for analysts' forecasting ability (forecast accuracy and forecast dispersion) and their tendency to follow the firm (analyst following). The most important **independent variables** are the test variables which indicate whether firms measure their tangible assets at fair value or at historical cost. As the study both investigates the effects of fair value measures of investment properties and PPE, each asset class is represented by its own independent variable in the regression estimation.[147]

5.1.1.2 Variables used within the regression analysis

5.1.1.2.1 Dependent variables

Because the study investigates the association between fair value accounting and different measures of financial analysts' forecasting ability (forecast accuracy and forecast dispersion) and analyst following, it is necessary to perform regression analyses for each one of these three measures. Therefore, the three measures forecast accuracy, forecast dispersion, and analyst following need to be specified in order to compute the dependent variables for the regression equation. To be able to compute these dependent variables, both actual EPS data (i.e. the realized EPS for the firm in one period) and forecasted consensus EPS figures are needed. The information is taken from the **FactSet/JCF database**[148] which collects earnings forecasts for European listed companies and has been used in empirical accounting research before.[149] Similar to the approach of several other studies (e.g., *Lang/Lundholm* (1996), p. 476; *Lang et al.* (2003), p. 324; *Hope* (2004), p. 29), the dependent variable to measure **forecast accuracy** is computed as follows:

$$(5.2) \qquad Accuracy = -\frac{|Actual\ EPS - Median\ forecasted\ EPS|}{Average\ stock\ price\ during\ the\ forecast\ month}$$

Forecast accuracy is defined as the negative of the absolute value of the analyst forecast error, deflated by stock price. Data from the eleventh month is used to obtain forecasted EPS figures and to construct the dependent variable. The eleventh month is chosen as the forecast month for the measurement of forecast accuracy as the study of *O'Brien/Bhushan* (1990) indicates that analyst activity decreases significantly after that date. The average stock price is needed to deflate forecast accuracy in a way to enable **cross-company comparisons**.[150] The average stock price is also computed on the basis of the eleventh month

---

146 Even when the natural logarithm of market capitalization is normally distributed across the sample, the remaining data is not normally distributed.

147 See chapter 2.1.3 for further details regarding the measurement practices of the two asset classes.

148 See the company's website www.factset.com for further details.

149 See for example the empirical research studies conducted by *Balboa et al.* (2008) or *Aubert/Dumontier* (2009).

150 Stock price data is taken from the database DataStream as the mean of all daily closing prices in the eleventh month, which is the same month where the forecasted EPS data is being extracted from.

to ensure consistency. In contrast to the study by *Lang/Lundholm* (1996), the variable forecast accuracy is computed on the basis of median forecasted EPS instead of using the mean. Since the median is less sensitive to possible **outliers** in the sample, this modification of the original model is used to compute the dependent variable (*Ernstberger et al.* (2008), p. 32).[151] The negative sign in front of the term ensures that lower estimated coefficients indicate a decrease in forecast accuracy. This information should be considered when the results are interpreted later.

The variable to measure **forecast dispersion** is defined as follows:[152]

$$(5.3) \qquad Dispersion = -\frac{Standard\ deviation\ of\ EPS\ forecasts}{Average\ stock\ price\ during\ the\ forecast\ month}$$

Forecast dispersion is defined similar to forecast accuracy. The standard deviation of EPS forecasts is deflated by the average stock price during the forecast month. The value for the standard deviation is included in the FactSet/JCF database. Because the standard deviation of individual analysts' forecasts is chosen from the eleventh month, the average stock price is computed for the eleventh month as well. Consistent with forecast accuracy, lower estimated coefficients indicate a decrease in forecast dispersion.

Finally, the third variable **analyst following** is simply defined as the number of analysts following the firm with no additional computations necessary.[153] Thus:

$$(5.4) \qquad Following = Number\ of\ analysts\ following\ the\ firm$$

After a definition of the dependent variables, the independent variables are specified in the next chapter.

5.1.1.2.2 Test and control variables

The dependent variables represent the left side of the regression equation. After the definition of the three dependent variables forecast accuracy, forecast dispersion, and analyst following, several independent variables need to be specified. The independent variables on the right side of the regression equation are both the **test variables**, which are representing fair value accounting for investment properties and PPE, and several control variables. Therefore, the test variables need to capture the effect of fair value or historical cost measurement in a way that the estimated coefficients for these variables describe the relationship between fair value measurement and the dependent variables.

The regression equation contains two test variables. Because it is examined whether investment properties and assets of property, plant, and equipment, which are measured at fair value or historical cost, have significant implications for analysts' behavior, the inde-

---

151 A sensitivity analysis is conducted with the mean which does not provide significant differences in the results compared to the median. See chapter 5.1.2.
152 See for example *Lang/Lundholm* (1996), p. 476 or *Bozzolan et al.* (2009), p. 443.
153 As the number of analysts following the firm is not available in the FactSet/JCF database, the number of forecasts by different analysts currently available for the regarding firm is applied instead.

pendent variables need to capture the measurement for these tangible assets. For investment properties (**FV_IP**) and assets of PPE (**FV_PPE**), a variable is constructed that ranges between 0 and 1 and represents the degree of fair value measurement in a financial statement. The two variables are constructed in the following way: By dividing the carrying amount of assets measured at fair value through the amount of total assets in the balance sheet, a ratio is received that ranges between 0 and 1. To provide an example, a value of 1 for the variable FV_IP in one observation would indicate that the company measures its investment properties at fair value and holds no other assets in the balance sheet in this period. Because the estimated coefficients of the two test variables provide direct evidence on the relationship between the dependent variables and fair value accounting, the hypotheses can be either verified or rejected on the basis of the value of FV_IP and FV_PPE. When it is assumed that fair value accounting has a significant influence on forecast accuracy, forecast dispersion and analyst following, these variables should be **significant** in an either positive or negative direction.

In addition to fair value accounting, there could be further influences on the dependent variables. Hence, it is necessary to control for these influences as the effect of the test variables would otherwise be superposed by influences which are not associated with the research question. Therefore, several control variables need to be added in order to complete the regression equation. First, the control variable **firm size** is included for a number of reasons. In general, size reflects information availability of the firm when it is expected that larger firms provide a higher amount of information to investors. Larger firms do typically have less volatile earnings and a better investor relations environment and do therefore usually provide more and better information to investors (*Jaggi/Jain* (1998), p. 187). Similar to the study by *Ernstberger et al.* (2008), the natural logarithm of the variable market capitalization (**Log(MCAP)**) is used to proxy for firm size as market capitalization itself is heavily skewed (*Ernstberger et al.* (2008), p. 34). In addition to Log(MCAP), the same regression is run with the natural logarithm of total assets in the balance sheet and the number of employees of the firm.[154] The results do not materially change when these alternative measures are applied to control for firm size.[155] Because it is predicted that firm size has a positive association with forecast accuracy, forecast dispersion, and analyst following, the coefficient for Log(MCAP) is expected to have a positive sign.

A further variable controls for the current **earnings situation** of the firm. As previous studies provide evidence that financial analysts find it more difficult to forecast earnings for companies which are reporting losses (e.g., *Hwang et al.* (1996); *Hope* (2004)), an indicator variable **LOSS** is included, taking the value of 1 (if the company reports a negative EPS) or 0 (in the case of a reported positive EPS). The reason for an increased difficulty in providing forecasts for firms reporting a loss could be unexpected *big bath accounting* etc. (*Hope* (2004), p. 30), where companies write down certain assets in one single year to report higher income in the following years. As loss firms are expected to cause higher errors

---

154 See for example *Lang et al.* (2003), p. 327, who use the natural logarithm of total assets to control for firm size.
155 See chapter 5.1.2 for further details.

in earnings forecasts, greater dispersion and a lower analyst following, it is predicted that the coefficient representing the variable LOSS has a negative value.

Similar to previous studies in this area (*Hope* (2004), p. 30; *Bozzolan et al.* (2009), p. 450), it is controlled for **leverage** as more highly levered firms are expected to feature more variable earnings. The variable **LEV** is defined as total liabilities divided by total assets. Due to more volatile earnings, which are more difficult to forecast, it is expected that the coefficient for the variable LEV has a negative relation with forecast accuracy, forecast dispersion, and analyst following.

A measure to control for the **number of analysts following the firm** is included into the regression when investigating the association between fair value accounting and forecast accuracy and forecast dispersion.[156] The control variable for analyst following is defined as **COV** (coverage). *Ernstberger et al.* (2008) refer to the increased competition among analysts if coverage for that company is higher (*Ernstberger et al.* (2008), p. 34). Other studies indicate that financial analysts improve their forecasting precision when analyst coverage increases and the number of analysts covering the firm proxies for the intensity of competition in the market (*Lys/Soo* (1995), p. 763). As the forecast accuracy (forecast dispersion) should be higher (lower) when more analysts produce estimates for the firm, a positive regression coefficient on COV is expected.

An additional control variable is included for **earnings surprise** that controls for the fact that forecasts are likely to be affected by the degree of earnings information which is reported (*Lang/Lundholm* (1996), p. 478; *Barron et al.* (1999), p. 89). Given the case that a company for example launches a major new product, expected earnings do presumably deviate substantially from realized earnings (*Lang/Lundholm* (1996), p. 478). While this has nothing to do with fair value accounting, consensus among analysts and forecast accuracy is likely to be low. Therefore, a measure of earnings surprise is included as an independent variable to control for such factors. Following *Barron et al.* (1999), the variable **EAR_SUR** is a scaled measure of the "random walk" change in earnings:

$$(5.5) \qquad EAR\_SUR = \left| \frac{EPS_t - EPS_{t-1}}{EPS_{t-1}} \right|,$$

with EPS_t and EPS_{t-1} indicating realized earnings per share in the current and prior year, respectively. Because it is projected that a high degree of earnings surprise in a period makes it more challenging to predict earnings, it is expected that the estimated coefficient for EAR_SUR has a negative sign.

Companies with a **cross-listing** in the U.S. have a different information environment, because they commit themselves to increased disclosure and also face strict enforcement through the supervision of the SEC (*Hail/Leuz* (2009), p. 429). *Lang et al.* (2003) provide evidence that cross-listed firms benefit from higher forecast accuracy than firms which are not cross-listed (*Lang et al.* (2003), p. 317). However, it could also be argued that cross-listed firms are more intensively involved in international operations and thus have earn-

---

156 This variable is not used as a control variable to investigate the third hypothesis, because analyst following functions as the dependent variable in this case.

ings which are more difficult to estimate (*Ernstberger et al.* (2008), p. 35). The variable **CROSSLIST** is included to control for the effect of cross-listings in the U.S. This binary variable indicates whether a company is cross-listed in the sample period (value 1) or not (value 0). Because it is expected that the increased disclosure requirements and the strict SEC enforcement have a positive impact on the dependent variables, it is predicted that the estimated coefficient for CROSSLIST has a positive sign.

A further dummy variable is included to capture the effect of a **first-time adoption** of IFRS. European capital market oriented firms must apply the IFRS for their consolidated financial statements from 2005 on. However, companies could have adopted the IFRS before 2005 on a voluntary basis. It is then expected that financial analysts find it more challenging to predict forecasts in the first year of the application of a new financial reporting system. Therefore, the variable **CHANGE** takes the value of 1 if the observation represents a firm-year from 2005 with a first-time adoption of IFRS (and 0 otherwise). Because of the demanding task to make forecasts for firms that are applying a financial reporting system for the first time, it is expected that the estimated coefficient for CHANGE has a negative sign.

Finally, **industry and country controls** are included into the regression equation. Dummy variables are included for each industry group, which are identified on the basis of the four-digit GICS code.[157] To control for country effects, dummy variables representing the different law systems in the countries are applied. The country control variables are based on two broad legal traditions, which are common law and civil law (*La Porta et al.* (1998), p. 1118). Whereas common law includes the law in England, there are three families of laws within the civil law tradition: French, German, and Scandinavian (*Mahoney* (2006), p. 93). The French law was written under Napoleon and did influence law systems in, among others, Belgium, the Netherlands, part of Poland, Italy, Portugal, and Spain (*La Porta et al.* (1998), p. 1118). Because Scandinavian countries are not contained in the sample, dummy variables for common law (Great Britain), French law (Belgium, France, the Netherlands, Italy, and Spain), and German law (Germany) countries are included.[158]

Taken together, the three measures of analyst behavior (forecast accuracy, forecast dispersion, and analyst following) are tested by using the following regression equations:

(5.6)
$$Accuracy = \beta_0 + \beta_1 FV\_IP_{i,t} + \beta_2 FV\_PPE_{i,t} + \beta_3 Log(MCAP)_{i,t} + \beta_4 LOSS_{i,t} + \beta_5 LEV_{i,t} + \beta_6 COV_{i,t} + \beta_7 EAR\_SUR_{i,t} + \beta_8 CROSSLIST_{i,t} + \beta_9 CHANGE_{i,t} + industry\ and\ country\ controls + \varepsilon_{i,t},$$

---

157 The GICS codes ("Global Industry Classification Standard") were developed by Standard & Poor's and MSCI Barra and consist of 24 industry groups. However, it is only controlled for 23 industry groups with "Capital Goods" representing the reference group. Results do not change when other industries function as the reference category.

158 To avoid the "dummy variable trap", only two of the three country controls can be included simultaneously in the regression. The results are based on dummy variables for French and German law. Results do not change when alternative combinations of country controls are applied.

$$(5.7) \quad \begin{aligned} Dispersion &= \beta_0 + \beta_1 FV\_IP_{i,t} + \beta_2 FV\_PPE_{i,t} + \beta_3 Log(MCAP)_{i,t} + \beta_4 LOSS_{i,t} + \\ &\beta_5 LEV_{i,t} + \beta_6 COV_{i,t} + \beta_7 EAR\_SUR_{i,t} + \beta_8 CROSSLIST_{i,t} + \beta_9 CHANGE_{i,t} + \\ &industry\ and\ country\ controls + \varepsilon_{i,t}, \end{aligned}$$

$$(5.8) \quad \begin{aligned} Following &= \beta_0 + \beta_1 FV\_IP_{i,t} + \beta_2 FV\_PPE_{i,t} + \beta_3 Log(MCAP)_{i,t} + \beta_4 LOSS_{i,t} + \\ &\beta_5 LEV_{i,t} + \beta_6 EAR\_SUR_{i,t} + \beta_7 CROSSLIST_{i,t} + \beta_8 CHANGE_{i,t} + \\ &industry\ and\ country\ controls + \varepsilon_{i,t}, \end{aligned}$$

where,

$FV\_IP_{i,t}$	a variable that ranges between 0 and 1 and represents the degree of fair value measurement of investment properties,
$FV\_PPE_{i,t}$	a variable that ranges between 0 and 1 and represents the degree of fair value measurement of PPE,
$Log(MCAP)_{i,t}$	the natural log of a firm's market capitalization,
$LOSS_{i,t}$	an indicator variable that takes the value of 1 if the firm is reporting a negative EPS,
$LEV_{i,t}$	a variable controlling for the leverage situation of a firm,
$COV_{i,t}$	the number of analysts following the firm ("analyst coverage"),
$EAR\_SUR_{i,t}$	a variable controlling for earnings surprises,
$CROSSLIST_{i,t}$	an indicator variable that takes the value of 1 if the firm is cross-listed in the U.S.,
$CHANGE_{i,t}$	an indicator variable that takes the value of 1 if the firm adopts IFRS for the first time in the regarding year,
$\varepsilon_{i,t}$	confounding factor,

and all variables are meant for company i in the year t.

5.1.2 Additional analyses

Using regression analysis enables making statements about the association between the dependent and independent variables. However, when investigating the association between analysts' forecasts and fair value accounting, there could be, besides fair value accounting, further influences on analysts' ability to forecasting even when these effects cannot effectively be controlled for. Additionally, variations of the dependent variables through time may cause the results of the regression analysis to be biased. In order to control for effects of **mitigated variables** and to address possible **time-series trends** of the variables, further analyses are necessary in a way to increase the confidence that is placed into the main results. Therefore, a matched sample design and a difference in differences analysis are employed to support the results. Both approaches are presented in the following two sections.

5.1.2.1 Matched sample design

An important problem in observational studies is to estimate the treatment effect. Unlike in experimental research, no systematic designs are used to maintain an explicit control group to the treatment group (*Dehejia/Wahba* (2002), p. 151).[159] The main problem of observational studies is seen in the fact that the treatments are not randomly assigned to the units in order to avoid **self-selection biases** (*Bloomfield/Rennekamp* (2009), p. 8). Thus, matched sampling is the procedure of data collection and organization designed to reduce bias and increase precision in observational studies (*Rubin* (1973), p. 159). The idea behind matching is to find a comparable non-treated unit with similar observable characteristics for any treated unit (*Dehejia/Wahba* (2002), p. 151). When these two units are matched and their average differences are estimated, it should be possible to compute, under some conditions, the pure effect of being treated. The idea behind the matching procedure is that pairwise matching causes a similar distribution of the control variables on the treatment group and non-treatment group, thus eliminating the **systematic variation** of the confounding factors between the two groups (*Gensler et al.* (2005), p. 43). In the case of the regarding fair value study, this would imply that it is necessary to match each fair value observation to a historical cost observation with similar firm characteristics.

Several methods do exist to match the treated with the non-treated groups. Whereas the first generation of matching studies paired the observations by focusing on either a single variable or on a weighted average of several variables,[160] problems with these approaches increase when the number of the observable characteristics is high. Referring to the fair value study, the firm-year observations for example differ in respect to the control variables (e.g., firm size, leverage, analyst following, earnings situation etc.). It is then difficult to determine along which dimensions to match units or which weighting scheme should be adopted (*Dehejia/Wahba* (2002), p. 151). Because the dimensionality of the observable characteristics is high in the sample which is used for the fair value study, a **propensity score matching method** is applied. Using this approach, a propensity score is computed for each observation of the original sample (i.e. treated and non-treated observations), which represents the conditional probability of assignment to a particular treatment given a vector of observed covariates.[161]

The propensity score reduces the **multidimensional problem** of treated and non-treated units to one single measure, with all unit characteristics incorporated into this measure. The matching partners are then determined in a way that their corresponding matches have similar propensity scores. The propensity score is a function of the control variables, which are used for the match, and is defined as the likelihood of participation in the treatment (*Gensler et al.* (2005), p. 44). It is obtained by running a **logistic regression** with the total sample where the dependent variable indicates the participation or non-participation in the treatment (i.e. a value of 1 indicates a fair value observation, whereas 0 indicates a historical cost observation). The logistic regression is performed with the variables that are expected to be associated with the participation in the treatment as independent variables, because these variables are assumed to cause the self-selection effect (*Gensler et al.* (2005), p. 44). Therefore, it is necessary to investigate the available dataset

---

159 For further information regarding experimental research see chapter 6.1.2.
160 See the studies cited by *Dehejia/Wahba* (2002), p. 151.
161 Both large and small sample theory indicates that the application of propensity scores is sufficient to remove the bias in observational studies. See *Rosenbaum/Rubin* (1983), p. 41.

to identify the variables with a significant influence on the dependent variables forecast accuracy, forecast dispersion, and analyst following.[162]

Because the propensity score incorporates all firm characteristics into one measure of equality, the **nearest neighbor algorithm** is then used to match each fair value observation with a non-fair value observation that is closest to its propensity score (*Gensler et al.* (2005), p. 46). The non-fair value observations are selected without replacement, which implies that the same match cannot be used twice.[163] After the units are matched, the unmatched comparisons (i.e. the historical cost observations that differed widely from any fair value observation) units are discarded and are not directly used in estimating the treatment impact (*Dehejia/Wahba* (2002), p. 151). Finally, the reduced sample with the same number of treated and non-treated observations is used to re-run the regression equations 5.6 - 5.8 presented in chapter 5.1.1.2.2.

5.1.2.2 Difference in differences analysis

The effects of accounting policy choices, such as the choice to apply fair value or historical cost accounting, is expected to be associated with analysts' ability to forecasting (forecast accuracy and forecast dispersion) and analyst following. However, statistical models may detect a significant influence of fair value accounting even if the significance is caused by other reasons, such as **time-series trends** in the outcomes of financial analysts' work. Thus, it could be the case that the effect of fair value accounting is overstated due to a varying degree of forecast accuracy, forecast dispersion, and analyst following through time for reasons other than assets measured at fair value. Therefore, a **difference in differences** design is used in order to mitigate the concern of time-series trends affecting the results.

Additional data for the companies included in the sample is needed for the period prior to IFRS adoption where it was not possible to measure tangible assets at fair value. To account for time trends unrelated to fair value accounting, the change experienced by the group subject to fair value accounting (referred to as the treatment group) is adjusted by the change experienced by a **control group** which is applying historical cost accounting (*Athey/Imbens* (2006), p. 431f.). According to this, the empirical outcomes (forecast accuracy, forecast dispersion, and analyst following) are observed for two groups in two time periods (*Meyer* (1995), p. 154). Whereas the firms included in the treatment group are exposed to fair value accounting in the second time period (the post period), they are not

---

162 The following variables have a significant influence and are used to compute the propensity scores: firm size, earnings situation, leverage, earnings surprise, first-time adoption of the IFRS, and analyst following. See chapter 5.2.4 for further details.

163 See *Dehejia/Wahba* (2002), p. 153, for further details on the advantages of matching units with replacement and without replacement. Even if choosing comparisons without replacement may cause estimates to be biased when treated units are matched to comparison units which are quite different in terms of propensity score, it could improve the precision of the estimates (*Dehejia/Wahba* (2002), p. 153).

exposed to the treatment in the first time period (the pre period).[164] The control group is not exposed to the treatment in either period and constantly applies historical cost accounting. The difference in differences analysis is then conducted by comparing the average gain in the treatment group with the average gain of the control group (i.e. by subtracting the average gain of the control group from the average gain of the treatment group). According to this, it is possible to use data on the treatment and control group in order to estimate a normal level of difference between the treated and non-treated group and then compare this with the difference after the treatment takes place. By analyzing the changes between the pre and the post period, each firm in the sample serves as its own control (*Hail/Leuz* (2009), p. 443). An illustrative example for the difference in differences analysis is depicted in Figure 5-1.

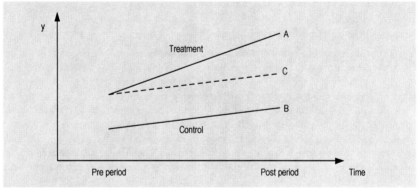

Figure 5-1: Difference in differences illustrative example
(Following *Without Author* (2011), p. 1)

Figure 5-1 provides the certain outputs (y) for the treatment group and the control group before (*pre period*) and after (*post period*) the units in the groups are exposed to a certain kind of treatment. Given the case that the analysis would be conducted only on the basis of the data of the post period, the treatment effect would be estimated as the distance AB (*Without Author* (2011), p. 1). This would be based on the assumption that the only reason for observing a difference in the outcome between the treatment and the control group would be the result of the treatment. However, this distance would overstate the treatment effect as the difference in differences estimator would only estimate the treatment effect as the distance AC (*Without Author* (2011), p. 2). The remaining distance CB refers to the "normal" difference between the treatment and the control group, resulting from time-series trends (*Without Author* (2011), p. 2).

The difference in differences estimators provide the possibility to perform univariate analyses and to compare the means of forecast accuracy, forecast dispersion, and analyst fol-

---

164 The pre period represents the period before IFRS adoption from 2001-2004, whereas the post period represents the period after IFRS adoption from 2005-2008. It is ensured that only firm-year observations not applying IFRS are included in the pre period.

lowing between groups and through time. However and in contrast to univariate analyses, multivariate regression analyses offer the **advantage** to control for factors such as firm size or leverage, which is important as firms are expected to often change their investment and financing policies around the adoption of a new accounting standard (*Hail/Leuz* (2009), p. 444f.). To account for the different time periods, prior and after the adoption of IFRS, and in order to include a measure for fair value or historical cost accounting, the following regression model is applied for each measure of financial analysts' output:

$$(5.9) \qquad y_{i,t} = \beta_0 + \beta_1 FV_{i,t} + \beta_2 TIME_{i,t} + \beta_3 FV_{i,t} * TIME_{i,t} + control\ variables + \varepsilon_{i,t},$$

where $y_{i,t}$ represents the three measures of financial analysts' output (forecast accuracy, forecast dispersion, and analyst following). FV is a dummy variable taking the value of 1 if the firm-year observation belongs to the treatment group (fair value) and 0 if it is in the control group (historical cost).[165] Because TIME is a dummy variable taking the value of 1 in the post period and 0 in the pre period, the **difference in differences estimator** is then the OLS estimate of β_3. This coefficient on the interaction between fair value accounting and the time period takes the value of 1 only for the fair value group in the post period and is 0 otherwise. It does therefore capture the effect of fair value accounting but simultaneously controls for time-series trends. In other words, β_3 is the true causal effect of the fair value treatment less time-series trends (*Meyer* (1995), p. 155). Such time-series trends are reflected by the coefficient for β_2. Finally, control variables are included to control for variations on the firm- and country-level.

5.2 Results

5.2.1 Data and sample

5.2.1.1 Sample selection procedure

In order to receive empirical data for the study, the time period of the years ranging from 2005-2008 is selected as the sample period. This four-year sample period from 2005 on is chosen as the starting point of the analysis for the following reason: European capital market oriented companies are obliged to prepare their consolidated accounts under IFRS from 2005 on. It is thus ensured that the companies in the sample report their figures under one single financial reporting regime. The sample is restricted to **seven European member states**, namely Belgium, France, Germany, Great Britain, the Netherlands, and Spain. These countries are the most important European member states with regard to their total GDP. The OSIRIS[166] database is used for the selection of the companies in the sample. All firms from the seven countries, which are contained in the OSIRIS database,

---

165 The variable *FV* can either indicate fair value accounting for investment properties (IP_D) and PPE (PPE_D).

166 The OSIRIS database is provided by Bureau van Dijk and contains listed companies, banks and insurance companies around the world. For further information see the company's website under www.bvdinfo.com.

are downloaded and it is additionally ensured that all companies included in the sample prepare their consolidated financial statements under IFRS. The companies downloaded from OSIRIS are then matched to the forecast data that is taken from the FactSet/JCF database. Similar to other studies (e.g., *Francis/Philbrick* (1993), p. 220; *Das et al.* (1998), p. 280), companies with a fiscal year-end that is not December 31 are excluded from the sample.[167]

In addition to forecast data and for the specification of the independent variables, information to the valuation method that is applied by each company and every single firm-year for investment properties and PPE is required. This information can be found in the notes section of the company's financial statements. As this information about the measurement method is not included in the OSIRIS database, it is necessary to hand-collect this data from the annual reports of the companies for every single year included in the sample. With this information taken from the annual reports, it is possible to construct the independent indicator variables indicating fair value or historical cost accounting. The annual reports are downloaded from each company's website and the information regarding the applied measurement method for tangible assets is used after reading the accounting policy section in the notes. In the case that annual reports were not available or when annual reports were only available in a language other than English or German, the regarding company was deleted from the sample. Furthermore, 1% at the top and bottom of the dependent and firm-specific control variables are removed from the sample to account for possible outliers.[168] All observations with fair value test variables outside the [0;1] interval are also removed due to plausibility reasons. Considering these restrictions, the total sample consists of **2,566 firm-year observations** with sufficient data available to compute the forecast measures.

5.2.1.2 Distribution of the sample

Table 5-1 refers to the distribution of the sample and presents the **number of observations** per country in each year. With a total of 1,448 firm-year observations, the observations from Germany and Great Britain represent a 56.43% stake out of the total sample. On the other hand, the firm-year observations from Belgium and Spain only stand for 12.51% of all observations. This large mismatch is explained by the fact that Germany and Great Britain face the largest number of listed companies and that their capital markets are amongst the largest capital markets in the European Union. However, the large difference might also result from the requirement that the firms' annual reports had to be available in either English or German language to be included in the sample. It has to be kept in mind that a large stake of the sample represents companies from Germany and Great Britain, because this may lower the explanatory power of the later regression results.[169] Referring to the distribution of the sample per country, the sample sizes in the years 2007 and 2008 are bigger than in the first two years of the sample period. This is

---

167 The December year-end criterion provides a basis for the industry-wide comparability across firms. See *O'Brien/Bhushan* (1990), p. 289.
168 Industry- and country-specific variables are not winsorized as they represent dummy variables.
169 This concern is addressed by a matched sample design. See chapter 5.1.2.1 for further details.

due to data availability. There are both more annual reports and analyst forecasts available in the near future compared to the first two years of the sample period.

Year	2005	2006	2007	2008	TOTAL	%
Country						
Belgium	37	44	48	46	175	6.82%
France	74	89	94	90	347	13.52%
Germany	93	125	153	139	510	19.88%
Great Britain	179	237	269	253	938	36.55%
Italy	52	65	61	59	237	9.24%
Netherlands	56	53	55	49	213	8.30%
Spain	31	36	42	37	146	5.69%
TOTAL	522	649	722	673	2,566	100.00%
%	20.34%	25.29%	28.14%	26.23%	100.00%	

Table 5-1: Number of firm-year observations per country

A distribution of the sample per **industry** is provided in Figure 5-2. The figure presents the distribution of the firm-year observations on the 10 industry sectors according to their GICS codes.[170] Absolute numbers of observations per industry sector are provided in brackets.

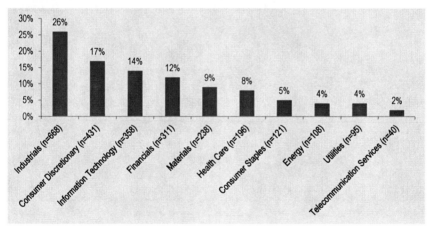

Figure 5-2: Distribution of the sample per industry sector[171]

Whereas observations from the industrial sector, as the largest sector in the sample, represent more than one quarter of the total sample, the sectors Consumer Discretionary, In-

---

170 Even if the distribution of the sample per industry sector is provided here, the single industry groups are later used as the industry dummy control variables. For a detailed distribution of the sample per industry group see Table A-1.

171 The percentage values do not sum up to 100% due to rounding differences.

formation Technology, and Financials[172] are still above 10%. On the other hand, the sectors Energy, Utilities, and Telecommunication Services each only account for less than 5% of the sample.

Because this study investigates the association of fair value accounting with characteristics of financial analysts, it is important to examine the sample with regard to the companies' valuation practices. Therefore, Table 5-2 presents the **number of fair value observations** for investment properties (IP) and assets of property, plant, and equipment (PPE), separately for each country and for the total sample. The last column shows the percentage of fair value observations, relative to the total number of firm-years included in every subsample. Similar to the study conducted by *Christensen/Nikolaev* (2009), the sample includes only a small number of fair value observations for assets of property, plant, and equipment (PPE). Only 8 firm-year observations out of the total sample feature the revaluation model for PPE and these observations are only based either in Great Britain or the Netherlands. The firms included in the other country samples measure their assets of PPE solely at historical cost. This evidence suggests that the vast majority of the companies prefer historical cost rather than fair value, perhaps due to higher complexity and input needed to determine the carrying values of PPE measured at fair value.

Year	2005		2006		2007		2008		TOTAL	%
Country	IP	PPE	IP	PPE	IP	PPE	IP	PPE		
Belgium (N = 175)	5	0	6	0	7	0	8	0	26	14.86%
France (N = 347)	4	0	5	0	7	0	6	0	22	6.34%
Germany (N = 510)	3	0	7	0	15	0	7	0	32	6.27%
Great Britain (N = 938)	10	1	15	1	17	1	15	1	61	6.50%
Italy (N = 237)	1	0	1	0	1	0	2	0	5	2.11%
Netherlands (N = 213)	4	1	4	1	4	1	3	1	19	8.92%
Spain (N = 146)	3	0	3	0	4	0	1	0	11	7.53%
TOTAL (N = 2,566)	30	2	41	2	55	2	42	2	176	6.86%

Table 5-2: Number of observations with fair value accounting per country

The companies in the sample are more likely to measure investment properties at fair value. The fair value model for investment properties is much more common than the revaluation model for PPE.[173] The largest proportion of firms adopting fair values can be found for companies based in Belgium and the Netherlands, whereas the largest absolute numbers of fair value firm-years for investment properties are available in Great Britain

---

172 While banks and insurance companies are not included in this sector, Financials refer to diversified financial and real estate firms.

173 Observations of investment properties are only indicated as fair value observations if they recognize their investment properties at fair value in the balance sheet rather than just disclosing the fair value in the notes.

and Germany. The decrease of fair value firm-years from 2007 to 2008 might be due to the financial crisis when market values were more difficult to determine. Overall, the data in Table 5-2 suggest that fair values are used **very rarely for tangible assets** with only 6.86% of all observations in the sample representing firm-years featuring fair value accounting. This finding stands in contrast to the view of the CFA Institute that favors fair values for all financial statement items to enhance information supply of users of financial statements (*CFA Institute Centre* (2008)).

In addition to country-based evidence, the application of fair value accounting may also **differ across industries**. Table 5-3 depicts the number of observations with fair value accounting per industry.

Year	2005		2006		2007		2008		TOTAL	%
Industry Sector	IP	PPE	IP	PPE	IP	PPE	IP	PPE		
Energy (N = 108)	2	1	2	1	2	1	1	1	11	10.19%
Materials (N = 238)	2	0	3	0	4	0	2	0	11	4.62%
Industrials (N = 668)	2	0	5	0	7	0	6	0	20	2.99%
Consumer Discretionary (N = 431)	5	1	8	1	7	1	8	1	32	7.42%
Consumer Staples (N = 121)	0	0	0	0	0	0	0	0	0	0.00%
Health Care (N = 196)	1	0	1	0	1	0	1	0	4	2.04%
Financials (N = 311)	14	0	18	0	29	0	19	0	80	25.72%
Information Technology (N = 358)	4	0	4	0	4	0	4	0	16	4.47%
Telecommunication Services (N = 40)	0	0	0	0	1	0	1	0	2	5.00%
Utilities (N = 95)	0	0	0	0	0	0	0	0	0	0.00%
TOTAL (N = 2,566)	30	2	41	2	55	2	42	2	176	6.86%

Table 5-3: Number of observations with fair value accounting per industry sector

The largest relative number of fair value observations is included in the industry sector Financials (25.72%), which contains both diversified financial firms and real estate firms. However, firms within this sector do only apply the fair value model for investment properties, but do not apply the revaluation model for PPE. The sectors Consumer Staples and Utilities do not feature any fair value observations. Fair value observations from the Energy and Consumer Discretionary sector represent 10.19% and 7.42%, respectively. The finding that firms from the Financials sector apply fair values most frequently confirms well with intuition. Real estate firms usually possess investment properties as a part of their core business. Unlike other firms, which use property in the course of the ordinary business, real estate firms are more likely to lease out property in order to earn a return. Thus, real estate firms are more interested to earn a return as a result from the holding of property rather than using the property to produce goods. With fair value accounting, real estate firms are able to earn a return when they expect fair value increases of their property. They are therefore less likely to apply historical cost accounting for investment properties than firms from other industry sectors.

The **distribution of the fair value test variables** is presented in Table 5-4. The table depicts the distribution of FV_IP and FV_PPE for each industry sector and for the total sample. The results suggest that, when assets are measured at fair value, investment properties' fair values (0.5071) represent, on average, a higher portion of the total assets than fair values for PPE (0.2488). The value of the variable FV_IP ranges from a lower zero up to one, thus indicating that there is at least one firm-year observation with an investment property's fair value which accounts for all of the total assets. The maximum value of FV_PPE is 0.3450, suggesting that fair value accounting for PPE does never exceed 35% of a firm's total asset value. This finding corroborates the view that fair value accounting is more important for investment properties than for assets of PPE. Referring to the single industry sectors, Health Care and Telecommunication Services reveal the highest mean values for FV_IP. However, these values are based on only four (Health Care) or two (Telecommunication Services) observations and should be interpreted with caution.

Industry Sector	Variable	Minimum	0.25 quartile	Mean	Median	0.75 quartile	Maximum
Energy (N = 11)	FV_IP	0.0821	0.1545	0.3969	0.3879	0.6126	0.7739
	FV_PPE	0.2148	0.2572	0.2932	0.3065	0.3425	0.3450
Materials (N = 11)	FV_IP	0.0010	0.0060	0.1849	0.0180	0.2390	0.9198
	FV_PPE	-	-	-	-	-	-
Industrials (N = 20)	FV_IP	0.0004	0.0634	0.5438	0.6224	0.9310	1.0000
	FV_PPE	-	-	-	-	-	-
Consumer D. (N = 32)	FV_IP	0.0007	0.0188	0.3717	0.2687	0.6857	0.9865
	FV_PPE	0.1828	0.1940	0.2045	0.1981	0.2086	0.2388
Consumer St. (N = 0)	FV_IP	-	-	-	-	-	-
	FV_PPE	-	-	-	-	-	-
Health Care (N = 4)	FV_IP	0.6224	0.6442	0.6852	0.6690	0.7099	0.7803
	FV_PPE	-	-	-	-	-	-
Financials (N = 80)	FV_IP	0.0024	0.4085	0.6377	0.7814	0.8989	1.0000
	FV_PPE	-	-	-	-	-	-
Information T. (N = 16)	FV_IP	0.0013	0.0040	0.2106	0.0150	0.2195	0.8626
	FV_PPE	-	-	-	-	-	-
Telecom Serv. (N = 2)	FV_IP	0.9635	0.9726	0.9817	0.9817	0.9909	1.0000
	FV_PPE	-	-	-	-	-	-
Utilities (N = 0)	FV_IP	-	-	-	-	-	-
	FV_PPE	-	-	-	-	-	-
TOTAL (N = 176)	FV_IP	0.0004	0.0432	0.5071	0.6208	0.8649	1.0000
	FV_PPE	0.1828	0.1983	0.2488	0.2268	0.2889	0.3450

Table 5-4: Distribution of the fair value test variables per industry sector

The distribution of the sample and the fair value test variables must be kept in mind for the later interpretation of the regression results. It is shown that a large number of fair value observations are available in the **Financials industry sector**. The empirical results may thus to a large extent be influenced by fair value accounting in this sector. Additionally, the fair values for investment properties are usually larger than fair values for PPE. This finding is important when it is expected that higher amounts of fair values have larger impacts of analysts' ability to forecasting than lower amounts. The next chapter presents descriptive statistics and a correlation analysis.

5.2.2 Descriptive statistics and correlation analysis

Table 5-5 presents descriptive statistics of the independent variables used as test or control variables. The values are stated separately for each country and for the total sample. The table presents the mean values for each measure and the standard deviations in brackets. For the columns that are presenting the number of loss observations, the number of change observations, and the number of firm-years with a cross-listing, the values in brackets indicate the percentage of the observations in relation to the total number of observations in that sub-sample.

As it can be seen in the table, when firms hold investment properties in the balance sheet, their carrying values are on average largest in France and Great Britain, whereas the mean values of investment properties in Germany and Italy are smallest. Spanish companies own on average the largest value of assets of property, plant, and equipment. Referring to the **total sample**, the mean value of investment property is higher than the mean value for PPE. This indicates that investment property does, on average, account for a larger portion of total assets than assets of PPE. According to market capitalization, total assets and number of employees, Table 5-5 shows that, on average, the largest firms are available in the French and Spanish sub-sample. The smallest companies with regard to these measures are based in Great Britain. This finding seems not surprising as the British sample is the largest overall sub-sample (N = 938), suggesting that even small British firms are more likely to use the capital markets. This would result in lower means for the firm size measures.

About 10% of all firm-year observations currently report a negative EPS (loss observation). As the variable LEV is defined as total liabilities divided by total assets, a mean leverage value of 0.5508 for the total sample indicates that companies in the sample have about 55% of debt in their balance sheet. The results for the **country-samples** suggest that Italian and Spanish companies are most highly levered, whereas Belgian and British firms feature the lowest leverage ratios. Companies in the sample are, on average, covered by 7.31 analysts with the larger Spanish firms having a higher analyst following than the smaller British firms in the sample. Firms in the German sample possess the highest earnings volatility, represented by the largest mean value for earnings surprise. A number of 233 firms have chosen to adopt IFRS in 2005 (i.e. the first year of the sample period), thus indicating that the majority of the companies voluntarily adopted the new accounting system at an earlier stage.

Variable Country	Investment property (th. EUR)	Property, plant and equipment (th. EUR)	Market capitalization (th. EUR)	Total assets (th. EUR)	Number of employees	Number of LOSS obs.	Leverage	Analyst coverage	Earnings surprise	Number of CHANGE obs.	Number of CROSS-LISTINGS
Belgium (N = 175)	316,740 (683,681)	633,831 (1,566,662)	1,837,081 (4,725,137)	2,606,342 (7,240,074)	9,369 (26,316)	25 (14.29%)	0.5219 (0.24)	6.4629 (6.13)	0.6543 (1.22)	25 (14.29%)	8 (4.57%)
France (N = 347)	2,597,414 (3,928,282)	1,516,995 (3,352,776)	3,478,364 (5,894,447)	9,269,575 (12,457,725)	27,183 (45,546)	29 (8.36%)	0.5807 (0.18)	10.1758 (6.62)	0.5031 (1.07)	50 (14.41%)	0 (0.00%)
Germany (N = 510)	251,017 (652,930)	903,286 (2,605,581)	2,395,465 (5,856,329)	5,242,640 (22,433,190)	16,177 (53,695)	36 (7.06%)	0.5574 (0.19)	8.4725 (8.34)	0.8992 (1.30)	75 (14.71%)	4 (0.78%)
Great Britain (N = 938)	1,621,555 (2,534,836)	232,621 (741,541)	1,381,144 (3,984,631)	1,545,241 (3,755,072)	7,794 (32,240)	120 (12.79%)	0.5100 (0.23)	4.6962 (4.88)	0.6613 (1.16)	45 (4.80%)	18 (1.92%)
Italy (N = 237)	77,065 (266,668)	1,837,281 (6,603,746)	2,469,878 (6,082,347)	5,022,324 (14,849,298)	10,198 (26,270)	19 (8.02%)	0.6076 (0.20)	7.8228 (6.99)	0.7704 (1.46)	2 (0.84%)	4 (1.69%)
Netherlands (N = 213)	954,462 (1,811,731)	647,913 (1,514,004)	2,387,678 (6,197,461)	2,810,889 (6,321,908)	12,240 (27,209)	21 (9.86%)	0.5508 (0.21)	9.9155 (7.40)	0.7017 (1.21)	34 (15.96%)	5 (2.35%)
Spain (N = 146)	1,353,224 (3,005,192)	2,407,163 (5,856,210)	3,970,608 (6,524,852)	7,650,283 (13,375,649)	14,753 (27,735)	11 (7.53%)	0.6602 (0.22)	11.1575 (6.48)	0.6016 (0.84)	2 (1.37%)	0 (0.00%)
TOTAL (N = 2,566)	928,307 (2,235,722)	856,490 (3,09,347)	2,228,888 (5,335,013)	3,900,151 (12,974,523)	13,349 (39,303)	261 (10.17%)	0.5508 (0.22)	7.3149 (6.88)	0.6968 (1.21)	233 (9.08%)	39 (1.52%)

Table 5-5: Descriptive statistics of the independent variables

Only 1.52% of all firm-year observations belong to firms with a cross-listing in the U.S. This finding seems surprising at the first sight as the sample mainly consists of large European listed companies which operate in a global context and are expected to benefit from an U.S. cross-listing. However, the increased regulatory effort, especially after the enactment of the Sarbanes-Oxley Act (SOX), may also prevent some companies from a cross-listing in the U.S.[174]

Table 5-6 provides descriptive statistics for the **dependent variables** forecast accuracy, forecast dispersion, and analyst following and presents univariate comparisons across the two samples to explore potential differences between fair value and historical cost accounting observations. The differences are presented both for the overall sample and separately for each country. The table presents the means of the three variables with p-values on the basis of a parametric t-test (test for equality of means without assuming equal variances in the two samples) stated in brackets. Indicators for tests of significance are also stated with *, **, and *** indicating significance at the 10%, 5%, and 1% levels (two-sided), respectively.[175] For the total sample, the mean of forecast accuracy of historical cost observations (-0.0258) is significantly higher than the mean of fair value observations (-0.0433), indicating that fair value accounting causes a significant decrease in forecast accuracy. Whereas the univariate analysis does not reveal a significant difference between historical cost and fair value observations for forecast dispersion, the findings for the total sample indicate a significant decrease of analyst following for fair value firms. Whereas historical cost observations have on average an analyst following of 7.4674, the analyst following for observations of fair value firms (5.1919) is significantly lower, which suggests that analysts are less likely to follow these firms. Therefore, it is assumed on the basis of these results that fair value accounting is negatively associated with forecast accuracy and analyst following. However, Table 5-6 only provides limited evidence of an incremental change in analysts' information environment for the fair value firms relative to the historical cost firms. Because these univariate comparisons do not control for correlated factors that potentially influence the change in analysts' information environment (e.g., changes in firm size or the earnings situation of the firm), the results only provide preliminary evidence on the hypotheses and should be interpreted with caution. Thus, hypothesis testing is conducted on the basis of multivariate regression analyses, which also incorporate firm- and country-specific factors influencing analysts' ability to forecasting.

Referring to the univariate comparisons on the **country level**, the results are not different from the findings for the total sample for the observations from France (see Table 5-6). Similar to the overall sample, forecast accuracy and analyst following are **significantly lower** for fair value firms than for historical cost firms. German fair value firms feature the lowest value for analysts' forecast dispersion (-1.9082) among all sub-samples. Even though, this somewhat low value does not cause forecast dispersion in the overall sample to result in a significant difference between historical cost and fair value observations. While the results for the other country samples also reveal differences between historical

---

174 See for example *Piotroski/Srinivasan* (2008), p. 383f., who report a significant decrease in the likelihood of small foreign firms to cross-list in the U.S.

175 This kind of presentation of significance levels is maintained in the entire study.

cost and fair value firms, the British and Italian samples yield some differences. There are no significant differences detected for forecast accuracy, forecast dispersion, and analyst following for these two country samples. This does not conform to the univariate findings of the overall sample. However, it is expected that the multivariate analyses in chapter 5.2.3 provide additional and helpful insights into the particularities of the single country samples.

Country	Variable	Historical cost observations	p-values	Fair value observations	TOTAL
Belgium (N = 175)	ACCURACY	-0.0219	(0.3179)	-0.0299	-0.0231
	DISPERSION	-1.3775	(0.2711)	-0.8957	-1.3059
	FOLLOWING	6.8926	***(0.0000)	4.0000	6.4629
France (N = 347)	ACCURACY	-0.0158	**(0.0316)	-0.0646	-0.0189
	DISPERSION	-1.0171	(0.2727)	-0.6732	-0.9953
	FOLLOWING	10.5138	***(0.0000)	5.1818	10.1758
Germany (N = 510)	ACCURACY	-0.0295	(0.1052)	-0.0550	-0.0311
	DISPERSION	-1.0729	(0.2036)	-1.9082	-1.1253
	FOLLOWING	8.7176	***(0.0002)	4.8125	8.4725
Great Britain (N = 938)	ACCURACY	-0.0310	(0.3028)	-0.0428	-0.0317
	DISPERSION	-0.1508	(0.4698)	-0.2550	-0.1572
	FOLLOWING	4.6844	(0.7562)	4.8772	4.6962
Italy (N = 237)	ACCURACY	-0.0228	(0.4929)	-0.0664	-0.0238
	DISPERSION	-2.3201	(0.1183)	-1.2577	-2.2977
	FOLLOWING	7.8448	(0.6153)	6.8000	7.8228
Netherlands (N = 213)	ACCURACY	-0.0227	(0.1833)	-0.0134	-0.0219
	DISPERSION	-1.5537	***(0.0022)	-0.5412	-1.4634
	FOLLOWING	9.3144	***(0.0000)	4.8421	8.9155
Spain (N = 146)	ACCURACY	-0.0178	*(0.0523)	-0.0415	-0.0196
	DISPERSION	-2.6576	**(0.0351)	-1.5113	-2.5712
	FOLLOWING	11.2000	(0.7842)	10.6364	11.1575
TOTAL (N = 2,566)	ACCURACY	-0.0258	***(0.0037)	-0.0433	-0.0270
	DISPERSION	-0.9941	(0.3877)	-0.8540	-0.9847
	FOLLOWING	7.4674	***(0.0000)	5.1919	7.3149
P-values are stated in brackets. *, **, and *** indicate significance at the 10%, 5%, and 1% levels (two-sided).					

Table 5-6: Descriptive statistics for the dependent variables

In addition to descriptive statistics, **pair-wise correlations** between the independent variables are presented in Table 5-7. The table shows both Pearson and Spearman correlation coefficients between the control variables and indicates whether these correlation coefficients are significantly (at the 5% level or better) different from zero (significant values stated in italics). Whereas Pearson coefficients are provided in the upper right of the table, Spearman coefficients are depicted in the lower left. Although the correlations provide evidence that over half of the coefficients are significant at least at the 5% level, the relatively low values for both Pearson and Spearman coefficients indicate that there is only a low overall correlation between the control variables. However, the control variable capturing size effects, Log(MCAP), and the variable controlling for analyst following (COV) reveal the highest correlations (Pearson: 0.7503; Spearman: 0.7955). This finding seems intuitively comprehensible as, on average, large corporations tend to have a higher analyst following than small firms. A significant and positive correlation is also documented between the variables COV and CROSSLIST. This suggests that analyst following is significantly increased when firms cross-list in the U.S., lending support to the argument that cross-listings increase the firm's information environment and attracting more analysts. COV is also significantly positively associated with LEV, thus indicating that analysts are not distracted from highly-levered firms.

	Log(MCAP)	LOSS	LEV	COV	EAR_SUR	CHANGE	CROSSLIST
Log(MCAP)		-0.2173	0.2479	0.7503	-0.1331	0.0096	0.1997
LOSS	-0.2231		-0.1814	-0.1678	0.2272	0.0058	-0.0313
LEV	0.2576	-0.1447		0.2346	-0.0220	0.0107	-0.0223
COV	0.7955	-0.2014	0.2540		-0.1362	0.0147	0.2138
EAR_SUR	-0.2103	0.2116	-0.0087	-0.2213		0.0273	-0.0137
CHANGE	0.0033	0.0058	0.0069	0.0076	0.0230		-0.0060
CROSSLIST	0.1756	-0.0313	-0.0182	0.1697	-0.0201	-0.0060	

Table 5-7: Correlations between the independent variables

It is important to avoid pair-wise correlations between variables in multivariate regression models. As high correlations among included variables increase the possibility of multicollinearity, the strength and reliability of the results may be decreased (*Ernstberger et al.* (2008), p. 40). In order to avoid multicollinearity in the regression results, two **specifications** of the full model are applied. These additional two regression models do only include either firm size or analyst following as a control factor, because these two variables are highly correlated on the basis of both Pearson and Spearman correlation coefficients. In the case that all specifications provide results similar to the full model, it is expected that reported correlations between the independent variables do not cause biased results.

5.2.3 Regression analyses and findings

This chapter presents the **multivariate regression results**. The regression results for the total sample are presented in chapter 5.2.3.1 (forecast accuracy), chapter 5.2.3.2 (forecast dispersion), and chapter 5.2.3.3 (analyst following). Chapter 5.2.3.4 depicts the coefficients for the industry and country control variables. Finally, the regression results for the country samples are reported in chapter 5.2.3.5.

5.2.3.1 Fair value accounting and forecast accuracy

The **multivariate regression results** for the measure forecast accuracy are presented in Table 5-8. The table depicts the results of OLS and rank regressions and provides several models for the dependent variable. The variables FV_IP and FV_PPE represent the test variables and capture the effect of fair value accounting for investment properties and assets of property, plant and equipment, respectively. As there is a significant correlation between the independent variables market capitalization and analyst coverage, the table provides, in addition to the full model (1), alternative models where only market capitalization or analyst coverage as firm-level controls are included, but never both. This results in three models for the measure forecast accuracy. The table provides estimators for the variables, t-statistics in brackets (two-sided) and significance indicators. *, **, and *** indicate significance at the 10%, 5%, and 1% levels, respectively. It is controlled for firm- and country-effects in all of the reported models. The coefficients for the industry dummies and the country controls are not reported in the table. This information can be found in the appendix, Table A-2 – Table A-4.

Variable	Pred. sign	OLS regression			Rank regression		
		Model (1)	Model (2)	Model (3)	Model (1)	Model (2)	Model (3)
(Intercept)	+/-	-0.1344 *** (-14.08)	-0.0149 *** (-3.55)	-0.0968 *** (-12.66)	1,238.9590 (1.55)	1,408.8657 * (1.73)	1,227.9799 (1.54)
FV_IP	+/-	-0.0329 *** (-4.82)	-0.0181 ** (-2.59)	-0.0261 *** (-3.84)	-0.1342 *** (-3.08)	-0.0613 (-1.39)	-0.1370 *** (-3.17)
FV_PPE	+/-	0.0048 (0.07)	0.0132 (0.18)	0.0205 (0.29)	0.0585 (0.33)	0.0500 (0.27)	0.0561 (0.31)
Log(MCAP)	+	0.0248 *** (13.82)		0.0167 *** (12.86)	0.3083 *** (10.49)		0.3183 *** (16.12)
LOSS	-	-0.0578 *** (-16.55)	-0.0635 *** (-17.67)	-0.0578 *** (-16.44)	-0.2911 *** (-8.37)	-0.3231 *** (-9.13)	-0.2915 *** (-8.39)
LEV	-	-0.0198 *** (-4.08)	-0.0151 *** (-3.00)	-0.0225 *** (-4.60)	-0.0968 *** (-5.28)	-0.0840 *** (-4.50)	-0.0960 *** (-5.26)
COV	+	-0.0015 *** (-6.48)	0.0007 *** (4.20)		0.0136 (0.46)	0.2441 *** (11.99)	
EAR_SUR	-	-0.0078 *** (-9.18)	-0.0081 *** (-9.18)	-0.0074 ** (-8.69)	-0.2747 *** (-15.17)	-0.2842 *** (-15.38)	-0.2755 *** (-15.29)
CHANGE	-	0.0128 *** (3.73)	0.0129 *** (3.61)	0.0130 *** (3.76)	0.1878 *** (5.44)	0.1882 *** (5.34)	0.1876 *** (5.43)
CROSSLIST	+	-0.0112 (-1.32)	-0.0014 (-0.16)	-0.0172 ** (-2.02)	-0.1338 (-1.59)	-0.0599 (-0.70)	-0.1314 (-1.57)
Industry & country controls		Included	Included	Included	Included	Included	Included
Adjusted R²		24.66%	19.01%	23.44%	26.10%	22.92%	26.12%

T-values are stated in brackets. *, **, and *** indicate significance at the 10%, 5%, and 1% levels (two-sided).

Table 5-8: Regression results for forecast accuracy

As reported in model (1) of the OLS regression, the estimated coefficient for FV_IP is -0.0329 (t-statistic: -4.82). It is **negative and significant** at the 1% level. In addressing the first hypothesis, this finding suggests that fair value accounting of investment properties, measured by a lower score for FV_IP, significantly decreases the forecast accuracy of financial analysts' annual earnings forecasts. The results do also hold when either Log(MCAP) or COV are not used within the regression model in the alternative specifications of the model (i.e. to avoid multicollinearity). The coefficient for FV_PPE (0.0048) is positive but not significant (t-statistic: 0.07), thus indicating that forecast accuracy is not affected when property, plant and equipment is measured at fair value. The difference to the finding for investment properties may be due to the fact that PPE is measured on the basis of the revaluation model, where changes are not recognized in the profit or loss for the period but in the OCI. By recognizing these fair value changes in the OCI, they are not part of the annual earnings that are forecasted by financial analysts.

The finding that fair value accounting for investment properties is more related with forecast accuracy conforms to the distribution of the fair value test variables reported in Table 5-4. When investment properties are measured at fair value, they do, on average, account for a larger stake of total assets than assets of PPE. The significant and negative coefficient for FV_IP reported in this chapter does therefore reflect the fact that the two test variables, FV_IP and FV_PPE, are constructed as **ratios**.[176] The results contradict the findings of *Fan et al.* (2006), who document a positive relation between forecast accuracy and fair value accounting. However, the authors concentrate on the insurance and financial services industry and do therefore use a more focused sample.

The results of the **firm-level control variables** are consistent with *Lang/Lundholm* (1996) as Log(MCAP), representing firm size, has a positive relation with forecast accuracy, which is consistent with the findings for their U.S. sample. In addition, the variable LOSS has a strong negative value, thus indicating that analysts find it significantly more difficult to make forecast predictions for firms currently reporting a loss. The problems of analysts with firms currently reporting a loss may result from unusual effects that are included in the loss reported during that period, such as for example big bath accounting. As expected, leverage is significantly negatively associated with forecast accuracy, suggesting that more highly levered firms have less accurate forecasts. Analyst coverage has a negative impact on accuracy, indicating that a greater analyst following does not cause forecasts to be more accurate. Although this finding is not consistent with the prediction in this study, the variable may be subject to multicollinearity as the coefficient becomes positive when firm size is not included in the model. The variable controlling for the volatility of earnings, EAR_SUR, is negative and significant in all three models. This conforms well with intuition when it is expected that greater earnings volatility causes less accurate forecasts.

The fact that the coefficient for the variable CHANGE is significantly positive indicates that analysts find it less challenging to predict earnings for firms that adopted IFRS in that regarding year. It could be hypothesized that due to the improved **information environment** provided by IFRS compared to local GAAP, the effect of a first-time adoption is overcompensated and causes more accurate forecasts. On the other hand, the different information environment, expected to result from a cross-listing in the U.S. (variable CROSSLIST), is only influencing the results in one of the three models. Finally, the adjusted R squared of model (1) is 24.66%, suggesting that the model explains a great deal of the variation in analyst forecast accuracy. The adjusted R squared is significantly decreased when Log(MCAP) is not included in the sample, suggesting that market capitalization helps explaining the variations among observations. It is therefore expected that there is a trade-off between the concern of multicollinearity in the analysis and the degree of variation that is explained by the model.

---

176 For a detailed description of the way of how the different variables are constructed see chapter 5.1.1.2.

Referring to the **rank regression** results included in Table 5-8, the outcomes for forecast accuracy do not significantly change when non-parametric rank data is used for the regression analysis. The coefficient for FV_IP is negative and significant (-0.1342 in the full model), thus suggesting that forecast accuracy is significantly decreased when investment properties are measured at fair value. However, significance is not reported in model (2) when Log(MCAP) is removed from the regression. Similar to the OLS regression, the coefficient for FV_PPE is positive, but never significant. However, this may also be due to the small number of fair value observations for assets of PPE available in the dataset. While the findings for the control variables do not materially change,[177] the adjusted R squared is significantly increased in all three models referring to forecast accuracy.[178] This finding points to a better model specification after the original sample is transformed into ranked data.

The finding that forecast accuracy is significantly associated with fair value accounting has implications for the **first hypothesis**. On the basis of theory and related literature, it has been assumed that there is no significant association between fair value accounting and forecast accuracy. Because fair values for investment properties cause forecasts to be significantly less accurate than forecasts for historical cost, the first hypothesis should be rejected. However, the results in this chapter provide only preliminary evidence. It is expected that further analyses do either corroborate or contradict the findings in this chapter.

5.2.3.2   Fair value accounting and forecast dispersion

The results regarding the association between analysts' forecast dispersion and fair value accounting are reported in Table 5-9. Similar to the previous chapter, the table presents coefficients for both an OLS and rank regression with different models used to avoid multicollinearity.

The results of the **OLS regression** reveal that the adjusted R squared of the full model (14.53%) is significantly lower than the adjusted R squared obtained when examining forecast accuracy. This indicates that the independent variables do not explain a similar amount of variation of the dependent variables when compared to forecast accuracy. The coefficients of the fair value indicator variables, FV_IP and FV_PPE, are not significant in all models,[179] thus indicating that fair value accounting for investment properties and property, plant, and equipment is not significantly related with the dispersion of individual forecasts. It is therefore expected that fair value measures do not significantly increase or reduce analysts' uncertainty with regard to future expectations. On the basis of this finding, it could be hypothesized that fair values do not affect financial analysts' information environment.

---

177 However, the only difference is reported for the variable COV, which is not significant when applying rank regression analysis (full model).

178 In the case of model (1), the value for the adjusted R squared increases from 24.66% to 26.10%.

179 The only exception is model (2) where FV_IP features a significantly positive coefficient.

Variable	Pred. sign	OLS regression			Rank regression		
		Model (1)	Model (2)	Model (3)	Model (1)	Model (2)	Model (3)
(Intercept)	+/-	-0.9298 * (-1.95)	0.6818 *** (3.36)	-0.1865 (-0.49)	1,330.3235 ** (2.06)	1,539.4866 ** (2.27)	1,938.6837 ** (2.54)
FV_IP	+/-	0.3686 (1.08)	0.5684 * (1.68)	0.5031 (1.49)	-0.1700 *** (-4.82)	-0.0802 ** (-2.20)	-0.0152 (-0.37)
FV_PPE	+/-	0.6585 (0.19)	0.7705 (0.22)	0.9681 (0.28)	0.1110 (0.76)	0.1006 (0.66)	0.2392 (1.40)
Log(MCAP)	+	0.3344 *** (3.72)		0.1743 *** (2.70)	0.3795 *** (15.98)		-0.1746 *** (-9.27)
LOSS	-	-2.0541 *** (-11.75)	-2.1313 *** (-12.25)	-2.0556 *** (-11.75)	-0.1563 *** (-5.56)	-0.1957 *** (-6.66)	-0.1324 *** (-4.00)
LEV	-	-1.1320 *** (-4.65)	-1.0678 *** (-4.39)	-1.1838 *** (-4.88)	-0.0313 ** (-2.11)	-0.0156 (-1.01)	-0.0715 *** (-4.11)
COV	+	-0.0293 ** (-2.56)	0.0003 (0.04)		-0.7550 *** (-31.49)	-0.4713 *** (-27.89)	
EAR_SUR	-	-0.1389 *** (-3.27)	-0.1428 *** (-3.35)	-0.1315 *** (-3.10)	-0.0641 *** (-4.38)	-0.0757 *** (-4.94)	-0.0204 (-1.19)
CHANGE	-	0.0831 (0.48)	0.0837 (0.48)	0.0873 (0.51)	0.0020 (0.07)	0.0025 (0.09)	0.0120 (0.36)
CROSSLIST	+	0.0706 (0.17)	0.2023 (0.48)	-0.0474 (-0.11)	0.2695 *** (3.97)	0.3605 *** (5.08)	0.1381 * (1.73)
Industry & country controls		Included	Included	Included	Included	Included	Included
Adjusted R²		14.53%	14.09%	14.34%	51.17%	46.27%	32.08%

T-values are stated in brackets. *, **, and *** indicate significance at the 10%, 5%, and 1% levels (two-sided).

Table 5-9: Regression results for forecast dispersion

Referring to the **firm-level controls**, Log(MCAP), LOSS, and LEV are significant in the expected direction, thus indicating that larger firms have less dispersed forecasts. Additionally, firms that currently report a loss and more highly levered firms face more dispersed forecasts. Similar to forecast accuracy, the findings regarding LOSS are comprehensible when it is assumed that analysts have problems to make forecasts for these firms due to unusual effects such as for example big-bath accounting. The coefficient for analyst coverage (COV) is also negative in the full model, whereas earnings volatility (EAR_SUR) has a significant and negative influence in all three models. The remaining firm-level controls (CHANGE, CROSSLIST) are not significant. Taken together, the results for forecast dispersion indicate that the dispersion of forecasts is less sensitive to the independent fair value test variables and control variables when compared to forecast accuracy. Additionally, the decreased adjusted R squared denotes that there could be further influences on forecast dispersion which are not included in the model such as differing information sources or time constraints. It could also be the case that analysts do largely differ in their personal skills when examining the future perspectives of the firm. However, a more adequate specification of the model remains an empirical question as only 14.53% of the variations of the dependent variable are explained by the model.

The results for the **rank regression** analysis regarding forecast dispersion are not consistent with the findings based on OLS. The coefficients on the basis of OLS should therefore be interpreted with caution. Contrary to the OLS regression, the rank regression reports negative significance for the variable FV_IP in two of the three models, assuming that fair value accounting for investment properties causes forecasts to be more dispersed. Only model (3) with analyst following not included as a control variable conforms to the findings of the OLS model. However, the coefficients for FV_PPE and for the control variables do not materially change.[180] Similar to forecast accuracy, the value for the adjusted R squared is significantly increased for the rank regression in all three models.

Taken the mixed results, it is not easy to provide evidence on the association between fair value accounting and forecast dispersion. Based on the findings in this chapter, the **second hypothesis** should not be rejected as fair value accounting is not associated with forecast dispersion. However, this conclusion does only hold in the case of the OLS regression, while the majority of the rank regressions corroborate the assumption of a significant and negative association.

5.2.3.3   Fair value accounting and analyst following

Table 5-10 reports the coefficients for OLS and rank regressions when fair value accounting and analyst following is examined. Two models are provided for both OLS and rank regression. Because analyst coverage is already used as a dependent variable, only two models are necessary for analyst following. Thus, model (2) does not include a measure for firm size, whereas model (1) represents the full model with all variables included.

The **OLS regressions** indicate that fair value accounting is significantly negatively associated with analyst following. Because the fair value coefficients for investment properties (FV_IP: -4.5857; t-statistics: -7.81) and property, plant, and equipment (FV_PPE: -10.5599; t-statistics: -1.74) are both negative, it is assumed that analysts are less likely to follow firms which are measuring their tangible assets at fair value, thus providing clear evidence on the third hypothesis. Additionally, the t-values and the significance levels suggest that analyst following is lower when investment property is measured at fair value compared to PPE, probably due to the fact that the fair value model causes greater volatility compared to the revaluation model.

---

180   However, the variable Log(MCAP) is significantly negative in model (3). In addition, the coefficients for CROSSLIST are significant and positive in all models when using ranked data.

Variable	Pred. sign	OLS regression		Rank regression	
		Model (1)	Model (2)	Model (1)	Model (2)
(Intercept)	+/-	-25.3502 *** (-38.41)	1.8777 *** (3.85)	-805.7395 (-1.51)	-888.9693 (-1.12)
FV_IP	+/-	-4.5857 *** (-7.81)	-2.5623 *** (-3.15)	-0.2051 *** (-7.09)	-0.0697 (-1.63)
FV_PPE	+/-	-10.5599 * (-1.74)	-16.9061 ** (-2.01)	-0.1698 (-1.41)	-0.4206 ** (-2.35)
Log(MCAP)	+	5.4617 *** (48.71)		0.7339 *** (55.49)	
LOSS	-	0.0530 (0.17)	-2.3400 *** (-5.61)	-0.0317 (-1.36)	-0.2387 *** (-6.98)
LEV	-	1.7652 *** (4.19)	5.4500 *** (9.45)	0.0532 *** (4.35)	0.1850 *** (10.37)
COV	+				
EAR_SUR	-	-0.2538 *** (-3.45)	-0.6140 *** (-6.02)	-0.0579 *** (-4.80)	-0.1779 *** (-10.07)
CHANGE	-	-0.1427 (-0.48)	-0.2571 (-0.62)	-0.0132 (-0.57)	-0.0269 (-0.73)
CROSSLIST	+	4.0226 *** (5.50)	11.9560 *** (12.04)	0.1740 *** (3.10)	0.7751 *** (9.45)
Industry & country controls		Included	Included	Included	Included
Adjusted R²		60.83%	24.19%	66.39%	25.58%

T-values are stated in brackets. *, **, and *** indicate significance at the 10%, 5%, and 1% levels (two-sided).

Table 5-10: Regression results for analyst following

This empirical evidence does not conform to the expectation that fair value measures provide a richer information set for making earnings forecasts. Moreover, it is hypothesized that analysts find it **more challenging** to predict fair values for assets that firms hold in their portfolio. When analysts are concerned of making wrong forecasts for the earnings of fair value firms, they may stop covering these firms, resulting in a lesser degree of overall analyst following in the case of fair value accounting. To give an example, it is interesting to note that fair value accounting for investment properties leads to a reduction in analyst following of about 4.5 analysts for that regarding firm (compared to the situation with property measured at historical cost).

Consistent with *Lang/Lundholm* (1996), the coefficient for the **control variable** Log(MCAP) is positive and significant, suggesting that the positive relation between analyst following and firm size may also be generalized to other countries which are not in the sample. In contrast to the findings for accuracy and dispersion, the coefficient for LOSS is only significant and negative in model (2). For the full model, the coefficient is not significant.[181] From the remaining variables, which do account for differences on the firm-level, the coefficients for LEV and CROSSLIST are significantly positively associated with analyst following. The results have to be interpreted in a way that a cross-listing in the U.S. significantly increases the attractiveness of firms which is represented by a higher analyst following for these firms. This finding has already been revealed in the course of the correlation analysis of chapter 5.2.2. Additionally, analysts are not distracted from high leverage ratios as they are more likely to follow firms with a large debt ratio. The coefficients for EAR_SUR conform to the findings for forecast accuracy and forecast dispersion as they are always significantly negative. Compared to the value for the models examining forecast accuracy and forecast dispersion, the adjusted R squared is significantly higher (60.83%). This indicates a fine goodness-of-fit and that the full model explains the majority of the variation of the dependent variable analyst following. The largest portion of the variation of analyst following is explained by the variable Log(MCAP), which faces the highest t-value of all explanatory variables. The adjusted R squared does therefore significantly decrease when the measure for firm size is removed from the model.

The results obtained when using **ranked data** do not materially change compared to the evidence based on the original OLS data. However, the coefficients for FV_IP and FV_PPE are negative and significant only in either model (1) (investment property) or model (2) (PPE). Nevertheless, the findings for the rank regression suggest that fair value accounting does negatively affect analysts' tendency to follow the firm. The control variables do not materially change in direction. The adjusted R squared, indicating the model's goodness-of-fit, is increased in the rank regression compared to OLS in the full model (1) by 5.56%. In the case of model (2), the adjusted R squared is only slightly increased.

Based on these findings of the OLS and rank regression, the **third hypothesis** should be rejected, because there is a significant association of analyst following and fair value accounting for investment properties and PPE. However, some concerns remain with regard to the mixed results of the rank regression. It is therefore expected that the further analyses provide additional evidence on the association of fair value accounting and analyst following.

5.2.3.4 Regression results for the industry and country controls

The OLS and rank regression coefficients for the industry and country controls are reported in appendix A. The coefficients for forecast accuracy are presented in Table A-2. Table A-3 and Table A-4 depict the coefficients for forecast dispersion and analyst following, respectively. The results show significance for the **country controls** indicating that different legal systems do have a significant influence on forecast accuracy, dispersion, and analyst following. The significance is highest in the case of forecast dispersion and analyst following. On the other hand, forecast accuracy is not that strongly related to differences

---

181 This finding seems surprising as the study finds that analysts' forecasts are less accurate and more dispersed when firms report a loss. If analysts are aware of this, they should not make earnings forecasts for firms that are expected to report a loss in the current period. However, the fact that they make earnings predictions anyhow may be explained by the long period of time that analysts usually cover firms.

in law systems, because the coefficients for French or German law are only significant in the reduced models (according to OLS). However, the tables only provide the coefficients for French and German law. The dummy variable for common law is not included as common law functions as the reference category.

Some **industry dummies** feature significant coefficients.[182] In the case of forecast accuracy, the coefficients for the industries "Consumer Services", "Pharmaceuticals" and "Semiconductors" are significantly positive according to OLS in the full model. This suggests that companies from these industries have, on average, higher forecast accuracy compared to the reference category. On the other hand, the industry "Food, Beverage & Tobacco" possesses a significantly negative coefficient in the three models, thus indicating decreased forecast accuracy. Referring to forecast dispersion, a clear significance in all three models is only demonstrated for the "Transportation", "Diversified Financials" and "Food & Staples" industries (according to the OLS regression). With significantly negative coefficients, the results indicate that such firms have more dispersed forecasts when compared to the remaining industries. Whereas only a few industries have significant coefficients in the case of forecast accuracy and forecast dispersion, the largest influence of different industries is reported for analyst following. According to the results stated, analysts are more likely to follow companies from a large number of industries (compared to the reference industry),[183] while a clear negative significance is not reported in the full model. The fact that industries by far have the largest association with analyst following seems intuitively comprehensible as the choice to follow a firm can directly be influenced by an analyst, whereas forecast accuracy and forecast dispersion are a matter of effort and skill.

5.2.3.5 Regression results for the country samples

The data sample comprises firm-year observations from seven European countries. It would be interesting to examine possible differences or similarities between the country samples. Thus, the results for **the country-specific OLS regression analyses** are provided in Table 5-11. The table shows the coefficients of the two test variables, FV_IP and FV_PPE, when they are regressed on the measures of forecast accuracy, forecast dispersion, and analyst following, separately for each country sub-sample.[184] The coefficients, which are provided for FV_IP and FV_PPE, are based on regression analyses with all firm-specific variables included (full model). To provide evidence on the goodness-of-fit of the regression analyses, the adjusted R squared values are also presented.

Referring to **forecast accuracy**, the French and British sample conform with the overall findings as these two samples provide significantly negative coefficients for FV_IP, indi-

---

182 The coefficient for the industry "Capital Goods" is not provided, because it functions as the reference category.

183 Industries with a positive and significant coefficient in both OLS models are: Energy, Materials, Transportation, Automobiles & Components, Consumer Services, Food & Staples Retailing, Household & Personal Products, Health Care Equipment & Services, Pharmaceuticals, and Telecommunication Services.

184 The complete regression results for the country samples are reported in Table A-8 – Table A-13 of appendix A.

cating that investment properties measured at fair value cause a bias in individual analysts' earnings forecasts. On the other hand, the coefficients for FV_IP in the remaining sub-samples are slightly positive, but not significant. Therefore, it is expected that especially the French and British country samples lead to the negative and significant coefficient for FV_IP in the overall sample.

Even though there is no significant value reported for the coefficient of **FV_PPE** in the overall sample, the Dutch sample reveals a significant and positive association between FV_PPE and forecast accuracy. This finding suggests that forecast accuracy is significantly higher for the Dutch sample when PPE is measured at fair value compared to historical cost. This difference between investment properties and PPE may be due to the fact that analysts may on the one hand benefit from the additional information provided by fair value accounting. However, on the other hand, an increased earnings volatility, which is only the case for investment properties, makes it more difficult to produce precise forecasts. The difference in the findings for FV_PPE between the overall and the Dutch sample may be explained by the small number of fair value firms from the Netherlands, which do not significantly influence the data in the overall sample. Contrarily to this, the coefficient for FV_PPE is not significant in the British sample. This may be due to the larger number of observations included in the British sample which makes it difficult to detect any significance of PPE measured at fair value.

Variable	Belgium	France	Germany	Great Britain	Italy	Nether- lands	Spain
	(N = 175)	(N = 347)	(N = 510)	(N = 938)	(N = 237)	(N = 213)	(N = 146)
ACCURACY							
FV_IP	0.0056 (0.24)	-0.0748 *** (-5.96)	0.0269 (1.22)	-0.0446 *** (-3.36)	1.4857 (1.06)	0.0064 (0.37)	0.0343 (1.07)
FV_PPE				-0.0394 (-0.39)		0.2521 ** (2.07)	
Adjusted R²	28.28%	36.54%	33.61%	29.55%	29.55%	30.87%	24.52%
DISPERSION							
FV_IP	0.4138 (0.25)	-0.3482 (-0.46)	0.9867 (-1.32)	-0.2703 (-1.11)	-21.2442 (-0.16)	0.6533 (0.55)	-0.2048 (-0.06)
FV_PPE				0.0399 (0.02)		6.6224 (0.80)	
Adjusted R²	26.01%	19.93%	26.56%	1.94%	15.98%	38.46%	40.60%
FOLLOWING							
FV_IP	0.6420 (0.38)	-8.6628 *** (-5.66)	0.0812 (0.04)	-2.8747 *** (-4.18)	-123.6009 (-0.88)	-4.1835 *** (-2.86)	4.2822 (0.98)
FV_PPE				-10.1382 * (-1.93)		0.4133 (0.04)	
Adjusted R²	85.72%	54.27%	61.99%	61.55%	69.21%	75.80%	59.69%
T-values are stated in brackets. *, **, and *** indicate significance at the 10%, 5%, and 1% levels (two-sided).							

Table 5-11: OLS regression results separately for each country

Referring to analysts' **forecast dispersion**, the results of each country do conform to the findings for the overall sample, as the coefficients for FV_IP and FV_PPE are never significant in either positive or negative direction, indicating that fair value accounting is not associated with dispersion among individual earnings forecasts. The values for the adjusted R squared are significantly different between the single country samples, ranging from a low 1.94% (British sample) to the top-end of 40.60% for the Spanish sample. Due to these large differences between the country samples, the results regarding forecast dispersion may have to be interpreted with caution. Similar to the total sample, there may be influences on forecast dispersion that cannot be accounted for adequately by the research design.

The results on the country-level regarding the number of **analysts following** the firm mainly conform to the findings for the overall sample. Four out of the seven countries examined feature a negative coefficient for FV_IP. Three coefficients feature negative significance. The Belgian, German, and Spanish sub-samples do not feature a significant coefficient for FV_IP. However, the findings indicate that fair value accounting for investment properties is negatively associated with analyst following. However, negative significance is only detected for French, British, and Dutch companies in the sample. A significant negative influence of fair value measures of assets of PPE is only reported for the British sample, whereas the Dutch sample features a positive, but not significant, coefficient. The adjusted R squared values range from 54.27% (France) to 85.72% (Belgium), indicating an adequate model specification explaining a large portion of the variation in analyst following.

The **rank regression** results accompany the regression results based on OLS and are meant to support the OLS findings. The rank regression results separately for each country are reported in Table 5-12.

Table 5-12 depicts the coefficients of the test variables, significance indicators and adjusted R squared values separately for each country. Contrariwise to the regression based on OLS, the single coefficients for FV_IP are not significant in the country samples in the case of **forecast accuracy**. That is a major difference compared to the analysis on the basis of OLS as the French and British country samples yield negative significance in the OLS regressions. However, both coefficients are also negative in rank regressions. The coefficient for FV_PPE is positive and significant only for the Dutch sample. A difference is also reported in the case of **forecast dispersion** for the British sub-sample with a coefficient for FV_IP that is negative and significant (-0.1425). The coefficient is not significant for the British sample in the OLS regression (see Table 5-11).

Three major differences are reported in the case of **analyst following**. First, the rank regression analysis reports a significant and positive coefficient for FV_IP (0.3932) in the Belgian sample, even though this significance is not reported under the OLS design. However, the Belgian OLS regression analysis features an unusually high adjusted R squared value of 85.72%, thus providing a possible explanation for the difference (the rank regression provides an adjusted R squared of 67.64%). Second, the coefficient for FV_IP within the Italian sample changes direction and is positive in the rank regression. Both OLS and rank regression coefficients are not significant. Finally, the coefficients for FV_IP within the German and Spanish samples also changes direction and are negative in the rank regression analysis (with both OLS and rank regression coefficients not significant).

Variable	Belgium (N = 175)	France (N = 347)	Germany (N = 510)	Great Britain (N = 938)	Italy (N = 237)	Netherlands (N = 213)	Spain (N = 146)
ACCURACY							
FV_IP	0.0556 (0.21)	-0.1858 (-1.40)	-0.0070 (-0.04)	-0.0692 (-0.95)	0.0180 (0.08)	0.0364 (0.11)	-0.1524 (-0.75)
FV_PPE				-0.4207 (-1.60)		0.6044 ** (2.04)	
Adjusted R²	30.21%	20.91%	28.71%	27.91%	41.94%	26.48%	37.53%
DISPERSION							
FV_IP	-0.1941 (-0.82)	-0.2034 (-1.63)	0.0721 (0.47)	-0.1425 ** (-2.28)	-0.1322 (-0.60)	-0.1794 (-0.62)	-0.2183 (-1.07)
FV_PPE				0.1328 (0.59)		0.2341 (0.88)	
Adjusted R²	45.23%	29.89%	42.60%	44.94%	38.23%	41.07%	36.80%
FOLLOWING							
FV_IP	0.3932 ** (2.20)	-0.5528 *** (-5.57)	-0.0424 (-0.36)	-0.1755 *** (-3.62)	0.1541 (0.97)	-0.1678 (-0.77)	-0.2276 (-1.45)
FV_PPE				-0.5584 *** (-3.19)		0.0401 (0.20)	
Adjusted R²	67.64%	51.26%	67.01%	66.36%	67.70%	65.60%	62.05%
T-values are stated in brackets. *, **, and *** indicate significance at the 10%, 5%, and 1% levels (two-sided).							

Table 5-12: Rank regression results separately for each country

Taken together, the results for the country-specific regression analyses suggest that there are **differences** between the country samples. The analyses for the total sample revealed a negative association of fair value accounting with forecast accuracy and analyst following (see Table 5-8 and Table 5-10). Even if it is not supported by the rank regressions, the findings in this chapter indicate that these significances are largely due the French and British data. The fair value test variables are also significant in these country samples. The remaining country samples feature fair value test variables that are not significant. However, observations from France and Great Britain account for half of the total observations. The findings for these two country samples do therefore have a large influence on the findings for the total sample. The country analysis also revealed that there are large differences of the adjusted R squared values, especially for forecast dispersion under OLS. These differences may be due to the variations of the dependent variables that are explained differently by the test and control variables in each country.

5.2.4 Robustness checks and matched sample design

The results of empirical analyses may depend on the empirical model applied and the available data. The confidence that is placed into the empirical findings can be increased when different models or data used do not cause differences in the main empirical results. This section does therefore report the results of robustness checks which are intended to increase the confidence in the main empirical results. Additionally, the results of a matched sample design are presented and interpreted.

In order to test the **sensitivity of the results** to alternative specifications of the model, it is first examined whether the results change when the dependent variable forecast accuracy is computed by using the mean of the forecasted EPS data instead of the median. Although it is expected that the median is less sensitive to possible outliers in the sample, an alternative specification of the model could provide additional insights regarding the strength and reliability of the results. The results do not materially change when the median is substituted by the mean to calculate forecast accuracy.[185] Second, it is investigated whether the results are robust to alternative measures that proxy for firm size. While the natural logarithm of market capitalization is used in the original analysis, it is alternatively substituted by the natural logarithm of total assets and the number of employees in that period. Basically, the results are robust to the alternative measures of firm size.[186] Finally, the full sample is used without an adjustment for outliers on the 1% and 99% quantile. The results do not materially change when the sample is not adjusted for outliers.[187]

Table 5-13 reports the coefficients for the OLS regression analysis with the **matched sample** which is obtained by using the propensity score matching procedure and the nearest neighbor algorithm.[188] Because every fair value observation is matched to a historical cost observation and there are 176 fair value observations in the original sample, the matched sample is reduced to 352 observations (from an original sample size of 2,566). The propensity scores are obtained by using the following indicators of similarity: firm size (Log(MCAP)), earnings situation (LOSS), leverage (LEV), earnings surprise (EAR_SUR), first-time adoption of the IFRS (CHANGE), and analyst following (COV). The coefficients reported in the table refer to the full models of forecast accuracy, forecast dispersion, and analyst following with all variables included.

The regression results for the matched sample design in Table 5-13 indicate that the sampling procedure was successful. The sample design helps to mitigate potential differences between fair value and non-fair value firm-year observations. Compared to the results for the non-sampled data reported in chapter 5.2.3, the results in Table 5-13 indicate that there is less difference among the observations. The firm-level controls are either non-significant or face a lower t-value. To provide an example, the coefficient for CHANGE is no longer significant in any of the three regressions, whereas it is significant for forecast accuracy in Table 5-8. The remaining firm-level controls face a significant decrease in their t-values, suggesting that the **propensity matching procedure** on the basis of the control variables was beneficial. However, even if the control variables are used for the matching procedure, it is not possible to achieve complete insignificance of all control variables as there is still an effect of the independent variables on the dependent variables.

---

185 The results for the variable forecast accuracy computed on the basis of the mean are reported in Table A-14 (appendix A).

186 See Table A-15 and Table A-16 of appendix A.

187 The results for the non-adjusted sample with outliers are reported in Table A-17 of appendix A.

188 See chapter 5.1.2.1 for further details.

Variable	Pred. sign	ACCURACY	DISPERSION	FOLLOWING
(Intercept)	+/-	-0.0888 *** (-2.86)	-2.3183 ** (-2.18)	-14.4901 *** (-7.81)
FV_IP	+/-	-0.0201 ** (-2.06)	0.1058 (0.32)	-1.5767 ** (-2.51)
FV_PPE	+/-	-0.0591 (-0.79)	0.1455 (0.06)	-4.3976 (-0.91)
Log(MCAP)	+	0.0142 *** (2.68)	0.5187 *** (2.86)	3.2038 *** (10.86)
LOSS	-	-0.1169 *** (-10.60)	-1.2916 *** (-3.43)	0.7995 (1.12)
LEV	-	-0.0190 (-1.30)	-0.4483 (-0.90)	1.8251 * (1.93)
COV	+	-0.0003 (-0.34)	-0.0812 *** (-2.77)	
EAR_SUR	-	-0.0093 *** (-5.41)	-0.1045 * (-1.79)	-0.1606 (-1.45)
CHANGE	-	0.0130 (1.18)	-0.3024 (-0.81)	-0.6849 (-0.96)
CROSSLIST	+	-0.0071 (-0.28)	-1.1519 (-1.32)	6.0968 *** (3.76)
Industry & country controls		Included	Included	Included
Adjusted R²		35.75%	16.65%	42.78%

T-values are stated in brackets. *, **, and *** indicate significance at the 10%, 5%, and 1% levels (two-sided).

Table 5-13: OLS regression results for the matched sample design

Referring to the two **test variables** measuring fair value accounting for investment property and assets of PPE (FV_IP and FV_PPE), the matched sample coefficients corroborate the results from the total sample. Analysts' forecast accuracy is significantly negatively associated with fair value accounting for investment properties, whereas the dispersion of individual forecasts is still not affected by fair value accounting. A negative association is also detected for fair value accounting and analyst following, even though significance is only reported in the case of investment properties.

The matched sample is also computed after transforming the data into **non-parametric measures**. The rank regression results for the matched sample design are reported in Table 5-14.

Referring to the **fair value test variables** of the rank regression, the results of the rank and OLS regression are not different in the case of forecast accuracy and forecast dispersion. The precision of forecasts is significantly negatively associated with fair value accounting for investment properties. The dispersion of forecasts is not affected. However, there is a difference reported for analyst following. Whereas the OLS regression reveals a negative and significant coefficient for FV_IP, the coefficient in the rank regression is also negative, but not significant. However, the t-value of -1.55 indicates that the coefficient is close to significance after transforming the matched sample into non-parametric data.

Variable	Pred. sign	ACCURACY	DISPERSION	FOLLOWING
(Intercept)	+/-	-329.3036 (-1.11)	465.0763 * (1.94)	-36.9800 (-0.15)
FV_IP	+/-	-0.1009 * (-1.67)	-0.0308 (-0.63)	-0.0789 (-1.55)
FV_PPE	+/-	-0.0332 (-0.18)	0.1646 (1.11)	-0.0909 (-0.59)
Log(MCAP)	+	0.1770 *** (2.80)	0.2921 *** (5.71)	0.5594 *** (12.87)
LOSS	-	-0.5327 *** (-5.10)	0.0294 (0.35)	0.1465 * (1.66)
LEV	-	-0.0220 (-0.45)	0.0052 (0.13)	0.0966 ** (2.33)
COV	+	0.0705 (1.07)	-0.6959 *** (-13.05)	
EAR_SUR	-	-0.3164 *** (-6.27)	-0.1182 *** (-2.89)	-0.1129 *** (-2.67)
CHANGE	-	0.2318 ** (2.30)	-0.0295 (-0.36)	-0.1234 (-1.45)
CROSSLIST	+	-0.1470 (-0.64)	0.2753 (1.49)	0.4393 ** (2.28)
Industry & country controls		Included	Included	Included
Adjusted R²		28.54%	52.55%	47.71%

T-values are stated in brackets. *, **, and *** indicate significance at the 10%, 5%, and 1% levels (two-sided).

Table 5-14: Rank regression results for the matched sample design

Taken together the findings in this chapter, the matched sample design provides further evidence on the **first hypothesis**, which investigates the association between fair value accounting and forecast accuracy. The matching procedure corroborates the findings from the original sample. There is a negative and significant influence of fair value accounting for investment properties on analysts' ability to produce precise forecasts. This assumption is supported by both OLS and rank regression analyses. Similar to the original sample, the matched sample reveals that there is no association between fair value accounting and individual analysts' forecast dispersion. The **second hypothesis** should therefore not be rejected. In the case of analyst following, OLS and rank regressions provide different results with regard to the fair value test variables. However, the coefficient for FV_IP in the rank regression is also negative. The findings in this chapter do corroborate the results from chapter 5.2.3.3. The **third hypothesis** should therefore be rejected.

Because the main results may also be influenced by time-series trends than cannot be controlled for in the original analysis, a difference in differences analysis is adequate to mitigate such effects. The results for the difference in differences analysis is therefore provided in the next chapter.

5.2.5   Difference in differences analysis

The regression results reported in chapter 5.2.3 provide evidence that fair value accounting for investment properties is negatively associated with forecast accuracy and analyst following. However, firms may face a varying degree of forecast accuracy and analyst following over time for reasons other than fair value accounting. As previously described in chapter 5.1.2.2, a difference in differences design can mitigate the concern subject to the caveat that firms not applying fair values during the same time period might not be affected in different time periods in similar ways. The following two chapters present the results of the difference in differences analysis. Whereas chapter 5.2.5.1 depicts univariate analyses, multivariate regression analyses are reported in chapter 5.2.5.2.

5.2.5.1   Univariate results of the difference in differences analysis

Additional data is used to perform a difference in differences analysis. Whereas the original sample of 2,566 firm-year observations from the time period 2005-2008 constitutes the post period, additional data is obtained for the time period 2001-2004 (the pre period). The time period 2001-2004 is chosen for basically two reasons: First, the time period represents four years of data and does therefore conform to the original time period of 2005-2008 regarding length. Second, the adoption of IFRS for consolidated financial statements became mandatory from the year 2005 on and by choosing the time period 2001-2004 it is assured that there are firms available in the sample which are still reporting their accounts under local GAAP. It is ensured that the sample obtained for the time period 2001-2004 does only include firm-year observations with firms reporting under local GAAP regulations where fair value accounting was not possible for the asset classes investigated.[189] If firms adopted IFRS prior to 2005 on a voluntary basis, the regarding IFRS firm-years are removed from the sample. Given these restrictions, the sample size for the period 2001-2004 amounts to **705 firm-year observations**. The reduction of the sample size compared to the original sample is due to data unavailability in earlier time periods and the requirement that IFRS firm-years should not be included.

Table 5-15 reports the means of the three **dependent variables**, forecast accuracy, forecast dispersion, and analyst following for the pre and post fair value adoption period. The values are provided separately for the historical cost and fair value group in a way to enable univariate comparisons. For each measure accuracy, dispersion, and following, the first row presents the univariate results for historical cost and fair value observations in the pre period, separately for investment properties and PPE. The second row presents the same values in the post period. Additionally, changes between the fair value and historical cost

---

189   The British and Dutch local GAAP regulations permitted fair value accounting for property under some circumstances (*Cairns et al.* (2011), p. 4f.) If firms from these countries measured their property at fair value under local GAAP regulations, they are removed from the sample.

group of firms are reported. Difference in differences estimators, which are supplemented by indicators representing significant difference from zero, are also provided in the table. Because there are not a sufficient number of observations available in the pre period for firms applying fair values for PPE from 2005 on, it is impossible to adequately implement a difference in differences design for PPE. The analysis in this chapter is therefore restricted to investment property only.

Variable	Time	Historical cost obs.	Investment property		Property, plant and equipment	
			Fair value obs.	FV-HC	Fair value obs.	FV-HC
ACCURACY	Pre	-0.0367	-0.0285	0.0082	- no data -	-
	Post	-0.0258	-0.0442	-0.0184***	-0.0140	0.0118
	Post-pre	0.0109***	-0.0157*		-	
DISPERSION	Pre	-3.2485	-1.4093	1.8393**	- no data -	-
	Post	-0.9941	-0.8712	0.1229	-0.0652	0.9289***
	Post-pre	2.2544***	0.5381		-	
FOLLOWING	Pre	10.6709	7.3404	-3.3305***	- no data -	-
	Post	7.4674	5.2083	-2.2591***	2.7500	-4.7174***
	Post-pre	-3.2035***	-2.1321*		-	

*, **, and *** indicate significance at the 10%, 5%, and 1% levels (two-sided).

Table 5-15: Univariate analysis of the difference in differences estimators

The results of the univariate analysis of the difference in differences estimators show that, for historical cost firms, the adoption of the IFRS caused a significant increase of **forecast accuracy**. Additionally, the coefficient for forecast dispersion is significantly increased, thus suggesting lower forecast dispersion for historical cost firms after the adoption of IFRS. These findings do basically agree with prior empirical studies dealing with the implications of IFRS adoption.[190] The fact that, in the post period, the means for forecast accuracy (-0.0258) and forecast dispersion (-0.9941) are significantly greater than in the pre period suggests that the adoption of IFRS provides an increased information environment for financial analysts. However, this finding does not hold for analyst following, as the number of analysts in the post period is significantly reduced by approximately three analysts per firm. It could be hypothesized that the adoption of IFRS did not cause a higher analyst following for historical cost firms. However, there could be further influences on this measure which cannot be captured in the course of a univariate analysis.

Referring to the forecast accuracy for **investment property** fair value firms (i.e. firms that are applying fair values in the post period but not in the pre period), the results indicate the opposite compared to historical cost firms. Although fair value firms feature a higher forecast accuracy in the pre period (with means of -0.0285 for fair value vs. -0.0367 for historical cost observations), they suffer from a large decline in forecast accuracy in the post period (-0.0442). However, the post period is the period when fair value accounting is applied in the financial statements. The results indicate that fair value accounting under IFRS causes forecasts to be less accurate, even when it is assumed that the

---

190 See for example the empirical studies dealing with the effects of IFRS adoption by *Ashbaugh/Pincus* (2001) or *Ernstberger et al.* (2008).

IFRS provide a better information environment for users of financial statements.[191] Figure 5-3 presents the difference in differences estimators for forecast accuracy in the pre and post period graphically.

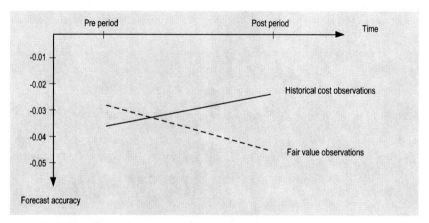

Figure 5-3: Difference in differences estimators for forecast accuracy

As Figure 5-3 shows, the forecast accuracy does slightly increase for historical cost observations, indicated by higher values in the post period compared to the pre period. The opposite is true for fair value observations with a decrease of forecast accuracy in the post period compared to the pre period. The fact that forecast accuracy for fair value firms is higher in the pre period compared to historical cost firms in the pre period rules out the possibility that time-series trends cause forecasts to be less accurate for fair value firms.

While the univariate analysis provides evidence that the effect of fair values on forecast accuracy is not influenced by time-series trends, the results for **forecast dispersion** are not that clear. For forecast dispersion, only two of the three difference in differences estimators take significant values. Nevertheless, the univariate analysis corroborates the prior findings regarding the negative influence of fair value measures on financial analysts' forecasting abilities. Whereas a significant finding with regard to forecast dispersion is not reported, the decrease in **analyst following** may be due to time-series changes. The fact that analyst following is decreased in the post period, no matter whether fair values are applied or not, may be explained through a general and steady decrease in analyst activity after the burst of the internet bubble in the year 2001. Additionally, it could be hypothesized that the financial crisis caused a decrease of analyst activity in the post period, especially in 2007 and 2008. Therefore, it could be hypothesized that the negative association of fair value accounting with analysts' tendency to follow firms might be overlapped by time-series trends, thus suggesting that the results reported in chapter 5.2.3.3 must be interpreted with caution. However, a univariate analysis does not account for firm- or

---

191 However, the decrease in forecast accuracy in the post period could also be due to the advent of the financial crisis in 2007.

country-specific factors, which are expected to influence the results as well. The next chapter does therefore present the results of multivariate regression analyses.

5.2.5.2   Regression results of the difference in differences analysis

To account for differences on the firm- and country-level, the results of a **multivariate OLS regression** analysis with the difference in differences estimators are reported in Table 5-16. The results are stated separately for investment properties and assets of PPE with IP_D and PPE_D representing dummy variables with a value of 1 if the firm-year observation is within the treatment group (fair value accounting) and 0 otherwise. The dummy variable TIME takes the value of 1 if the observation belongs to the second time period (post period after IFRS adoption) and is 0 otherwise. The difference in differences estimators of interest are therefore IP_D*TIME and PPE_D*TIME which are measuring the joint effect of time and the treatment. In other words, the difference in differences estimators account for time-series effects and depict the pure effect of the treatment.

The results reported in Table 5-16 support the original findings presented in 5.2.3. The coefficient for the difference in differences estimator of **investment properties**, IP_D*TIME, is significantly negative for **forecast accuracy** (-0.0244, t-value: -2.70), suggesting that time-series and self-selection effects are not responsible for the prior findings. The multivariate regression analysis does therefore support the univariate analysis of chapter 5.2.5.1 that time-series trends are not responsible for the decrease in forecast accuracy. The time-series effect can also be measured and is represented by the coefficient for TIME, which has a value of -0.0025. Basically, the results regarding forecast accuracy indicate that the decrease in forecasting precision is caused by a pure time-series effect (measured by the coefficient for TIME) and a pure fair value effect (measured by the coefficient for IP_D*TIME). TIME is not significant, thus suggesting that the decrease in forecast accuracy, which has already reported in the original model, is solely due to fair value accounting. There is no difference reported when turning to the control variables which have similar significance as in the original analysis (full model). The only difference to the original model is reported for the variable COV. Whereas the coefficient for COV is significant and negative in the original regression analysis, it is significant and positive in the difference in differences analysis. However, a positive coefficient for COV conforms more with intuition when it is expected that higher analyst following increases the competition among individual analysts to produce precise forecasts. The model for forecast accuracy provides an adjusted R squared of 21.04%. Even if this is below the value obtained for the original regression of chapter 5.2.3.1, it still indicates an adequate model specification.

Referring to **forecast dispersion** of investment property, the difference in differences estimator highlights the negative influence of fair value accounting for investment properties. With a coefficient of -1.4719 (t-value: -1.66), IP_D*TIME is significant at the 10% level. This negative association is not detected in the original analysis (in the case of the full model). The significant and positive coefficient for TIME (1.5430) indicates that the overall forecast dispersion decreased over time. As already revealed in the course of the univariate analysis, this means that individual analysts' forecasts became more similar, probably due to the better information available after the adoption of IFRS. However, the same caveat that holds for the original analysis is also true here: The low value for the adjusted R squared indicates a poor model specification for forecast dispersion when compared to forecast accuracy and analyst following. This suggests that the findings regarding forecast dispersion should be interpreted with more caution compared to the other results.

Variable	Pred. sign	Investment property			Property, plant and equipment		
		ACCURACY	DISPERSION	FOLLOWING	ACCURACY	DISPERSION	FOLLOWING
(Intercept)	+/-	-0.0286 *** (-5.37)	-0.7255 (-1.38)	-3.6369 *** (-6.02)	-0.0270 *** (-5.07)	-0.6420 (-1.23)	-3.6222 *** (-6.00)
IP_D	+/-	0.0074 (0.92)	1.4840 * (1.88)	-3.0207 *** (-3.31)			
PPE_D	+/-				-0.0046 (-0.17)	0.6088 (0.22)	-5.6764 * (-1.78)
TIME	+/-	-0.0025 (-0.84)	1.5430 *** (5.35)	-5.1846 *** (-16.13)	-0.0038 (-1.31)	1.4407 *** (5.09)	-5.1245 *** (-16.21)
IP_D*TIME	+/-	-0.0244 *** (-2.70)	-1.4719 * (-1.66)	0.8919 (0.87)			
PPE_D*TIME	+/-				0.0053 (0.16)	-0.8686 (-0.26)	1.9366 (0.50)
Log(MCAP)	+	0.0039 *** (4.72)	0.0556 (0.68)	2.0168 *** (23.08)	0.0037 *** (4.49)	0.0566 (0.70)	2.0021 *** (22.86)
LOSS	-	-0.0664 *** (-20.66)	-3.9694 *** (-12.56)	-1.0412 *** (-2.85)	-0.0662 *** (-20.56)	-3.9636 *** (-12.53)	-1.0646 *** (-2.90)
LEV	-	-0.0179 *** (-3.74)	-1.8279 *** (-3.88)	4.7564 *** (8.83)	-0.0178 *** (-3.71)	-1.8085 *** (-3.84)	4.7187 *** (8.73)
COV	+	0.0006 *** (3.65)	0.0091 (0.60)		0.0006 *** (3.85)	0.0076 (0.50)	
EAR_SUR	-	-0.0071 *** (-9.14)	-0.1368 * (-1.80)	-0.4481 *** (-5.11)	-0.0072 ** (-9.32)	-0.1403 * (-1.85)	-0.4627 *** (-5.26)
CHANGE	-	0.0127 *** (3.28)	0.1952 (0.51)	-0.3383 (-0.77)	0.0129 *** (3.33)	0.1992 (0.52)	-0.3079 (-0.70)
CROSSLIST	+	-0.0025 (-0.31)	-0.5275 (-0.67)	13.0377 *** (14.78)	-0.0032 (-0.40)	-0.4310 (-0.55)	12.7802 *** (14.47)
Industry & country controls		Included	Included	Included	Included	Included	Included
Adjusted R²		21.04%	10.13%	37.09%	20.68%	10.03%	36.70%

T-values are stated in brackets. *, **, and *** indicate significance at the 10%, 5%, and 1% levels (two-sided).

Table 5-16: OLS regression results of the difference in differences analysis

The opposite is true for **analyst following** in the case of investment property. An adjusted R squared of 37.09% indicates a good specification of the model with a great deal of variation explained by the independent variables. The goodness-of-fit of the model is almost four times higher when compared to the model measuring forecast dispersion. Thus, more confidence is put into the finding that the negative influence of fair value accounting on analyst following may in large parts be attributed to time-series effects, as the coefficient for TIME (-5.1846) is highly significant at the 1% level (t-value: -16.13). The difference in differences estimator IP_D*TIME is positive, but not significant. This indicates that there is a slightly and positive influence of investment properties measured at fair value on the tendency of individual analysts to follow these firms. This finding is not supported by the original analysis. However, the coefficient for IP_D is still negative and significant.

When turning to the implications of fair value accounting for **property, plant and equipment**, the results in Table 5-16 conform to the results reported in the original regression analysis presented in chapter 5.2.3. Similar to the prior findings, the coefficients of interest (here: the difference in differences estimator PPE_D*TIME) are never significant in any of the reported regressions for forecast accuracy, dispersion, and analyst following. On the other hand, the coefficient for TIME takes significant values in the case of forecast dispersion and analyst following, suggesting that the variation of the dependent variables is caused by time-series trends unrelated to fair value accounting.[192] But the finding that the coefficient for PPE_D (-5.6764) is still negative and significant (at the 10% level) in the case of analyst following conforms to the original analysis in chapter 5.2.3. However, the problems with the small number of fair value observations for PPE still remain, which leads to the conclusion that a matched sample design (as conducted in chapter 5.2.4) leads to more appropriate results for PPE. Table 5-17 reports the **rank regression** results of the difference in differences analysis.

The rank regression results do largely conform to the results based on OLS. Referring to **investment properties** and forecast accuracy, the coefficient for the difference in differences estimator IP_D*TIME is negative and significant (-0.1424), even if the significance is not that great as the significance of the regarding OLS estimator (t-values of -2.70 in the OLS vs. -1.73 in the rank regression). While there is no significance reported for the difference in differences estimator in the case of analyst following (similar to the findings for the OLS regression), the estimator is also no longer significant in the case of forecast dispersion. Referring to **assets of PPE**, the results of the rank regression are basically not different to the results based on OLS. The coefficient for the difference in differences estimator PPE_D*TIME is never significant.

---

192 This interpretation is not without any problems due to the following reason: Because there are no observations for PPE fair value firms in the pre period, the coefficient for TIME captures the comprehensive difference between the two time periods. The difference in differences analysis for property, plant and equipment is still advantageous as the sample size is significantly increased when an additional time period is investigated.

Variable	Pred. sign	Investment property			Property, plant and equipment		
		ACCURACY	DISPERSION	FOLLOWING	ACCURACY	DISPERSION	FOLLOWING
(Intercept)	+/-	2,609.7275 *** (2.86)	1,300.1562 * (1.75)	-542.8692 (-0.77)	2,499.8026 *** (2.62)	1,150.6035 (1.47)	-182.6096 (-0.25)
IP_D	+/-	0.0453 (0.61)	-0.0805 (-1.32)	-0.1405 ** (-2.42)			
PPE_D	+/-				-0.1487 (-0.57)	0.0459 (0.21)	-0.5094 ** (-2.52)
TIME	+/-	0.0055 (0.21)	-0.0937 *** (-4.44)	-0.3605 *** (-18.92)	-0.0020 (-0.08)	-0.0929 *** (-4.46)	-0.3618 *** (-19.33)
IP_D*TIME	+/-	-0.1424 * (-1.73)	-0.0764 (-1.14)	-0.0312 (-0.49)			
PPE_D*TIME	+/-				0.1631 (0.53)	-0.0184 (-0.07)	0.2046 (0.86)
Log(MCAP)	+	0.1572 *** (6.57)	0.2770 *** (14.16)	0.6579 *** (45.22)	0.1513 *** (6.35)	0.2669 *** (13.69)	0.6517 *** (44.76)
LOSS	-	-0.3251 *** (-11.04)	-0.1840 *** (-7.65)	-0.0485 ** (-2.13)	-0.3249 *** (-11.02)	-0.1832 *** (-7.59)	-0.0505 ** (-2.20)
LEV	-	-0.0998 *** (-6.07)	-0.0263 * (-1.96)	0.0750 *** (5.91)	-0.0996 *** (-6.05)	-0.0259 * (-1.92)	0.0747 *** (5.86)
COV	+	0.1658 *** (7.33)	-0.6487 *** (-35.08)		0.1694 *** (7.50)	-0.6403 *** (-34.62)	
EAR_SUR	-	-0.2630 *** (-16.18)	-0.0775 *** (-5.84)	-0.0693 *** (-5.52)	-0.2649 *** (-16.29)	-0.0800 *** (-6.01)	-0.0731 *** (-5.81)
CHANGE	-	0.1780 *** (5.06)	0.0024 (0.09)	-0.0257 (-0.94)	0.1794 *** (5.10)	0.0039 (0.14)	-0.0230 (-0.84)
CROSSLIST	+	-0.0483 (-0.67)	0.3319 *** (5.67)	0.4002 *** (7.25)	-0.0505 (-0.71)	0.3198 *** (5.46)	0.3874 *** (7.01)
Industry & country controls		Included	Included	Included	Included	Included	Included
Adjusted R²		25.81%	49.71%	54.73%	25.69%	49.39%	54.45%

T-values are stated in brackets. *, **, and *** indicate significance at the 10%, 5%, and 1% levels (two-sided).

Table 5-17: Rank regression results of the difference in differences analysis

Taken together, the difference in differences design increases the confidence in the results in a way that investment properties measured at fair value cause forecasts to be less accurate. Whereas the change in analyst following might go back to time-series changes, there is also a slight and negative association between fair value accounting and analyst dispersion, even if this finding is not supported by the rank regression. However, the results of the difference in differences analysis with regard to fair value accounting for PPE need to be interpreted with caution. There are no observations for PPE fair value firms in the pre period. The matched sample design is expected to yield better results in this respect.

The difference in differences design provides further evidence for either rejecting or not rejecting the three hypotheses. According to the first hypothesis, it is assumed that fair value accounting is not associated with analysts' forecast accuracy. The difference in differences results corroborate the prior findings of a negative association and rule out time-series trends responsible for the outcomes in the previous chapters. The **first hypothesis** should therefore be rejected. Even if the OLS regression in this chapter reveals a negative impact of fair value accounting for analyst dispersion, this finding is not supported by the ranked data. The **second hypothesis** should therefore not be rejected. This conforms to the findings regarding forecast dispersion for the original and the matched sample. Referring to analyst following, the results of the difference in differences analysis reveal that the prior findings are largely due to time-series effects. However, there is still a slight evidence of a negative association of fair value accounting with analyst following. Nevertheless, and based on the difference in differences analysis in this chapter, the **third hypothesis** should not be rejected.

The difference in differences analysis completes the presentation of the empirical results. The next chapter summarizes the findings, draws conclusions and derives implications.

5.3   Discussion

The study investigates whether fair value accounting for two classes of tangible assets is associated with three measures of financial analysts' when producing earnings forecasts: forecast accuracy, forecast dispersion, and analyst following. While the results of the archival-based study indicate that there is a **significant influence** of fair value accounting in general, there is a different influence of fair value measures for investment properties and property, plant and equipment. On the one hand, the analysis provides strong evidence that the ability of analysts to produce precise forecasts is negatively affected by fair value accounting for investment properties. On the other hand, the results suggest that fair value accounting for PPE is not associated with forecast accuracy. It is expected that these different findings for investment property and PPE are due to differences in fair value accounting under the fair value model (investment property) and the revaluation model (PPE). Whereas the fair value model demands that fair value changes are recognized in the profit or loss for the period, such changes are part of the OCI under the revaluation model. Even if there is a strong impact of fair values on forecast accuracy, forecast dispersion is not affected in a similar way, thus suggesting that there may be further influences on the dispersion of individual analysts' forecasts rather than fair value accounting. The results regarding forecast dispersion also need to be interpreted with caution due to a relatively low model specification according to the value for the adjusted R squared. Referring to analyst following, the regression and several sensitivity analyses yield a significantly negative influence of fair value accounting on analysts' tendency to follow the firm. The results indicate a clear negative significance for investment properties measured at fair value. In the case of PPE, negative significance is only reported in one of the empirical models applied.

Referring to the firm-level control variables, the results of the study do largely conform to the expectations from chapter 5.1.1.2.2. Forecasts that are made for larger firms are more accurate than forecasts for smaller firms and analyst following is significantly increased in the case of large corporations. Whereas analysts find it **challenging** to predict earnings for firms currently reporting a loss with forecast accuracy (forecast dispersion) significantly decreased (increased), their tendency to follow the firm is not affected by its current earnings situation. Analysts' forecast accuracy is also negatively affected by earnings surprises, thus suggesting that analysts find it easier to produce forecasts for firms with a steady earnings trend rather than for firms with more volatile earnings. Conforming to expectation, forecast accuracy is also decreased for more highly-levered firms. Analysts are more likely to follow firms with a cross-listing in the U.S., which indicates that analysts may benefit from the increased disclosure requirements and the enforcement through the supervision of the SEC. Additionally, analysts benefit from IFRS adoption in the first year of the change, even if it is expected that analysts should find it more challenging to produce earnings forecasts for firms that switch to the new financial reporting system in that regarding year.

In chapter 4.2.2, it is argued on the basis of the **signaling theory** that managers may have an incentive to voluntarily measure the assets that their firm holds in the portfolio at fair value. This context holds under the assumption that fair values provide an increased information environment for financial analysts. When fair values provide this increased information environment and if managers are aware of this potential relationship, firms should more heavily rely on fair values rather than historical cost. However, managers may also rely more on historical cost accounting due to the fact that fair values are more difficult to determine than historical cost.[193] The composition of the sample indicates that historical cost accounting is by far dominating fair value accounting with only 6.86% of all firm-year observations featuring investment properties or property, plant, and equipment at fair value.[194] Although this finding is consistent with prior empirical evidence, especially when focusing on PPE,[195] it does not concord to the recommendation of the IASB and the CFA Institute. Both institutions intend to increase the application of fair values in financial statements in order to increase the quality of the information supply for users of financial statements (*CFA Institute Centre* (2008); *Foster/Shastri* (2010), p. 20). Taken the findings from the study, it is therefore expected that managers avoid the increased time and effort that is needed for fair value determination and do therefore more rely on historical cost accounting.

The finding that fair value accounting is negatively associated with financial analysts' forecast accuracy does not conform to **prior empirical literature**. *Fan et al.* (2006) provide evidence that a requirement to report fair values under U.S. GAAP enhances the accuracy of analysts' forecasts for a sample of insurance companies. However, the authors focus on one industry and do not examine analyst following. *Lang/Lundholm* (1996) and *Eng/Teo* (2000) find that forecast accuracy is significantly increased for firms with more informative and higher levels of disclosures. If fair values decrease forecast accuracy, fair value ac-

---

193 Additionally, fair value measures require extensive disclosures, especially when they are determined mark-to-model. See chapter 2.1.2.5.
194 A great deal of the fair value observations account for diversified financial firms. See chapter 5.2.1.2.
195 See for example the studies by *Christensen/Nikolaev* (2009) and *Cairns et al.* (2011).

counting should thus not be considered as more informative disclosures compared to historical cost accounting. Moreover, this would suggest that historical costs are more appropriate to serve the needs of users of financial statements. However, both studies are not based on IFRS archival data. The findings from the studies may thus not be transferred to fair value accounting under IFRS.

Referring to the **first hypothesis**, the results obtained for investment properties provide clear evidence against the assumption that fair value accounting is not associated with analysts' forecast accuracy. The results of the study suggest that investment properties measured at fair value cause forecast accuracy to be significantly decreased. The fact that this finding is also supported by the matched sample design and the difference in differences analysis strengthens the confidence in this relationship. In the case of assets of property, plant and equipment, the effect of fair value accounting is not that clear. Whereas the original regression analysis does only reveal a slightly positive (but not significant) association, the matched sample design yields a negative t-value for fair value accounting of PPE and forecast accuracy. However, the coefficient for PPE is still not significant even if it is expected that a matched sample design mitigates the problem of the small number of PPE fair value observations. The difference in differences analysis is only of limited advantage for PPE, because of data unavailability in the pre period. It is assumed that the different implications of fair value accounting for investment properties and PPE are caused by the different valuation models in IAS 40 and IAS 16. Even though both refer to *fair value accounting*, the fair value model is more challenging for analysts than the revaluation model, where fair value changes are not recognized in the profit or loss for the period.

Summarizing these findings, the **hypothesis H_1 is rejected:** There is a difference of forecast accuracy for firms that measure their tangible assets at fair value compared to firms that measure their tangible assets at historical cost. Analysts' forecast accuracy is significantly decreased in the case of investment property measured at fair value. There is no clear evidence in the case of PPE due to a lack of significance.

In addressing the **second hypothesis** that fair value accounting is unrelated with the dispersion of individual analysts' forecasts, the study provides similar results for both asset classes. Even if the difference in differences analysis provides evidence of a negative association between fair value accounting for investment property and forecast dispersion, this finding needs to be interpreted with caution. It is the only approach in the course of the study that yields a significant influence. Neither the original regression analysis nor the matched sample design provides similar results. However, the fact that the significance is only detected by the difference in differences design may be traced back to time-series trends in the variation of the dependent variables. However, a large issue is the poor model specification of all analyses in the study investigating forecast dispersion, suggesting that there are further influences on forecast dispersion that cannot be accounted for by such an archival research design. The same holds in the case of fair values for PPE with no empirical model in the study revealing significance for the dependent variable.

Therefore, the **hypothesis H_2 cannot be rejected:** There is no difference detected of forecast dispersion for firms that measure their tangible assets at fair value compared to firms that measure their tangible assets at historical cost. Most of the empirical models applied provide no significance for the fair value test variables.

The **third hypothesis** refers to the association of fair value accounting and analysts' tendency to follow the firm. Similar to the second hypothesis, fair value measures of investment property and assets of PPE provide conforming results. The regression analysis indicates a negative and significant influence of fair value accounting on analyst following, no matter whether the assets are accounted for under the fair value model (investment properties) or the revaluation model (PPE). These results are supported by most of the models applied. Even if the difference in differences analysis demonstrates that a large portion of the decrease in analyst following is caused by time-series trends, evidence remains that fair values have a negative influence. Given this finding, it is expected that fair values do not increase the richness of a firm's information environment, thus leading to a decrease in analyst following. Moreover, it could be hypothesized that analysts find it challenging to make earnings forecasts for fair value firms, which could prevent them from undertaking coverage for these firms. This assumption seems comprehensible in the context of the finding that forecast accuracy is significantly decreased for (investment property) fair value firms and due to the fact that analysts have an intention to produce precise forecasts (chapter 2.2.2.5).

Hypothesis H_3 is therefore rejected: There is a difference of analyst following for firms that measure their tangible assets at fair value compared to firms that measure their tangible assets at historical cost. Analyst following is significantly decreased for fair value firms. Figure 5-4 summarizes the results of the hypotheses tests regarding financial analysts' forecasting abilities (forecast accuracy and forecast dispersion) and analyst following.

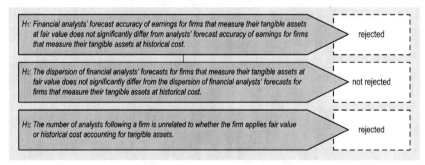

H_1: Financial analysts' forecast accuracy of earnings for firms that measure their tangible assets at fair value does not significantly differ from analysts' forecast accuracy of earnings for firms that measure their tangible assets at historical cost. — rejected

H_2: The dispersion of financial analysts' forecasts for firms that measure their tangible assets at fair value does not significantly differ from the dispersion of financial analysts' forecasts for firms that measure their tangible assets at historical cost. — not rejected

H_3: The number of analysts following a firm is unrelated to whether the firm applies fair value or historical cost accounting for tangible assets. — rejected

Figure 5-4: Results of the hypotheses tests for the archival study

In contrast to the assumption that fair value measures in financial statements increase the quality and the richness of a firm's information environment, evidence is provided that fair values are not always beneficial for financial analysts when making forecasts. However, fair value accounting cannot be made responsible for a bias in forecasting. The fact that only fair value accounting for investment properties causes this bias in forecast accuracy, but not fair value accounting for property, plant and equipment, leads to the conclusion that fair value accounting is not a problem by itself. Moreover, the increased **earnings**

volatility caused by fair value changes of recognized investment properties makes it challenging for financial analysts to produce precise forecasts. Analysts employ long-run time-series models to predict earnings in the future, which are not taking into account short-time changes of the fair value. The confidence in this argumentation is also increased by the fact that fair value changes of property, plant and equipment are not recognized in the profit or loss for the period. The fair value changes of PPE need not to be forecasted and analysts' long-run time-series models would be more adequate to forecast earnings for PPE fair value firms. According to this, the forecast accuracy for PPE fair value firms would not be as negatively affected as the forecast accuracy for investment property fair value firms. This assumption conforms to the empirical findings.

The question that remains is whether increased earnings volatility, caused by fair value changes, constitutes a problem. When it is argued from an investor's perspective, this should not be the case when the earnings volatility better reflects the true **economic condition** of the company. Fair values would then be proven to be more value relevant than historical cost measures that are depreciated without any respect to changing economic conditions. However, problems certainly arise when model-based fair values are used and offer scope for managerial discretion. If managers are able to manipulate the fair value measures in a favorable direction in a way that changing fair values can be made responsible for changes in earnings, fair value accounting would be blamed to cause unexpected earnings volatility. The fair value conception would then not be of advantage for users of financial statements.

The study with financial analysts offers significant **implications** for accounting practitioners and users of financial statements. First of all, the results yield implications for **investors**. Deriving such implications is important, because IFRS financial statements do mainly intend to serve the informational needs of investors. In addition, investors are the main users of the research reports and earnings forecasts by financial analysts. Even if the results also suggest that analysts are less likely to follow fair value firms, the finding that forecast accuracy is negatively affected by fair value accounting (for investment properties) should be of main interest for investors. The causality between fair value accounting and the accuracy for earnings forecasts by financial analysts should be interpreted by investors in the following way: Under the condition that investors expect that research reports are in general beneficial in a way that they use these reports in making investment decisions, investors should pay an increased attention to the companies' financial statements. Thus, it would not be sufficient to solely rely on the research reports without taking into account the financial statement information. Given the case that investors notice that the company measures a large portion of its assets at fair value, they should eventually **adjust the earnings forecast** for this company, because the study shows that forecasts are then likely to deviate more from the later realized figures. On the other hand, firms relying more on historical cost measures should face more accurate forecasts by financial analysts. Thus, investors should view fair value accounting as an additional parameter that is affecting analysts' ability to forecasting.

The study has also implications for **corporate managers** who make decisions on whether to recognize tangible assets at fair value or historical cost. The study indicates that an increased earnings volatility, caused by fair value accounting for investment properties, has negative effects on financial analysts forecast accuracy and their tendency to follow the firm. This implies that fair value accounting causes less precise forecasts for the firm. In addition, analysts are less likely to follow fair value firms as they find forecasting more challenging for these firms. However, prior accounting literature indicates that firms benefit from more precise forecasts as well as from a larger analyst following (*Gebhardt et al.* (2001), p. 165ff.; *Lang et al.* (2004), p. 612). According to this, more precise forecasts and greater analyst coverage are associated with lower cost of capital and increased firm valuation. Managers should therefore prefer a historical cost accounting environment instead of fair values. If managers take actions that are for the best sake of the company they work for, they may even be obligated to measure assets in the company's portfolio at historical cost in order to ensure certain benefits for their employer.

The study also provides **standard setters** like the IASB or the FASB with helpful empirical evidence regarding the influence of fair value accounting on users of financial statements. Additionally, the distribution of the sample shows that fair values are only used very seldom in practice for the asset classes examined. These findings indicate that, especially in the case of PPE, managers view the time-consuming efforts to determine the fair values as disproportional. However, the new standard IFRS 13 could be a first step in producing greater acceptance for fair value accounting as it provides one single framework for fair value measurement that is easier to understand compared to the prior dispersed regulations.

Several **limitations** have to be made as the study is not without caveats. The first limitation is a lack of **generalizability** of the results, because the study focuses solely on fair value accounting for non-financial assets. The results are to a large extent driven by fair value accounting for investment properties as the highest number of fair value observations is available within the real estate industry. Financial institutions are not included in the comprehensive sample of firm-year observations due to its special regulatory environment. The study does therefore only investigate the implications of fair value accounting for a limited group of assets. It does not empirically examine fair value accounting in a more comprehensive way. Additionally, the study only examines the association of earnings forecasts with fair value accounting and does not take into account the implications of **fair value determination**. It could be hypothesized that forecast accuracy, dispersion and analyst following are different for mark-to-market and mark-to-model fair values.[196]

A further limitation concerns aspects of **data availability**. The study provides empirical evidence primarily for larger companies, because it is more likely that financial analysts follow so-called blue-chips than small-caps. Even if company size functions as an important firm-specific control factor, the concern remains that many smaller companies are not included in the comprehensive sample when financial analysts' forecasts are not available for these firms during the sample period. Therefore, the sample is biased towards larger companies at the cost of smaller companies. In addition, there is a bias resulting from the language skills of the researcher as only these companies are included in the sample that have an annual report either available in English or German language.

---

196 However, the aspect of fair value determination is addressed in the course of the second empirical study. See chapter 6.

The final limitation concerns **causality**. The results of the study are interpreted in a way that it is expected that firms face a decrease in forecast accuracy or analyst following after they chose to measure their assets at fair value. It is believed that the choice of corporate managers to apply fair values is endogenous. Therefore, the reason for the decrease in forecast accuracy or the lower analyst following is seen in the fact that assets are measured at fair value. However, causality could also run the other way round with firms choosing to apply fair value accounting after they face less precise forecasts and poor analyst coverage. Managers may have this intention when they expect a solely positive influence of fair value accounting to increase forecasting precision and to attract more analysts. Given this case, the fair value decision would then be exogenous and the causality would not hold as expected. Unfortunately, this question cannot be sufficiently addressed by the research method and remains an open issue.

After a presentation and discussion of the results of the first empirical study in this chapter, the research design and the results of the experiment conducted with nonprofessional investors are presented in the next chapter.

6 Analysis of investors' judgments and investment decisions

6.1 Methodological approach

6.1.1 Preliminary considerations

In the previous chapter, archival data was used to examine the implications of fair value accounting on properties of financial analysts' forecasts. This approach is viewed as adequate because analysts' forecasts are easily observable and can therefore be used for empirical research. However, when doing archival research, problems could emerge in circumstances when archival data cannot easily be obtained from databases or other sources such as annual reports or when data cannot be collected. In addition, another disadvantage of archival research is that the effect of an independent variable cannot be isolated from other factors. In many circumstances it might also be the case that archival data is created for a special purpose, such as various political, legal, or financial reasons other than for the intended analysis and does not provide the exact information needed (*Wang* (2010), p. 31). Therefore, when examining the implications of fair value measures on investors' judgments and investment decisions, an archival-based approach seems not to be appropriate as the behavior of investors cannot easily be observed. For this reason, an **experimental-based approach** is used in order to examine investors' behavior when confronted with fair value measures.

A major advantage of doing experimental-based research is that it allows making **causal statements** in a way that a circumstance caused a change in behavior (*Martin* (2000), p. 26). Experiments are research studies in which the variance of all, or nearly all, of the possible influential independent variables not pertinent to the immediate problem of the investigation is kept to a minimum (*Kerlinger/Lee* (2000), p. 579). This is achieved by isolating the research in a physical situation apart from the routine of ordinary living, and by manipulating one or more independent variables under rigorously specified, operationalized, and controlled conditions (*Hogg/Vaughan* (2008), p. 10). A fundamental difference between experimental and non-experimental research is the fact that experimental research is conducted by an investigator who is actively engaged and influences the course of the experiment (*Huber* (1995), p. 62). Contrary to archival research, where variables are collected and observed, experimental research is conducted in a way that the researcher actively manipulates variables or treatments and observes the influences of these treatments on other variables. Using an archival-based approach, the researcher has no control over the variables examined as they do already exist in a certain form or cannot intrinsically be manipulated (*Sterzel* (2011), p. 102). Overcoming these limitations, an experiment causes significant changes in observed variables with a simultaneously control or elimination of unintentional influences or confounding factors (*Rack/Christophersen* (2009), p. 18).

Taken together, conducting an experiment emerges to be an appropriate research approach to examine investors' judgments and investment decisions under a fair value accounting environment. Going more into detail, it is investigated whether recognized or disclosed fair values cause a change in investors' belief with regard to the performance of a certain company share and whether fair values significantly affect the investment decisions of nonprofessional investors. Additionally, it is investigated whether there is a different impact of mark-to-market or mark-to-model fair value accounting on the judgments and investment decisions.

The next chapter presents the research design of the experiment used to assess investors' judgments and investment decisions. It presents the procedure for doing laboratory experiments and describes the variables which are used and observed during the experiment. Beside a description of possible confounding factors (and ways to eliminate or control for confounding), the experiment design is described. Empirical results are presented in chapter 6.2.

6.1.2 Research design

6.1.2.1 Laboratory experiment

Basically, experimental-based research may be conducted either by doing field experiments or laboratory experiments (*Sarris* (1990), p. 228f.). A **field experiment** is a research study conducted in a realistic situation in which one or more independent variables are manipulated under conditions as carefully controlled as the situation permits (*Kerlinger/Lee* (2000), p. 581). In contrast to laboratory experiments, field experiments are conducted in a natural environment. To give an example, in the course of a field experiment, members of work teams may be examined in the organization for which they work for. Because field experiments are conducted in a realistic natural environment, an advantage of this approach is seen in the fact that the results of a field experiment may easily be generalized and transferred to other circumstances (*Rack/Christophersen* (2009), p. 18). This fact refers to the issue of the **external validity** of field experiments and to the possibility that the causal relationship of the field experiment may be transferred to further populations and situations (*Shadish et al.* (2002), p. 21; *Sterzel* (2011), p. 111). The more realistic setting of field experiments is also expected to have an influence on the variables that are observed as the variables in a field experiment usually have a stronger effect than those of laboratory experiments.[197] In addition, it is argued that field experiments are suited both to testing hypotheses derived from theory and to finding answers to practical problems while laboratory experiments are suited mainly for testing aspects of theories (*Kerlinger/Lee* (2000), p. 583). On the other hand, the realistic setting of field experiments may generate influences which are not appreciated and cannot sufficiently be controlled for, which results in a lack of precision of the experimental results.[198] As the dependent variables are sometimes inadequate or cannot precisely be measured in a realistic scenario, the dependent variables cannot pick up all the variance that has been provoked by the manipulation of the independent variables (*Kerlinger/Lee* (2000), p. 584f.).

---

197 Concerning this point, it is stated in literature that "the more realistic the research situation, the stronger the variables". See *Kerlinger/Lee* (2000), p. 582.

198 Given the case that work teams are examined in their natural environment, problems may occur when participants take telephone calls or are influenced by construction noise (*Rack/Christophersen* (2009), p. 18).

Whereas field experiments are conducted in a natural environment, **laboratory experiments** (as the name implies) are conducted within a non-natural setting or a laboratory. In such an experiment, the research situation can be isolated from the life around the laboratory by eliminating extraneous influences that may otherwise affect the independent and dependent variables (*Rack/Christophersen* (2009), p. 18f.). Thus, the laboratory experiment has the inherent virtue of relatively complete control (*Kerlinger/Lee* (2000), p. 579). In the above example of the work teams, the participants may then be cut off from the phone line to eliminate the effect of incoming telephone calls in order to create an isolated research situation. In addition to control, a laboratory experiment provides a high degree of both specificity in the operational definition of variables and precision of measurements (*Kerlinger/Lee* (2000), p. 579). The advantages of doing experimental research in the laboratory result in a high degree of **internal validity** of the derived results: Because further influences on the dependent variables are eliminated or effectively controlled for, the variance of the independent variables can solely be traced back to the manipulation of the independent variable (*Sterzel* (2011), p. 111). However, a disadvantage of laboratory experiments is seen in the lack of external validity when results may not always be generalized (*Hogg/Vaughan* (2008), p. 10). In addition, the lack of strength of the independent variables is also viewed as a problem. Since laboratory situations are situations which are created for special purposes, the effects of experimental manipulations are expected to be weak (*Kerlinger/Lee* (2000), p. 580).

Whereas field experiments possess a relatively high degree of external validity, laboratory experiments feature a relatively high degree of internal validity. It is important to note that the degree of external and internal validity is mutually dependent in a way that a high degree of external validity causes a low degree of internal validity and vice versa (*Rack/Christophersen* (2009), p. 28). Thus, in doing experimental research, there is a trade-off between external and internal validity. Even if internal and external validity may not be realized at the same time, they are both important issues (*Sterzel* (2011), p. 112). However, when it is postulated that external validity cannot be achieved without a certain degree of internal validity, the criterion of internal validity is viewed as more important because it is assumed as a condition to achieve a certain degree of external validity (*Stier* (1999), p. 210). The study to examine investors' behavior is therefore conducted as a **laboratory experiment** which enables to efficiently eliminate or control for influences that are not appreciated. In addition, using the approach of a field experiment would be challenging as investors' behavior had to be examined when they act in their familiar environment. According to this, participants' behavior or trading activities had under these circumstances to be monitored at the location where they usually make their investment decisions or read companies' financial statements. In addition to difficulties during the implementation of the experiment (i.e. control for confounding factors), this approach would be very time-consuming and costly (*Grüning* (2011), p. 265) which makes it necessary to standardize the investors' environments within a research laboratory. Therefore, conducting a laboratory experiment is viewed as appropriate to examine investors' behavior and decision-making in the present setting. However, it has to be noted that laboratory experiments are conducted within an artificial environment with materials created solely for the purpose of the research question.

6.1.2.2 Variables used within the experiment

As already stated above, there are different variables which need to be differentiated when doing experimental research. The variables are as follows:

- The **independent variable** is the measure of influence which needs to be examined. Due to this purpose, the independent variable is systematically manipulated during the course of the experiment (*Stier* (1999), p. 210). This means that the independent variable is manipulated within different factor levels and specifications (*Rack/Christophersen* (2009), p. 413). Therefore, the independent variable is often referred to as the treatment effect within an experiment. As an experiment is not limited to just one treatment effect, it may also feature a couple of independent variables, depending on the research design.[199]

- The **dependent variable** is the measure that is subject to investigation within an experiment. It is of interest whether the independent variable has an influence on the dependent variable (*Stier* (1999), p. 210). Therefore, it is examined whether the variation of the hypothesized independent variable has an effect on the dependent variable in order to validate a certain causal statement (*Rack/Christophersen* (2009), p. 19). Similar to independent variables, experimental studies may feature more than just one dependent variable.

- Beside of the systematic effects of the independent variables, there could be further influences on the dependent variables. These factors, whose effect on the dependent variable is not intended, are therefore referred to as **confounding factors** (*Rack/Christophersen* (2009), p. 19). Confounding factors in the course of an experiment could for example consist of a participant's age, sex, or knowledge. Although independent variables and confounding factors do both have an influence on the dependent variables, confounding factors are not manipulated by the researcher (*Stier* (1999), p. 210). Moreover, the influences of confounding factors need to be eliminated or controlled for as it is aimed to examine the causality between independent and dependent variable in an unbiased manner.

An experiment faces confounding errors when the **variation** of the dependent variable, which needs to be examined, may be caused not only by the manipulation of the treatment effect (independent variable) but additionally by the confounding factors (*Stier* (1999), p. 210). In this case, both the independent and the confounding variables are responsible for a change of the measured value of the dependent variable. This problem occurs when confounding factors cannot be eliminated and are not sufficiently controlled for.[200]

The empirical study which is presented in this chapter features two independent variables, with each having two dimensions or factors. Consistent with the fair value model and the measurement of investment property, the first independent variable is concerned with the different kinds of **accounting treatment**. According to IAS 40, investment properties may either be recognized at fair value or at historical cost. In the latter case, the fair value must

---

199 The research design of the study is presented in chapter 6.1.2.4.
200 For a detailed description of the dealing with confounding factors in the study see chapter 6.1.2.3.

be disclosed in the notes. Therefore, the first independent variable (**fair value presentation**) is two-dimensional, because it is varied in a way that it has either the specification of fair value recognition or fair value disclosure. In the case of a fair value disclosure in the notes, the asset is measured at historical cost and depreciated on a regular basis.

The second independent variable is needed in order to model **fair value determination**. Because it is of interest whether and how participants differentiate between model- and market-based fair values, the second independent variable is also two-dimensional in a way that it either represents a fair value based on the DCF method or a fair value that has been derived from an active market. These two possibilities are consistent with the fair value hierarchy included in IFRS 13 which demands a model-based fair value determination when objective market values (Level 1 or Level 2 inputs) are not available.[201] According to the hypotheses that have been developed in chapter 4.2.3, it is expected that recognition and disclosure as well as the kind of fair value determination have a significant influence on investors' judgments and investment decisions.

The dependent variables are designed in a way that they are appropriate to capture and operationalize investors' judgments and investment decisions when confronted with fair values. More specifically, the variation of the two independent variables modeling fair value accounting is examined whether it influences certain measures of investors' behavior and market measures. The first dependent variable concerns **investors' judgment** about the future performance of the companies' shares: Do participants expect the future prospects of a company to be either more or less dispersed when the company uses either disclosed or recognized mark-to-market or mark-to-model fair value measures? Second, the **participant's confidence** that they place into their judgment concerning the share's future performance is surveyed. If fair values provide more useful information, participants should be happier with their decision made for a company recognizing fair values rather than just disclosing them. Third, investors are asked whether they would invest in the share or not (**willingness-to-invest**). Here, it is expected that fair value accounting has a significant influence on the participant's willingness to invest in the share which would also result in a significant change of market liquidity. Furthermore, it is of interest whether investors adjust the **amount to invest** when confronted with the experimental treatments. In addition to these dependent variables which are needed for hypotheses testing, additional variables are collected in order to investigate influences on investors' judgments and investment decisions.

The assumed causal relationship between independent and dependent variable must not necessarily go straight-line. Despite of the unintentional effects of confounding factors which need to be eliminated or controlled for (see chapter 6.1.2.3), there could be further effects influencing the causality between independent and dependent variable (*Rack/Christophersen* (2009), p. 19). When examining these effects, it has to be distinguished between moderator variables and mediator variables, depending upon the kind of influence on the causal relationship between independent and depending variable (*Sterzel* (2011), p. 105). Whereas **moderator variables** affect the direction or the degree of causality, **mediator variables** are able to provide statistical evidence of causality between the

---

201 For further information see chapter 2.1.2.4.

independent and dependent variables that could otherwise not be detected by statistical instruments (*Rack/Christophersen* (2009), p. 19).

It is not expected that moderator or mediator variables have an influence on the causal relationship between fair value accounting and investors' behavior. There is a direct causal relationship between fair value accounting and investors' judgments, confidence and their willingness to invest. The relationship does therefore not depend on a third variable (moderation) and the independent variables do not affect a third variable that in turn affect the dependent variable (mediation). Figure 6-1 presents the causality between the independent and dependent variables in the fair value study.

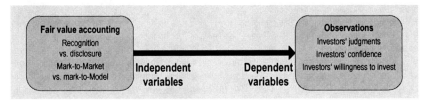

Figure 6-1: Causality between independent and dependent variables
            (Following *Müller* (2009), p. 239)

Figure 6-1 shows that the causal relationship is modeled in a way that fair value accounting is expected to influence investors' judgments, confidence, and their willingness to invest. The next chapter deals with confounding facpators which may have an additional influence on the causality between independent and dependent variables.

6.1.2.3 Dealing with confounding factors

As already mentioned in the previous chapter, there could be further influences which are referred to as **confounding factors**. The different kinds of confounding factors that may occur when doing experimental research can be classified as follows (*Hussy et al.* (2010), p. 115f.):

- **Subject's biases** are connected with the participants of an experiment. A possible confounding factor does emerge when the participants differ within the experimental treatments and dimensions of the independent variable in regard to various personal attributes, such as age, sex, intelligence, education, or religion (*Hussy et al.* (2010), p. 115). To give an example, if an experiment involves the problem-solving ability of participants under certain conditions, their intelligence, which may be measured by the intelligence quotient, constitutes a possible confounding factor.

- **Situation's biases** result from the context of the research. A possible confounding factor does emerge when the situations' characteristics are different for the participants within the experimental treatments and dimensions of the independent variable with regard to time of day, illumination, or experiment material (*Hussy et al.*

(2010), p. 116). Referring to the example above, confounding is present if the participants solve the problem in different rooms or at different day times.

- **Experimenter's biases** are connected with the person who conducts the experiment. Possible confounding factors do emerge when there are different experimenters within the experimental treatments and dimensions of the independent variable (*Hussy et al.* (2010), p. 116). Experimenter's biases may therefore consist of several factors such as age or sex. In addition, a confounding is also present when the same experimenter treats different groups of participants significantly differently for example with regard to expression or speech.

Situation's biases and experimenter's biases are not of relevance for the fair value study. As the situation and environment as well as the experimenter remain constant during the whole process of conducting the experiment, the only possible confounding may emerge due to subject's biases. It is expected that subjects differ in regard to various personal attributes. As aforementioned, the confounding factors are influencing the results in a nonintentional way and should therefore be either eliminated or controlled for (*Rack/Christophersen* (2009), p. 19). The following control methods may be applied in general for confounding factors:

- A **stabilization** of confounding factors is commonly applied for situation's biases or experimenter's biases with situation and experimenter remain constant for all participants during the experiment (*Hussy et al.* (2010), p. 116). In addition, the experimenter should pay attention to an identical course of the experiment which also includes a foremost identical appearance in all experiment sessions (*Sterzel* (2011), p. 117).

- The procedure of setting the influence of confounding factors to zero is referred to as **elimination**. Situation's biases such as construction noise may be best eliminated when performing a laboratory experiment which is conducted in specific rooms (*Stier* (1999), p. 214).

- **Systematic variation** describes the procedure to reclassify a possible confounding factor into an independent variable (*Hussy et al.* (2010), p. 117). Given the case that the age of participants is expected to have an influence on the problem-solving ability, the transformation of the variable "age" into an independent variable would be helpful.

- In the course of the **random variation**, a large number of values of the potential confounding factor are randomly allocated to the participants in order to prevent a systematic variation on the level of the independent variable (*Hussy et al.* (2010), p. 117). Given the case of construction noise, differing degrees of construction noise are randomly allocated to the participants as it is expected that all experimental dimensions then face the same number of participants suffering from comparable amounts of construction noise (*Hussy et al.* (2010), p. 117).

- The method of **randomization** is commonly applied to control for subject's biases (*Kay* (2005), p. 121). The approach involves randomly allocating the participants across the treatment groups in order to reach statistical equivalence of all treatment groups in regard to the confounding factors (*Hussy et al.* (2010), p. 117). For example, if a new drug should be compared against a standard drug, then the patients should be allocated to either the new drug or to the standard drug by chance.

- The method of **parallelization** also addresses subject's biases. Using this control, the dependent variable is measured before the start of the experiment and the participants are placed in a ranking order (*Rack/Christophersen* (2009), p. 29). In the case of a two-dimensional independent variable, two participants are taken of this ranking order each time and are allocated randomly to the two dimensions (*Hussy et al.* (2010), p. 118). This approach can also be applied for relatively small sample sizes.

- Using **blind trial** controls, the researcher does not know the underlying hypothesis and who belongs to the control group and the experimental group. The researcher has no group specific expectations about differences in the behavior due to the treatment effects which he can unconsciously pass to the participants (*Hussy et al.* (2010), p. 118). Thus, the method of blind trials is used to control for experimenter bias.

In the course of the fair value experiment, possible situation's biases are addressed by the methods of **stabilization** and **elimination**. Because it is assured that all participants receive the same materials (beside of the different treatments) for conducting the experiment and take the experiment in the same room at almost the same time, a possible confounding resulting from situation's biases can be eliminated. Additionally, it is paid attention to the fact that the participants are not disturbed during the completion of the experimental tasks in a way that the experiment was conducted under testing conditions (i.e. participants had to switch off their mobile phones and it was ensured that no other persons could enter the experiment room). The same holds for experimenter's biases which are eliminated in a way that the experiment is conducted by only one single person. A record is prepared in order to ensure an identical appearance in regard to word choice, gesture, and facial expression.

While situation's biases and experimenter's biases can easily be controlled for by stabilization and elimination, controlling for subject's characteristics is more challenging. The approach of **randomization** is used to control for subject's biases. Therefore, the participants of the study are randomly allocated to the different treatments of the effect to ensure that confounding cannot arise. The participant's characteristics are captured by a questionnaire which is handed out to the participants after the end of the experiment and involves several characteristics such as education, sex, and risk preference. The answers which are given to these questions enable an ex post examination in a way to investigate whether randomization was successful and that all treatment groups face similar subject's characteristics.

Controlling for confounding factors is important when doing experimental research in order to ensure the validity of the results. On the other hand, **quasi-experimental designs** refer to situations when participants are not randomly assigned to the treatment effects being studied or when confounding factors cannot fully be controlled for (*Shadish et al.* (2002), p. 14). The first key difference of a quasi-experimental approach to an experimental design is therefore the lack of random assignment which results in a decreased internal validity when confounding cannot be controlled for by the methods of parallelization without randomization (*Hussy et al.* (2010), p. 135f.). Additionally, it is argued that quasi-experimental designs are characterized in a way that a comprehensive control of confounding factors cannot be ensured (*Sterzel* (2011), p. 125). According to this, the influences of at least one confounding factor cannot be eliminated or controlled which results in a lack of internal validity (*Rack/Christophersen* (2009), p. 21). Thus, the most important difference between experiments and quasi-experiments is seen in the degree of control for possible confounding (*Hüttner/Schwarting* (2002), p. 169).

The experiment is conducted as a **between-subjects design** with a (random) allocation of all participants to the treatment groups.[202] Each participant receives experiment materials for his or her treatment and is not exposed to further treatments. However, a further possible experiment design is the **within-subjects design** with all participants running through all the treatments of the independent variables. Although a within-subjects design has several advantages, such as the smaller sample size required, the application of such an experiment design inserts further possible confounding into the experiment (*Hussy et al.* (2010), p. 119). Whereas participants can be part of the treatment group or the control group in a between-subjects design but cannot be part of both, each participant faces the complete set of treatment effects in a within-subjects design. Therefore, the fundamental disadvantage of a within-subjects design can be referred to as **carryover effects**. This means that the participation in one condition may affect the performance in other conditions, thus creating a confounding extraneous variable that varies with the independent variable (*Hussy et al.* (2010), p. 119).

The participation in the conditions may affect the participant's performance in the subsequent conditions either positively or negatively. For example, it could be the case that participants in the fair value study learn how to deal with fair values, which results in **learning effects** that influence the subsequent conditions positively. On the other hand, participants may fatigue during the experiment which has a negative influence on the later conditions and participants face **end-game biases**.[203] In addition, within-subjects designs are usually more time consuming than between-subjects designs. This is due to the fact that within-subject experiments usually last for a couple of rounds instead of just one in the case of between-subject experiments.

Taken together and due to the disadvantages of a within-subjects design, the fair value experiment is constructed as a between-subjects design. Possible confounding effects are addressed by elimination, stabilization, and randomization. The experiment design is presented in detail in the next chapter.

---

202 For a detailed description of the experimental design see chapter 6.1.2.4.

203 However, the method of counterbalancing may be applied in such a case to overcome some of the disadvantages of a within-subjects design. See *Greenwald* (1976), p. 316.

6.1.2.4 Experiment design

The participants of the fair value experiment are graduate **master students** with a major or minor in accounting that are studying at Muenster University, Germany. Additionally and in an attempt to increase the number of subjects, third-year bachelor students with a major in accounting have also been invited to take part in the experiment. This participant pool is selected for at least three reasons. First, it is mentioned in the IFRS framework that primary users of financial reporting are investors who provide risk capital to the entity (F 10). Additionally, SFAC No. 2 indicates that financial statements are intended for users who have "a reasonable understanding of business and economic activities" (*Frederickson et al.* (2006), p. 1081). Master and third-year bachelor students with a major or minor in accounting meet this criterion. This implies that the participants should have sufficient knowledge to make informed judgments and decisions within the experimental setting. Second and contrary to the first empirical study, it was decided to avoid consuming limited available analyst resources because it was of interest whether and how nonprofessional investors would react when they are confronted with fair values. This is also emphasized by the fact that standard setters have expressed an explicit interest in understanding how financial reporting standards affect the group of nonprofessional investors (*Levitt* (1998), p. 79ff.). Third, *Elliott et al.* (2007) find that second-year master students (i.e. to a large extent similar to the participants in this experiment) are suitable proxies for nonprofessional investors. This evolves them as an important constituent group for accounting standard setters and regulators (*Elliott et al.* (2007), p. 166).

The effect of fair value accounting on investors' judgments and investment decisions is examined in a **2×2 between-subject design** which indicates that the experiment faces two independent variables, which are each two-dimensional. When all combinations are realized, the experiment consists of in sum four cells. The two independent variables which are manipulated are (1) recognition vs. disclosure of fair values (**financial statement presentation**) and (2) mark-to-market vs. mark-to-model fair values (**fair value determination**). Figure 6-2 presents the experimental design and highlights the different cells including the four different treatment conditions.

Figure 6-2 shows that the experiment consists of four cells with different combinations of the two independent variables. Before the start of the experiment, each participant is allocated randomly to one of the four cells, meaning that he or she can only participate in one of the four combinations (between-subjects design). The study materials consist of three components: general instructions to the experiment, an excerpt of the annual report of a hypothetical company including a short notes section, and two question sets that are performed computer-based. The financial statement information of the hypothetical listed company **Union Estate AG** involves two year information of the balance sheet and the income statement, which is accompanied by some information from the notes. Because the experimental design is largely based on IAS 40 and this standard is especially relevant for real estate firms, Union Estate does also belong to the real estate industry. To enable a more realistic scenario, the balance sheet and the income statement are constructed in a way that the figures and ratios do largely conform to listed firms operating in the German real estate industry.[204]

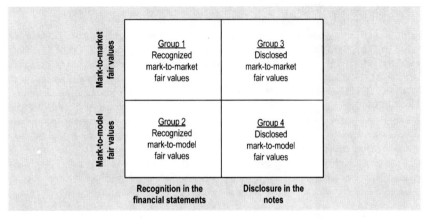

Figure 6-2: Experimental design

A **pre-test** was conducted before the regular experiment was initiated. The pre-test was necessary in order to ensure the quality of the experimental design and to assure that the experiment materials were easy to understand for the participants. The pre-test was conducted with members from the Accounting Center of Muenster University. The pre-test was conducted under real experimental conditions to prepare for the experimental sessions. The comments received after the pre-test suggested that the experiment design and the experiment materials were viewed as adequate for the analysis.[205] The results of the pre-test are not included in the experiment sample.

Participation in the experiment is voluntary and each participant receives **remuneration** as a compensation for the time and effort that he or she spends in taking part in the experiment. The remuneration depends on the performance of the participants in the experiments and ranges between 15 and 25 Euros, which is viewed as adequate for the amount of time needed for the experiment.[206] Each participant receives the same company-specific information of Union Estate which only differs in regard to the two manipulation effects. The remaining information is held constant for all participants. This means that all participants receive two year financial statements and the information that the company holds an asset with a major portion of the company's total assets. In addition, it is noted that this asset increased significantly in value compared to the prior year.

---

204 The short annual report of the company Union Estate AG (for the first group) is included in appendix C.
205 However, small changes were made to increase the understandability of the experiment materials.
206 The participants received 20 Euros on average.

The experiment manipulation is implemented as follows (see Figure 6-2):

- In the financial statements of the **first group**, the fair value is recognized in the balance sheet with all fair value gains recorded in the profit or loss for the period. This leads to a significant upward change of the carrying value of the asset and the stockholders' equity due to a larger earnings number in the income statement. In addition, participants receive the information that objective market values are available and are used for the fair value of the asset.

- The **second group** received the same financial statement figures, but finds information in the notes section that the fair value is computed on the basis of a DCF model and is additionally provided with the DCF computation and some managerial assumptions regarding interest rate, terminal values etc.

- Because fair values are only disclosed for the **third group** of participants, financial statement information differs in regard to carrying value, shareholders' equity, and earnings which are significantly lower compared to the case with recognized fair values. However, the fair values, which are disclosed in the notes, are determined mark-to-market.

- Finally, the **fourth group** receives financial statements similar to the third group, but is provided with information that the disclosed fair value amount is determined mark-to-model with the corresponding information concerning the DCF calculation.

During the experiment, the participants receive the general instructions and the company specific information in two separate envelopes. The two question sets, consisting of questions regarding the valuation task and questions concerning participants' background information, are presented on a computer screen. The participants made their inputs then solely computer-based.[207] It has to be noted that the participants are seated in a way that they cannot view other participants' screens. In a first step of the experiment, the participants are advised to read the **general instructions** of the experiment. Then, participants are instructed to study the **company specific information** regarding the Union Estate AG carefully in a way that they are able to provide a valuation for the company's stock. Thus, participants are asked to indicate a price bid for one share of Union Estate AG. Because an industry P/E ratio and the EPS figures for two fiscal years are provided as part of the bottom line of the income statement, participants should be able to compute a certain price for one share of Union Estate AG. Even if the formula for the computation is not provided, participants are under some circumstances able to compute a benchmark value for their price judgment.[208] After the participant has assessed the value of the firm, based on the information given, he or she must answer the following **key questions** (questions 1 to 4):

---

207 The software z-Tree ("Zurich Toolbox for Readymade Economic Experiments") of the University of Zurich is used for the computer-based experiment procedure. The software is freely available.

208 However, it is expected that participants significantly deviate from this value when they incorporate the additional information in the financial statements, especially when referring to the fair value information.

- In capturing the participant's **judgment** in regard to the future performance of the share, the participant must post a price bid for the share, which is the maximum amount of money he or she is willing to pay for one share upon public release of the financial information.

- Then, the participant is asked about the **confidence** that he/she places into his/her prior price judgment. The participant's level of confidence is captured by using a 7-point likert-scale, ranging from "very unconfident" to "very confident".

- The participant is then asked whether he or she would make an **investment** in the share (yes or no).

- If participants indicated "yes" for the prior question, he or she is asked about the **amount of money** that he or she is willing to invest in the company. This answer is captured on the basis of a 7-point likert-scale, ranging from "very low amount" to "very high amount".

In addition to the four key questions that have to be answered by the participants, a second set of **additional questions** is provided to the participant to accompany the judgment and investment decision on various elements. In particular, participants are asked to indicate their judgment concerning:[209]

- the company's overall financial condition (question 5),

- the volatility of Union Estate's net income (question 6),

- Union Estate's growth prospects (question 7),

- the usefulness of Union Estate's net income as a predictor of future years' net income (question 8),

- the usefulness of Union Estate's disclosure in the notes as a predictor of future years' net income (question 9),

- the risk of investing in the company (question 10),

- the potential for managerial discretion (question 11),

- the relevance of Union Estate's company information (question 12), and

- the overall reliability of Union Estate's company information (question 13).[210]

For the additional questions 5-13, participants circled a number on a likert scale ranging from 1 to 7. For questions 5, 7-9, and 12-13, a high score on the scale indicates that the variable is judged very good and a low score indicates that it is judged very poor. For questions 6 and 10-11, a high score on the scale indicates that volatility, risk, and reliability are judged very high, whereas a low score indicates that these measures are assessed very low.

Prior to the experiment procedure and in the course of the application for the experiment,[211] participants are asked for some **background information**, for example with re-

---

209 The additional questions do largely conform to the questions used by *Belzile et al.* (2006).
210 The full set of questions (in German language) is included in appendix C.

gard to their age, gender, level of education, investment experience, and attitude toward risk. The participant's attitude towards risk is addressed by presenting experimental subjects with a couple of simple choice tasks which can be used to measure the degree of risk aversion.[212] To address possible overconfidence issues,[213] three types of knowledge questions are provided where participants made judgments and indicated the confidence that they put into their judgments. Because the level of difficulty increases from question 1 (i.e. very easy to give the right answer) to question 3 (i.e. almost impossible to give the right answer), the level of overconfidence of each participant can be measured. Finally, participants are asked two questions in order to examine whether the manipulation was sufficiently effective (**manipulation checks**). Therefore, the participants are asked to indicate (by yes or no) whether the company in the experiment recognized fair values in the financial statements and whether fair values were derived from an active market.[214]

The results of the experiment are presented in the next chapter.

6.2   Results

6.2.1   Data and sample

6.2.1.1   Characteristics of the experiment participants

The experiment was conducted between May 9th and May 12th, 2011. **Four experiment sessions** were offered to the participants (one session each day). This ensured that every student with a general interest could participate in the experiment due to possible time constraints. Each day, the experiment was conducted in the evening hours to prevent possible overlapping with regular MBA or undergraduate courses. Similar day times for the experimental sessions were also chosen in order to prevent potential biases and to provide similar experimental environments for each participant. Because the experimental sessions were conducted computer-based, the computer pool of the University of Muenster was used for the four experimental sessions.

91 students participated in the experiment. This number reflects about 70% of the total participant pool, consisting of MBA students with a major or minor in accounting as well as third-year bachelor students with a major in accounting. During the time of the experiment, the participants were on average 24.97 years old (standard deviation: 1.55) and

---

211 Participants were able to apply for the experiment online. The unipark online survey system was used to implement the online application proposal. See www.unipark.info.

212 The participants are provided with ten paired lottery choices with differing expected payoffs. Whereas this approach to determine risk attitude was first used by *Binswanger* (1980) to measure the amount of risk aversion for farmers in India, the ten lottery-choices in the fair value study conform to the lottery-choices used by *Holt/Laury* (2002), p. 1645. See appendix C.

213 Overconfidence biases are viewed as a systematic overestimation of the precision of own knowledge and imply an underestimation of the variance of random variables. See *Menkhoff et al.* (2010), p. 4.

214 The original question sets (in German language) are included in appendix C.

were all enrolled in the business administration programs of the University of Muenster.[215] Figure 6-3 provides information concerning participants' sex and their program.

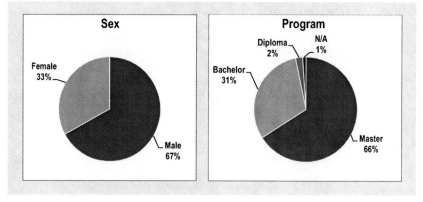

Figure 6-3: Sex and program of the experiment participants

The majority of the participants' sex is male (67%), only one third of all students doing the experiment is female (33%). It is expected that the greater share of male students corresponds to the overall majority of male students in the accounting department of the University of Muenster, whereas other departments (i.e. marketing or management) feature a greater share of female students. With a share of 66%, the majority of the students is enrolled in the **master program**, whereas only 31% of the participants are bachelor students.[216] The great share of master students is due to the original focus of the study on graduate students, from whom it is expected that they yield the best results with regard to the research question. Bachelor students have also been recruited in an attempt to increase the participant pool. However, it is expected that also bachelor students with a major in accounting yield adequate results.

Master students are, on average, enrolled in their course of study for 2.73 semesters (SD: 1.06) and do currently feature an average grade of 2.21 (SD: 0.51). Students in the bachelor program are enrolled for, on average, 5.68 semesters (SD: 1.52) and feature an average grade of 2.36 (SD: 0.46). The difference in the duration of study between master and bachelor students is due to the longer regular period of study in the bachelor program (six semesters) compared to the master program (four semesters) and due to the fact that only third-year bachelor students were asked to participate in the experiment. As master students represent the largest group among the experiment participants, their respective majors and minors are depicted in Figure 6-4.

---

215 One student indicated "Other" when he was asked for his program. However, as only students of business administration were invited to participate to the experiment, it is expected that the regarding student indicated the wrong field in this question. This has been corrected manually.

216 There are also two diploma students included in the sample. One student indicated "N/A" when asked for his or her program.

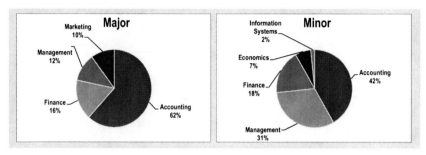

Figure 6-4: Participants' majors and minors in the master program

Master students at the University of Muenster may choose among four majors and six minors. Figure 6-4 shows that accounting is the major most frequently chosen by the experiment participants. **62%** of all master students participating in the experiment have their **major in accounting**, whereas the remaining four, finance (16%), management (12%), and marketing (10%), are not that prominent among the respondents. Even if accounting is still most frequently chosen as the minor (42%), management is also popular among the master students (31%),[217] while finance (18%), economics (7%), and information systems (2%) are less often selected.[218]

Experiment participants were also asked about the number of accounting and finance courses which they had already attended. With, on average, 7.57 (SD: 5.10) accounting courses, participants had attended significantly more accounting courses than finance courses (mean: 3.31; SD: 2.84). This finding therefore corresponds to the data provided for the selected majors and minors. Because experience besides the university can be an important influential factor when examining subjects' behavior, Figure 6-5 depicts the practical experience of the experiment participants.

In order to measure the **practical experience** of the experiment participants, students were first asked whether they had received any kind of vocational training prior to the beginning of their master or bachelor courses at the university. The results show that 30% of the participants had received such training, whereas the majority had gone to university right after completing their A-levels. Second, participants were asked about their professional experience in the field of business studies, including not only vocational training, but also working as an intern or student trainee. Most of the students indicated that they have between one and two years of professional experience (55%), whereas one third (34%) answered that they have at least three years of professional experience (probably coupled with vocational training). Only 11% of the participants have less than one year of professional experience.

---

217 The 31% of the participants' minor reported here for "management" also includes the minor "hospital management".

218 Even if only master students with a major or minor in accounting have been invited for the experiment, there are also eight master students included with majors and minors different from accounting. These observations are not excluded to increase the sample size and to maintain similar group sizes.

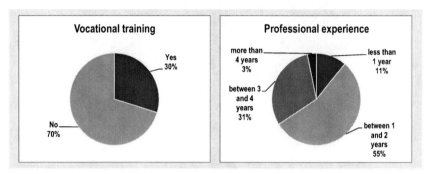

Figure 6-5: Practical experience of the experiment participants

Examining **investment experience**, the participants were asked whether they had already invested in bonds (i.e. corporate or government bonds) and shares on the stock exchange. Even if the subjects were asked separately for bonds and shares, the results for the two questions are the same with 55% of the respondents having investment experience with both bonds and shares. Because there is variation of the responses for bonds and shares in the full dataset (i.e. not every participant with investment experience in bonds has also investment experience in shares and vice versa), this coincidence can be interpreted as random. Additionally, the participants' own assessment concerning their investment experience and risk attitude was of interest. Figure 6-6 presents the results.

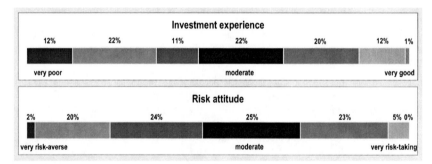

Figure 6-6: Investment experience and risk attitude of the experiment participants

On a 7-point likert-scale, participants were asked to assess their own investment experience, ranging from 1 (= "very poor") to 7 (= "very good"). The mean over all participants is 3.56, thus indicating that participants have on average less than moderate (4) experience with investing. While 12% indicated that they only have very poor investment experience, one participant (1%) assessed his own investment experience as "very good". Referring to participants risk attitude, participants are on average more risk-averse than risk-taking (mean: 3.64). However, the majority of participants assessed their own attitude towards risk as more or less moderate. In addition to their own attitude towards risk, participants were also asked to make a **fictitious investment decision**. Thus, they were informed that they received 50,000 Euros and should decide about which percentage of the total amount they would like to invest in shares on the stock exchange (i.e. the risky investment) or, alternatively, in a fixed income investment based on the EURIBOR interest rate (i.e. the risk-free investment). Figure 6-7 presents the results.

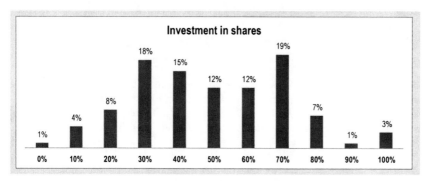

Figure 6-7: Risk attitude based on investment decision of the experiment participants

The results for this question support the findings on the basis of the participant's self-assessment of risk attitude. Figure 6-7 provides evidence that participants' risk attitude is on average **moderate**. Over three quarters (76%) of all subjects intend to invest between 30% and 70% of the 50,000 Euros in shares. Only a minority of the respondents intends to underweight or overweight shares or fixed income investments.

Another instrument to indirectly measure the participants' attitude towards risk is to present experiment subjects with a couple of simple choice tasks, such as a modest **lottery**. To measure the degree of risk aversion, the approach developed by *Holt/Laury* (2002) is used where participants are provided ten times with two hypothetical lotteries, resulting in a 20 Euros or 16 Euros payoff in lottery X and a 38.50 Euros and 1 Euro payoff in lottery Y. The probability of the payoffs changes in the course of the lottery. Whereas the higher payoff is less probable at the beginning of the lottery, this situation changes with the higher payoff being more probable at the end of the lottery. Risk-averse participants are expected to choose lottery X in the first four rounds before they select lottery Y in the remaining six rounds. *Holt/Laury* (2002) develop a classification into risk classes which is based on the number of choices for lottery X (which represent the "safe choices"). The regarding results for the experiment in this study are presented in Table 6-1.

The analysis supports the prior findings regarding risk attitude and provides evidence that the subjects in the sample exhibit a **tendency to moderate risk aversion**. However, the results of the lottery also provide evidence that the participants are more risk averse than risk loving, even if 21% of all participants are exactly risk neutral and some respondents are classified as (very) risk loving. The mean of 5.62 also indicates a slight tendency upon risk aversion. 4% of the participants are classified into the highest risk aversion category with at least nine safe choices.

Number of safe choices	Risk preference classification	Proportion of participants
0-1	highly risk loving	0%
2	very risk loving	2%
3	risk loving	4%
4	risk neutral	21%
5	slightly risk averse	23%
6	risk averse	24%
7	very risk averse	10%
8	highly risk averse	11%
9-10	stay in bed	4%

Table 6-1: Participants' risk-aversion classification based on lottery choices

The questions measuring the level of **overconfidence** are included in appendix C. Prior research demonstrated that people are often more confident in their judgments that is warranted by the facts (*Griffin/Tversky* (1992), p. 411). Therefore, controlling for over-confidence biases is important to rule out the possibility that differences in the participants' self-confidence in decision-making significantly influence the results. Participants were asked three questions with an increasing level of difficulty. While the first question is very easy to answer, it is expected that the last question is almost impossible to be answered correctly with general knowledge. Each of the three questions is accompanied by an additional question where participants could indicate the confidence that they put into their judgment, ranging on a scale from 1 ("I could also toss a coin") to 7 ("I am sure as hell"). As expected, the percentage of right answers is significantly lower for questions 2 and 3 than for question 1. Whereas 89% of all participants answered question 1 correctly, only 40% and 52% responded correctly to questions 2 and 3, respectively. The finding that question 3 is more frequently answered correctly than question 2 is somewhat surprising, as it was expected that question 3 is more challenging for the participants. However, participants may have viewed both questions as equally difficult, thus resulting in a random choice for questions 2 and 3. The results for the confidence that the respondents place into their judgments on the three questions are visualized in Figure 6-8.

The analysis of confidence supports the results obtained from the right or wrong answers for the questions. Whereas more than 30% of the participants are "sure as hell" that they gave the right answer to question 1 (mean: 5.36), confidence on questions 2 and 3 is markedly lower (means of 1.29 and 1.14). For both questions 2 and 3, the respondents agree that they would rather toss a coin than giving the correct answer with both lines running in parallel. There is thus evidence that participants did indeed view the two questions as **equally difficult** and place only little confidence into their judgments, thus resulting in a sharp increase of the lines for question 2 and 3 above 80% when indicating "toss a coin". Based on these results, an overconfidence bias cannot be confirmed for the overall sample. As the trend for the more difficult questions 2 and 3 is rather different from the trend for question 1, participants are, on average, not overconfident with regard to their judgments.

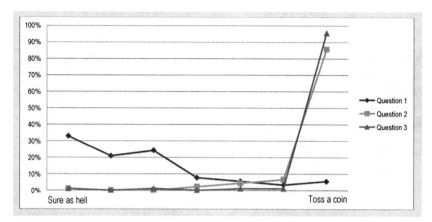

Figure 6-8: Confidence placed into knowledge questions

6.2.1.2 Preliminary checks

Before the results of the experiment can be presented and interpreted, it is important to perform several preliminary checks. These checks intend to corroborate the quality of the experiment procedure in a way to ensure that the participants understood the treatments through manipulation checks (chapter 6.2.1.2.1). Additionally, the validity of the results can be increased through an effective dealing with confounding factors, which is achieved through a random allocation of the participants to the treatments (chapter 6.2.1.2.2).

6.2.1.2.1 Manipulation checks

Manipulation checks measure the perception of manipulation of the independent variables (*Stangor* (2011), p. 238). They test whether the **variation** in the independent variables is included in the dataset as it was intended by the research design (*Webster/Sell* (2007), p. 129). In other words, manipulation checks assess whether the experiment participants understood the manipulation of the variables in a way that variation among groups can be traced back solely to the manipulation. Otherwise, differences among groups would be due to coincidences when participants did not make notice of the manipulation and viewed the different circumstances as equal.

The experimental questions contained **two manipulation check questions**. The first question pertained to the reporting environment for fair values. It was asked whether the Union Estate AG measures its portfolio at fair value or at historical cost (i.e. where the fair value was only disclosed in the notes). The second question addresses the kind of fair value determination as it was asked whether the fair value was determined mark-to-market (i.e. derived from an active market, Level 1) or mark-to-model on the basis of a DCF model (Level 3). The results for the manipulation checks are stated in Table 6-2. Whereas the first two rows of the table (Panel A) depict the percentage of correct answers with regard to the manipulation checks, the second part (Panel B) of the table refers to the combination of the two manipulation checks pertaining to each treatment group.

Panel A: Overall manipulation checks per question	Percentage of correct answers
Manipulation check 1 (fair value vs. historical cost)	100%
Manipulation check 2 (mark-to-market vs. mark-to-model)	93%
Panel B: Combination of manipulation checks per group	**Percentage of correct answers**
Group 1 (recognized mark-to-market fair values)	91%
Group 2 (recognized mark-to-model fair values)	57%
Group 3 (disclosed mark-to-market fair values)	87%
Group 4 (disclosed mark-to-model fair values)	73%

Table 6-2: Results for the manipulation checks

The results presented in Table 6-2 provide evidence that the different treatments resulted in significantly **different responses** to the manipulation checks. While the first question is answered correctly by all participants in the sample, the second question is answered by the vast majority of 93%. This difference indicates that experiment participants found it slightly more challenging to detect the variation of the fair value determination (mark-to-market vs. mark-to-model) than the kind of measurement of the (fair value vs. historical cost). Referring to the combination of manipulation checks per group, the percentage of correct answers corresponds to the participants that answered both questions of their respective treatment correctly. Similar to the analysis for the overall manipulation checks, the results show that participants face greater problems to detect the variation in fair value measurement. Whereas Groups 1 and 3 provide correct answers in 91% and 87% of all cases, Groups 2 and 4 have significantly lower percentages of correct answers. Especially the finding for Group 2 with the combination of model-based and recognized fair values is striking as there are only 57% of correct answers. This should be kept in mind when the results for each group are interpreted. However, the data suggests that the experiment participants did on average understand the two manipulations in the study.[219]

6.2.1.2.2   Allocation of the participants to the treatments

As described in chapter 6.1.2.3, the approach of randomization is used to control for subject's biases and address possible issues of confounding. Therefore, the students with an interest to take part in the experiment have been allocated randomly to the four treatments or groups. In order to ensure the validity of the experimental results, it is necessary to examine the success of the random allocation, thus comparing the mean values of participant's characteristics per group. Table 6-3 presents the results for group-wise comparisons of the means for several demographic and educational characteristics of the participants.

---

219   To increase the confidence in empirical evidence, the regression analyses in chapter 6.2.3 are performed with the total sample as well as with the reduced sample, where all participants with false manipulation checks are removed. The results for the reduced sample regression analyses are provided in appendix B.

Participants' characteristics	Group 1 (N = 23)	Group 2 (N = 23)	Group 3 (N = 23)	Group 4 (N = 22)	Total (N = 91)
Current age	25.30 ** (-2.22)	25.17 (-1.54)	24.22 *** (3.48)	24.82 (0.31)	24.97
% of male participants	73.91% (-1.41)	65.22% (0.41)	65.22% (0.41)	63.64% (0.61)	67.00%
% of master students	52.17% *** (2.79)	60.87% (0.99)	65.22% (0.19)	86.36% *** (-4.02)	65.93%
Number of semesters	4.96 *** (-4.10)	4.22 (-1.11)	3.65 (1.19)	2.91 *** (4.18)	3.95
Current grade	2.34 (-1.44)	2.19 (1.45)	2.48 *** (-4.14)	2.04 *** (4.34)	2.27
% of master students with major accounting	66.67% (-0.84)	57.14% (0.74)	80.00% *** (-2.90)	47.37% ** (2.32)	61.67%
% of master students with minor accounting	41.67% (-0.05)	50.00% (-1.30)	40.00% (0.26)	36.84% (0.73)	41.67%
% of participants with vocational training	39.13% * (-1.94)	26.09% (0.76)	30.43% (-0.07)	22.73% (1.39)	29.67%
Years of professional experience	2.09 * (-1.69)	1.78 (0.56)	1.70 (1.14)	1.86 (-0.02)	1.86
Number of accounting courses	8.83 ** (-2.36)	7.65 (-0.15)	7.09 (0.90)	6.68 * (1.67)	7.57
Number of finance courses	2.91 (1.34)	3.00 (1.04)	3.74 (-1.46)	3.59 (-0.95)	3.31

The table provides mean values, parametric t-statistics in brackets (two-sided) and significance indicators, where *, **, and *** indicate significance at the 10%, 5%, and 1% levels, respectively. The t-values and the tests for significance are determined on the basis of comparisons of group-wise mean values with the overall mean value in the total sample.

Table 6-3: Demographic and educational characteristics per group

The number of experiment participants is almost equally distributed among the four treatments with Groups 1-3 each comprising 23 participants, whereas the fourth group has 22 participants. The results in Table 6-3 demonstrate that the process of randomizing was **successful** in three aspects of demographic and educational characteristics (sex, % of master students, number of finance courses) in a way that no group value significantly deviates from the overall mean. In addition, the second treatment group does not face significant values in any of the categories, thus suggesting that participants of Group 2 are closest to the overall mean.

The remaining categories and groups face some significant values, highlighting the fact that random allocation might not produce groups that are always **equal in every respect**. While Group 3 faces significance in three categories, Groups 4 and 1 deviate significantly from the overall mean in 5 and 6 cases, respectively. Based on the findings, it can be hypothesized that the first group includes, on average, older students in higher semesters with a greater percentage of students with vocational training and professional experience. Whereas students of the first group also attended the largest number of accounting cours- es, the number of master students in the first group is below average. When these findings hold for the first group, it could be said that the fourth group functions as the opposite with the largest share of master students and lowest number of accounting courses. This can be explained by the fact that only 47.37% of all master students in Group 4 have their major in accounting (compared to two third of the master students in Group 1), thus re- sulting in a lower number of accounting courses. Compared to Group 1 and 4, the re- maining Groups 2-3 are closer to the overall means.

Table 6-4 provides group-wise comparisons for the investment, risk, and confidence char- acteristics per group.

Participants' characteristics	Group 1 (N = 23)	Group 2 (N = 23)	Group 3 (N = 23)	Group 4 (N = 22)	Total (N = 91)
% of participants that invested in bonds	52.17% (0.56)	56.52% (-0.39)	69.57% *** (-2.87)	40.91% *** (2.66)	54.95%
% of participants that invested in shares	69.57% *** (-2.87)	47.83% (1.32)	56.52% (-0.39)	45.45% * (1.90)	54.95%
Participants' investment experience	4.00 ** (-2.56)	3.35 (1.22)	3.48 (0.47)	3.41 (0.87)	3.56
Participants' risk attitude	3.83 (-1.47)	3.39 * (1.89)	3.96 ** (-2.46)	3.36 ** (2.11)	3.64
Amount invested in shares rather than EURIBOR	58.26% *** (-3.79)	45.65% (1.57)	50.87% (-0.65)	42.27% *** (3.00)	49.34%
Number of safe choices in the lottery	5.91 * (-1.67)	5.17 ** (2.51)	5.57 (0.27)	5.82 (-1.15)	5.62
Confidence for question 1	5.96 *** (-3.35)	5.17 (1.08)	5.13 (1.30)	5.18 (1.02)	5.36
Confidence for question 2	1.26 (0.28)	1.04 *** (2.69)	1.57 *** (-3.11)	1.27 (0.17)	1.29
Confidence for question 3	1.26 (-1.43)	1.00 * (1.74)	1.13 (0.16)	1.18 (-0.45)	1.14
T-values are stated in brackets. *, **, and *** indicate significance at the 10%, 5%, and 1% levels (two-sided).					

Table 6-4: Investment, risk and confidence characteristics per group

There is no aspect of investment, risk or confidence that is equally distributed among all treatments. Similar to the results for the demographic and educational variables, the first group does significantly deviate from the overall mean in the greatest number of catego- ries, thus supporting the prior findings. However, the majority of the values included in Table 6-4 as well as the values included in Table 6-3 are not significantly different from the mean.

Taken together, the analysis in this chapter supports the argument that **random allocation** was to a great extent successful and that a possible confounding due to subject's biases can be excluded. However, there are still some cases where the mean group values significantly deviate from the overall mean. This fact should be kept in mind when interpreting the results.

6.2.2 Descriptive statistics and correlation analysis

The previous chapter analyses participants' characteristics in order to address concerns of possible confounding. The quality of the results is increased when the participants' characteristics are distributed equally across the treatments, which is achieved through random allocation. The descriptive and univariate analysis in this chapter focuses on the **variation of the test variables** (dependent variables). Whereas it was of interest that there is no difference between participants' characteristics among groups, it is expected that the manipulation causes significant changes in the test variables. The following two chapters present descriptive statistics and the results of univariate comparisons of the four key measures (6.2.2.1) and the additional questions (6.2.2.2).

6.2.2.1 Descriptive statistics for the dependent variables

Table 6-5 presents the results for univariate comparisons between groups for the first dependent variable which refers to a **price bid** for one share of Union Estate AG. Because it is in the focus of the first hypothesis of the experimental study, Panel C reports Levene's test statistics for pair-wise tests of variance equality. Tests of variances are only provided for the first key measure "price bid", because the focus of the remaining test variables is on the comparisons of the mean values and not of the variances.

The price judgments of participants included in Group 1 (mean: 24.00) are significantly higher than the price judgments of the remaining groups, thus suggesting that participants view a company's performance as better when fair values are **recognized and determined mark-to-market**. This difference is significant at the 5% and 10% level when compared to the Groups 2 (p-value: 0.0367) and 3 (p-value: 0.0583), respectively. The fact that a difference is only detected in the case of recognized Level 1 fair values might be due to participants who viewed these values as more reliable, resulting in higher price bids. The standard deviations per group point to almost equal values in Groups 2 and 4 (i.e. mark-to-model fair values are not interpreted differently whether they are recognized or disclosed). On the other hand, there is an increase reported for the standard deviation in Group 3. The highest value reported for Group 3 (4.9893) might result from a greater degree of uncertainty associated with the disclosure of a fair value (and with the recognition of historical cost). However, Levene's test for equality of variances does not report significance for differences of standard deviations between groups.

Panel A: Price bid for one share – mean and [standard deviation]			
Fair value determination	Recognition	Fair value presentation Disclosure	Row data
Mark-to-market	Group 1 24.00 [3.3439]	Group 3 21.57 [4.9893]	22.78 [4.3284]
Mark-to-model	Group 2 21.96 [3.0819]	Group 4 21.50 [3.0519]	21.73 [3.0067]
Column data	22.98 [3.3067]	21.53 [4.0639]	

Panel B: Tests of means		
Comparison	t-statistic	p-value
Recognition vs. disclosure (mark-to-market)	1.9441	0.0583
Recognition vs. disclosure (mark-to-model)	0.4991	0.6202
Mark-to-market vs. mark-to-model (recognition)	2.1551	0.0367
Mark-to-market vs. mark-to-model (disclosure)	0.0526	0.9583

Panel C: Tests of variances		
Comparison	Levene's test statistic	p-value
Recognition vs. disclosure (mark-to-market)	0.0010	0.9749
Recognition vs. disclosure (mark-to-model)	0.2186	0.6425
Mark-to-market vs. mark-to-model (recognition)	2.2188	0.1435
Mark-to-market vs. mark-to-model (disclosure)	0.3810	0.5403

Panel A provides mean values and standard deviations (stated in brackets) for each group, accompanied by row and column data. Panel B depicts t-statistics and p-values for pair-wise group comparisons. Panel C reports Levene's statistics for pair-wise tests of variance equality, which are also supplemented by p-values to indicate significance.

Table 6-5: Descriptive statistics for share price judgment

Table 6-6 reports the results for the question focusing on the **confidence** that participants place into their price judgments.[220]

Referring to Panel A of Table 6-6, the confidence placed into the price judgment is, on average, higher on the basis of market values than on the basis of model-based fair values in both the recognition and disclosure case. This finding seems comprehensible when it is expected that not much confidence is put into decisions which are based on **subjective model-based fair values**. The higher mean value for mark-to-market fair values is also reflected in Panel B which presents pair-wise indicators of significance. However, a significant difference (on the 10% level) is only reported in the disclosure case for the group-wise comparison of Group 3 and Group 4 (p-value: 0.0772). This suggests that the implications of market values are greatest when historical costs are recognized with fair values only disclosed in the notes and implies that participants view historical costs as more reliable measures.

---

220 The participants made their judgment on a 7-point likert-scale where higher values represented a greater degree of confidence.

Panel A: Confidence placed into price judgment – mean and [standard deviation]			
Fair value determination	**Recognition**	**Fair value presentation** **Disclosure**	**Row data**
Mark-to-market	Group 1 3.91 [1.4114]	Group 3 4.26 [1.3218]	4.09 [1.3634]
Mark-to-model	Group 2 3.39 [1.3731]	Group 4 3.45 [1.6541]	3.42 [1.4998]
Column data	3.65 [1.4019]	3.87 [1.5315]	

Panel B: Tests of means		
Comparison	**t-statistic**	**p-value**
Recognition vs. disclosure (mark-to-market)	-0.8627	0.3930
Recognition vs. disclosure (mark-to-model)	-0.1398	0.8895
Mark-to-market vs. mark-to-model (recognition)	1.2707	0.2105
Mark-to-market vs. mark-to-model (disclosure)	1.8106	0.0772

Panel A provides mean values and standard deviations (stated in brackets) for each group, accompanied by row and column data. Panel B depicts t-statistics and p-values for pair-wise group comparisons.

Table 6-6: Descriptive Statistics for confidence placed into price judgment

Table 6-7 depicts the results for participants' **investment decision**, i.e. whether participants would either invest in shares of Union Estate AG or not.[221] This represents a major difference to the prior key measures as it is now asked for a particular investment decision rather than a judgment.

Similar to the prior measure with the confidence that is placed into a judgment, the greatest mean value is again reported for Group 3 (0.65), thus suggesting that 65% of all participants would make an investment in shares of Union Estate AG. Whereas the majority of participants would generally invest in shares over all treatments, the lowest value is reported for Group 4 (0.55). Participants exposed to the treatments 1 and 2 conform in their investment decision (0.61). Even if there are differences reported between the mean values, Panel B makes clear that these differences are **not significant**. Thus, fair value determination and its presentation in the financial statements are not associated with changes in investment decisions.

---

221 Participants could either indicate "yes" or "no", resulting in values of either 1 or 0.

Panel A: Investment decision (yes = 1; no = 0) – mean and [standard deviation]			
Fair value determination	Recognition	Fair value presentation Disclosure	Row data
Mark-to-market	Group 1 0.61 [0.4990]	Group 3 0.65 [0.4870]	0.63 [0.4880]
Mark-to-model	Group 2 0.61 [0.4990]	Group 4 0.55 [0.5096]	0.58 [0.4995]
Column data	0.61 [0.4934]	0.60 [0.4954]	

Panel B: Tests of means		
Comparison	t-statistic	p-value
Recognition vs. disclosure (mark-to-market)	-0.2990	0.7663
Recognition vs. disclosure (mark-to-model)	0.4206	0.6762
Mark-to-market vs. mark-to-model (recognition)	0.0000	1.0000
Mark-to-market vs. mark-to-model (disclosure)	0.7183	0.4764

Panel A provides mean values and standard deviations (stated in brackets) for each group, accompanied by row and column data. Panel B depicts t-statistics and p-values for pair-wise group comparisons.

Table 6-7: Descriptive statistics for investment decision

Table 6-8 presents the results for the **amount** that participants are willing to invest in shares of Union Estate AG. Because it is of interest to further examine participants' investment behavior when they are in general willing to buy shares of the company, this measure is collected as an add-on to the prior key measure. Only participants who indicated "yes" in the prior question were able to answer this question. The remaining experiment participants skipped this question. Thus, the results depicted in Table 6-8 are based on a reduced sample of subjects.[222] Participants indicated their decision on a 7-point likert-scale ranging from 1 ("very low amount") to 7 ("very high amount").

The results presented in Table 6-8, Panel A, indicate that subjects of Group 1 are, on average, willing to invest the greatest amount into the company (mean: 3.50), thus suggesting that recognized mark-to-market fair values provide participants with the best environment to making good investments. On the other hand, the lowest value for the invested amount is reported for the case when mark-to-market fair values are only disclosed (2.80). However, the t-statistics and p-values reported in Panel B do not report significance for any of the group-wise comparisons. According to this, the results for the amount that participants are willing to invest are not different to the finding for the investment decision in general. Thus, fair value accounting (i.e. fair value presentation and determination process) seems to have **no significant association** with participants' investment decision.

---

222 A total number of 55 participants indicated that they would generally invest in the company.

Panel A: Amount to be invested in the company – mean and [standard deviation]			
Fair value determination	**Recognition**	**Fair value presentation Disclosure**	**Row data**
Mark-to-market	Group 1 3.50 [1.1602]	Group 3 2.80 [1.2071]	3.13 [1.1955]
Mark-to-model	Group 2 3.07 [1.7305]	Group 4 3.17 [1.1146]	3.12 [1.4231]
Column data	3.28 [1.4357]	3.96 [1.1379]	

Panel B: Tests of means		
Comparison	**t-statistic**	**p-value**
Recognition vs. disclosure (mark-to-market)	1.5899	0.1235
Recognition vs. disclosure (mark-to-model)	-0.1635	0.8715
Mark-to-market vs. mark-to-model (recognition)	0.7697	0.4484
Mark-to-market vs. mark-to-model (disclosure)	0.8110	0.4250

Panel A provides mean values and standard deviations (stated in brackets) for each group, accompanied by row and column data. Panel B depicts t-statistics and p-values for pair-wise group comparisons.

Table 6-8: Descriptive statistics for the amount to be invested

However, it must be noted that univariate comparisons only provide **limited evidence** as they do not incorporate further measures with a possible influence on the test variables. Variations of the test variables may be due to overlapping effects or may be caused by participant's characteristics. Therefore, it is expected that multivariate regression analyses provide more adequate results through the synchronous consideration of such factors. Additionally, regression analyses are able to examine the specific influence of single variables on the variation of a certain dependent variable which is the central question of experimental research.[223]

6.2.2.2 Descriptive statistics for the independent variables

Table 6-9 presents the group-wise and overall results for the independent variables. The questions refer to several questions regarding the financial condition of the firm, such as i.e. growth prospects or the usefulness of different parts of the financial statements to assess net income. Because it is expected that participants' response differ significantly between groups, it is important to incorporate these measures into the analysis. Subjects made their responses on a 7-point likert-scale.

---

223 For the results of the regression analyses see chapter 6.2.3.

Participants' assessment	Group 1 (N = 23)	Group 2 (N = 23)	Group 3 (N = 23)	Group 4 (N = 22)	Total (N = 91)
Company's overall financial condition	5.78 *** (-3.21)	5.35 (0.84)	5.13 *** (2.91)	5.50 (-0.57)	5.44
Volatility of company's net income	4.96 *** (-2.67)	4.09 *** (2.32)	5.39 *** (-5.14)	3.50 *** (5.71)	4.49
Company's growth prospects	4.17 *** (2.88)	5.00 *** (-3.42)	4.61 (-0.46)	4.41 (1.06)	4.55
Usefulness of net income as predictor of future net income	3.43 * (1.94)	3.87 (-0.95)	3.57 (1.02)	4.05 ** (-2.13)	3.73
Usefulness of notes disclosures as predictor of future net income	4.09 (-0.08)	4.22 (-0.82)	4.00 (0.44)	4.00 (0.44)	4.08
Risk of investing in the company	3.52 (0.65)	3.48 (0.92)	4.22 *** (-4.11)	3.23 *** (2.62)	3.62
Potential for managerial discretion	5.26 *** (-3.05)	4.22 *** (2.88)	5.57 *** (-4.81)	3.82 *** (5.16)	4.73
Relevance of company information	5.13 (-1.34)	5.13 (-1.34)	4.70 * (1.97)	4.86 (0.74)	4.96
Reliability of company information	4.04 *** (3.45)	5.00 *** (-3.20)	4.39 (1.03)	4.73 (-1.33)	4.54

T-values are stated in brackets. *, **, and *** indicate significance at the 10%, 5%, and 1% levels (two-sided).

Table 6-9: Participants' assessments for the independent variables

With an average mean value of 5.44, the **company's overall financial condition** is ranked as favorable by the participants. While the values for Group 2 and 4 do not significantly differ from the overall mean, the results for Group 1 (Group 3) indicate an above average (below average) value, which is significant. Thus, recognized mark-to-market fair values cause the assessment of the financial condition to be significantly increased compared to the case where these values are only disclosed (with recognized historical cost instead). When asked for the **volatility of the company's net income**, results indicate that the manipulation caused significant differences for all treatments. The cases with mark-to-market fair values, no matter whether these values are recognized or disclosed, lead to a significantly increased assessment of volatility, whereas model-based fair values cause a decrease. This finding suggests that participants view the net income as less sensitive to DCF calculations than to objective market values, probably due to an increased implied volatility of market value changes. This assumption is also supported by the fact that the American and European debt crisis caused an increase in the overall volatility on the stock exchanges. Even if the participants were told at the beginning of the experiment that they should make their assessments without taking into account such developments, a certain influence cannot be excluded. Concerning the **company's growth prospects**, significant differences of the group means from the overall means are reported for the first two groups, whereas there is no significant deviation in the remaining two groups. However, the fact that significance is only reported when fair values are recognized advocates for the assumption that the financial statement presentation format has a stronger influence on participants than the way of how fair values are determined.

Because it is expected that differences in the presentation format and fair value determination affect participants' assessment of the usefulness of financial statements as a predictor for future income, two questions were implemented to analyze the direction and strength of the manipulation. The first question concerns the **usefulness of net income as predictor of future net income**. While there is only a slight significance (10% level) reported for Group 1 (below average), usefulness is assessed significantly highest of participants in Group 4. Thus, usefulness is increased when historical costs are applied and fair values are only disclosed in the notes. This finding ties nicely into the expectation as it is anticipated that participants may forecast historical cost more easily than market values (probably due to increased volatility).[224] The second question in this field refers to the **usefulness of notes disclosures as predictor of future net income**. The way of fair value determination and the financial statement presentation format was specified in the notes of Union Estate AG. Contrary to the prior findings, there is no significant difference among groups, thus suggesting that the manipulation is not reflected in participants' assessment of notes' usefulness. This finding corroborates with the expectation that the notes are not viewed as equally important as quantitative financial statement data and are, by some investors (as represented by the experiment participants), not taken into account at all.

Referring to the **risk of investing in the company**, participants of Group 3 (disclosed mark-to-market fair values) assess the investment risk as significantly greatest (1% level). Therefore, it is assumed that participants find it challenging to deal with mark-to-market fair values, when these values are only disclosed. However, that finding conforms to the assumption that nonprofessional investors view disclosed information as less reliable compared to information that is recognized (*Frederickson et al.* (2006), p. 1077). As a result, participants assess the investment risk as significantly higher when information is only disclosed. The experiment manipulations cause great variation in participants' assessment of Union Estate's **potential for managerial discretion**. Contrary to the expectation that market values are superior, participants view mark-to-market accounting as containing a greater risk of managerial discretion than mark-to-model accounting, indicated by significantly greater values for the Groups 1 and 3. Managerial discretion seems not to be of such a great issue when model-based fair values are applied. This somewhat surprising finding is not in line with the assumption that market values are free from managerial discretion, while DCF calculations are highly subjective. However, this issue needs further consideration in the course of multivariate regression analyses.

Finally, two questions were included to gain insights into the degree of relevance and reliability that participants assign to the financial statements which are subject to the experiment manipulations. When asked for the **relevance of company information**, the responses indicate that the manipulations did not cause relevance assessments to significant-

---

224 This assumption is also corroborated by the findings of the archival study with financial analysts. See chapter 5.2.3.1.

ly differ from the overall mean. However, a slight and positive significance (10% level) is documented for Group 3, suggesting that mark-to-market disclosure, holding all else equal, provides greatest relevance. The question concerning the **reliability of company information** is to some extend related with the potential for managerial discretion. Responses indicate significance only for the recognition case (on the 1% level). Similar to managerial discretion, participants view mark-to-model accounting significantly more reliable than mark-to-market accounting. This finding does not conform to intuition. However, it could be due to the way in which the DCF calculation for the determination of the mark-to-model fair values has been presented in experiment materials. The detailed information provided could have been viewed as reliable of the experiment participants.

6.2.2.3   Correlation analysis for the independent variables

Before several regression analyses and empirical findings are presented in chapter 6.2.3, correlations between the independent variables are provided. The **pair-wise correlations** are presented in Table 6-10. The correlation analysis is not only helpful in a way that the results provide information with regard to the association of the different measures. It is also necessary to omit possible multicollinearity in the course of the later multivariate regression analysis.

	Fin. Cond.	Volati- lity	Growth	Net Income	Notes	Risk	Discre- tion	Rele- vance	Reliab- ility
Fin. Cond.		-0.2162	0.1309	0.2262	0.0457	-0.4732	-0.0459	0.2814	0.2426
Volati- lity	-0.1694		-0.1313	-0.2512	-0.1668	0.4440	0.1931	0.0053	-0.1904
Growth	0.1784	-0.1347		0.0105	0.0858	-0.1746	-0.2335	0.0514	0.1544
Net Income	0.2517	-0.2510	0.0385		0.2389	-0.3626	-0.1501	0.3144	0.3523
Notes	0.0021	-0.1543	0.0897	0.1923		-0.1300	0.0556	0.3151	0.1468
Risk	-0.4236	0.4462	-0.1949	-0.3505	-0.1099		0.1294	-0.3487	-0.3571
Discre- tion	-0.0475	0.2336	-0.2736	-0.1607	0.0355	0.1520		0.1668	-0.2485
Rele- vance	0.3169	-0.0131	0.0340	0.2871	0.3152	-0.3138	-0.1837		0.3858
Reliab- ility	0.2809	-0.2012	0.1319	0.3234	0.1173	-0.3715	-0.2433	0.3632	

Pearson coefficients are provided in the upper right of the table, Spearman coefficients are depicted in the lower left. Significant correlation coefficients (at the 5% level or better) are stated in italics.

Table 6-10: Correlations between the independent variables

Table 6-10 shows that over half of the coefficients are significant at least at the 5% level. The relatively low values for both Pearson and Spearman coefficients indicate that there is only a **low correlation** between the variables. However, the highest correlations are reported for the variable risk, which is significantly negatively related to the overall financial condition of the company (Pearson: -0.4732; Spearman: -0.4236) and positively associated with the volatility of the company's net income (Pearson: 0.4440; Spearman: 0.4462). This finding is intuitively comprehensible when it is assumed that a better financial condition corresponds to a lower assessment of risk and that higher volatility causes an increase in risk.

Because the correlation analysis only reveals a relatively low association between the variables (with only a few coefficients above 0.4), a synchronous inclusion of the variables into regression analyses is not expected to cause biased results due to multicollinearity. The results for the regression analyses are presented in the next chapter.

6.2.3 Regression analyses and findings

The empirical analysis in this chapter is conducted on the basis of multivariate regression analyses using **ordinary least squares** (OLS). The regression analysis enables an examination of the effects of several independent variables on one dependent variable. The variation of the dependent variable is explained by variations of the independent variables. Thus, regression analyses provide a great opportunity to analyze the association of the experiment manipulations as independent variables on the four key measures serving as the basis for the hypotheses. In general, the regression analyses conducted in this chapter do not materially differ from the analyses performed in order to investigate financial analysts' forecasting behavior in chapter 5.2.3.[225]

OLS regression analyses assume a normal distribution of all variables included in the model. Because not all variables included in the model are normally distributed, a regression analysis based on OLS might provide biased estimators. Even if it could be argued on the basis of the *central limit theorem* that a sufficiently large number of observations helps in mitigating this bias (*Downing/Clark* (2010), p. 198), concerns regarding the reliability of the results remain. Therefore, the results of **rank regressions** are additionally provided to support the OLS results as transformed rank data avoids the skewness of the regular data.[226] In addition, the dataset is controlled for multicollinearity. However, the **variance inflation factors** do not indicate that multicollinearity is an issue in the sample.[227] **White's test** does not provide evidence for heteroscedasticity, thus making it not necessary to perform weighted least squares regressions (WLS) with the variables responsible for

---

225 As the general approach is very similar, the same assumptions when performing OLS regressions do also apply in this chapter. For a detailed description of the assumptions see chapter 5.1.1.1.

226 Performing rank regressions, the dataset is first transformed into ranks. Second, the OLS regression is re-run with the transformed data.

227 The VIFs of the OLS regressions in this chapter are all below a value of 3. Thus, multicollinearity is not present in the dataset.

the multicollinearity bias.[228] In every regression computed, the **Durbin-Watson statistic** does not detect autocorrelation of the confounding factors. Therefore, it is not expected that the regression estimators are biased due to auto correlated confounding factors.

The following three sub-chapters examine the association of the independent variables (experiment manipulations) with the dependent variables (key measures). The two experiment manipulations function as test variables and are included as dummy/indicator variables. First, it is indicated whether fair values are recognized (value "1") or disclosed (value "0"). Second, it is indicated whether fair values are determined mark-to-market (value "1") or mark-to-model (value "0"). In addition to the two test variables, the additional measures are included as independent variables to investigate the effects of various participants' assessments on the dependent variables. The association between fair value accounting and participants' dispersion of individual share price judgments is examined in chapter 6.2.3.1. Chapter 6.2.3.2 presents the results for the confidence that participants place into their price judgment and chapter 6.2.3.3 reports the outcomes for participants' investment decision.

6.2.3.1   Fair value accounting and participants' dispersion of share price judgments

The two hypotheses H_{4a} and H_{4b} for the experimental study concern the dispersion of participants' share price judgments. To provide empirical evidence on this issue, the dependent variable **price deviation** (PRICE_DEV) is the standardized absolute value for the share price judgment of each participant. A standardization of the values reduces skewness and better enables comparisons between groups. The variable is standardized on the basis of group-wise means and standard deviations. Because the variable is computed in this way, greater values for PRICE_DEV indicate greater dispersion of the participants' share price judgments. Taken together, the first hypothesis is tested by using the following regression equation:

$$
\begin{aligned}
PRICE\_DEV_{i,m} = {} & \beta_0 + \beta_1 REC\_DISC_{i,m} + \beta_2 MA\_MO_{i,m} + \beta_3 FIN\_COND_{i,m} + \\
& \beta_4 VOLA\_INC_{i,m} + \beta_5 GROWTH_{i,m} + \beta_6 INC_{i,j} + \beta_7 NOTES_{i,m} + \beta_8 RISK_{i,m} + \\
& \beta_9 DISCR_{i,m} + \beta_{10} RELEV_{i,m} + \beta_{11} RELIA_{i,m} + \varepsilon_{i,m},
\end{aligned}
$$

(6.1)

where,

$REC\_DISC_{i,m}$	*an indicator variable that takes the value of 1 if the firm recognizes investment properties at fair values,*
$MA\_MO_{i,m}$	*an indicator variable that takes the value of 1 if the firm determines the fair value of investment properties mark-to-market,*
$FIN\_COND_{i,m}$	*the overall financial condition of the company,*
$VOLA\_INC_{i,m}$	*the volatility of the company's net income,*
$GROWTH_{i,m}$	*the company's growth prospects,*
$INC_{i,m}$	*the usefulness of the company's net income to predict future income,*
$NOTES_{i,m}$	*the usefulness of the company's notes disclosures to predict future income,*

---

228   The p-values for any of the OLS regressions in this chapter are at least 0.1351, thus indicating that the hypothesis of heteroscedasticity must be rejected in all cases.

$RISK_{i,m}$	the risk of investing in the company,
$DISCR_{i,m}$	the potential for managerial discretion,
$RELEV_{i,m}$	the relevance of company information,
$RELIA_{i,m}$	the reliability of company information,
$\varepsilon_{i,m}$	confounding factor,

and all variables are meant for experiment subject i in group m. Table 6-11 depicts the results for both an OLS regression analysis and for an regression analysis based on ranked data. The variables REC_DISC and MA_MO represent the test variables and capture the effects of the two manipulations (recognition vs. disclosure and mark-to-market vs. mark-to-model).

Variable	OLS regression	Rank regression
(Intercept)	0.1740 (0.19)	46.0115 ** (2.53)
REC_DISC	0.0633 (0.32)	0.1898 (1.25)
MA_MO	0.0805 (0.48)	0.0068 (0.05)
FIN_COND	0.0986 (1.04)	-0.0216 (-0.16)
VOLA_INC	-0.0686 (-1.10)	-0.0659 (-0.47)
GROWTH	-0.1114 (-1.62)	-0.1295 (-1.08)
INC	-0.0565 (-0.87)	-0.0629 (-0.50)
NOTES	0.0223 (0.41)	-0.0658 (-0.54)
RISK	0.0938 (1.20)	0.0194 (0.14)
DISCR	0.0217 (0.38)	0.0326 (0.25)
RELEV	0.0031 (0.04)	-0.0593 (-0.43)
RELIA	0.0772 (1.10)	0.1561 (1.21)
Adjusted R^2	-4.08%	-6.59%
T-values are stated in brackets. *, **, and *** indicate significance at the 10%, 5%, and 1% levels (two-sided).		

Table 6-11: OLS and rank regression results for dispersion of share price judgments

The coefficients obtained for the OLS and the rank regression indicate no significant association between fair value accounting and dispersion of participants' share price judgments. The coefficients for the two test variables REC_DISC and MA_MO are positive, suggesting that fair values, which are determined mark-to-market, cause an increase in variance of estimated share prices. However, the coefficients are not significant at least at the 10% level, thus providing no evidence on this issue. There is also no significant difference reported for the remaining independent variables, even if it was expected that these variables have an influence on participants' judgments. The adjusted R squared values in both OLS and rank regression are negative, suggesting that only a small fraction of the deviations of prices to the mean is explained by the model. As the adjusted R squared coefficient accounts for the explanatory power when a larger number of variables are included in the model, negative values indicate a possible **misspecification** of the model. Additionally, there is the question of adequate specification of the dependent variable as standardized value on the basis of means and standard deviations per group.

Several **variations** of the model are applied in order to address the concern of possible model misspecification. The model presented in this chapter is robust to alternative specifications of the dependent variable, such as for example the simple standard deviation or the variance. Results do not change when these alternative specifications are applied.[229] In addressing the concern that there are too many variables in the model causing negative R squared values, the regression is re-run with only the two test variables, REC_DISC and MA_MO, included as independent variables. Under this approach, significance is also not reported for the two variables, suggesting that the further variables are not overlapping the effects of fair value accounting (both presentation format and kind of determination).

Taken together, the results in this chapter for the deviation of participants' share price judgments indicate that there might be **further influences** that are not captured by the model and experimental approach. It therefore remains an empirical question whether fair value accounting is significantly associated with a greater or lesser extent in dispersion of individual investors' price judgments under an experimental setting. However, this finding does not surprise when it is referred to the archival study conducted with financial analysts in chapter 5, as a significant association between analyst dispersion and fair value accounting is also not reported. Additionally, the adjusted R squared values are significantly decreased in the case of forecast dispersion when compared to forecast accuracy and analyst following, even if they are not negative. This indicates that there is no significant association between fair value accounting and both professional and nonprofessional investors' behavior. The experimental evidence in this chapter corroborates the prior archival-based results.[230] The two hypotheses H_{4a} and H_{4b}, **should therefore be rejected.**

6.2.3.2   Fair value accounting and confidence placed into share price judgment

The two hypotheses H_{5a} and H_{5b} of the experimental study concern the confidence that participants place into their share price judgments. It is expected that fair value presentation (i.e. recognition or disclosure of fair values) significantly affects participants' confidence. Additionally, it is anticipated that the way of fair value determination has a signifi-

---

229 For the regression results when several alternative specifications of PRICE_DEV are used as dependent variable see Table B-1 of appendix B.

230 The regression results for the reduced sample measuring dispersion (i.e. where all participants with false manipulation checks are removed) are provided in Table B-2 of appendix B. No material differences to the full sample have been detected.

cant influence on the measure to be tested. To provide empirical evidence on this issue, the variable **CONFIDENCE**, which represents the participants' responses to this question in the experimental setting, is included as the dependent variable in the equation. Similar to the prior chapter, the regression equation is as follows:

(6.2)
$$CONFIDENCE_{i,m} = \beta_0 + \beta_1 REC\_DISC_{i,m} + \beta_2 MA\_MO_{i,m} + \beta_3 FIN\_COND_{i,m} + \beta_4 VOLA\_INC_{i,m} + \beta_5 GROWTH_{i,m} + \beta_6 INC_{i,m} + \beta_7 NOTES_{i,m} + \beta_8 RISK_{i,m} + \beta_9 DISCR_{i,m} + \beta_{10} RELEV_{i,m} + \beta_{11} RELIA_{i,m} + \varepsilon_{i,m},$$

where the subscripts indicate that all variables are meant for experiment subject i in group m. The specifications of the independent variables in the equation are not different from the specifications in Equation 6.1.[231] The variables REC_DISC and MA_MO again represent the test variables and estimators for the variables. The results for the OLS and rank regression with participants' confidence are presented in Table 6-12.

Variable	OLS regression	Rank regression
(Intercept)	3.7109 ** (2.22)	38.5956 ** (2.35)
REC_DISC	0.8492 ** (2.42)	0.3380 ** (2.45)
MA_MO	-0.2481 (-0.83)	-0.1263 (-1.09)
FIN_COND	-0.1208 (-0.71)	-0.1131 (-0.93)
VOLA_INC	0.1647 (1.48)	0.1933 (1.54)
GROWTH	-0.1171 (-0.96)	-0.1018 (-0.94)
INC	0.1070 (0.92)	0.1067 (0.95)
NOTES	0.0132 (0.14)	-0.0003 (0.00)
RISK	-0.1078 (-0.78)	-0.1302 (-1.01)
DISCR	-0.2156 ** (-2.13)	-0.2363 * (-1.97)
RELEV	0.1971 (1.34)	0.1746 (1.39)
RELIA	0.0381 (0.30)	0.0563 (0.48)
Adjusted R²	10.80%	11.28%

T-values are stated in brackets. *, **, and *** indicate significance at the 10%, 5%, and 1% levels (two-sided).

Table 6-12: OLS and rank regression results for share price confidence

---

231 For a detailed description of the variables see chapter 6.2.3.1.

The results provided in Table 6-12 indicate no difference between the OLS and the rank regression, thus suggesting that the lack of normal distribution is not of a problem in the regression equation. It is now referred to the results of the OLS regression as these outcomes are easier to interpret than the ranked results. The coefficient for **REC_DISC** (0.8492) is positive and significantly different from zero (at the 5% level). This indicates a significant increase in participants' confidence when fair values of investment properties are recognized rather than disclosed (with recognized historical cost). Participants are thus more confident with their share price judgments when fair values are included in the balance sheet. This finding conforms to the expectation that recognized information functions as a signal for the degree of information reliability. Additionally, the more conform presentation of the fair value information may cause participants to believe that they possess information of higher quality. Because REC_DISC is developed as a dummy variable, the coefficient can be interpreted in a way that fair value recognition causes confidence to be increased by, on average, about 0.85 points on a 7-point scale.

The way of fair value determination does not seem to have an influence on confidence. Even if the reported coefficient for **MA_MO** is negative, it is not significant at least at the 10% level. This is on the first sight not conforming to intuition when it is expected that participants feel more comfortable when they can make their judgments based on market data. But the finding may be explained by master and bachelor students as experiment participants, representing nonprofessional investors. Even if the difference between mark-to-market and mark-to-model fair values is material in academic research and practice, it is not considered that important by nonprofessional investors. Moreover, the negative coefficient for MA_MO (even if it is not significant) implies a slightly higher confidence for model-based fair values, probably due to the detailed information available for the DCF calculation.[232] However, it could on the other hand be the case that information in the notes was in general not considered that important during the experiment when compared to information contained in the financial statements. That would more conform to the expectation that nonprofessional investors solely focus on the balance sheet and the income statement.

While there is no significance reported for the **additional variables**, the only exception is the coefficient for the variable DISCR (-0.2156) which is representing the potential for managerial discretion. Because the coefficient is significant and negative (at the 5% level), the degree of confidence is adversely associated with the expected potential for managerial discretion. This relationship could be expected as it should be intuitively clear that participants' place less confidence into their share price judgments when they expect a substantial degree of managerial discretion. The direction of influence (even if not significant) of the remaining variables in the equation vary, with financial condition, growth prospects, and risk having a negative influence and volatility of income, usefulness of income or notes as predictors, and both relevance and reliability are negatively associated with confidence. The adjusted R squared values for the OLS and the rank regression are 10.80% and 11.28%, indicating that the model is more adequate to explain variations of participants' confidence than the dispersion of share price judgments (see chapter 6.2.3.1).

---

232 See the experiment materials in appendix C.

Results in this chapter suggest that recognized fair values are superior to historical cost with regard to participants' confidence. No significant influence could be detected for the determination process of fair values, i.e. whether fair values are determined mark-to-market or mark-to-model.[233] As such, hypothesis H_{5a} that participants' place more confidence into recognized than disclosed fair values **cannot be rejected**. On the other hand, hypothesis H_{5b}, dealing with the determination process of fair values, could not be confirmed as there is no significant association H_{5b} between fair value determination and participants' confidence. Hypothesis H_{5b} **should therefore be rejected**.

6.2.3.3 Fair value accounting and participants' investment decision

The third hypothesis in the course of the experimental analysis concerns the participants' investment decision, thus referring to an investors' **willingness to invest** on the basis of the information provided. Participants were first asked whether they would make a concrete investment in the firm (i.e. to buy shares of Union Estate AG). Second (if they indicated "yes" for the prior question), participants were asked for the amount to invest in the company which could be indicated on a 7-point likert-scale ranging from 1 ("very low") to 7 ("very high"). When it is expected that fair value presentation and determination cause differences in investors' perception concerning the constitution of the firm, the experiment manipulations should have a significant influence on participants' investment decision. According to this, participants should be more or less likely to invest in the firm when mark-to-market or mark-to-model fair values are either recognized or disclosed and should adjust the amount to invest that they are willing to invest in the firm.

The investment decision in general and the amount to be invested is analyzed by computing two regression equations with one equation for participants' general investment decision and the amount to be invested. There is one problem when investigating the investment decision as this variable is a dummy variable that can only take the values of 1 and 0, indicating that participants are willing to invest or not. Because OLS regressions with a dummy variable as dependent variable produce biased results,[234] the **logistic regression** is alternatively applied. This approach makes predictions of the probability for the occurrence of an event (*Backhaus et al.* (2011), p. 250). It examines the influence (i.e. the increased or decreased probability to invest) of the two test variables (REC_DISC, MA_MO) on the dependent variable capturing the investment decision (**INVEST**).

In order to compute and interpret the obtained **probabilities**, the logistic regression assumes that there are only indicator variables included in the equation. Thus, the variables capturing the additional measures, such as the answers for relevance and reliability, need to be transformed into indicator variables before the logistic regression can be performed. The 7-point likert-scales which were used to survey the independent variables are transformed as follows: Values ranging from 1 to 4 are transformed into the new value 0,

---

233 The regression results for the reduced sample measuring participants' confidence (i.e. where all participants with false manipulation checks are removed) are provided in Table B-3 of appendix B. There are no material differences to the results obtained for the full sample.

234 The OLS regression produces biased results for dependent dummy variables for mainly three reasons. See *Backhaus et al.* (2011), p. 253f.

whereas values from 5 to 7 are transformed into the value 1.[235] Taken together, the following (logistic) regression equation is formulated in order to provide evidence on participants' investment decision:[236]

(6.3)
$$INVEST_{i,m} = \beta_0 + \beta_1 REC\_DISC_{i,m} + \beta_2 MA\_MO_{i,m} + \beta_3 FIN\_COND\_D_{i,m} + \\ \beta_4 VOLA\_INC\_D_{i,m} + \beta_5 GROWTH\_D_{i,m} + \beta_6 INC\_D_{i,m} + \beta_7 NOTES\_D_{i,m} + \\ \beta_8 RISK\_D_{i,m} + \beta_9 DISCR\_D_{i,m} + \beta_{10} RELEV\_D_{i,m} + \beta_{11} RELIA\_D_{i,m} + \varepsilon_{i,m},$$

where,

$REC\_DISC_{i,m}$	an indicator variable that takes the value of 1 if the firm recognizes investment properties at fair values,
$MA\_MO_{i,m}$	an indicator variable that takes the value of 1 if the firm determines the fair value of investment properties mark-to-market,
$FIN\_COND\_D_{i,m}$	the overall financial condition of the company (transformed dummy variable),
$VOLA\_INC\_D_{i,m}$	the volatility of the company's net income (transformed dummy variable),
$GROWTH\_D_{i,m}$	the company's growth prospects (transformed dummy variable),
$INC\_D_{i,m}$	the usefulness of the company's net income to predict future income (transformed dummy variable),
$NOTES\_D_{i,m}$	the usefulness of the company's notes disclosures to predict future income
$RISK\_D_{i,m}$	the risk of investing in the company,
$DISC\_D_{i,m}$	the potential for managerial discretion (transformed dummy variable),
$RELEV\_D_{i,m}$	the relevance of company information (transformed dummy variable),
$RELIA\_D_{i,m}$	the reliability of company information (transformed dummy variable),
$\varepsilon_{i,m}$	confounding factor,

and all variables are meant for experiment subject i in group m. Even if some of the variables are now transformed into indicators, the specification of the two test variables REC_DISC and MA_MO remains unchanged. Unlike investment decision, the association of fair value accounting with participants' amount to invest (variable AMOUNT) is tested by a regular OLS regression. This is possible as the dependent variable **AMOUNT** is not an indicator variable, but has been surveyed on a 7-point likert-scale instead. Thus, the following regression equation needs to be tested:

(6.4)
$$AMOUNT_{i,m} = \beta_0 + \beta_1 REC\_DISC_{i,m} + \beta_2 MA\_MO_{i,m} + \beta_3 FIN\_COND_{i,m} + \\ \beta_4 VOLA\_INC_{i,m} + \beta_5 GROWTH_{i,m} + \beta_6 INC_{i,m} + \beta_7 NOTES_{i,m} + \beta_8 RISK_{i,m} + \\ \beta_9 DISCR_{i,m} + \beta_{10} RELEV_{i,m} + \beta_{11} RELIA_{i,m} + \varepsilon_{i,m},$$

with the subscripts again indicating that all variables are meant for experiment subject i in group m. For a detailed description of the variables included see chapter 6.2.3.1.

---

235 The transformation of a 7-point likert-scale is not without problems as the scale possesses a middle point (4). This raises the question of allocating this value to either the first or second group. To address this problem, the analysis in this chapter is also performed with an allocation of the middle point to the first group (indicator value 0). The results do not materially change. Results do also not materially change when the means of each measure are chosen as the middle point.

236 The add-on "_D" in the case of the additional measures indicates that the transformed variables are included in the regression in order to highlight this difference to the other regression approaches.

The results for participants' willingness to invest are depicted in Table 6-13. The table presents the coefficients for the logistic regression examining participants' investment decisions and the OLS regression results for the amount that participants are willing to invest, each accompanied by rank regression coefficients.

| Variable | Investment decision | Amount to invest | |
	Logistic regression	OLS regression	Rank regression
(Intercept)	0.2100 (2.17)	1.9918 (0.82)	16.6348 (1.04)
REC_DISC	1.5206 (0.50)	0.7897 * (1.76)	0.2515 ** (2.06)
MA_MO	0.8052 (0.19)	0.1948 (0.52)	0.0602 (0.62)
FIN_COND (_D)	2.0809 (0.83)	-0.0084 (-0.03)	0.0022 (0.02)
VOLA_INC (_D)	1.5959 (0.55)	-0.2331 (-1.49)	-0.2093 * (-1.73)
GROWTH (_D)	1.5650 (0.76)	0.4797 *** (2.70)	0.2257 ** (2.26)
INC (_D)	1.5296 (0.55)	0.1404 (0.98)	0.0631 (0.67)
NOTES (_D)	1.1720 (0.08)	-0.1626 (-1.38)	-0.1388 (-1.55)
RISK (_D)	0.4193 (1.77)	-0.1727 (-0.86)	-0.0592 (-0.48)
DISCR (_D)	1.0197 (0.00)	0.0073 (0.05)	-0.0397 (-0.37)
RELEV (_D)	2.7481 (2.65)	0.1413 (0.70)	0.0797 (0.73)
RELIA (_D)	1.1707 (0.09)	-0.1325 (-0.74)	-0.0250 (-0.22)
Adjusted R^2		11.69%	10.16%
Nagelkerke's R^2	22.69%		

T-values are stated in brackets. In case of the logistic regression, the statistics and indicators of significance are based on the Wald test, which is similar to the regular t-statistic but is better applied for logistic approaches. *, **, and *** indicate significance at the 10%, 5%, and 1% levels (two-sided).

Table 6-13: Logistic, OLS and rank regression results for investment decision

The results concerning **participants' general willingness to invest** in the company are depicted in the left part of Table 6-13 (second column). Because of the logistic regression, the results of a rank regression are not provided in the case of the willingness to invest. It is important to note that the table does not report the regular coefficients for the logistic regression (the so-called "logits"), because these are not easy to interpret. Instead, the table shows the so-called **odds ratios**, which represent the probability of the regarding variable relative to its converse probability.[237] The design of the odds ratio as a kind of probability implies that the coefficients in the column for the logistic regression can only take positive values. Interpreting the odds ratios, values greater than 1 indicate an increase in probability, whereas values below 1 imply a decrease, which would correspond to negative regression coefficients in a regular OLS regression.

Another particularity concerns the measure for the goodness-of-fit of the model. For logistic regressions, the **Nagelkerke's R squared** is used to indicate whether the model is specified well enough. As its value is in a range between 0 and 1 (with higher values indicating better explanation through the model), it can be interpreted in the same way as the adjusted R squared in an OLS model.[238] As a rule of thumb, Nagelkerke's R squared values above 0.2 do in general indicate that the model specification is adequate (*Backhaus et al.* (2011), p. 276). The Nagelkerke's R squared is provided for the logistic regression, whereas the regular adjusted R squared values are provided for the remaining computations included in the table.

The Nagelkerke's R squared for the logistic regression takes the value of 22.69%, which can be viewed as an adequate specification of the model. When focusing on the **single coefficients** (i.e. the odds ratios) of the logistic model, the Wald statistics indicate that the coefficients for the test variables are not significant. However, interpreting the results should to some extent be possible, even if significance could not be reported. The odds ratio for the test variable **REC_DISC** is 1.5206. This value implies that the probability for making an investment in the company (i.e. choosing "yes" during the experiment) is increased by about 50% when the company recognizes fair values instead of just disclosing them. The odds ratio for the second test variable **MA_MO** is 0.8052. The fact that the value is below 1 indicates that the probability resulting from this variable is decreased. When the company determines the fair values mark-to-market, the probability to invest in the shares is thus decreased by about 20%. Even if this finding does not conform with intuition (e.g. when it is expected that market-based fair values should normally be ranked superior to model-based fair values), it is not different to the results obtained for the confidence question reported in chapter 6.2.3.2. However, the coefficient for MA_MO should not be overstated as it is not significant. Moreover, the results indicate that the difference in fair value determination is not material for the experiment participants. The finding for this question does therefore corroborate to the prior findings. It could be assumed that the fair value determination issue is not of great relevance for nonprofessional investors, even if it is subject to material discussion in academic community. Additionally, the insignificant coefficient for MA_MO could also be due to the small number of observations in the experiment, which makes it difficult to detect any significant association.

The odds ratios of the **remaining variables** are also not significant, even if some variables reveal higher probabilities than others. The coefficient measuring the overall financial

---

237 To give an example, an odds ratio of 4 for a certain variable in a logistic regression would imply that the probability for this variable (if it takes the value of 1) with regard to the dependent variable is four times higher. See *Backhaus et al.* (2011), p. 265.

238 The Nagelkerke's R squared is viewed as the preferred "pseudo R squared" measure for logistic regressions (*Backhaus et al.* (2011), p. 270).

condition (FIN_COND) is positive (2.0809), thus suggesting that a high assessment of financial condition induces an increase in investment probability of about 100%. It is also necessary to mention the odds ratios for the variables RISK (0.4193) and RELEV (2.7481), because the coefficients indicate considerable changes in the probability to invest, even if they are not significant. The coefficients obtained for the two variables conform well to intuition: Whereas an increase in risk assessment is negatively related to investment probability,[239] a higher degree of relevance correlates positively with the probability that experiment participants choose to invest in the company.

Taken together, the findings for the key measure investment decision provide evidence that participants are more likely to make an investment in the company when fair values are recognized rather than disclosed. In addition, model-based fair values also increase the probability of making an investment when compared with fair values which are derived from an active market. However, the results for the logistic regression are not significant, thus limiting the explanatory power of the fair value test variables. As aforementioned, the insignificance may be due to the small number of observations available. The two hypotheses H_{6a} and H_{6c} **are therefore rejected**. There is no significant association of fair value presentation or fair value determination with participants' general willingness to invest. Similar to the prior findings, it is thus assumed that differences in the fair value determination and presentation are not important for nonprofessional investors.

In addition to participants' general willingness to invest, the right side of Table 6-13 depicts the regression results for the **amount to be invested in the company**. This measure was collected in addition to the prior question in order to further examine participants' behavior when they are in general willing to invest in the company. For this question, the table shows only the results for the participants who have chosen to invest in the company in the course of the prior question. Therefore, the regression results are based on a reduced sample of 55 subjects. Whereas the third column shows the coefficients for the regular OLS regression, the rank regression coefficients are depicted in the fourth and last column on the right of the table.

The results obtained in the course of the OLS regression do in general conform to the results based on ranked data. This implies that the lack of normal distribution of some variables included does not cause the OLS approach to produce biased coefficients and t-statistics. The coefficient for the first test variable, **REC_DISC**, is positive and significant (0.7897) at the 10% level. This leads to the suggestion that participants do significantly invest a higher amount of their capital into the firm when this firm choses to recognize fair values instead of just disclosing them. The fact that the regarding coefficient of the rank regression (0.2515) is positive and significant even at the 5% level highlights the importance of this variable in the equation. The finding conforms to intuition when it is expected that participants are more likely to invest a greater share of their funds into companies with a better supply of information provided to investors.[240] Additionally, this outcome also corroborates the finding for investors' confidence, where it is also reported that

---

239 The coefficient for RISK (-0.2178) is significantly negative in the rank regression (at the 10% level).
240 However, this assumption only holds under the condition that fair values provide more and better information to investors than historical costs.

the confidence that is placed into a price judgment is significantly increased when fair values are recognized. Referring to the second test variable, the results suggest no considerable influence of the kind of fair value determination on the amount invested. The coefficient of 0.1948 for **MA_MO** is positive but not significant. Even if this finding seems surprising at first sight, it is in line with prior findings with regard to this variable.[241] Whereas the kind of fair value presentation has, to some extent, a significant influence on participants' behavior, participants' behavior is not affected significantly different by the fair value determination process.

The reported **differences** between REC_DISC and MA_MO could be explained by the fact that nonprofessional investors focus more on the financial statements than information contained in the notes (*Ernst et al.* (2009)). Because differences in the fair value determination are only reported in the notes, these differences are not considered by the experiment participants, thus resulting in a coefficient for MA_MO that is not significant. On the other hand, the coefficient for REC_DISC reflects a variation in the balance sheet and the income statement which is considered material. The regarding coefficient is therefore significant.

Referring to the **independent variables** included in the regression, significance is only reported for the coefficient of GROWTH.[242] The coefficient (0.4797) is positive and highly significant at the 1% level. Conforming to expectation, this implies that better growth perspectives significantly tempt investors to "open their pockets" and to invest more money into the regarding company. The positive association of GROWTH is supported by the regarding coefficient of the rank regression. Concerning the indicators for model specification, both adjusted R squared values indicate that the model is adequate. With values of 11.69% for the OLS and 10.16% for the rank regression, respectively, the measures for the goodness-of-fit indicate that the independent variables explain a significant percentage of the variation of the dependent variable.

Taken together, the **results** with regard to the amount that participants would be prepared to invest in the company indicate the following: Whereas fair value presentation is significantly associated with the amount to be invested, fair value determination is not considered by the participants. In the case of recognized fair values, participants are willing to invest a significantly greater amount of money compared to the case of fair value disclosure.[243] Due to this reason, the results provide clear evidence on hypothesis H_{6b}: The hypothesis that the amount invested is smaller for recognized fair values during times of fair value increases **should be rejected**. There is also no evidence provided that mark-to-market fair values cause a significantly greater amount invested. Thus, hypothesis H_{6d} **should be rejected**. After the empirical results have been depicted in detail in this chapter,

---

241 See for example the findings reported for share price judgment (chapter 6.2.3.1) or the findings reported for the confidence that participants place into their price judgment (chapter 6.2.3.2).

242 In contrast to OLS, the rank regression provides a significant and negative influence of VOLA_INC (coefficient: -0.2093), indicating that an increase in volatility makes participants spending less into the regarding company. Even if not significant, OLS also provides a negative coefficient.

243 The regression results of participants' investment decisions for the reduced sample are provided in Table B-4 of the appendix. Beside of the fact that the variable REC_DISC is not significant when measuring the amount to be invested, no material differences have been detected.

the next chapter presents a summary of the experimental study and reviews the outcomes that have been obtained during the investigation of investors' judgments and investment decisions. Implications and limitations of the study are also discussed.

6.3 Discussion

The study in this chapter investigates the effect of fair value presentation and determination on several measures around investors' judgments and investment decisions. To provide evidence on this issue, a **laboratory experiment** has been conducted with master and bachelor students of the University of Muenster accounting department. The two treatment effects included the fair value presentation format (recognition vs. disclosure) and the kind of fair value determination (mark-to-market vs. mark-to-model). Results indicate that fair values are significantly associated only with the **confidence** that participants' place into their judgments and with the **amount of money** that they are willing to invest into the exemplary enterprise "Union Estate AG". Both measures are significantly positively affected when fair values are recognized. This means that participants feel more confident about their price judgment and are willing to invest a larger amount of money into the firm when fair values are recognized rather than disclosed. However, there is no difference in investors' behavior when fair values are either determined mark-to-market or mark-to-model. The dispersion of individual participants' share price judgments are also not different between groups which suggests that participants' judgments are not sensitive to the mark-to-market or mark-to-model fair value determination or in which way these values are presented. The same holds in the case of participants' general willingness to invest: Whereas the majority of all subjects in the experiment would generally buy shares of the company, their general investment decision is not related to the kind of fair value presentation and how fair values are determined.

The preliminary checks included in the experiment suggest that the random allocation of participants on the four treatments was successful. In addition, the manipulation checks provide evidence for the assumption that the participants included in the sample generally understood the information that has been presented to them. However, participants found it more challenging to detect differences in fair value determination than fair value presentation format. This is foremost clear in the treatment combination of recognized fair values which are determined model-based, where only a slight majority was able to answer both manipulation questions correctly. However, it is assumed that this finding must be interpreted in association to participants' assessment of the usefulness of **notes** in general. Because participants' do, on average, assess the usefulness of disclosures in the notes to be limited, this helps to understand why participants found it more difficult to detect the information regarding the fair value determination in the notes. This assumption is also helpful when interpreting the somewhat surprising finding that model-based fair values sometimes reveal higher confidence of willingness to invest than market-based fair values. Even if this is not conforming to intuition, it could be argued that only few participants did read the notes carefully. Additionally, it could be put into question whether all participants did in general understand the material differences between a fair value determination mark-to-market and mark-to-model.[244] Given this case, participants could have viewed the detailed information that has been provided in the mark-to-model treatment as more reliable.

Referring to the **fourth hypothesis** (i.e. hypotheses H_{4a} and H_{4b}) constructed in chapter 4.2.3.1, it was argued that the functional fixation hypothesis is likely to cause a greater dispersion of participants' judgments when fair values are disclosed in the notes rather than recognized in the financial statements. It was also assumed that participants are more likely to reach an "overload cognitive state" before reaching the notes section, thus resulting in greater dispersion of fair value disclosures. In addition, it was expected that dispersion increases when fair values are determined mark-to-model. However, the results obtained in the course of the experiment do not provide support for these expectations. Based on the multivariate regression results, a significant influence of fair value accounting on the dispersion of participants' judgments cannot be reported. This finding holds for both the kind of fair value presentation and determination. The univariate comparisons and the tests for equality of the group variances do provide similar results. Taken together, this indicates that variations in fair value accounting are not associated with the dispersion of participants' judgments. However, this finding from the experiment conforms to the finding of the archival study for forecast dispersion reported in chapter 5.2.3.2. Similar to forecast dispersion, the value for the R squared is significantly lower when the dispersion of nonprofessional investors is examined. The insignificance may also be due to the small number of observations in the experiment. Thus, the **hypotheses H_{4a} and H_{4b} are rejected**: First, the dispersion of participants' judgments for firms disclosing fair values is not greater than for firms recognizing these amounts. Second, the dispersion of participants' judgments for firms applying mark-to-model fair values is not greater than for firms applying mark-to-market fair values.

The signaling theory suggests that participants should place greater confidence into their price judgment when this is based on recognized fair value information. In addition, participants should be more confident with market-based fair values rather than model-based fair values. Referring to the **fifth hypothesis** (i.e. hypotheses H_{5a} and H_{5b}), clear evidence is only provided for the presentation format of fair values in the financial statements. The regression results support the argument that recognized fair values cause an increase in participants' confidence, whereas disclosed fair values lead to a confidence decrease. But participants make no difference whether these fair values are determined mark-to-market or mark-to-model. Therefore, **hypothesis H_{5a} is not rejected**: Investors' confidence is greater when they make their judgments on the basis of recognized fair values rather than disclosed fair value information. However, **hypothesis H_{5b} is rejected**: Investors' confidence is not greater when they make their judgments on the basis of mark-to-market fair values rather than on mark-to-model fair values.

---

244 The regressions are re-run only with the master students included. The results do not materially change with regard to the test variables. The only difference is reported for the variable REC_DISC, which is no longer significant in the case of the amount invested, even if it is still positive (t-value 1.38). It is expected that the lack of significance is due to the smaller number of observations (60 master students vs. 91 students in the total sample).

The **sixth hypothesis**, which incorporates both participants' general willingness to invest (i.e. hypotheses H_{6a} and H_{6c}) and the amount to be invested (i.e. hypotheses H_{6b} and H_{6d}), is based on the signaling theory and investors' tendency to adopt some kind of vagueness avoidance. During times of increasing fair values, as it is modeled in the experiment, it is expected that participants are less likely to invest in firms recognizing fair values as they expect less favorable earnings in the future. Participants should also be less likely to invest in mark-to-model fair value firms, because it is assumed that these measures contain a high degree of uncertainty. In order to address the hypotheses, clear empirical evidence is only reported for the amount to be invested in the company. No significance is reported for participants' general willingness to invest in the company. It is therefore assumed that differences in fair value reporting and determination are not strong enough to have a significant influence on a general investment decision. However, significance is reported when participants show a general interest in investing in the company. For the reduced sample of participants with a general willing to invest, recognizing fair values makes them investing a greater amount into the company when compared to just disclosing these values. This is the complete opposite from which was expected as it was assumed that participants adjust the amount to be invested downwards in the case of recognized fair value increases. Because this is not supported by the outcomes of the study, it is therefore expected that participants prefer the short-term gains of fair value increases and do not consider possible decrease of earnings in the future. Concerning differences in fair value determination, significance is not detected. Therefore, the **hypotheses capturing investors' willingness to invest and the amount to be invested are rejected**: First, investors' willingness to invest and the amount to be invested during times of increasing fair values is not smaller for firms recognizing fair values than for firms only disclosing fair value information (hypotheses H_{6a} and H_{6b}). Second, investors' willingness to invest and the amount to be invested is not greater for firms that use mark-to-market fair values rather than for firms that use mark-to-model fair values (hypotheses H_{6c} and H_{6d}).

Figure 6-9 summarizes the results of the hypotheses tests for investors' judgments and investment decisions. The basic outcome of the experiment is the finding that **fair value presentation** is to some extent significantly associated with judgments and investment decisions, whereas the kind of fair value determination seems not to be of relevance for participants. This difference in perception should be interpreted in the following way: The experiment has been conducted with bachelor and master students which are representing nonprofessional investors. As already mentioned before, it is not clear how these participants weight the information included in the notes when compared to the information contained in the balance sheet or the statement of income. When quantitative data is assessed more important, notes disclosures including the determination process for fair values are not taken into account. This might explain the discrepancy in the findings for fair value presentation and determination, when it is true that information in the notes is assessed less relevant and reliable than quantitative financial statement data (*Maines/McDaniel* (2000), p. 185).

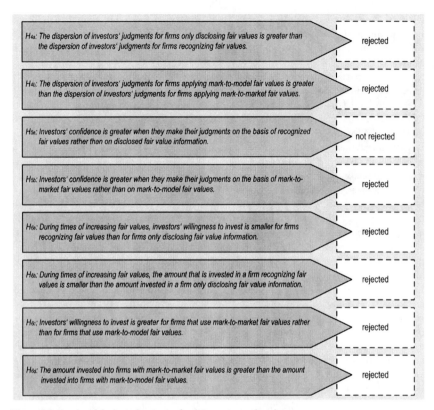

Figure 6-9: Results of the hypotheses tests for the experimental study

Even if some of the participants view quantitative data and notes as equally important, they could experience an overload cognitive state due to the fact that the notes are placed at the very end of the annual report (*Hodge et al.* (2004), p. 688). However, these assumptions are also supported by participants' responses when asked for the usefulness of information contained in the notes as a predictor for future income: With a mean of 3.73, participants indicated that they assess the usefulness of such information as below average.[245]

When only focusing on the case of fair value presentation in the financial statements (fair value recognition vs. fair value disclosure), significance is solely reported for confidence and the amount to invest, but not for dispersion and the general willingness to invest. What is striking here is the fact that fair values are only of relevance when subjects are asked to give an assessment on a **7-point likert-scale**. On the other hand, participants' price judging behaviors as a basis for their dispersion and their two-dimensional choices do not cause any significance. Under the experimental setting, they find it challenging to

---

245 See the descriptive statistics in chapter 6.2.2.2.

process non-conforming information in the balance sheet and the notes as it is the case when historical cost are recognized and fair values are disclosed. However, this view is only revealed when participants are able to actively choose and make an indication on a certain scale rather than on the basis of simple yes/no questions. This view is also not detected when examining participants' price judgment behavior resulting in dispersion. This indicates that participants, even if they subjectively would prefer fair values, are affected not differently by fair values and historical cost in such an experimental setting. Thus, it is assumed that there remains a discrepancy between participants' activities and their opinion when asked about fair values.

The results yield **implications** for users and preparers of financial statements. First, the experiment provides implications for **investors**. The experiment revealed that participants were more confident with fair values and invested larger amounts into fair value firms. It is therefore expected that investors may benefit from an increase in share prices of fair value firms. This finding is consistent with the assumption that fair values provide more decision-useful information to investors, thus increasing the liquidity of the regarding stock. However, even if the invested amounts increase when firms apply fair values, the absolute number of investors for the fair value company remains constant. This is due to the fact that the general investment decision was not related to fair value accounting, thus suggesting that no investor made his investment decision solely dependent on differences in the measurement for tangible assets. Nevertheless, investors benefit from fair values, because an increase in liquidity is also likely to cause lower bid ask spreads of the regarding stock.

The experiment provides also implications for **corporate managers**. Nonprofessional investors tend to invest higher amounts of money into fair value firms, which results in greater liquidity and higher share prices. Managers should therefore rely more on fair value accounting. This incentive would be given especially if managers receive parts of their compensation as share-based payments with greater share prices directly causing greater compensation. However, advantages would also arise for the company when higher share prices are more likely to prevent unfriendly takeover bids. According to the outcomes of the experiment, fair value accounting would even be beneficial for assets with no active market where the fair value has to be determined model based. This is because the experiment participants made no difference between mark-to-market and mark-to-model fair values, probably due to the fact that information contained in the notes was not considered important.

The experimental study does also provide implications for the **standard setter**. Even if fair values for tangible assets are not common in practice,[246] the results in this chapter provide evidence that these measures contribute to well-functioning capital markets through an increase in **liquidity** in the market. This finding corroborates to the standard setter's view that fair values are in general beneficial for investors (*Ball* (2006), p. 11). However, an interesting finding of the study is that investors made no difference between market- and model-based fair values. Beside of some problems when interpreting this result, this fact could attenuate several subjectivity concerns of model-based fair values, which have espe-

---

246 See the distribution of the sample of the first empirical study in chapter 5.2.1.2. Only 6.86% of all observations included in the sample are fair value observations (see Table 5-2).

cially been raised during the recent financial crisis. In addition, the findings provide insights into the process of how nonprofessional investors use and read financial reports. It is indicated that investors read financial reports in the order in which it is presented, thus resulting in greater importance of quantitative data rather than notes disclosures.

Finally, the results have implications for **auditors** and **enforcement institutions**, such as for example the German Financial Reporting Enforcement Panel (FREP). The outcomes of the experimental study suggest that recognized fair values are viewed as important and are used to make performance assessments, whereas disclosed fair values are not equally considered. According to this, auditors and enforcement institutions should put more time and effort on the verification of recognized rather than disclosed fair values. These findings conform to prior findings in empirical literature that recognized information is considered more important than information that is disclosed (*Sami/Schwartz* (1992); *Maines/McDaniel* (2000)). Anyway, the notes disclosures are still of relevance as there are also users of financial statements that rely on such information. It would thus be advisable to set out clear priorities for auditing and supervision with recognized information viewed as most important.

The experimental study is not without **limitations**. Similar to the first empirical study presented in chapter 5, the results of the experiment may also not easily be **generalized**. The experiment manipulations of the study did largely conform to the treatment for investment property as it is specified in IAS 40. The experiment did therefore focus on the measurement of tangible assets under the fair value model for investment properties. It is not clear whether these findings may be transferred to further applications of fair values.

A limitation of the study with financial analysts is that the kind of **fair value determination** (mark-to-market vs. mark-to-model) was not considered. Even if this shortcoming was mitigated by the experimental study, concerns remain with regard to the empirical outcomes. According to the results of the study in this chapter, nonprofessional investors made no difference between market- and model-based fair values. Even if this finding could be attributed to the fact that the participants did not view notes disclosures as important, it is not conforming to the empirical evidence reported in prior literature.[247] In addition, the finding is not conforming to intuition when it is expected that model-based estimates carry a significant degree of subjectivity and potential for discretion. The discrepancy may be explained in a way that not all students did fully understand the differences between mark-to-market and mark-to-model fair value accounting, even if they answered correctly to the manipulation checks. It is suggested that a different sample consisting of professional investors (i.e. financial analysts or funds managers) in a similar experimental setting would have provided different results. However, the fact that nonprofessional investors did not feel uncomfortable when confronted with model-based estimates is nevertheless an important finding of the study.

The limitation just mentioned is also related to the question of **data quality**. According to this, master and bachelor students were used as experiment participants in order to proxy for nonprofessional investors. Even if literature suggests that this group of subjects may

---

247 See for example *Khurana/Kim* (2003), *Gassen/Schwedler* (2010) or *Song et al.* (2010).

sufficiently proxy for the behavior of nonprofessional investors (*Elliott et al.* (2007)), it is still questionable whether the participants in the sample are not different from nonprofessional investors. However, the preliminary checks indicate that the majority of the students understood the manipulations and that investment experience was equally distributed among the treatments. This does, at least to some extent, mitigate the concern of data quality.

The final limitation concerns the experimental design and the **degree of realism.** The participants of the experiment were only provided with a subset of the information typically available to most investors in a way that they could complete the task in a reasonable amount of time. Compared to a comprehensive annual report, participants only received a reduced version of the annual report, containing three pages (plus front page). It is hard to believe that such a reduced annual report would exist in reality. Moreover, such reports consist of hundreds of pages nowadays, often including not only the financial statements and the management report, but in addition further information about the company. However, investors would in reality not solely rely on financial statement information. Investors would rely on further information sources such as newspapers or analyst recommendations. These additional features could not be incorporated into the experiment, thus reducing the degree of realism. Even though, it is expected that the laboratory experiment provided the best trade-off between reality and practicability with regard to the research question.

7 Conclusion

This research work examines the implications of fair value accounting for users of financial statements. After theory and the empirical results of two empirical studies have been presented in the previous chapters, this chapter concludes the research by presenting the main findings of the research (chapter 7.1). Implications and the contribution of the research are reported in chapter 7.2. In addition, limitations and perspectives for the future of fair value accounting are presented (chapter 7.3).

7.1 Summary and main findings

Fair value accounting is of growing importance in accounting research and practice. IFRS became mandatory for the consolidated financial statements of capital-market oriented companies in the European Union in 2005. This did not only bring about convergence in accounting, but also introduced the fair value approach for certain assets and liabilities as fair value accounting was not possible under many local GAAP systems. Especially the financial crisis caused the fair value discussion, which has before been mainly of interest for accounting academics and practitioners, into a debate of public interest. However, fair values are not only relevant for financial instruments. Indeed, IFRS allows fair value accounting for a wide range of assets or liabilities, including for example investment property or assets of PPE. The growing importance of fair value accounting is also reflected by the fact that the IASB released the **new standard IFRS 13** *Fair Value Accounting*, which must be applied from 2013 on. The new IFRS is part of the Memorandum of Understanding project between the IASB and the FASB and intends to provide a single framework for fair value measurement in financial statements. While the guidelines for fair value measurement were before dispersed over several IFRS, thus lacking of consistent specifications about fair value determination, recognition and disclosure, IFRS 13 consolidates these guidelines into one single standard. Even if the new standard also addresses some concerns which were especially raised for Level 3 fair values during the financial crisis, fair value accounting is still discussed controversially. Whereas proponents argue that fair values do in general provide more relevant and decision-useful information for investors, opponents mainly focus on the potential for managerial discretion when fair values cannot be determined reliably.

The adoption of IFRS did also change the **focus of financial reporting**. While especially in Continental Europe, the local GAAP requirements were supposed to fulfill the informational needs of various stakeholders of the company (i.e. tax authorities, creditors, suppliers etc.), IFRS focuses primarily on the informational needs of the investor. As IFRS restricts the purpose of accounting to serve the informational needs of investors, the implications of the reported IFRS data on investors are in the center of the discussion. Thus, it is of specific interest whether and how investors react when firms apply fair value accounting. However, when investors buy shares of a certain company, they are rather interested in the future prospects of their investment to earn a significant return. Therefore, there remains the question of the predictive power of IFRS financial statements, which means whether IFRS financial statements are appropriate to enable forecasting of accounting numbers by professional or nonprofessional investors.

The review of related empirical literature identified a significant **research gap** in this field. Due to these reasons, the present study examined the implications of fair value accounting for users of financial statements. The following sub-objectives were addressed in the course of the study:

- The implications of fair value accounting on the **forecasting ability** of financial analysts,

- the implications of fair value accounting on **judgments and investment decisions** of nonprofessional investors,

- differences between **full fair value accounting** for investment properties (fair value model) and **piecemeal fair value accounting** for PPE (revaluation model), and

- the implications of fair value presentation (recognition vs. disclosure) and determination (market- vs. model-based).

The research question and the sub-objectives just stated made it necessary to apply two different empirical research approaches. In a first step, the implications of fair value accounting on the forecasting ability of financial analysts have been examined by using an **archival-based** approach. Second, the behavior of nonprofessional investors when confronted with fair values has been captured by using an **experimental study**.

Several methodological issues needed to be considered as groundwork for the two empirical studies. Therefore, the **fair value approach** under IFRS was presented in detail in the second chapter. The chapter did also deal with the fair value model and the revaluation model for investment properties and PPE, because these assets were in the center of the later empirical studies. The second chapter did also go into further detail concerning **financial analysts** and the way they perform coverage. Because the research work combines several streams of literature, the third chapter reviewed **related empirical literature** concerning the relevance and reliability of fair value accounting as well as the predictability of accounting numbers. However, the review of related empirical literature was also necessary to identify the research gap and for a further specification of the research question. Based on the reviewed empirical literature, chapter 4 presented **theory** which was used to develop hypotheses. In the fifth chapter, it was examined whether financial analysts' **forecast accuracy, forecast dispersion, and their tendency to follow the firm** is significantly affected by fair value accounting. Because a cross-country sample of seven countries from the European Union was employed, the sample amounted to a comprehensive size of 2,566 firm-year observations. The regression results were accompanied by several robustness checks and a difference in differences approach in order to increase the confidence that was placed into the results. The results of an experiment conducted with 91 master and third-year bachelor students of the University of Muenster were presented in the sixth chapter. During the experiment, participants were provided with different financial statement data, featuring different kinds of fair value presentation and determination, and had to respond to several questions. Here, it was examined whether **participants' judgments** with regard to firm constitution and performance and their investment decisions do significantly differ depending on the fair value information provided to them.

Referring to the sub-objectives (i.e. derived from the main research question) presented in the first chapter of this research work, the following empirical results could be obtained on the basis of the two empirical studies.

The results of the archival-based study suggested that there is a significant association of fair value accounting and **financial analysts' forecast accuracy** and their **tendency to follow the firm**, while there is no significant association of fair value accounting and the dispersion of individual analysts' forecasts. Whereas the ability of financial analysts to produce precise earnings forecasts was negatively affected by fair value accounting for investment properties, there is no association documented between fair value accounting for assets of PPE and forecast accuracy. Financial analysts were also less likely to follow fair value firms, no matter whether they measured investment properties or assets of PPE at fair value instead of historical cost. Because the dispersion of individual forecasts was not significantly affected by fair value accounting, it was hypothesized that analysts interpreted the financial statement information in similar ways and that fair value accounting did not cause divergences in beliefs. The results suggest that financial analysts do not benefit from fair values in financial statements. It could also be argued that fair values decrease the predictive power of financial reporting, thus reflected by a significant decrease in forecast accuracy. As the archival study was based on a comprehensive sample of firm-year observations from seven European countries, the empirical results also provided evidence on the application of fair values in practice. However, and not conforming to the signaling theory that managers should have an incentive to measure firm assets at fair value, only the minority of the sample firms chose fair value accounting instead of historical cost.

Referring to the implications of fair value accounting for the **judgments and investment decisions of nonprofessional investors**, master and third-year bachelor students enrolled at the University of Muenster were used to proxy for nonprofessional investors' behavior. The study was conducted as a laboratory experiment where participants were provided with different financial statement information of an exemplary firm. Participants then indicated the estimated share price, the confidence placed into their assessments, their investment decisions, and the amount of money that they were willing to invest into the exemplary company. The results showed that participants' confidence that is placed into their investment decisions was significantly increased when a firm recognized tangible assets at fair value. In addition, participants were more likely to invest a greater amount of money when fair values were recognized compared to the case when fair values were disclosed. However, fair value accounting was not significantly associated with the investment decision in general and the dispersion of individual share price judgments. Therefore, the experiment with nonprofessional investors provided results that are not different to the results obtained for financial analysts in the first study in the case of dispersion.

The first study conducted with financial analysts provided empirical evidence on differences between **full and piecemeal fair value accounting** as represented by the fair value model and the revaluation model, respectively. As mentioned above, properties of analysts' forecasts have been examined whether they are significantly affected by fair value accounting for two classes of tangible assets, namely investment properties and assets of PPE. Because these two asset classes were chosen, the research design provided a unique setting to compare some kind of full and piecemeal fair value accounting. While only forecast accuracy is differently affected, the results suggest that full fair value accounting decreases accuracy of earnings, whereas piecemeal fair values do not influence forecast accuracy. However, this finding may be traced back to the increase in earnings volatility in the case of the fair value model for investment properties. On the other hand, the revaluation model for PPE captures fair value changes in the OCI. Given this fact, financial analysts may have found it more challenging to predict companies' earnings when they had to predict fair value changes of assets as well.

The laboratory experiment allowed drawing conclusions regarding the financial statement **presentation and determination of fair values**. The experimental design included different kinds of fair value presentation (i.e. recognized fair values or fair values which were only disclosed in the notes) and the way in which fair values were determined (mark-to-market vs. mark-to-model. Results suggest that fair value presentation did significantly affect the experimental participants' behavior, whereas the kind of determination of fair values did not seem to be of great relevance for the respondents. More precisely, the positive implications of fair values on participants' confidence and their willingness to invest could only be reported for the case of fair value recognition, but not for disclosure. These results are consistent with the assumption that information in the notes is not considered as important as quantitative information contained in the balance sheet or the statement of comprehensive income. On the other hand, the finding that fair value determination was not influential does not conform to intuition. The difference between mark-to-market and mark-to-model is considered material among accounting academics and practioners. However, results suggest that nonprofessional investors do not view that difference as material. They are rather interested in a consistent presentation of fair values, no matter whether fair values are determined mark-to-market or mark-to-model. Figure 7-1 presents the basic outcomes of the two empirical studies, separately for each sub-objective.

A closer investigation of the key results of the two empirical studies reveals some significant similarities as well as differences between the fair value perception of financial analysts and nonprofessional investors. On the one hand, there is striking evidence that investors' dispersion is not affected by fair values, thus suggesting that the way in which fair value information is interpreted by different individuals does not vary with the degree of professionalism. This means that fair value information is not interpreted differently by different types of investors and that fair values do not increase the **variance of investors' expectations** with regard to future firm performance. On the other hand, significant differences between financial analysts and nonprofessional investors constitute of the following: Whereas financial analysts find it more challenging to predict earnings and are less likely to follow firms under the fair value accounting regime, the participants of the experiment are more confident and invest greater amounts of money into fair value firms. Even if this **controversy** does only exist in the full fair value case (i.e. fair value model for investment properties), a possible explanation for this is a difference in *perception* and *impact*. While users of financial statements feel more confident when they can make judgments on the basis of fair value information, their ability to make appraisals about the future performance of the firm is reduced, perhaps due to an increase of volatility. However, volatility should not constitute a problem by itself when it reflects the true economic conditions of the company. Nevertheless, these differences may also be due to the different research designs and the focus that has been made in the course of the two studies.

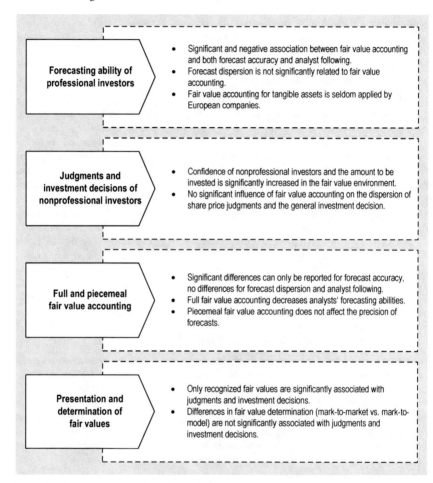

Forecasting ability of professional investors
- Significant and negative association between fair value accounting and both forecast accuracy and analyst following.
- Forecast dispersion is not significantly related to fair value accounting.
- Fair value accounting for tangible assets is seldom applied by European companies.

Judgments and investment decisions of nonprofessional investors
- Confidence of nonprofessional investors and the amount to be invested is significantly increased in the fair value environment.
- No significant influence of fair value accounting on the dispersion of share price judgments and the general investment decision.

Full and piecemeal fair value accounting
- Significant differences can only be reported for forecast accuracy, no differences for forecast dispersion and analyst following.
- Full fair value accounting decreases analysts' forecasting abilities.
- Piecemeal fair value accounting does not affect the precision of forecasts.

Presentation and determination of fair values
- Only recognized fair values are significantly associated with judgments and investment decisions.
- Differences in fair value determination (mark-to-market vs. mark-to-model) are not significantly associated with judgments and investment decisions.

Figure 7-1: Empirical outcomes for each sub-objective

Summarizing the findings, the research documented a significant association between fair value accounting and both the forecasting abilities and the investment behavior of users of financial statements. The research examines fair value accounting for tangible assets under IFRS by using a comprehensive setting and provides multifaceted evidence on the implications of fair values for both financial analysts and nonprofessional investors. The next chapter presents the contribution of the two empirical studies and points to possible implications for accounting research and practice.

7.2   Implications and contribution

The study contributes to research in the field of accounting and financial reporting in several ways. First, the study contributes to accounting research regarding the **implications of financial reporting**. Financial reporting is primarily focused on the informational needs of investors. Thus, financial reporting aims to reduce information asymmetries between management and the owners of the firm. In ensuring an adequate information supply for their investors, preparers of financial statements are interested in whether exercising voluntary fair value options increase or decrease the quality of information that is available in the market. Furthermore, standard setters expressed a specific interest in accounting research on the implications of financial statements for investors (*Levitt* (1998), p. 79ff.). As such, the results of the study provide evidence that analysts and nonprofessional investors are significantly affected by voluntary fair values in financial statements. The study also corroborates the findings reported in prior literature with regard to the importance of disclosures in the notes as recognized fair values do bear a somewhat greater importance for investors than disclosed values do.

The study also contributes to the ongoing debate regarding the **usefulness of fair values in financial statements**. Even if the financial crisis from 2008 highlighted some of the problems of fair value accounting, the IASB still has a tendency towards fair values in financial statements (*Foster/Shastri* (2010), p. 20; *Küting/Kaiser* (2010), p. 376). A further step away from the so-called mixed-model approach with both historical and market values in the accounts is brought by the single fair value standard IFRS 13. Even if the IASB mentions that the new standard is only intended to provide guidance on fair value measurement, there is the concern that it could be used as the basement for the further expansion of fair value accounting in the future (*Berndt/Eberli* (2009), p. 897). However, the problem with prior literature in this field of research is that most of the research was conceptual-based rather than based on empirical data. Contrariwise, this study is the first study that deals with the implications of fair value accounting by using a comprehensive research design which is both incorporating professional and nonprofessional investors. As such, the study provides both proponents and opponents of the fair value idea with good arguments: Whereas the volatility of fair values makes forecasting more challenging, the investors' community feels more confident when they can make their decisions on the basis of fair values rather than on the basis of historical cost. This implies that fair value accounting cannot be viewed as either *good* or *bad*. Moreover, it is important to form an opinion about fair value accounting in the context in which it is applied and with regard to the purpose that it has to fulfill.

As the review of related literature demonstrated, much of the prior research focused on the implications of fair values on professional investors, such as for example financial advisors or managers of mutual funds. This narrow focus is justified by the argument that financial statements are mainly used by professional investors, whereas nonprofessional investors prefer other information sources (*Ernst et al.* (2009), p. 29). However, **nonprofessional investors** should not be ignored in a comprehensive analysis as it is also conceivable that they read annual reports, even if the information contained in the reports is evaluated differently depending on the degree of professionalism of the reader. Even if there have been some empirical studies examining fair values and nonprofessional investors, these studies were primarily based on surveys or remained largely abstract. Therefore, the study contributes to prior literature as it provides empirical evidence on the fair value perception of nonprofessional investors under laboratory conditions.

Prior research did to a large extent focus on the implications of fair values for financial instruments which are held by banks or insurance companies. However, other studies that also incorporate fair value accounting for tangible assets remained largely descriptive and only documented that these assets are measured mostly at historical cost. Multivariate regression analyses have not been performed. As such, the study does not only corroborate the prior descriptive results concerning the measurement of tangible assets, it does also expand the empirical evidence with regard to the implications of fair value accounting for **non-financial assets**. Because the study is not restricted to financial institutions, a larger sample size could be used for the analyses. Taken together, the study is the first empirical study that applies multivariate tools of data analysis on fair value measures for tangible assets in IFRS financial statements and examines their association with professional and nonprofessional investors' behavior. The accounting community should thus welcome this kind of empirical evidence when fair value measures are further expanded in the future.

Furthermore, the study provides evidence on the **application of fair values** in accounting practice. As mentioned in the conceptual part of the text, several institutions like the IASB or the CFA Institute believe that fair values are superior to historical cost as they provide more timely and relevant information. If this view is accepted, these institutions should have an interest in a wide application of fair values. Conforming to prior results, the results of the study reveal the opposite. The descriptive results on fair value accounting in prior studies were reduced to either single industries or countries. On the other hand, the results of this study may easily be generalized with a comprehensive cross-country sample applied. Fair value accounting for tangible assets is not common in the financial statements of European firms which are included in the sample. This leads to the suggestion that accounting practitioners and preparers do not share the views of the IASB or the CFA Institute or, alternatively, do fear the increased expense of a measurement of tangible assets at fair value. On the other hand, the reasons for the scarce application of fair values could also be due to the accounting tradition in continental Europe with a strict focus on historical cost measures.

The results also contribute to existing **theory**. According to the functional fixation hypothesis, individuals are likely to concentrate on a certain number in the financial statements which is not adjusted, even if further information is provided (*Tinic* (1990), p. 783). The outcomes of the experiment showed that nonprofessional investors only reacted differently on recognized information, but ignored information that has just been disclosed. That finding conforms to prior literature as individuals kept interpreting the net income in the same way no matter what information is provided in the notes (*Viger et al.* (2008), p. 97). The concept of functional fixation provides an explanation for the fact that the differences between mark-to-market and mark-to-model are not viewed as material by nonprofessional investors. It can thus also be applied to the case fair value accounting with the method of determination only disclosed in the notes.

Related empirical literature shows that forecast accuracy is significantly increased for firms with more informative disclosure policies (*Lang/Lundholm* (1996)), higher levels of annual report disclosure (*Eng/Teo* (2000)), and higher levels of forward looking non-financial disclosures (*Vanstraelen et al.* (2003)). The results of the fair value study with financial analysts do not corroborate the results of **prior literature** as it is reported that forecast accuracy is significantly decreased for fair value firms. Additionally, the study yields different results with regard to fair values than the study by *Fan et al.* (2006), who report more precise forecasts for fair value firms under U.S. GAAP. However, the authors used a more focused sample. Nevertheless, the results of this study with financial analysts should be interpreted that fair values cannot be viewed as a kind of beneficial disclosure that is primarily of advantage for users of financial statements. Moreover, it is suggested that the increased earnings volatility compensates possible advantages of more informative fair values in financial statements.

Implications for accounting practitioners and users of financial statements have been presented separately for the results of each empirical study in every chapter. Even if the two studies examined the implications of fair value accounting, they focused on different types of financial statement users. Whereas the first study focused on the earnings forecasts of financial analysts, the second study was concerned with the judgments and investment decisions of nonprofessional investors. Despite of those differences, the results of both studies yield **complementing implications** for users and preparers of financial statements.

Both studies provide important implications for **investors**. The outcomes of the experimental study provided evidence that the confidence placed into a price judgment is increased under the fair value environment. The amount invested into a fair value company is higher, resulting in greater liquidity and lower bid-ask spreads for the regarding stock. Taken solely the findings from the experiment, investors would benefit from fair value accounting when the capital markets are better able to transfer financial resources between market participants. However, the first study showed that financial analysts are less likely to produce precise earnings forecasts for fair value firms, probably due to increased earnings volatility. The benefits of fair value accounting are then foiled by less precise forecasts. Investors should therefore interpret analysts' research reports for fair value firms with caution. Anyhow, it could be supposed that investors may take advantage of the different implications of fair value accounting for financial analysts and nonprofessional investors. In the case of fair value firms, investors should focus less on the earnings forecasts but should rely more on other information sources or personal intuition. They are then able to, at least to some extent, benefit from fair value accounting without making investment decisions on the basis of biased forecasts. In the case of historical cost firms, the forecasts could be used for decision-making as they are more accurate than for fair value firms. The decreases in confidence and invested amounts are then compensated by more accurate forecasts.

The implications for **corporate managers** are also twofold. As more precise forecasts and higher analyst following increases firm valuation and lowers the cost of capital (*Gebhardt et al.* (2001); *Lang et al.* (2004)), managers should more rely on historical cost accounting. On the other hand, nonprofessional investors prefer recognized fair values rather than disclosed ones. Even if fair values for tangible assets are not common in practice, managers should more rely on fair value accounting to attract more nonprofessional investors. Given that different findings, the implications of fair value accounting for corporate managers largely depend on the focus on either financial analysts or nonprofessional investors. If institutional investors hold large stakes in the company, managers may more rely on historical cost accounting. This is because such investors usually refer to the earnings forecasts of financial analysts (*Davis/Steil* (2001), p. 260f.). Contrariwise, investors should focus more on fair values when their company is dependent on free float holders with a large number of nonprofessional investors or if managers intend to increase the investor base. Additionally, the problems of financial analysts with fair values may also be mitigated through a better **explanation of the fair value changes** in each period. This implies that managers make clear specifications of the assets measured at fair value, including both the method of determination and the expected fair value changes in the forthcoming periods. If analysts possess such comprehensive information, the concern of earnings volatility may be mitigated, thus resulting in more precise forecasts even in the fair value environment.

7.3 Limitations and perspectives

The limitations of the two studies have already been presented in each chapter where the results of the studies have been reported. The limitations of both studies do primarily refer to aspects of generalizability and data availability and quality. Referring to aspects of **generalizability**, it is questionable whether the results of the studies also hold for different samples or research designs. Because the first study focused on tangible assets, further asset classes, such as for example financial instrument, were not included. Additionally, the experiment design conformed to IAS 40 and the accounting for investment properties, thus also providing evidence solely for one class of tangible assets. Concerning **data availability**, the results of the first study are primarily based on large public-traded companies located in the European Union. It is thus questionable whether the results would also hold for companies from other regions. Finally, data quality refers to the experiment as it is not clear whether master and bachelor students proxy for nonprofessional investors' behavior.

The limitations just mentioned indicate that there is plenty of room to expand the empirical research with regard to the implications of fair value accounting for users of financial statements. First, further research could incorporate financial institutions and fair value accounting for **financial instruments**. However, prior empirical literature did focus on the value relevance of fair values in the financial statements of financial institutions. The implications on financial analysts' forecasts and nonprofessional investors' behavior have not been examined. It would also make sense to examine the implications of fair value accounting for financial institutions' financial assets as these firms measure their financial instruments usually to a large extent at fair value. Fair value accounting of financial assets leaves also plenty of room due to the new standard IFRS 9, which intends to facilitate accounting regulations and replaces IAS 39 by the second half of 2011. As there is no IFRS 9 archival data available yet, a further experimental approach could reflect the new regulations in a way to examine its implications for users of financial statements. Such an approach would in addition enable making comparisons between IAS 39 and IFRS 9 as the new standard makes significant changes to the accounting for financial instruments (*Spector* (2010), p. 36).

The first empirical study investigated implications of fair value accounting for seven European countries. Complementing research could broaden the **sample** and could focus on countries outside of the EU. However and in order to ensure comparability, the companies within the sample should prepare their accounts under IFRS. Thus, it is expected that especially larger companies with pronounced capital markets such as for example Australia would yield interesting results. It would also be interesting to expand the study to the United States capital markets. An expansion to the United States capital markets is possible in the long-term as the U.S. regulator published plans to allow domestic companies to use IFRS not before 2015 (*DeFelice/Lamoreaux* (2010), p. 22).

The experiment was conducted with master and bachelor students which were used as proxies for nonprofessional investors. Further research could expand the findings in a way that a similar research design is used with **professional investors**. Because professional investors are more familiar with the fair value issue, it is expected that the outcomes of such a study yield interesting results for the standard setter and preparers of financial statements. When financial analysts or funds managers are used as proxies for professional investors, a comparison to the archival-based results of the study in this research would also be possible. However, it is expected that gathering a sufficient number of participants could be more challenging due to professional investors' time constraints.

The discussion around fair value accounting gained momentum with the upcoming financial crisis in 2008. The problems and concerns that resulted in this context caused, among others, recent developments such as for example *IFRS 13 Fair Value Measurement* as a consistent basement for the fair value accounting under IFRS. Generally, the issuance of IFRS 13 is strongly welcomed as it provides one single framework for fair value measurement and attempts to accomplish greater acceptance for fair values. However, the world economy did not remain unchanged during the time the IASB developed the new fair value standard. After a time period of a prospering world economy, the financial crisis was superseded by a **public debt and currency crisis** with many developed countries suffering from large budget deficits. This boosted the pressure on prices of government bonds especially of some countries within the European Union and significantly increased the refinancing costs of the heavily indebted countries. Finally, this caused the European Union to set up a rescue plan and the European Central Bank (ECB) to purchase government bonds of these countries. Although these developments changed the focus of the public and took fair value accounting out of the line of fire, fair values still remain important and retain their place in accounting practice. According to this, the recent debt crisis also demanded fair value expertise as the valuation of the impaired Greek government bonds in the IFRS statements of European banks remained largely unclear. Whereas some banks used the current price of the bonds and suffered from significant depreciations, others have used differing methods not without raising the concerns of the standard setter (*IASB* (2011)).

Backed with the empirical evidence of two comprehensive fair value studies, it should finally be referred to the question raised at the very beginning of this research: *Are fair val-*

ues rather foul or fair? Even if the results suggested that fair values lowered the predicting value of financial statements due to increased earnings volatility (*foul*), it should not be disregarded that fair values also caused higher confidence (*fair*). The findings imply a differentiated view on fair value accounting rather than reasoning that fair values are *foul* or *fair*. As it is often the case in reality, the opinion that someone puts into something largely depends on the eye of the beholder. Thus, providing additional information in the form of fair values should not be detrimental when it reflects economic conditions. When economic conditions are volatile and fair values reflect this volatility, this should not be a concern of fair value accounting by itself.

Appendix A: Empirical analysis of financial analysts' forecasts

Table A-1: Distribution of the sample per industry[248]

Sector		Industry group		No.	TOTAL	%
10	Energy	1010	Energy	108	108	4.21%
15	Materials	1510	Materials	238	238	9.28%
20	Industrials	2010	Capital Goods	432		
		2020	Commercial Services & Supplies	157		
		2030	Transportation	79	668	26.03%
25	Consumer Discretionary	2510	Automobiles & Components	64		
		2520	Consumer Durables & Apparel	137		
		2530	Consumer Services	36		
		2540	Media	149		
		2550	Retailing	45	431	16.80%
30	Consumer Staples	3010	Food & Staples Retailing	19		
		3020	Food, Beverage & Tobacco	83		
		3030	Household & Personal Products	19	121	4.71%
35	Health Care	3510	Health Care Equipment & Services	69		
		3520	Pharmaceuticals, Biotechnology & Life Sciences	127	196	7.64%
40	Financials	4020	Diversified Financials	146		
		4040	Real Estate	165	311	12.12%
45	Information Technology	4510	Software & Services	215		
		4520	Technology Hardware & Equipment	110		
		4530	Semiconductors & Semiconductor Equipment	33	358	13.95%
50	Telecommunication Services	5010	Telecommunication Services	40	40	1.56%
55	Utilities	5510	Utilities	95	95	3.70%
TOTAL				**2,566**	**2,566**	**100%**

---

248 Banks and insurance companies are not included in the sample. Therefore, the sector "Financials" contains of the industry groups "Diversified Financials" and "Real Estate" only.

Table A-2: Coefficients of the industry and country control variables for forecast accuracy

Industry controls	Pred. sign	OLS regression			Rank regression		
		Model (1)	Model (2)	Model (3)	Model (1)	Model (2)	Model (3)
Energy	+/-	0.0066	0.0057	0.0046	0.0225	0.0224	0.0233
Materials	+/-	-0.0001	0.0006	-0.0011	*** -0.1290	*** -0.1145	*** -0.1289
Commercial Serv.	+/-	0.0009	-0.0005	0.0012	-0.0087	-0.0141	-0.0093
Transportation	+/-	-0.0025	-0.0022	-0.0045	-0.0810	-0.0607	-0.0809
Automobiles	+/-	-0.0033	-0.0051	-0.0055	-0.0027	-0.0123	-0.0020
Cons. Durables	+/-	-0.0002	-0.0029	-0.0014	0.0207	0.0063	0.0211
Cons. Services	+/-	*** 0.0231	** 0.0196	** 0.0185	0.0382	0.0207	0.0404
Media	+/-	-0.0072	* -0.0088	* -0.0082	-0.0503	-0.0474	-0.0506
Retailing	+/-	0.0049	0.0035	0.0048	-0.0288	-0.0450	-0.0285
Food & Staples	+/-	0.0260	0.0162	0.0186	* 0.1973	0.1497	* 0.2006
Food & Beverage	+/-	** -0.0142	** -0.0152	** -0.0147	* -0.1098	* -0.1104	* -0.1099
Household	+/-	0.0150	0.0099	0.0082	0.1503	0.1328	0.1528
Health Care	+/-	0.0083	0.0057	0.0060	0.0534	0.0457	0.0545
Pharmaceuticals	+/-	*** 0.0147	** 0.0137	** 0.0127	0.0496	0.0493	0.0502
Div. Financials	+/-	-0.0021	-0.0016	-0.0020	-0.0333	-0.0267	-0.0336
Real Estate	+/-	0.0048	0.0033	0.0050	-0.0143	-0.0090	-0.0154
Software	+/-	0.0067	0.0019	0.0049	** 0.0835	0.0578	** 0.0840
Hardware	+/-	0.0075	0.0045	0.0080	* 0.0953	0.0671	* 0.0952
Semiconductors	+/-	** 0.0219	0.0154	** 0.0211	*** 0.2667	* 0.1803	0.2694
Telecoms	+/-	-0.0011	-0.0041	-0.0055	-0.0438	-0.0410	-0.0426
Utilities	+/-	0.0042	0.0064	0.0036	0.0546	0.0881	0.0537
Country controls							
French law	+/-	0.0000	** 0.0053	-0.0011	*** -0.0921	*** -0.0683	*** -0.0908
German law	+/-	-0.0046	-0.0049	** -0.0075	-0.0413	-0.0383	-0.0398

*, **, and *** indicate significance at the 10%, 5%, and 1% levels (two-sided).

Table A-3: Coefficients of the industry and country control variables for forecast dispersion

Industry controls	Pred. sign	OLS regression Model (1)	Model (2)	Model (3)	Rank regression Model (1)	Model (2)	Model (3)
Energy	+/-	0.2827	0.2701	0.2433	** 0.0969	** 0.0968	0.0545
Materials	+/-	0.1836	0.1922	0.1631	** 0.0666	** 0.0844	0.0622
Commercial Serv.	+/-	-0.0387	-0.0584	-0.0333	0.0218	0.0151	0.0545
Transportation	+/-	** -0.6163	** -0.6124	** -0.6543	-0.0275	-0.0026	-0.0293
Automobiles	+/-	0.0744	0.0505	0.0318	0.0427	0.0309	0.0023
Cons. Durables	+/-	-0.2058	-0.2416	-0.2299	* 0.0740	0.0562	0.0526
Cons. Services	+/-	* -0.7489	* -0.7962	* -0.8410	0.0740	0.0524	-0.0512
Media	+/-	* 0.3929	0.3706	0.3726	** 0.0917	** 0.0952	** 0.1099
Retailing	+/-	0.5241	0.5062	0.5231	** 0.1342	* 0.1142	0.1182
Food & Staples	+/-	*** -1.8699	*** -2.0018	*** -2.0162	0.0601	0.0014	-0.1180
Food & Beverage	+/-	0.3692	0.3553	0.3595	0.0409	0.0402	0.0492
Household	+/-	0.6665	0.5989	0.5322	0.1420	0.1204	0.0023
Health Care	+/-	-0.0253	-0.0607	-0.0712	** 0.1306	** 0.1212	0.0692
Pharmaceuticals	+/-	0.3759	-0.3902	-0.4153	-0.0338	-0.0342	-0.0651
Div. Financials	+/-	0.3359	0.3432	0.3391	*** 0.1063	*** 0.1143	*** -0.1274
Real Estate	+/-	0.1160	0.0952	0.1187	** 0.0909	** 0.0975	*** 0.1515
Software	+/-	0.1772	0.1120	0.1413	*** 0.1423	*** 0.1107	*** 0.1113
Hardware	+/-	-0.1086	-0.1489	-0.0978	-0.0279	-0.0626	-0.0209
Semiconductors	+/-	-0.9309	** -1.0181	** -0.9461	-0.0860	** -0.1923	*** -0.2356
Telecoms	+/-	-0.5912	-0.6318	-0.6777	0.1067	0.1101	0.0430
Utilities	+/-	-0.4648	-0.4353	-0.4772	-0.0428	-0.0016	0.0091
Country controls							
French law	+/-	*** -1.4397	*** -1.3677	*** -1.4616	*** -0.4981	*** -0.4687	*** -0.5731
German law	+/-	*** -0.9164	*** -0.9193	*** -0.9735	*** -0.3272	*** -0.3236	*** -0.4099

*, **, and *** indicate significance at the 10%, 5%, and 1% levels (two-sided).

Table A-4: Coefficients of the industry and country control variables for analyst following

Industry controls	Pred. sign	OLS regression Model (1)	OLS regression Model (2)	Rank regression Model (1)	Rank regression Model (2)
Energy	+/-	*** 1.3409	*** 2.2000	0.0562	** 0.1241
Materials	+/-	** 0.8988	*** 1.6267	0.0059	** 0.0894
Commercial Serv.	+/-	-0.1844	* -0.9784	-0.0433	*** -0.1245
Transportation	+/-	** 1.2963	*** 2.6335	0.0024	* 0.1118
Automobiles	+/-	** 1.4539	*** 2.0604	0.0535	0.0678
Cons. Durables	+/-	* 0.8216	0.4606	0.0282	-0.0133
Cons. Services	+/-	*** 3.1395	*** 4.4853	*** 0.1658	*** 0.2749
Media	+/-	* 0.6926	0.6363	-0.0241	-0.0382
Retailing	+/-	0.0325	-0.5036	0.0212	-0.0387
Food & Staples	+/-	*** 4.9887	** 5.4887	*** 0.2359	** 0.2710
Food & Beverage	+/-	0.3315	0.2023	-0.0110	-0.0274
Household	+/-	*** 4.5772	*** 6.7278	** 0.1850	*** 0.3173
Health Care	+/-	** 1.5664	** 1.9138	* 0.0814	** 0.1399
Pharmaceuticals	+/-	*** 1.3459	*** 2.1523	0.0414	* 0.0900
Div. Financials	+/-	-0.1093	0.0194	-0.0280	-0.0276
Real Estate	+/-	-0.0940	-0.8402	** -0.0803	*** -0.1497
Software	+/-	*** 1.2246	0.3112	0.0410	-0.0444
Hardware	+/-	-0.3689	*** -1.9888	-0.0093	*** -0.1694
Semiconductors	+/-	0.5203	-1.7512	*** 0.1982	-0.0162
Telecoms	+/-	*** 2.9491	*** 4.4270	0.0843	** 0.2013
Utilities	+/-	0.4236	** 1.7548	* -0.0687	0.0239
Country controls					
French law	+/-	*** 0.7464	*** 3.7248	*** 0.0993	*** 0.3458
German law	+/-	*** 1.9474	*** 3.6773	*** 0.1095	*** 0.2584

*, **, and *** indicate significance at the 10%, 5%, and 1% levels (two-sided).

Table A-5: Results for the WLS analysis with weighted factor Log(MCAP)

Variable	Pred. sign	ACCURACY			DISPERSION			FOLLOWING	
		Model (1)	Model (2)	Model (3)	Model (1)	Model (2)	Model (3)	Model (1)	Model (2)
(Intercept)	+/-	-0.0979	-0.0081	-0.0688	-1.3258	0.6887	-0.5135	-20.7885	1.7305
		*** (-10.91)	** (-2.18)	*** (-9.66)	*** (-2.68)	*** (3.39)	(-1.31)	*** (-36.20)	*** (4.05)
FV_IP	+/-	-0.0294	-0.0198	-0.0244	0.3403	0.5681	0.4824	-3.9689	-1.6347
		*** (-5.07)	*** (-3.36)	*** (-4.23)	(1.04)	* (1.72)	(1.49)	*** (-7.02)	** (-2.13)
FV_PPE	+/-	-0.0043	-0.0058	0.0053	0.5753	0.6424	0.8604	-10.9089	-13.5128
		(-0.07)	(-0.09)	(0.08)	(0.16)	(0.18)	(0.24)	** (-2.01)	* (-1.83)
Log(MCAP)	+	0.0179		0.0118	0.4045		0.2350	4.7280	
		*** (10.94)		*** (10.07)	*** (4.46)		*** (3.61)	*** (46.90)	
LOSS	-	-0.0566	-0.0614	-0.0568	-2.2264	-2.2638	-2.2305	-0.0854	-1.7565
		*** (-16.92)	*** (-18.08)	*** (-16.88)	*** (-12.12)	*** (-12.58)	*** (-12.13)	(-0.34)	*** (-5.11)
LEV	-	-0.0186	-0.0148	-0.0204	-1.1458	-1.0655	-1.1971	1.6378	4.5416
		*** (-4.31)	*** (-3.36)	*** (-4.72)	*** (-4.75)	*** (-4.39)	*** (-4.97)	*** (4.32)	*** (8.89)
COV	+	-0.0010	0.0004		-0.0284	0.0034			
		*** (-5.29)	*** (3.18)		*** (-2.68)	(0.43)			
EAR_SUR	-	-0.0081	-0.0082	-0.0078	-0.1511	-0.1505	-0.1427	-0.1936	-0.5612
		*** (-10.57)	** (-10.39)	*** (-10.15)	*** (-3.54)	*** (-3.51)	*** (-3.34)	*** (-2.98)	*** (-6.37)
CHANGE	-	0.0114	0.0109	0.0113	0.1050	0.0916	0.1045	-0.2765	-0.1947
		*** (3.81)	*** (3.55)	*** (3.76)	(0.62)	(0.54)	(0.62)	(-1.00)	(-0.51)
CROSSLIST	+	-0.0074	0.0000	-0.0106	0.0127	0.1872	-0.0844	5.0725	12.6127
		(-1.22)	(0.00)	* (-1.75)	(0.04)	(0.50)	(-0.24)	*** (5.99)	*** (11.10)
Industry & country controls		Included	Included	Included	Included	Included	Included	Included	Included
Adjusted R²		23.48%	19.89%	22.67%	14.86%	14.16%	14.65%	58.67%	22.97%

T-values are stated in brackets. *, **, and *** indicate significance at the 10%, 5%, and 1% levels (two-sided).

Table A-6: Results for the WLS analysis with weighted factor COV

Variable	Pred. sign	ACCURACY Model (1)	Model (2)	Model (3)	DISPERSION Model (1)	Model (2)	Model (3)	FOLLOWING Model (1)	Model (2)
(Intercept)	+/-	-0.1040 ***(-11.55)	-0.0075 **(-2.01)	-0.0665 ***(-9.43)	-0.4990 (-1.21)	0.5529 ***(3.03)	0.3361 (0.96)	-1.5027 ***(-7.30)	1.2616 ***(12.52)
FV_IP	+/-	-0.0276 ***(-4.30)	-0.0177 ***(-2.70)	-0.0212 ***(-3.32)	0.3634 (1.22)	0.5050 *(1.72)	0.5173 *(1.75)	-0.3333 **(-2.18)	0.0434 (0.28)
FV_PPE	+/-	0.0050 (0.06)	0.0025 (0.03)	0.0187 (0.24)	-0.0657 (-0.02)	0.1045 (0.04)	0.3756 (0.14)	-2.2003 *(-1.91)	-1.3890 (-1.16)
Log(MCAP)	+	0.0194 ***(11.71)		0.0115 ***(9.93)	0.2249 ***(2.85)		0.0361 (0.59)	0.5996 ***(15.20)	
LOSS	-	-0.0684 ***(-19.99)	-0.0738 ***(-21.21)	-0.0688 ***(-19.94)	-1.3355 ***(-9.25)	-1.3735 ***(-9.54)	-1.3274 ***(-9.17)	-0.1050 (-1.54)	-0.1525 **(-2.14)
LEV	-	-0.0216 ***(-4.99)	-0.0173 ***(-3.90)	-0.0236 ***(-5.40)	-0.7772 ***(-3.57)	-0.7416 ***(-3.40)	-0.8491 ***(-3.90)	0.2568 **(2.26)	0.3402 ***(2.87)
COV	+	-0.0012 ***(-6.60)	0.0003 **(2.54)		-0.0472 ***(-3.81)	-0.0251 ***(-2.60)			
EAR_SUR	-	-0.0089 ***(-11.04)	-0.0091 ***(-10.90)	-0.0096 ***(-10.59)	-0.0692 *(-1.95)	-0.0722 **(-2.03)	-0.0588 *(-1.66)	-0.0519 ***(-3.11)	-0.0648 ***(-3.73)
CHANGE	-	0.0122 ***(4.21)	0.0116 ***(3.91)	0.0120 ***(4.12)	0.0139 (0.09)	0.0228 (0.14)	0.0271 (0.17)	-0.0390 (-0.44)	0.0167 (0.18)
CROSSLIST	+	-0.0086 (-1.56)	-0.0012 (-0.22)	-0.0119 **(2.14)	0.2549 (0.44)	0.3423 (0.59)	-0.0503 (-0.09)	12.7807 ***(7.54)	14.0028 ***(7.92)
Industry & country controls		Included	Included	Included	Included	Included	Included	Included	Included
Adjusted R²		27.63%	23.74%	26.42%	11.75%	11.50%	11.28%	12.67%	4.74%

T-values are stated in brackets. *, **, and *** indicate significance at the 10%, 5%, and 1% levels (two-sided).

Table A-7: Results for the WLS analysis with weighted factor LEV

Variable	Pred. sign	ACCURACY			DISPERSION			FOLLOWING	
		Model (1)	Model (2)	Model (3)	Model (1)	Model (2)	Model (3)	Model (1)	Model (2)
(Intercept)	+/-	-0.1321 ***(-13.95)	-0.0136 ***(-3.26)	-0.0951 ***(-12.52)	-0.9314 *(-1.95)	0.6772 ***(3.33)	-0.1904 (-0.50)	-25.3534 ***(-38.35)	1.8535 ***(3.79)
FV_IP	+/-	-0.0328 ***(-4.84)	-0.0181 ***(-2.61)	-0.0261 ***(-3.87)	0.3706 (1.08)	0.5698 *(1.68)	0.5046 (1.49)	-4.5857 ***(-7.81)	-2.5639 ***(-3.15)
FV_PPE	+/-	0.0043 (0.06)	0.0125 (0.17)	0.0197 (0.28)	0.6590 (0.19)	0.7703 (0.22)	0.9674 (0.28)	-10.5535 *(-1.74)	-16.8836 **(-2.00)
Log(MCAP)	+	0.0246 ***(13.82)		0.0166 ***(12.89)	0.3338 ***(3.71)		0.1742 ***(2.69)	5.4599 ***(48.61)	
LOSS	-	-0.0583 ***(-16.84)	-0.0640 ***(-17.95)	-0.0584 ***(-16.73)	-2.0618 ***(-11.78)	-2.1389 ***(-12.26)	-2.0636 ***(-11.78)	0.0611 (0.20)	-2.3214 ***(-5.56)
LEV	-	-0.0216 ***(-4.46)	-0.0168 ***(-3.36)	-0.0242 ***(-4.98)	-1.1262 ***(-4.61)	-1.0613 ***(-4.34)	-1.1785 ***(-4.83)	1.7867 ***(4.22)	5.5071 ***(9.51)
COV	+	-0.0015 ***(-6.44)	0.0007 ***(4.24)		-0.0292 **(-2.55)	0.0003 (0.03)			
EAR_SUR	-	-0.0077 ***(-9.19)	-0.0080 ***(-9.19)	-0.0074 ***(-8.70)	-0.1380 ***(-3.25)	-0.1418 ***(-3.33)	-0.1305 ***(-3.07)	-0.2546 ***(-3.46)	-0.6138 ***(-6.02)
CHANGE	-	0.0129 ***(3.76)	0.0128 ***(3.62)	0.0131 ***(3.80)	0.0831 (0.48)	0.0826 (0.48)	0.0875 (0.51)	-0.1508 (-0.50)	-0.3084 (-0.74)
CROSSLIST	+	-0.0120 (-1.43)	-0.0023 (-0.26)	-0.0179 **(-2.13)	0.0693 (0.16)	0.2012 (0.47)	-0.0496 (-0.12)	4.0342 ***(5.51)	11.9714 ***(12.06)
Industry & country controls		Included	Included	Included	Included	Included	Included	Included	Included
Adjusted R²		24.92%	19.29%	23.72%	14.54%	14.11%	14.36%	60.77%	24.17%

T-values are stated in brackets. *, **, and *** indicate significance at the 10%, 5%, and 1% levels (two-sided).

Table A-8: OLS regression results separately for each country measuring forecast accuracy

Variable	Belgium (N = 175)	France (N = 347)	Germany (N = 510)	Great Britain (N = 938)	Italy (N = 237)	Netherlands (N = 213)	Spain (N = 146)
(Intercept)	-0.2013 *** (-4.46)	-0.0301 (-1.32)	-0.1319 *** (-5.42)	-0.1933 *** (-11.37)	-0.1913 *** (-4.78)	-0.1536 *** (-3.60)	-0.0705 (-1.65)
FV_IP	0.0056 (0.24)	-0.0748 *** (-5.96)	0.0269 (1.22)	-0.0446 *** (-3.36)	1.4857 (1.06)	0.0064 (0.37)	0.0343 (1.07)
FV_PPE				-0.0394 (-0.39)		0.2521 ** (2.07)	
Log(MCAP)	0.0344 *** (4.11)	0.0093 ** (2.40)	0.0271 *** (6.10)	0.0351 *** (10.80)	0.0360 *** (4.61)	0.0281 *** (3.54)	0.0068 (0.93)
LOSS	-0.0212 ** (-2.13)	-0.0653 *** (-7.95)	-0.0984 *** (-10.01)	-0.0594 *** (-9.67)	-0.0586 *** (-4.70)	-0.0620 *** (-4.33)	-0.0522 *** (-4.45)
LEV	0.0075 (0.51)	-0.0455 *** (-3.80)	-0.0428 *** (-3.03)	-0.0050 (-0.56)	-0.0329 ** (-2.13)	-0.0164 (-1.00)	0.0136 (0.96)
COV	-0.0025 ** (-2.26)	-0.0005 (-1.07)	-0.0014 *** (-2.95)	-0.0032 *** (-5.05)	-0.0009 (-1.39)	-0.0014 (-1.63)	-0.0005 (-0.76)
EAR_SUR	-0.0124 *** (-5.67)	-0.0036 * (-1.82)	-0.0076 *** (-3.94)	-0.0065 *** (-3.83)	-0.0038 * (-1.78)	-0.0155 *** (-5.91)	-0.0055 * (-1.70)
CHANGE	0.0037 (0.52)	0.0080 (1.45)	0.0128 * (1.96)	0.0128 (1.43)	0.0211 (0.72)	0.0211 ** (2.54)	-0.0052 (-0.24)
CROSSLIST	-0.0355 (-1.45)		-0.0087 (-0.30)	-0.0193 (-1.26)	-0.0160 (-0.76)	-0.0107 (-0.45)	
Industry controls	Included	Included	Included	Included	Included	Included	Included
Adjusted R²	28.28%	36.54%	31.61%	24.80%	29.55%	30.87%	24.52%

T-values are stated in brackets. *, **, and *** indicate significance at the 10%, 5%, and 1% levels (two-sided).

Table A-9: Rank regression results separately for each country measuring forecast accuracy

Variable	Belgium (N = 175)	France (N = 347)	Germany (N = 510)	Great Britain (N = 938)	Italy (N = 237)	Nether-lands (N = 213)	Spain (N = 146)
(Intercept)	164.3078 (0.97)	97.7729 (0.40)	477.3117 (1.41)	859.9651 (1.58)	346.5635 * (1.77)	79.7471 (0.42)	-171.5959 * (-1.72)
FV_IP	0.0556 (0.21)	-0.1858 (-1.40)	-0.0070 (-0.04)	-0.0692 (-0.95)	0.0180 (0.08)	0.0364 (0.11)	-0.1524 (-0.75)
FV_PPE				-0.4207 (-1.60)		0.6044 ** (2.04)	
Log(MCAP)	0.2584 ** (2.03)	0.1371 ** (1.99)	0.3770 *** (5.57)	0.4420 *** (9.23)	0.6326 *** (6.07)	0.4927 *** (4.32)	0.0017 (0.01)
LOSS	-0.3405 ** (-2.30)	-0.3178 *** (-2.78)	-0.3451 *** (-3.74)	-0.2641 *** (-5.11)	-0.2459 * (-1.87)	-0.4384 *** (-2.63)	-0.2953 (-1.64)
LEV	-0.1332 (-1.41)	-0.2109 *** (-3.75)	-0.1464 *** (-3.30)	-0.0037 (-0.12)	-0.1991 *** (-3.17)	0.0230 (0.33)	0.1105 (1.28)
COV	0.1088 (0.91)	0.1343 * (1.89)	0.0044 (0.06)	-0.1050 ** (-2.11)	-0.2522 ** (-2.72)	-0.2239 ** (-2.09)	0.1577 (1.38)
EAR_SUR	-0.3386 *** (-4.60)	-0.2034 *** (-3.84)	-0.1883 *** (-4.49)	-0.2471 *** (-8.36)	-0.4434 *** (-6.98)	-0.2756 *** (-4.36)	-0.2129 *** (-2.75)
CHANGE	0.2248 ** (2.06)	0.2020 ** (2.51)	0.1175 * (1.90)	0.2503 *** (3.30)	0.3238 (0.96)	0.2038 ** (2.10)	-0.1020 (-0.30)
CROSSLIST	-0.7775 ** (-2.33)		-0.4210 (-1.32)	-0.0926 (-0.74)	-0.2619 (-1.09)	0.0874 (0.36)	
Industry controls	Included	Included	Included	Included	Included	Included	Included
Adjusted R^2	30.21%	20.91%	28.71%	27.91%	41.94%	26.48%	37.53%

T-values are stated in brackets. *, **, and *** indicate significance at the 10%, 5%, and 1% levels (two-sided).

Table A-10: OLS regression results separately for each country measuring forecast dispersion

Variable	Belgium (N = 175)	France (N = 347)	Germany (N = 510)	Great Britain (N = 938)	Italy (N = 237)	Nether-lands (N = 213)	Spain (N = 146)
(Intercept)	-7.0327 ** (-2.22)	-8.5811 *** (-6.24)	-0.1317 (-0.12)	-0.4958 (-1.59)	-5.2303 (-1.36)	-2.6141 (-0.90)	-20.6518 *** (-4.77)
FV_IP	0.4138 (0.25)	-0.3482 (-0.46)	0.9867 (0.99)	-0.2703 (-1.11)	-21.2442 (-0.16)	0.6533 (0.55)	-0.2048 (-0.06)
FV_PPE			0.0399 (0.02)			6.6224 (0.80)	
Log(MCAP)	1.1769 ** (2.00)	1.2991 *** (5.58)	0.1876 (0.94)	0.0759 (1.27)	1.2540 * (1.67)	0.2052 (0.38)	3.4049 *** (4.56)
LOSS	-3.5875 *** (-5.13)	-2.0361 *** (-4.12)	-2.3286 *** (-5.24)	-0.6015 *** (-5.35)	-0.0096 (-0.01)	-1.7029 * (-1.74)	-5.4155 **** (-4.55)
LEV	0.3810 (0.36)	0.1710 (0.24)	-2.5264 *** (-3.96)	-0.1681 (-1.03)	-4.5064 *** (-3.03)	1.3116 (1.17)	-0.6218 (-0.43)
COV	-0.1509 * (-1.93)	-0.0454 * (-1.74)	-0.0429 ** (-2.07)	-0.0119 (-1.02)	-0.0998 (-1.52)	-0.0368 (-0.64)	-0.1263 * (-1.91)
EAR_SUR	-0.3904 ** (-2.54)	0.0071 (0.06)	-0.1815 ** (-2.07)	0.0179 (0.58)	-0.2889 (-1.40)	-0.0286 (-0.16)	-0.1000 (-0.30)
CHANGE	0.4354 (0.86)	0.4298 (1.30)	-0.4042 (-1.36)	0.0028 (0.02)	-5.6288 ** (-1.99)	-0.6011 (-1.06)	-3.1991 (-1.42)
CROSSLIST	-0.3119 (-0.18)		-3.9405 *** (-2.99)	0.1694 (0.60)	1.4902 (0.73)	0.5940 (0.37)	
Industry controls	Included	Included	Included	Included	Included	Included	Included
Adjusted R²	26.01%	19.93%	26.56%	1.94%	15.98%	38.46%	40.60%

T-values are stated in brackets. *, **, and *** indicate significance at the 10%, 5%, and 1% levels (two-sided).

Table A-11: Rank regression results separately for each country measuring forecast dispersion

Variable	Belgium (N = 175)	France (N = 347)	Germany (N = 510)	Great Britain (N = 938)	Italy (N = 237)	Netherlands (N = 213)	Spain (N = 146)
(Intercept)	344.0982 ** (2.30)	-303.5491 (-1.30)	-59.0554 (-0.20)	547.6284 (1.18)	451.1926 ** (2.24)	247.9504 (1.47)	77.4131 (0.77)
FV_IP	-0.1941 (-0.82)	-0.2034 (-1.63)	0.0721 (0.47)	-0.1425 ** (-2.28)	-0.1322 (-0.60)	-0.1794 (-0.62)	-0.2183 (-1.07)
FV_PPE				0.1328 (0.59)		0.2341 (0.88)	
Log(MCAP)	0.6743 *** (5.98)	0.5799 *** (8.92)	0.3325 *** (5.52)	0.3556 *** (8.68)	0.7123 *** (6.64)	0.4358 *** (4.27)	0.3974 *** (3.17)
LOSS	-0.0947 (-0.72)	-0.3919 *** (-3.64)	-0.0918 (-1.12)	-0.0972 ** (-2.19)	0.1714 (1.27)	0.0569 (0.38)	-0.8744 *** (-4.84)
LEV	-0.0949 (-1.14)	-0.2052 *** (-3.88)	-0.1467 *** (-3.72)	0.0981 *** (3.78)	-0.2452 *** (-3.80)	-0.0186 (-0.30)	0.2176 ** (2.51)
COV	-0.8088 *** (-7.63)	-0.3808 *** (-5.70)	-0.8172 *** (-13.58)	-0.9910 *** (-23.30)	-0.9035 *** (-9.48)	-0.8287 *** (-8.65)	-0.1657 (-1.44)
EAR_SUR	-0.1428 ** (-2.19)	-0.0349 (-0.70)	-0.1001 *** (-2.68)	-0.0007 (-0.03)	-0.1024 (-1.57)	-0.1467 ** (-2.60)	-0.0980 (-1.26)
CHANGE	-0.0739 (-0.77)	0.0662 (0.87)	-0.0313 (-0.57)	-0.1399 ** (-2.15)	-0.0811 (-0.23)	-0.0494 (-0.57)	-0.5683 * (-1.68)
CROSSLIST	-0.4450 (-1.51)		-0.3457 (-1.21)	0.6998 *** (6.49)	0.2262 (0.92)	0.0162 (0.07)	
Industry controls	Included	Included	Included	Included	Included	Included	Included
Adjusted R²	45.23%	29.89%	42.60%	44.94%	38.23%	41.07%	36.80%

T-values are stated in brackets. *, **, and *** indicate significance at the 10%, 5%, and 1% levels (two-sided).

Table A-12: OLS regression results separately for each country measuring analyst following

Variable	Belgium	France	Germany	Great Britain	Italy	Nether-lands	Spain
	(N = 175)	(N = 347)	(N = 510)	(N = 938)	(N = 237)	(N = 213)	(N = 146)
(Intercept)	-28.8477 *** (-12.40)	-25.6449 *** (-10.02)	-29.1770 *** (-14.46)	-15.6440 *** (-21.59)	-38.1397 *** (-12.48)	-31.7751 *** (-11.08)	-33.7853 *** (-6.77)
FV_IP	0.6420 (0.38)	-8.6628 *** (-5.66)	0.0812 (0.04)	-2.8747 *** (-4.18)	-123.6009 (-0.88)	-4.1835 *** (-2.86)	4.2822 (0.98)
FV_PPE				-10.1382 * (-1.93)		0.4133 (0.04)	
Log(MCAP)	5.6491 *** (13.99)	5.4504 *** (13.90)	6.5327 *** (20.19)	3.6177 *** (29.93)	8.0834 *** (14.56)	6.9122 *** (14.78)	6.6714 *** (8.24)
LOSS	-1.4235 ** (-1.98)	-0.3847 (-0.37)	1.3720 (1.41)	-0.4726 (-1.47)	1.2923 (1.03)	1.2877 (1.04)	2.3300 (1.47)
LEV	3.6435 *** (3.49)	5.8687 *** (3.92)	2.1961 (1.57)	2.0068 *** (4.36)	-2.1982 (-1.42)	0.0357 (0.03)	3.3555 * (1.75)
COV	Not included	Not included	Not included	Not included	Not included	Not included	Not included
EAR_SUR	-0.0705 (-0.44)	-0.4649 * (-1.82)	-0.4924 ** (-2.58)	0.0841 (0.95)	-0.2905 (-1.35)	-0.0455 (-0.20)	-0.1805 (-0.41)
CHANGE	-0.8475 (-1.63)	1.3546 * (1.94)	-0.6353 (-0.98)	-1.5551 *** (-3.33)	-0.6398 (-0.22)	0.3487 (0.49)	2.4005 (0.79)
CROSSLIST	6.2849 *** (3.66)		5.0836 * (1.77)	4.9620 *** (6.31)	-2.1702 (-1.02)	11.1887 *** (8.26)	
Industry controls	Included	Included	Included	Included	Included	Included	Included
Adjusted R²	85.72%	54.27%	61.99%	61.55%	69.21%	75.80%	59.69%

T-values are stated in brackets. *, **, and *** indicate significance at the 10%, 5%, and 1% levels (two-sided).

Table A-13: Rank regression results separately for each country measuring analyst following

Variable	Belgium (N = 175)	France (N = 347)	Germany (N = 510)	Great Britain (N = 938)	Italy (N = 237)	Nether- lands (N = 213)	Spain (N = 146)
(Intercept)	-133.6919 (-1.18)	262.0611 (1.36)	338.1082 (1.48)	535.0189 (1.48)	63.5691 (0.44)	-80.1549 (-0.62)	-66.2679 (-0.86)
FV_IP	0.3932 ** (2.20)	-0.5528 *** (-5.57)	-0.0424 (-0.36)	-0.1755 *** (-3.62)	0.1541 (0.97)	-0.1678 (-0.77)	-0.2276 (-1.45)
FV_PPE				-0.5584 *** (-3.19)		0.0401 (0.20)	
Log(MCAP)	0.7382 *** (11.90)	0.5337 *** (11.79)	0.7264 *** (23.14)	0.7235 *** (34.26)	0.7280 *** (12.34)	0.7759 *** (14.58)	0.7124 *** (9.70)
LOSS	-0.0049 (-0.05)	-0.2137 ** (-2.40)	0.0759 (1.22)	-0.1061 *** (-3.09)	-0.0972 (-1.00)	0.0712 (0.63)	0.2270 (1.64)
LEV	0.0477 (0.75)	0.1777 *** (4.14)	0.0435 (1.46)	0.1002 *** (5.02)	0.0137 (0.29)	0.0286 (0.61)	0.0195 (0.29)
COV	Not included	Not included	Not included	Not included	Not included	Not included	Not included
EAR_SUR	0.0038 (0.08)	-0.0161 (-0.39)	-0.0851 *** (-3.04)	-0.0280 (-1.42)	-0.11392 *** (-3.02)	-0.0402 (-0.94)	-0.1020 * (-1.71)
CHANGE	-0.0459 (-0.62)	0.0719 (1.14)	-0.0331 (-0.80)	-0.1341 *** (-2.65)	-0.0878 (-0.35)	0.0414 (0.63)	0.1137 (0.43)
CROSSLIST	0.2063 (0.92)		0.3504 (1.63)	0.2301 *** (2.75)	-0.1340 (-0.75)	0.2486 (1.50)	
Industry controls	Included	Included	Included	Included	Included	Included	Included
Adjusted R²	67.64%	51.26%	67.01%	66.36%	67.70%	65.60%	62.05%

T-values are stated in brackets. *, **, and *** indicate significance at the 10%, 5%, and 1% levels (two-sided).

Table A-14: OLS regression results with the mean used to compute forecast accuracy

Variable	Pred. sign	FORECAST ACCURACY		
		Model (1) Full Model	Model (2)	Model (3)
(Intercept)	+/-	-0.0929 *** (-12.23)	-0.0123 *** (-2.94)	-0.1192 *** (-15.30)
FV_IP	+/-	-0.0209 *** (-3.08)	-0.0150 *** (-2.16)	-0.0203 *** (-2.86)
FV_PPE	+/-	0.0164 (0.24)	-0.0026 (-0.04)	0.0394 (0.54)
Log(MCAP)	+	0.0162 *** (12.54)		0.0192 *** (14.32)
LOSS	-	0.0004 (1.13)	0.0007 * (1.74)	0.0019 *** (4.73)
LEV	-	-0.0221 *** (-4.55)	-0.0109 ** (-2.22)	-0.0111 ** (-2.20)
COV	+	-0.0578 *** (-16.09)	-0.0643 *** (-17.57)	
EAR_SUR	-	-0.0074 *** (-8.73)	-0.0084 *** (-9.69)	-0.0100 *** (-11.47)
CHANGE	-	0.0130 *** (3.77)	0.0126 *** (3.56)	0.0124 *** (3.43)
CROSSLIST	+	-0.0170 ** (-2.02)	0.0065 (0.76)	-0.0179 ** (-2.02)
Industry & country controls		Included	Included	Included
Adjusted R²		23.64%	18.93%	15.86%

T-values are stated in brackets. *, **, and *** indicate significance at the 10%, 5%, and 1% levels (two-sided).

Table A-15: OLS regression results with total assets used to represent firm size

Variable	Pred. sign	ACCURACY			DISPERSION			FOLLOWING	
		Model (1)	Model (2)	Model (3)	Model (1)	Model (2)	Model (3)	Model (1)	Model (2)
(Intercept)	+/-	-0.1347 ***(-14.13)	-0.0155 ***(-3.68)	-0.0091 ***(-12.89)	-0.9329 *(1.96)	0.6580 ***(3.24)	-0.2575 (-0.67)	-24.9426 ***(-37.68)	2.0856 ***(4.30)
FV_IP	+/-	-0.0329 ***(-4.83)	-0.0180 ***(-2.58)	-0.0263 ***(-3.87)	0.3685 (1.08)	0.5569 *(1.68)	0.4939 (1.47)	-4.6305 ***(-7.93)	-2.6515 ***(-3.29)
FV_PPE	+/-	0.0062 (0.09)	0.0145 (0.20)	0.0215 (0.31)	0.7224 (0.21)	0.8330 (0.24)	1.0117 (0.29)	-10.6838 *(-1.77)	-16.9982 **(-2.04)
Log(total assets)	+	0.0248 ***(13.82)		0.0170 ***(13.06)	0.3303 ***(3.69)		0.1839 ***(2.84)	5.4047 ***(48.13)	
LOSS	-	-0.0572 ***(-16.34)	-0.0629 ***(-17.45)	-0.0571 ***(-16.21)	-2.0201 ***(-11.54)	-2.0960 ***(-12.03)	-2.0194 ***(-11.53)	-0.0258 (-0.08)	-2.4262 ***(-5.85)
LEV	-	-0.0196 ***(-4.03)	-0.0147 ***(-2.92)	-0.0219 ***(-4.49)	-1.1266 ***(-4.64)	-1.0608 ***(-4.37)	-1.1709 ***(-4.83)	1.6330 ***(3.88)	5.1914 ***(9.07)
COV	+	-0.0014 ***(-6.24)	0.0008 ***(4.42)		-0.0271 **(-2.36)	0.0021 (0.26)			
EAR_SUR	-	-0.0077 ***(-9.11)	-0.0080 ***(-9.12)	-0.0074 ***(-8.63)	-0.1354 ***(-3.19)	-0.1393 ***(-3.28)	-0.1284 ***(-3.03)	-0.2590 ***(-3.53)	-0.6155 ***(-6.09)
CHANGE	-	0.0128 ***(3.71)	0.0128 ***(3.58)	0.0131 ***(3.76)	0.0746 (0.43)	0.0745 (0.43)	0.0792 (0.46)	-0.1705 (-0.57)	-0.3282 (-0.79)
CROSSLIST	+	-0.0123 (-1.52)	-0.0020 (-0.24)	-0.0186 **(-2.30)	0.0664 (0.16)	0.2033 (0.50)	-0.0534 (-0.13)	4.4220 ***(6.34)	12.7626 ***(13.65)
Industry & country controls		Included	Included	Included	Included	Included	Included	Included	Included
Adjusted R^2		24.56%	18.89%	23.43%	14.33%	13.90%	14.17%	60.66%	24.67%

T-values are stated in brackets. *, **, and *** indicate significance at the 10%, 5%, and 1% levels (two-sided).

Table A-16: OLS regression results with number of employees used to represent firm size

Variable	Pred. sign	ACCURACY			DISPERSION			FOLLOWING	
		Model (1)	Model (2)	Model (3)	Model (1)	Model (2)	Model (3)	Model (1)	Model (2)
(Intercept0)	+/-	-0.1343	-0.0155	-0.0982	-0.9274	0.6794	-0.1961	-25.0647	2.0510
		***(-14.10)	***(-3.68)	***(-12.83)	*(-1.95)	***(3.35)	(0.52)	***(-38.03)	***(4.21)
FV_IP	+/-	-0.0329	-0.0180	-0.0262	0.3635	0.5642	0.4985	4.6281	-2.6363
		***(-4.82)	***(-2.58)	***(-3.87)	(1.07)	*(1.67)	(1.48)	***(-7.93)	***(-3.26)
FV_PPE	+/-	0.0059	0.0144	0.0212	0.6846	0.7994	0.9949	-10.6374	-16.9488
		(0.08)	(0.20)	(0.30)	(0.20)	(0.23)	(0.29)	*(-1.76)	**(-2.02)
Log(number of employees)	+	0.0247		0.0169	0.3339		0.1755	5.4285	
		***(13.79)		***(13.01)	***(3.73)		***(2.73)	***(48.58)	
LOSS	-	-0.0573	-0.0629	-0.0573	-2.0151	-2.0917	-2.0157	0.0207	-2.3657
		***(-16.36)	***(-17.46)	***(-16.24)	***(-11.52)	***(-12.01)	***(-11.51)	(0.07)	***(-5.68)
LEV	-	-0.0195	-0.0146	-0.0218	-1.1581	-1.0913	-1.2035	1.5578	5.1076
		***(-4.02)	***(-2.90)	***(-4.46)	***(-4.77)	***(-4.49)	***(-4.96)	***(3.70)	***(8.86)
COV	+	-0.0014	0.0008		-0.0292	0.0005			
		***(-6.28)	***(4.43)		**(-2.55)	(0.06)			
EAR_SUR	-	-0.0077	-0.0080	-0.0074	-0.1359	-0.1397	-0.1283	-0.2609	-0.6229
		***(-9.11)	***(-9.11)	***(-8.63)	***(-3.20)	***(-3.28)	***(-3.02)	***(-3.54)	***(-6.12)
CHANGE	-	0.0128	0.0127	0.0129	0.0869	0.0668	0.0897	-0.0983	-0.1936
		***(3.71)	***(3.57)	***(3.72)	(0.51)	(0.50)	(0.52)	(-0.33)	(-0.47)
CROSSLIST	+	-0.0123	-0.0025	-0.0191	0.1763	0.3087	0.0393	4.6950	13.2340
		(-1.53)	(-0.30)	**(-2.37)	(0.44)	(0.77)	(0.10)	***(6.79)	***(14.23)
Industry & country controls		Included	Included	Included	Included	Included	Included	Included	Included
Adjusted R²		24.51%	18.87%	23.37%	14.53%	14.09%	14.35%	61.05%	24.76%

T-values are stated in brackets. *, **, and *** indicate significance at the 10%, 5%, and 1% levels (two-sided).

Table A-17: OLS regression results for the sample with outliers

Variable	Pred. sign	ACCURACY			DISPERSION			FOLLOWING	
		Model (1)	Model (2)	Model (3)	Model (1)	Model (2)	Model (3)	Model (1)	Model (2)
(Intercept)	+/-	-0.1809	-0.0107	-0.1462	-1.8838	0.7348	-0.7793	-26.7003	1.4820
		***(-13.01)	*(-1.76)	***(-12.90)	**(-2.20)	**(2.03)	(-1.16)	***(-40.64)	***(3.01)
FV_IP	+/-	-0.0584	-0.0385	-0.0569	-0.2911	0.0146	-0.0967	-4.7007	-2.9319
		***(-5.94)	***(-3.77)	***(-5.87)	(-0.47)	(0.02)	(-0.16)	***(-7.91)	***(-3.53)
FV_PPE	+/-	0.0719	0.0936	0.1082	0.3217	0.5025	0.7334	-9.9521	-15.7996
		(0.68)	(0.77)	(1.15)	(0.05)	(0.08)	(0.11)	(-1.58)	*(-1.79)
Log(MCAP)	+	0.0352		0.0221	0.5408		0.3063	5.6707	
		***(13.50)		***(11.71)	***(3.37)		***(2.67)	***(50.76)	
LOSS	-	-0.0827	-0.0924	-0.0830	-3.6900	-3.8387	-3.6946	0.1120	-2.8379
		***(-17.28)	***(-18.90)	***(-17.34)	***(-12.52)	***(-13.15)	***(-12.53)	(0.39)	***(-7.20)
LEV	+	-0.0423	-0.0368	-0.0003	-1.3723	-1.2872	-1.4497	1.8699	5.4161
		***(-6.11)	***(-5.15)	(-0.06)	***(-3.22)	***(-3.02)	***(-3.41)	***(4.51)	***(9.46)
COV	+	-0.0018	0.0012		-0.0414	0.0054			
		***(-5.64)	***(5.16)		**(-2.09)	(0.38)			
EAR_SUR	-	-0.0003	-0.0003	-0.0002	0.0028	0.0026	0.0030	-0.0050	-0.0122
		**(-2.26)	**(-2.25)	**(-2.03)	(0.39)	(0.38)	(0.42)	(-0.74)	(-1.28)
CHANGE	-	0.0172	0.0175	0.0184	0.4444	0.4501	0.4517	-0.1783	-0.2323
		***(3.36)	***(3.32)	***(3.48)	(1.41)	(1.43)	(1.44)	(-0.58)	(-0.54)
CROSSLIST	+	-0.0160	-0.0122	-0.0248	0.5775	0.6354	0.2211	8.6154	18.0850
		(-1.54)	(-1.14)	**(-2.34)	(0.90)	(0.99)	(0.36)	***(14.27)	***(22.50)
Industry & country controls		Included	Included	Included	Included	Included	Included	Included	Included
Adjusted R²		21.01%	15.66%	18.54%	9.76%	9.41%	9.64%	64.90%	31.20%

T-values are stated in brackets. *, **, and *** indicate significance at the 10%, 5%, and 1% levels (two-sided).

Appendix B: Empirical analysis of investors' judgments and investment decisions

Table B-1: OLS regression results for alternative specifications of dispersion of share price judgment

Variable	Original model	Alternative 1	Alternative 2	Alternative 3
	absolute standardized values	squared standardized values	absolute deviation of means minus the group means	squared deviation of means minus the group means
(Intercept)	0.1740 (0.19)	-0.4322 (-0.14)	0.3831 (0.11)	3.1475 (0.06)
REC_DISC	0.0633 (0.32)	0.2215 (0.34)	0.9294 (1.26)	13.9048 (1.21)
MA_MO	0.0805 (0.48)	0.0202 (0.04)	-0.1303 (-0.21)	-5.9496 (-0.61)
FIN_COND	0.0986 (1.04)	0.0973 (0.31)	0.2819 (0.79)	-0.8049 (-0.15)
VOLA_INC	-0.0686 (-1.10)	-0.1781 (-0.87)	-0.2469 (-1.05)	-2.3622 (-0.65)
GROWTH	-0.1114 (-1.62)	-0.1432 (-0.64)	-0.2634 (-1.02)	0.9004 (0.22)
INC	-0.0565 (-0.87)	-0.1154 (-0.54)	-0.1674 (-0.68)	0.0773 (0.02)
NOTES	0.0223 (0.41)	0.1327 (0.74)	0.0932 (0.45)	2.0238 (0.63)
RISK	0.0938 (1.20)	0.2569 (1.01)	0.2985 (1.02)	1.6111 (0.35)
DISCR	0.0217 (0.38)	-0.0235 (-0.13)	0.0632 (0.30)	-1.1140 (-0.34)
RELEV	0.0031 (0.04)	0.0288 (0.11)	-0.0468 (-0.15)	-0.2183 (-0.05)
RELIA	0.0772 (1.10)	0.2558 (1.11)	0.3014 (1.14)	1.9562 (0.48)
Adjusted R^2	-4.08%	-8.87%	-5.21%	-9.89%

T-values are stated in brackets. *, **, and *** indicate significance at the 10%, 5%, and 1% levels (two-sided).

Table B-2: OLS and rank regression results for dispersion of share price judgment
(reduced sample less false manipulation checks)

Variable	OLS regression	Rank regression
(Intercept)	-0.0282 (-0.01)	32.7712 ** (2.07)
REC_DISC	0.2429 (0.33)	0.0220 (0.11)
MA_MO	0.4776 (0.85)	0.1286 (0.90)
FIN_COND	0.3684 (1.14)	0.1424 (0.91)
VOLA_INC	-0.1951 (-0.85)	0.0605 (0.35)
GROWTH	-0.4878 ** (-2.20)	-0.2987 ** (-2.23)
INC	-0.4625 * (-1.94)	-0.1716 (-1.18)
NOTES	0.0185 (0.10)	0.0348 (0.25)
RISK	0.3557 (1.37)	0.0987 (0.61)
DISCR	0.1293 (0.69)	0.0572 (0.38)
RELEV	0.0789 (0.31)	-0.1167 (-0.77)
RELIA	0.4919 ** (2.13)	0.1197 (0.81)
Adjusted R²	6.21%	0.54%

T-values are stated in brackets. *, **, and *** indicate significance at the 10%, 5%, and 1% levels (two-sided).

Table B-3: OLS and rank regression results for share price confidence
(reduced sample less false manipulation checks)

Variable	OLS regression	Rank regression
(Intercept)	4.3346 ** (2.28)	30.6579 ** (2.13)
REC_DISC	1.0727 ** (2.46)	0.4682 *** (2.67)
MA_MO	-0.2317 (-0.69)	-0.1463 (-1.12)
FIN_COND	-0.1415 (-0.73)	-0.1586 (-1.11)
VOLA_INC	0.1347 (0.98)	0.1422 (0.90)
GROWTH	-0.2721 ** (-2.05)	-0.2336 * (-1.91)
INC	0.0686 (0.48)	0.0755 (0.57)
NOTES	0.0386 (0.36)	0.0098 (0.08)
RISK	-0.1242 (-0.80)	-0.1471 (-0.99)
DISCR	-0.1764 (-1.58)	-0.1916 (-1.39)
RELEV	0.2184 (1.43)	0.2259 (1.63)
RELIA	0.0503 (0.36)	0.0918 (0.68)
Adjusted R²	13.00%	16.17%

T-values are stated in brackets. *, **, and *** indicate significance at the 10%, 5%, and 1% levels (two-sided).

Table B-4: Logistic, OLS and rank regression results for investment decision
(reduced sample less false manipulation checks)

Variable	Investment decision Logistic regression	Amount to invest OLS regression	Rank regression
(Intercept)	0.1228 * (2.74)	3.3876 (1.15)	26.5277 * (1.87)
REC_DISC	0.4890 (0.86)	0.3686 (0.65)	0.1372 (0.94)
MA_MO	0.8714 (0.05)	0.3265 (0.68)	0.0841 (0.73)
FIN_COND (_D)	2.3629 (0.67)	0.0545 (0.17)	0.0286 (0.23)
VOLA_INC (_D)	2.9236 (1.85)	-0.2828 (-1.44)	-0.2161 (-1.50)
GROWTH (_D)	2.0000 (1.22)	0.5014 ** (2.22)	0.2027 * (1.76)
INC (_D)	1.7026 (0.54)	-0.1483 (-0.76)	-0.1142 (-0.98)
NOTES (_D)	1.4762 (0.37)	-0.1809 (-1.29)	-0.1094 (-1.08)
RISK (_D)	0.2876 (2.42)	-0.3956 (-1.65)	-0.2124 (-1.58)
DISCR (_D)	1.7605 (0.67)	0.0515 (0.34)	-0.0059 (-0.05)
RELEV (_D)	2.8278 (2.29)	0.1917 (0.82)	0.0777 (0.64)
RELIA (_D)	1.1692 (0.07)	-0.2001 (-0.95)	-0.0809 (-0.62)
Adjusted R²		15.00%	11.97%
Nagelkerke's R²	30.41%		

T-values are stated in brackets. *, **, and *** indicate significance at the 10%, 5%, and 1% levels (two-sided).

Appendix C: Experiment materials

Part 1: Questions that had to be answered during the experiment

Teil 1: Angaben zum Experiment

1. Der Ihnen vorliegende Geschäftsbericht der Union Estate AG wurde heute veröffentlicht. Welchen <u>Kurs für eine Aktie der Union Estate AG</u> würden Sie heute unter Berücksichtigung der Ihnen vorliegenden Informationen erwarten? *(Angaben in Euro, bitte runden Sie auf Werte ohne Dezimalstellen)*

   EINGABE: _____ €

2. Der von Ihnen erwartete Kurs für eine Aktie der Union Estate AG beträgt XXX Euro. Wie <u>sicher</u> sind Sie sich, dass diese Einschätzung dem tatsächlichen Kurs heute nach Börsenschluss <u>entspricht</u>?

sehr unsicher			mittel- mäßig			sehr sicher	keine Angabe
❑	❑	❑	❑	❑	❑	❑	❑

3. Wären Sie bereit, auf Basis der Informationen im Geschäftsbericht 2010, in Aktien der Union Estate AG <u>zu investieren</u>?

   ❑ ja   ❑ nein   ❑ keine Angabe

4. Bei Antwort „ja":
   Welchen Anteil Ihres Gesamtvermögens würden Sie in Aktien der Union Estate AG <u>investieren</u>?

sehr wenig			mittel- mäßig			sehr viel	keine Angabe
❑	❑	❑	❑	❑	❑	❑	❑

5. Wie schätzen Sie auf der Basis des Geschäftsberichts 2010 die <u>finanzielle Lage</u> der Union Estate AG ein?

sehr schlecht			mittel- mäßig			sehr gut	keine Angabe
❑	❑	❑	❑	❑	❑	❑	❑

6. Wie schätzen Sie auf der Basis des Geschäftsberichts 2010 die <u>Volatilität des Jahresergebnisses</u> der Union Estate AG ein?

sehr gering			mittel- mäßig			sehr hoch	keine Angabe
❑	❑	❑	❑	❑	❑	❑	❑

7. Wie schätzen Sie auf der Basis des Geschäftsberichts 2010 die <u>Wachstumsperspektiven</u> der Union Estate AG ein?

sehr schlecht			mittel- mäßig			sehr gut	keine Angabe
❑	❑	❑	❑	❑	❑	❑	❑

8. **Wie schätzen Sie auf der Basis des Geschäftsberichts 2010 die Nützlichkeit des Jahresergebnisses für die Prognose von zukünftigen Gewinnen der Union Estate AG ein?**

sehr gering			mittel- mäßig			sehr hoch	keine Angabe
❑	❑	❑	❑	❑	❑	❑	❑

9. **Wie schätzen Sie auf der Basis des Geschäftsberichts 2010 die Nützlichkeit der Informationen im Anhang für die Prognose von zukünftigen Gewinnen der Union Estate AG ein?**

sehr gering			mittel- mäßig			sehr hoch	keine Angabe
❑	❑	❑	❑	❑	❑	❑	❑

10. **Wie schätzen Sie auf der Basis des Geschäftsberichts 2010 das Risiko einer Investition in Aktien der Union Estate AG ein?**

sehr gering			mittel- mäßig			sehr hoch	keine Angabe
❑	❑	❑	❑	❑	❑	❑	❑

11. **Wie schätzen Sie auf der Basis des Geschäftsberichts 2010 den bilanzpolitischen Ermessensspielraum der Union Estate AG ein?**

sehr gering			mittel- mäßig			sehr hoch	keine Angabe
❑	❑	❑	❑	❑	❑	❑	❑

12. **Wie schätzen Sie die Relevanz der Informationen im Geschäftsbericht 2010 der Union Estate AG ein?**

sehr gering			mittel- mäßig			sehr hoch	keine Angabe
❑	❑	❑	❑	❑	❑	❑	❑

13. **Wie schätzen Sie die Verlässlichkeit der Informationen im Geschäftsbericht 2010 der Union Estate AG ein?**

sehr gering			mittel- mäßig			sehr hoch	keine Angabe
❑	❑	❑	❑	❑	❑	❑	❑

Teil 2: Manipulationschecks

14. **Bilanziert die Union Estate AG ihr Immobilienportfolio im Rahmen der Folgebewertung zum beizulegenden Zeitwert (Fair Value)?**

   ❑ ja   ❑ nein   ❑ keine Angabe

15. **Werden bei der Ermittlung der beizulegenden Zeitwerte für das Immobilienportfolio der Union Estate AG beobachtbare Marktwerte herangezogen?**

   ❑ ja   ❑ nein   ❑ keine Angabe

Part 2: Questions that had to be answered subsequently to the experiment

1. **Welche Stadt hat mehr Einwohner?**

   ❑ Essen

   ❑ Münster

   Wie sicher sind Sie sich, dass Ihre Antwort richtig ist?

„Ich könnte auch eine Münze werfen."					„Ich bin mir todsicher."
50%	60%	70%	80%	90%	100%
❑	❑	❑	❑	❑	❑

2. **Wie hoch ist der Messeturm in Frankfurt am Main?**

   ❑ 243 Meter

   ❑ 257 Meter

   Wie sicher sind Sie sich, dass Ihre Antwort richtig ist?

„Ich könnte auch eine Münze werfen."					„Ich bin mir todsicher."
50%	60%	70%	80%	90%	100%
❑	❑	❑	❑	❑	❑

3. **Wie hoch ist die spezifische Dichte von Osmium unter Normalbedingungen?**

   ❑ 22,61 g/cm^3

   ❑ 36,28 g/cm^3

   Wie sicher sind Sie sich, dass Ihre Antwort richtig ist?

„Ich könnte auch eine Münze werfen."					„Ich bin mir todsicher."
50%	60%	70%	80%	90%	100%
❑	❑	❑	❑	❑	❑

4. Im Folgenden erhalten Sie mehrmals die Möglichkeit, sich zwischen zwei Lotterien zu entscheiden, bei denen Sie unterschiedliche Auszahlungen zu unterschiedlichen Wahrscheinlichkeiten erhalten. Bitte geben Sie jeweils an, für welche Option (A oder B) Sie sich jeweils (pro Zeile) entscheiden würden.

Option A	Option B	Bitte jeweils ankreuzen	
zu 1/10 erhalten Sie 20,00 EUR, zu 9/10 erhalten Sie 16,00 EUR	zu 1/10 erhalten Sie 38,50 EUR, zu 9/10 erhalten Sie 1,00 EUR	❏ Option A	❏ Option B
zu 2/10 erhalten Sie 20,00 EUR, zu 8/10 erhalten Sie 16,00 EUR	zu 2/10 erhalten Sie 38,50 EUR, zu 8/10 erhalten Sie 1,00 EUR	❏ Option A	❏ Option B
zu 3/10 erhalten Sie 20,00 EUR, zu 7/10 erhalten Sie 16,00 EUR	zu 3/10 erhalten Sie 38,50 EUR, zu 7/10 erhalten Sie 1,00 EUR	❏ Option A	❏ Option B
zu 4/10 erhalten Sie 20,00 EUR, zu 6/10 erhalten Sie 16,00 EUR	zu 4/10 erhalten Sie 38,50 EUR, zu 6/10 erhalten Sie 1,00 EUR	❏ Option A	❏ Option B
zu 5/10 erhalten Sie 20,00 EUR, zu 5/10 erhalten Sie 16,00 EUR	zu 5/10 erhalten Sie 38,50 EUR, zu 5/10 erhalten Sie 1,00 EUR	❏ Option A	❏ Option B
zu 6/10 erhalten Sie 20,00 EUR, zu 4/10 erhalten Sie 16,00 EUR	zu 6/10 erhalten Sie 38,50 EUR, zu 4/10 erhalten Sie 1,00 EUR	❏ Option A	❏ Option B
zu 7/10 erhalten Sie 20,00 EUR, zu 3/10 erhalten Sie 16,00 EUR	zu 7/10 erhalten Sie 38,50 EUR, zu 3/10 erhalten Sie 1,00 EUR	❏ Option A	❏ Option B
zu 8/10 erhalten Sie 20,00 EUR, zu 2/10 erhalten Sie 16,00 EUR	zu 8/10 erhalten Sie 38,50 EUR, zu 2/10 erhalten Sie 1,00 EUR	❏ Option A	❏ Option B
zu 9/10 erhalten Sie 20,00 EUR, zu 1/10 erhalten Sie 16,00 EUR	zu 9/10 erhalten Sie 38,50 EUR, zu 1/10 erhalten Sie 1,00 EUR	❏ Option A	❏ Option B
zu 10/10 erhalten Sie 20,00 EUR, zu 0/10 erhalten Sie 16,00 EUR	zu 10/10 erhalten Sie 38,50 EUR, zu 0/10 erhalten Sie 1,00 EUR	❏ Option A	❏ Option B

Part 3: Application form for the experiment[249]

Teil 1: Begrüßung

Liebe Teilnehmerinnen und Teilnehmer,

herzlich Willkommen und vielen Dank für Ihr Interesse an unserem Experiment. Auf den folgenden Seiten werden einige Daten erhoben, die für die Anmeldung notwendig sind. Die Eingabe wird nur 2–3 Minuten dauern. Ihre Angaben werden anonym behandelt und nicht in Verbindung mit Ihren persönlichen Daten gespeichert (diese sind nur für die Kontaktaufnahme und für Ihre Vergütung notwendig).

Das Experiment wird in der Zeit vom 9. bis 12. Mai 2011 stattfinden und dauert ca. 50 Minuten. Sie erhalten für die Teilnahme eine Vergütung, die im Durchschnitt 20 € betragen wird.

Nachdem Sie sich erfolgreich registriert haben, werden wir in den nächsten Tagen per E-Mail mit Ihnen in Kontakt treten.

Vielen Dank für Ihre Bemühungen!

Prof. Dr. Peter Kajüter

Teil 2: Erfassung personenbezogener Daten

5. **Bitte geben Sie Ihre Daten an:**

    Name: _____   Vorname: _____

    Geburtsjahr: _____

    Geschlecht: ❏ männlich   ❏ weiblich

6. **Bitte geben Sie eine E-Mail-Adresse an, über die wir Sie kontaktieren sollen:**

    E-Mail: _____

    E-Mail: _____ (Wiederholung)

7. **Bitte geben Sie die Kontoverbindung an, auf welche die Experimentvergütung überwiesen werden soll:**

    Kontoinhaber: _____

    Kontonummer: _____

    Bankleitzahl: _____

    Geldinstitut: _____

---

249 Participants applied for the experiment online via the unipark system. See www.unipark.info.

8. **Bitte kreuzen Sie die Termine an, an denen Sie an unserem Experiment teilnehmen können. Je mehr Termine Sie ankreuzen, desto höher ist die Teilnahmechance.**

   ☐ Montag, 9. Mai 2011, 18:15-19:15 Uhr

   ☐ Dienstag, 10. Mai 2011, 18:15-19:15 Uhr

   ☐ Mittwoch, 11. Mai, 16:15-17:15 Uhr

   ☐ Donnerstag, 12. Mai, 18:15-19:15 Uhr

Teil 3: Erfassung des Wissensniveaus, der Investitionserfahrung und der Risikoeinstellung

Hinweis: Diese Daten werden anonym (ohne Ihre zuvor eingegebenen persönlichen Daten) gespeichert!

9. **Welches Studienfach belegen Sie?**

   ☐ Betriebswirtschaftslehre

   ☐ Volkswirtschaftslehre

   ☐ Wirtschaftsinformatik

   ☐ anderes

10. **Welchen Studienabschluss streben Sie an?**

    ☐ Bachelor

    ☐ Master

    ☐ Diplom

    ☐ anderen

11. **Nur bei Master: Welchen Major und welchen Minor belegen Sie?**

    Major: _____

    Minor: _____

12. **In welchem Semester studieren Sie?** _____

13. **Wie ist Ihr aktueller Notendurchschnitt?** _____

14. **Haben Sie vor Ihrem Studium eine Ausbildung absolviert?** ☐ ja   ☐ nein

15. **Wie viele Jahre Berufserfahrung haben Sie im betriebswirtschaftlichen Bereich?**
    (inklusive Praktika, Ausbildung und Nebenjobs, bitte auf volle Jahre aufrunden)

    _____ Jahre

16. **Wie viele Lehrveranstaltungen zum Thema Accounting (Rechnungswesen/-legung, Controlling, Steuern) haben Sie bislang belegt?**

    _____ Lehrveranstaltungen

17. **Wie viele Lehrveranstaltungen zum Thema Finanzierung (Wertpapiermanagement, Banken, etc.) haben Sie bislang belegt?**

    _____ Lehrveranstaltungen

18. Haben Sie in der Vergangenheit einmal Geld in festverzinsliche Anlagen (z.B. Anleihen) angelegt?

❏ ja   ❏ nein

19. Haben Sie in der Vergangenheit einmal Geld in Aktien angelegt?

❏ ja   ❏ nein

20. Wie schätzen Sie Ihre Anlageerfahrung ein?

sehr gering			mittel- mäßig			sehr groß
❏	❏	❏	❏	❏	❏	❏

21. Sie erhalten 50.000 Euro, die Sie festverzinslich zum EURIBOR-Zinssatz anlegen können. Alternativ könnten Sie das Geld auch an der deutschen Börse in Aktien investieren. Welchen Anteil würden Sie in Aktien investieren?

0%	10%	20%	30%	40%	50%	60%	70%	80%	90%	100%
❏	❏	❏	❏	❏	❏	❏	❏	❏	❏	❏

22. Wie schätzen Sie Ihre Risikoeinstellung bei finanziellen Anlagen ein?

sehr risikoavers			mittel- mäßig			Sehr risikofreudig
❏	❏	❏	❏	❏	❏	❏

Part 4: Annual report of Union Estate AG

Group 1: Recognized mark-to-market fair values

Lagebericht	1

Die Union Estate AG ist ein Immobilienunternehmen, das sich auf deutsche Gewerbeimmobilien speziali-siert hat. Im Fokus der Union Estate AG stehen langfristig vermietete Büroimmobilien an nachgefragten Wirtschaftsstandorten deutscher Ballungszentren.

Ziel der Union Estate AG ist die Steigerung der Mieterlöse. Das Immobilienportfolio umfasst ertragsstarke Objekte mit variierenden Mietvertragslaufzeiten und bonitätsstarken Mietern. Selbst in wirtschaftlich schwierigen Zeiten besteht kein Abwertungsbedarf des Immobilienportfolios, da sich die Objekte der Uni-on Estate AG durch gute urbane Lagen in deutschen Metropolen mit Wachstumspotential auszeichnen.

Zum 31.12.2010 notierte die Aktie von Union Estate zu einem Jahresschlusskurs von 20 Euro. Dies liegt leicht über der branchenüblichen Bewertung für Immobilienaktien (Branchen-KGV: 15).

Leerstandsentwicklung - Gewerbeimmobilien

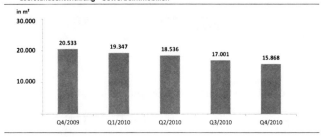

Laufzeitstruktur der Mietverträge

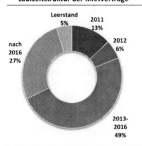

Immobilienbestand nach Region

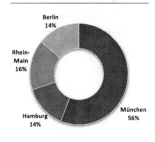

Bilanz zum 31. Dezember 2010

AKTIVA

in TEUR	Anhang	2010	2009
Immaterielle Vermögensgegenstände		336	311
Sachanlagen		3.923	5.897
Als Finanzinvestition gehaltene Immobilien	1	1.482.578	1.425.440
Langfristige Vermögenswerte		**1.486.837**	**1.431.648**
Forderungen aus Lieferungen und Leistungen		5.694	4.099
Liquide Mittel		146.818	51.426
Kurzfristige Vermögenswerte		**152.512**	**55.525**
Gesamte Aktiva		**1.639.349**	**1.487.173**

PASSIVA

in TEUR	Anhang	2010	2009
Gezeichnetes Kapital		56.000	56.000
Kapitalrücklage		237.450	237.450
Gewinnrücklagen		339.036	241.574
Eigenkapital		**632.486**	**535.024**
Rückstellungen		1.550	1.200
Finanzverbindlichkeiten		1.000.752	947.257
Langfristige Schulden		**1.002.302**	**948.457**
Verbindlichkeiten aus Lieferungen und Leistungen		4.561	3.692
Kurzfristige Schulden		**4.561**	**3.692**
Gesamte Passiva		**1.639.349**	**1.487.173**

Gewinn- und Verlustrechnung für das Geschäftsjahr 2010

in TEUR	Anhang	2010	2009
Umsatzerlöse aus Vermietung		142.698	119.857
Aufwand aus Vermietung		-10.189	-8.833
Nettogewinn aus der Fair Value-Anpassung von als Finanzinvestition gehaltenen Immobilien	1	57.138	4.432
Personalaufwand		-5.321	-4.990
Zinsaufwand		-50.037	-47.362
Sonstige betriebliche Aufwendungen		-1.866	-516
Ergebnis vor Ertragsteuern		**132.423**	**62.588**
Ertragsteuern		-19.863	-9.388
Jahresergebnis		**112.560**	**53.200**
Ergebnis je Aktie in EUR		**2,01**	**0,95**

| Anhang | 3 |

1 Als Finanzinvestition gehaltene Immobilien

Als Finanzinvestition gehaltene Immobilien werden bei erstmaliger Bewertung zu Anschaffungs- oder Herstellungskosten bewertet. Im Rahmen der Folgebewertung werden die als Finanzinvestition gehaltenen Immobilien zu ihrem beizulegenden Zeitwert (Fair Value) bilanziert, der die Marktbedingungen am Bilanzstichtag widerspiegelt. Gewinne oder Verluste aus der Änderung der Zeitwerte werden in der Gewinn- und Verlustrechnung erfasst.

Bei der Ermittlung des beizulegenden Zeitwerts werden beobachtbare Marktwerte herangezogen, die aufgrund von einer großen Anzahl von Käufen und Verkäufen für weitgehend identische Immobilien in ähnlichen Lagen zustande gekommen sind.

Im Geschäftsjahr 2010 ergab sich aufgrund der guten wirtschaftlichen Entwicklung sowie des gesunkenen allgemeinen Leerstands eine Erhöhung des beizulegenden Zeitwerts. Mit einem Gesamtwert von TEUR 1.482.578 (Vorjahr: TEUR 1.425.440) liegt der Wert des Immobilienportfolios über dem Wert des Vorjahres.

BESTÄTIGUNGSVERMERK

Wir haben den von der Union Estate AG aufgestellten Jahresabschluss sowie den Lagebericht für das Geschäftsjahr vom 1. Januar bis zum 31. Dezember 2010 geprüft. Wir haben unsere Abschlussprüfung nach den gesetzlichen Regelungen vorgenommen.

Unsere Prüfung hat zu keinen Einwendungen geführt.

Hamburg, den 10. Februar 2011

Hamburger Treuhand AG
Wirtschaftsprüfungsgesellschaft

Bibliography

A

Aboody, D./Barth, M. E./Kasznik, R. (1999): Revaluations of fixed assets and future firm performance: Evidence from the UK, in: Journal of Accounting and Economics, 26 (1-3), p. 149-178.

Aboody, D./Barth, M. E./Kasznik, R. (2004): Firms' Voluntary Recognition of Stock-Based Compensation Expense, in: Journal of Accounting Research, 42 (2), p. 123-150.

Achleitner, A.-K./Bassen, A./Pietzsch, L. (2001): Kapitalmarktkommunikation von Wachstumsunternehmen – Kriterien zur effizienten Ansprache von Finanzanalysten, Stuttgart 2001.

Achleitner, P./Wichels, D. (2003): Management von Kapitalmarkterwartungen, in: Ebel, B./Hofer, M. B. (eds.): Investor Marketing. Aktionäre erfolgreich gewinnen, Investoren langfristig binden, Börsenkurse nachhaltig steigern, 1st ed., Wiesbaden 2003, p. 51-62.

Acker, D./Horton, J./Tonks, I. (2002): Accounting standards and analysts' forecasts: the impact of FRS3 on analysts' ability to forecast EPS, in: Journal of Accounting and Public Policy, 21 (3), p. 193-217.

Aharony, J./Barniv, R./Falk, H./Routledge (2010): The Impact of Mandatory IFRS Adoption on Equity Valuation of Accounting Numbers for Security Investors in the EU, in: European Accounting Review, 19 (3), p. 535-579.

Ahmed, A. S./Kilic, E./Lobo, G. J. (2006): Does Recognition versus Disclosure Matter? Evidence from Value-Relevance of Banks' Recognized and Disclosed Derivative Financial Instruments, in: Accounting Review, 81 (3), p. 567-588.

Akerlof, G. A. (1970): The Market for "Lemons": Quality Uncertainty and the Market Mechanism, in: Quarterly Journal of Economics, 84 (3), p. 488-500.

Albert, H. (2000): Kritischer Rationalismus – Vier Kapitel zur Kritik illusionären Denkens, Tübingen 2000.

Al-Laham, A. (1997): Strategieprozesse in deutschen Unternehmungen – Verlauf, Struktur und Effizienz, Diss., Wiesbaden 1997.

Ameln, F. v. (2004): Konstruktivismus – Die Grundlagen systemischer Therapie, Beratung und Bildungsarbeit, Stuttgart 2004.

Anandarajan, A./Viger, C./Curatola, A. P. (2002): An Experimental Investigation of Alternative Going-Concern Reporting Formats: A Canadian Experience, in: Canadian Accounting Perspectives, 1 (2), p. 1-26.

Arnold, J./Moizer, P. (1984): A Survey of the Methods Used by UK Investment Analysts to Appraise Investments in Ordinary Shares, in: Accounting & Business Research, 14 (55), p. 195-208.

Arrow, K. J. (1985): The Economics of Agency, in: Pratt, J. W./Zeckhauser, R. J. (eds.): The Structure of Business, Boston, Mass. 1985, p. 37-51.

Ashbaugh, H./Pincus, M. (2001): Domestic Accounting Standards, International Accounting Standards, and the Predictability of Earnings, in: Journal of Accounting Research, 39 (3), p. 417-434.

Athanasakou, V. E./Strong, N. C./Walker, M. (2009): Earnings management or forecast guidance to meet analyst expectations?, in: Accounting & Business Research, 39 (1), p. 3-35.

Athey, S./Imbens, G. W. (2006): Identification and Inference in Nonlinear Difference-in-Differences Models, in: Econometrica, 74 (2), p. 431-497.

Aubert, F./Dumontier, P. (2009): Analyzing Brokers' Expertise: Did Analysts Fully Anticipate the Impact of IFRS Adoption on Earnings? The European Evidence, Working Paper.

Auer, L. v. (2011): Ökonometrie – Eine Einführung, 5th ed., Berlin 2011.

B

Backhaus, K./Erichson, B./Plinke, W./Weiber, R. (2011): Multivariate Analyse-methoden – Eine anwendungsorientierte Einführung, 13th ed., Berlin 2011.

Baetge, J./Zülch, H. (2001): Fair Value-Accounting, in: Betriebswirtschaftliche Forschung und Praxis, 53 (6), p. 543-562.

Bailey, W./Andrew Karolyi, G./Salva, C. (2006): The economic consequences of increased disclosure: Evidence from international cross-listings, in: Journal of Financial Economics, 81 (1), p. 175-213.

Balboa, M./Gomez-Sala, J. C./Lopez-Espinosa, G. (2008): Does the value of recommendations depend on the level of optimism? A country-based analysis, in: Journal of Multinational Financial Management, 18 (4), p. 405-426.

Ball, R. (1978): Anomalies in relationships between securities' yields and yield-surrogates, in: Journal of Financial Economics, 6 (2-3), p. 103-126.

Ball, R. (2006): International Financial Reporting Standards (IFRS): pros and cons for investors, in: Accounting & Business Research, 36 (Special Issue), p. 5-27.

Ball, R. (2009): The Global Financial Crisis and the Efficient Market Hypothesis: What Have We Learned?, in: Journal of Applied Corporate Finance, 21 (4), p. 8-16.

Barlev, B./Haddad, J. R. (2003): Fair Value Accounting And The Management Of The Firm, in: Critical Perspectives on Accounting, 14 (4), p. 383-415.

Barron, O. E./Byard, D./Kim, O. (2002): Changes in Analysts' Information around Earnings Announcements, in: Accounting Review, 77 (4), p. 821-846.

Barron, O. E./Kile, C. O./O'Keefe, T. B. (1999): MD&A Quality as Measured by the SEC and Analysts' Earnings Forecasts, in: Contemporary Accounting Research, 16 (1), p. 75-109.

Bartel, R. (1990): Charakteristik, Methodik und wissenschaftsmethodische Probleme der Wirtschaftswissenschaften, in: Wirtschaftswissenschaftliches Studium, 19 (2), p. 54-59.

Barth, D. (2009): Prognoseberichterstattung – Praxis, Determinanten und Kapitalmarktwirkungen bei deutschen börsennotierten Unternehmen, Frankfurt am Main 2009.

Barth, M. E. (1994): Fair Value Accounting: Evidence from Investment Securities and the Market Valuation of Banks, in: Accounting Review, 69 (1), p. 1-25.

Barth, M. E. (2000): Valuation-based accounting research: Implications for financial reporting and opportunities for future research, in: Accounting & Finance, 40 (1), p. 7-31.

Barth, M. E./Beaver, W. H./Landsman, W. R. (1996): Value-Relevance of Banks' Fair Value Disclosures under SFAS No. 107, in: Accounting Review, 71 (4), p. 513-537.

Barth, M. E./Beaver, W. H./Landsman, W. R. (2001): The relevance of the value relevance literature for financial accounting standard setting: another view, in: Journal of Accounting and Economics, 31 (1-3), p. 77-104.

Barth, M. E./Clinch, G. (1998): Revalued Financial, Tangible, and Intangible Assets: Associations with Share Prices and Non-Market-Based Value Estimates, in: Journal of Accounting Research, 36 (Supplement), p. 199-233.

Barth, M. E./Hodder, L. D./Stubben, S. R. (2008): Fair Value Accounting for Liabilities and Own Credit Risk, in: Accounting Review, 83 (3), p. 629-664.

Barth, M. E./Landsman, W. R. (1995): Fundamental Issues Related to Using Fair Value Accounting for Financial Reporting, in: Accounting Horizons, 9 (4), p. 97-107.

Barth, M. E./Landsman, W. R./Wahlen, J. M. (1995): Fair value accounting: Effects on banks' earnings volatility, regulatory capital, and value of contractual cash flows – The Role of Capital in Financial Institutions, in: Journal of Banking & Finance, 19 (3-4), p. 577-605.

Bartlett, S. A./Chandler, R. A. (1997): The Corporate Report and the Private Shareholder: Lee and Tweedie Twenty Years on – Bartlett, Susan A.; Chandler, Roy A., in: British Accounting Review, 29 (3), p. 245-261.

Beatty, A./Weber, J. (2006): Accounting Discretion in Fair Value Estimates: An Examination of SFAS 142 Goodwill Impairments, in: Journal of Accounting Research, 44 (2), p. 257-288.

Beaver, W. H. (1983): Zur Effizienz des Kapitalmarkts: Gegenwärtiger Stand der Forschung, in: Betriebswirtschaftliche Forschung und Praxis, 35 (4), p. 344-358.

Beaver, W. H./Ryan, S. G. (1985): How Well Do Statement No. 33 Earnings Explain Stock Returns?, in: Financial Analysts Journal, 41 (5), p. 66-71.

Belzile, R./Fortin, A./Viger, C. (2006): Recognition versus Disclosure of Stock Option Compensation: An Analysis of Judgements and Decisions of Nonprofessional Investors, in: Canadian Accounting Perspectives, 5 (2), p. 147-179.

Beneish, M. D. (1991): Stock Prices and the Dissemination of Analysts' Recommendations, in: Journal of Business, 64 (3), p. 393-416.

Benston, G. J. (2008): The shortcomings of fair-value accounting described in SFAS 157, in: Journal of Accounting and Public Policy, 27 (2), p. 101-114.

Benston, G. J./Smith, C. W., JR. (1976): A Transactions Cost Approach to the Theory of Financial Intermediation, in: Journal of Finance, 31 (2), p. 215-231.

Berkau, C. (2009): Bilanzen, 2nd ed., Konstanz 2009.

Bernard, V. L./Merton, R. C./Palepu, K. G. (1995): Mark-to-Market Accounting for Banks and Thrifts: Lessons from the Danish Experience, in: Journal of Accounting Research, 33 (1), p. 1-32.

Bernard, V. L./Ruland, R. G. (1987): The Incremental Information Content of Historical Cost and Current Cost Income Numbers: Time-Series Analyses for 1962-1980, in: Accounting Review, 62 (4), p. 707-722.

Berndt, T./Eberli, P. (2009): Die Fair-Value-Konzeption des IASB – Aktueller Stand und künftige Entwicklung, in: Der Schweizer Treuhänder, 83 (11), p. 895-898.

Bertoni, M./Rosa, B. de (2007): Financial Performance According to IFRS and the Role of Comprehensive Income, in: Kumar, A./Kandzija V. (eds.): Economic Integration: Prospects and Dilemmas, Ljubljana 2007, p. 145-159.

Beyer, A./Guttman, I. (2011): The Effect of Trading Volume on Analysts' Forecast Bias, in: The Accounting Review, 86 (2), p. 451-481.

Bhushan, R. (1989): Firm characteristics and analyst following, in: Journal of Accounting and Economics, 11 (2-3), p. 255-274.

Bieg, H./Bofinger, P./Küting, K./Kußmaul, H./Waschbusch, G./Weber, C.-P. (2008): Die Saarbrücker Initiative gegen den Fair Value, in: Der Betrieb, 61 (47), p. 2549-2552.

Binswanger, H. P. (1980): Attitudes toward Risk: Experimental Measurement in Rural India, in: American Journal of Agricultural Economics, 62 (3), p. 395-407.

Bittner, T. (1996): Die Wirkungen von Investor Relations-Maßnahmen auf Finanzanalysten, Diss., Bergisch Gladbach 1996.

Black, E. L./Sellers, K. F./Manly, T. S. (1998): Earnings Management Using Asset Sales: An International Study of Countries Allowing Noncurrent Asset Revaluation, in: Journal of Business Finance & Accounting, 25 (9-10), p. 1287-1317.

Black, F./Jensen, M. C./Scholes, M. (1972): The capital asset pricing model – Some empirical tests, in: Jensen, M. C. (ed.): Studies in the theory of capital markets, New York 1972, p. 79-121.

Black, F./Scholes, M. (1973): The Pricing of Options and Corporate Liabilities, in: Journal of Political Economy, 81 (3), p. 637-654.

Blackledge, M. (2009): Introducing Property Valuation, London 2009.

Blaufus, K. (2005): Fair Value Accounting – Zweckmäßigkeitsanalyse und konzeptioneller Rahmen, Wiesbaden 2005.

Bloomfield, R./Rennekamp, K. (2009): Experimental Research in Financial Reporting – From the Laboratory to the Virtual World, Hanover, Mass. 2009.

Böckem, H./Schurbohm, A. (2002): Die Bilanzierung von Immobilien nach den International Accounting Standards, in: Zeitschrift für internationale und kapitalmarktorientierte Rechnungslegung, 2 (1), p. 38-51.

Böcking, H.-J./Benecke, B. (2000): Die fair value-Bewertung von Finanzinstrumenten, in: Ballwieser, W. (ed.): US-amerikanische Rechnungslegung. Grundlagen und Vergleiche mit dem deutschen Recht, 4th ed., Stuttgart 2000, p. 193-239.

Bolstad, W. M. (2007): Introduction to Bayesian statistics, 2nd ed., Hoboken, NJ 2007.

Bondt, W. F. M. de/Thaler, R. H. (1990): Do Security Analysts Overreact?, in: American Economic Review, 80 (2), p. 52-57.

Bortz, J./Döring, N./Bortz-Döring (2006): Forschungsmethoden und Evaluation – Für Human- und Sozialwissenschaftler, 4th ed., Heidelberg 2006.

Botosan, C. A. (2006): Disclosure and the cost of capital: what do we know?, in: Accounting & Business Research, 36 (International Accounting Policy Forum), p. 31-40.

Bouwman, M. J./Frishkoff, P./Frishkoff, P. A. (1995): The Relevance of GAAP-Based Information: A Case Study Exploring Some Uses and Limitations, in: Accounting Horizons, 9 (4), p. 22-47.

Bowen, R. M./Chen, X./Cheng, Q. (2008): Analyst Coverage and the Cost of Raising Equity Capital: Evidence from Underpricing of Seasoned Equity Offerings, in: Contemporary Accounting Research, 25 (3), p. 657-699.

Bozzolan, S./Trombetta, M./Beretta, S. (2009): Forward-Looking Disclosures, Financial Verifiability and Analysts' Forecasts: A Study of Cross-Listed European Firms, in: European Accounting Review, 18 (3), p. 435-473.

Brennan, M. J./Chordia, T. (1993): Brokerage Commission Schedules, in: Journal of Finance, 48 (4), p. 1379-1402.

Brink, H. L. (1992): A history of Philips' accounting policies on the basis of its annual reports, in: European Accounting Review, 1 (2), p. 255-275.

Brown, L. D. (1983): Accounting Changes and the Accuracy of Analysts' Earnings Forecasts, in: Journal of Accounting Research, 21 (2), p. 432-443.

Brown, L. D. (1993): Earnings forecasting research: its implications for capital markets research, in: International Journal of Forecasting, 9 (3), p. 295-320.

Brown, P./Izan, H. Y./Loh, A. L. (1992): Fixed Asset Revaluations and Managerial Incentives, in: Abacus, 28 (1), p. 36-57.

Buschhüter, M./Striegel, A. (2009): Internationale Rechnungslegung – IFRS Praxis, 1st ed., Wiesbaden 2009.

C

Cairns, D. (2003): Applying International Accounting Standards, 3rd ed., London 2003.

Cairns, D./Massoudi, D./Taplin, R./Tarca, A. (2011): IFRS fair value measurement and accounting policy choice in the United Kingdom and Australia, in: British Accounting Review, 43 (1), p. 1-21.

Callsen-Bracker, H.-M. (2007): Finanzanalysten und Preiseffizienz, Diss., 1st ed., Baden-Baden 2007.

Capistrán, C./Timmermann, A. (2009): Disagreement and Biases in Inflation Expectations, in: Journal of Money, Credit and Banking, 41 (2), p. 365-396.

Carroll, T. J./Linsmeier, T. J./Petroni, K. R. (2003): The Reliability of Fair Value versus Historical Cost Information: Evidence from Closed-End Mutual Funds, in: Journal of Accounting, Auditing & Finance, 18 (1), p. 1-23.

Carruthers, B. G. (1995): Accounting, Ambiguity, and the New Institutionalism, in: Accounting, Organizations & Society, 20 (4), p. 313-328.

Castedello, M. (2009): Fair Value Measurement – Der neue Exposure Draft 2009/5, in: Die Wirtschaftsprüfung, 62 (18), p. 914-917.

CFA Institute Centre (2008): Official Position concerning Fair Value Reporting.

Chang Joon Song/Thomas, W. B./Han Yi (2010): Value Relevance of FAS No. 157 Fair Value Hierarchy Information and the Impact of Corporate Governance Mechanisms, in: Accounting Review, 85 (4), p. 1375-1410.

Chen, C. R./Chan, K. C./Steiner, T. L. (2002): Are All Security Analysts Equal?, in: Journal of Financial Research, 25 (3), p. 415-430.

Chen, I. J. (2005): The Investigation of the Relationship among Analyst Following, Managerial Ownership and Firm Valuation: From the Perspective of Agency Theory, in: Journal of Social Sciences, 1 (1), p. 9-15.

Chen, J. (2010): Essentials of technical analysis for financial markets, Hoboken N.J. 2010.

Cheng, Y./Liu, M. H./Qian, J. (2006): Buy-Side Analysts, Sell-Side Analysts, and Investment Decisions of Money Managers, in: Journal of Financial and Quantitative Analysis, 41 (1), p. 51-83.

Choi, F. D. S./Meek, G. K. (2005): International accounting, 5th ed., Upper Saddle River, NJ 2005.

Christensen, H. B./Nikolaev, V. (2009): Who uses fair value accounting for non-financial assets after IFRS adoption?, University of Chicago Booth School of Business Working Paper (09-12).

Chugh, L. C./Meador, J. W. (1984): The Stock Valuation Process: The Analysts' View, in: Financial Analysts Journal, 40 (6), p. 41-48.

Chung, K. H./Jo, H. (1996): The Impact of Security Analysts' Monitoring and Marketing Functions on the Market Value of Firms, in: Journal of Financial and Quantitative Analysis, 31 (4), p. 493-512.

Clement, M. B./Tse, S. Y. (2005): Financial Analyst Characteristics and Herding Behavior in Forecasting, in: Journal of Finance, 60 (1), p. 307-341.

Coase, R. H. (1937): The Nature of the Firm, in: Economica, 4 (16), p. 386-405.

Cornett, M. M./Rezaee, Z./Tehranian, H. (1996): An investigation of capital market reactions to pronouncements on fair value accounting, in: Journal of Accounting and Economics, 22 (1-3), p. 119-154.

Cotter, J./Richardson, S. (2002): Reliability of Asset Revaluations: The Impact of Appraiser Independence, in: Review of Accounting Studies, 7 (4), p. 435-457.

Cotter, J./Zimmer, I. (2003): Disclosure versus recognition: The case of asset revaluations, in: Asia-Pacific Journal of Accounting & Economics, 10 (1), p. 81-99.

Craig, S./Weil, J. (2004): SEC Targets Morgan Stanley Values, in: Wall Street Journal, 2004, 11-8-2004, p. C3.

Crookham, J. (1995): Sales Comparison Approach: Revisited, in: Appraisal Journal, 63 (2), p. 177-181.

D

Damodaran, A. (2002): Investment valuation – Tools and techniques for determining the value of any asset, 2nd ed., New York 2002.

Danbolt, J./Rees, W. (2008): An Experiment in Fair Value Accounting: UK Investment Vehicles, in: European Accounting Review, 17 (2), p. 271-303.

Das, S./Levine, C. B./Sivaramakrishnan, K. (1998): Earnings Predictability and Bias in Analysts' Earnings Forecasts, in: The Accounting Review, 73 (2), p. 277-294.

Davis, E. P./Steil, B. (2001): Institutional Investors, Hong Kong 2001.

Day, J. F. S. (1986): The Use of Annual Reports by UK Investment Analysis, in: Accounting & Business Research, 16 (64), p. 295-307.

Deaconu, A./Buiga, A./Nistor, C. S. (2010): The Value Relevance of Fair Value: Evidence for Tangible Assets on the Romanian Market, in: Transition Studies Review, 17 (1), p. 151-169.

DeBondt, W. F. M./Thaler, R. H. (1990): Do security analysts overreact?, in: American Economic Review, 80 (2), p. 52-57.

Decker, R. O. A. (1994): Eine Prinzipal-Agenten-theoretische Betrachtung von Eigner-Manager-Konflikten in der Kommanditgesellschaft auf Aktien und in der Aktiengesellschaft, Bergisch Gladbach 1994.

DeFelice, A./Lamoreaux, M. G. (2010): The SEC's IFRS Work Plan, in: Journal of Accountancy, 209 (4), p. 22-25.

Dehejia, R. H./Wahba, S. (2002): Propensity Score-Matching Methods for Nonexperimental Causal Studies, in: Review of Economics & Statistics, 84 (1), p. 151-161.

Deng, Z./Lev, B. (2006): In-process R&D: To capitalize or expense?, in: Journal of Engineering and Technology Management, 23 (1-2), p. 18-32.

Diamond, D. W. (1984): Financial Intermediation and Delegated Monitoring, in: Review of Economic Studies, 51 (166), p. 393-414.

Diamond, D. W./Verrecchia, R. E. (1991): Disclosure, Liquidity, and the Cost of Capital, in: The Journal of Finance, 46 (4), p. 1325-1359.

Dietrich, R. J./Harris, M. S./Muller, K. A. (2001): The reliability of investment property fair value estimates, in: Journal of Accounting and Economics, 30 (2), p. 125-158.

Dinauer, J. W. (1977): Methoden der Aktienanalyse und Anlageberatung und ihre Integration zu einem praxisorientierten Entscheidungskonzept unter Einbeziehung psychologischer Aspekte, Augsburg 1977.

Ding, Y./Jeanjean, T./Lesage, C./Stolowy, H. (2009): An Experiment in the Economic Consequences of Additional Disclosure: The Case of the Fair Value of Unlisted Equity Investments, Working Paper.

DiPiazza, S. A./Eccles, R. G. (2002): Building Public Trust – The Future of Corporate Reporting, New York, NY 2002.

Dohrn, M. (2004): Entscheidungsrelevanz des Fair Value-Accounting am Beispiel von IAS 39 und IAS 40, Diss., Lohmar 2004.

Doukas, J. A./Chansog Kim/Pantzalis, C. (2000): Security Analysis, Agency Costs, and Company Characteristics, in: Financial Analysts Journal, 56 (6), p. 54-63.

Downing, D./Clark, J. (2010): Business Statistics, 5th ed., Hauppauge NY 2010.

Dreman, D. N./Berry, M. A. (1995): Analyst Forecasting Errors and Their Implications for Security Analysis, in: Financial Analysts Journal, 51 (3), p. 30-41.

Du, N./Budescu, D. V. (2005): The Effects of Imprecise Probabilities and Outcomes in Evaluating Investment Options, in: Management Science, 51 (12), p. 1791-1803.

Düsterlho, J.-E. v. (2000): Der Umgang mit den Analysten, in: Deutscher Investor-Relations-Kreis (ed.): Investor Relations. Professionelle Kapitalmarktkommunikation, Wiesbaden 2000, p. 73-79.

E

Eagly, A. H./Chaiken, S. (1975): An Attribution Analysis of the Effect of Communicator Characteristics on Opinion Change: The Case of Communicator Attractiveness, in: Journal of Personality and Social Psychology, 32 (1), p. 136-144.

Easton, P. D./Eddey, P. H./Harris, T. S. (1993): An Investigation of Revaluations of Tangible Long-Lived Assets, in: Journal of Accounting Research, 31 (3), p. 1-38.

Eberts, M. (1986): Das Berufsbild des Finanzanalysten in der Bundesrepublik Deutschland, Darmstadt 1986.

Eccher, E. A./Ramesh, K./Thiagarajan, S. R. (1996): Fair value disclosures by bank holding companies, in: Journal of Accounting and Economics, 22 (1-3), p. 79-117.

Eccles, R. G./Herz, R. H./Keegan, E. M./Phillips, D. M. H. (2001): The ValueReporting Revolution – Moving Beyond The Earnings Game, New York, Chichester 2001.

Eckstein, P. P. (2010): Statistik für Wirtschaftswissenschaftler – Eine realdatenbasierte Einführung mit SPSS, 2nd ed., Wiesbaden 2010.

Edwards, E. O./Bell, P. W. (1995): The Theory and Measurement of Business Income, New York 1995.

Elliott, W. B./Hodge, F. D./Jackson, K. E. (2008): The Association between Non-professional Investors' Information Choices and Their Portfolio Returns: The Importance of Investing Experience, in: Contemporary Accounting Research, 25 (2), p. 473-498.

Elliott, W. B./Hodge, F. D./Kennedy, J. J./Pronk, M. (2007): Are M.B.A. Students a Good Proxy for Nonprofessional Investors?, in: Accounting Review, 82 (1), p. 139-168.

Ellsberg, D. (1961): Risk, Ambiguity, and the Savage Axioms, in: Quarterly Journal of Economics, 75 (4), p. 643-669.

Ellsworth, R. (2001): The Sales Comparison Approach and the Appraisal of Complete Facilities, in: Appraisal Journal, 69 (3), p. 266-269.

Eng, L. L./Teo, H. K. (2000): The Relation Between Annual Report Disclosures, Analysts' Earnings Forecasts and Analyst Following: Evidence From Singapore, in: Pacific Accounting Review, 11 (2), p. 219-239.

Engel-Ciric, D. (2002): Einschränkung der Aussagekraft des Jahresabschlusses nach IAS durch bilanzpolitische Spielräume, in: Deutsches Steuerrecht, 40 (18), p. 780-784.

Ernst, E./Gassen, J./Pellens, B. (2009): Verhalten und Präferenzen deutscher Aktionäre – Eine Befragung von privaten und institutionellen Anlegern zum Informations-verhalten, zur Dividendenpräferenz und zur Wahrnehmung von Stimmrechten, No. 43, ed. by v. Rosen 2009.

Ernstberger, J./Krotter, S./Stadler, C. (2008): Analysts' Forecast Accuracy in Germany: The Effect of Different Accounting Principles and Changes of Accounting Principles, in: Business Research, 1 (1), p. 26-53.

F

Fama, E. F. (1970): Efficient Capital Markets: A Review of Theory and Empirical Work, in: Journal of Finance, 25 (2), p. 383-417.

Fama, E. F. (1991): Efficient Capital Markets: II, in: Journal of Finance, 46 (5), p. 1575-1617.

Fama, E. F./MacBeth, J. D. (1973): Risk, Return, and Equilibrium: Empirical Tests, in: Journal of Political Economy, 81 (3), p. 607-636.

Fan, D. K. K./So, R. W./Yeh, J. J. (2006): Analyst Earnings Forecasts for Publicly Trad-ed Insurance Companies, in: Review of Quantitative Finance and Accounting, 26 (2), p. 105-136.

Feng, M./McVay, S. (2010): Analysts' Incentives to Overweight Management Guidance When Revising Their Short-Term Earnings Forecasts, in: Accounting Review, 85 (5), p. 1617-1646.

Fischer, D. T. (2009): Der Standardentwurf "Fair Value Measurement" (ED/2009/5), in: PiR - Praxis der internationalen Rechnungslegung, 13 (11), p. 341-342.

Fischer, D. T. (2010): Offenlegungspflichten im Rahmen des Standardentwurfs "Fair Value Measurement" (ED/2009/5) – Vergleich zu US-GAAP, in: PiR - Praxis der internationalen Rechnungslegung, 12 (3), p. 82-84.

Fiske, S. T./Taylor, S. E. (2008): Social Cognition – From Brains to Culture, Boston 2008.

Flesher, D. L./Marquette, P. (1998): The Theory and Measurement of Business Income (Book), in: Issues in Accounting Education, 13 (1), p. 239-240.

Foster, B. P./Shastri, T. (2010): The Subprime Lending Crisis and Reliable Reporting: Limitations to the Use of Fair Value in Unstable Markets, in: CPA Journal, 80 (4), p. 20-25.

Francis, J./Philbrick, D. (1993): Analysts' Decisions as Products of a Multi-task Environment, in: Journal of Accounting Research, 31 (2), p. 216-230.

Frank, U. (2007): Wissenschaftstheorie, in: Köhler, R./Küpper, H.-U./Pfingsten, A. (eds.): Handwörterbuch der Betriebswirtschaft, 6th ed., Stuttgart 2007, col. 2010-2017.

Franke, G. (1993): Agency-Theory, in: Wittmann, W./Kern, W. (eds.): Enzyklopädie der Betriebswirtschaftslehre, 5th ed., Stuttgart 1993, p. 37-49.

Franke, G./Hax, H. (2009): Finanzwirtschaft des Unternehmens und Kapitalmarkt, 6th ed., Berlin 2009.

Franken, L. (2001): Gläubigerschutz durch Rechnungslegung nach US-GAAP – Eine Ökonomische Analyse, Frankfurt am Main 2001.

Frederickson, J. R./Hodge, F. D./Pratt, J. H. (2006): The Evolution of Stock Option Accounting: Disclosure, Voluntary Recognition, Mandated Recognition, and Management Disavowals, in: Accounting Review, 81 (5), p. 1073-1093.

Friedl, B. (2003): Controlling, Stuttgart 2003.

Friedrich, N. (2007): Die Rolle von Analysten bei der Bewertung von Unternehmen am Kapitalmarkt: das Beispiel Telekommunikationsindustrie, Lohmar 2007.

Fuchs, D. A. (2003): An institutional basis for environmental stewardship – The structure and quality of property rights, Dordrecht 2003.

Fülbier, R. U. (2005): Wissenschaftstheorie und Betriebswirtschaftslehre, in: Horsch, A./Meinhövel, H./Paul, S. (eds.): Institutionenökonomie und Betriebswirtschaftslehre, München 2005, p. 15-29.

Funke, A. (2006): Konglomeratsabschlag und Transaktionskostentheorie – Theoretische Erklärung und empirische Befunde in Europa, Wiesbaden 2006.

Furubotn, E. G./Pejovich, S. (1974): The economics of property rights, Cambridge, Mass. 1974.

G

Gassen, J./Schwedler, K. (2010): The Decision Usefulness of Financial Accounting Measurement Concepts – Evidence from an Online Survey of Professional Investors and their Advisors, in: European Accounting Review, 19 (3), p. 495-510.

Gebhardt, W. R./Lee, C. M. C./Swaminathan, B. (2001): Toward an Implied Cost of Capital, in: Journal of Accounting Research, 39 (1), p. 135-176.

Gensler, S./Skiera, B./Böhm, M. (2005): Einsatzmöglichkeiten der Matching Methode zur Berücksichtigung von Selbstselektion, in: Journal für Betriebswirtschaft, 55 (1), p. 37-62.

Gibbons, M. R. (1982): Multivariate Tests of Financial Models, in: Journal of Financial Economics, 10 (1), p. 3-27.

Gill, M. J./Swann, W. B. J./Silvera, D. H. (1998): On the Genesis of Confidence, in: Journal of Personality and Social Psychology, 75 (5), p. 1101-1114.

Givoly, D./Lakonishok, J. (1984): Properties of analysts' forecasts of earnings: A review and analysis of research, in: Journal of Accounting Literature, 3 , p. 117-152.

Göbel, E. (2002): Neue Institutionenökonomik – Konzeption und betriebswirtschaftliche Anwendungen, Stuttgart 2002.

Göres, U. L. (2004): Die Interessenkonflikte von Wertpapierdienstleistern und -analysten bei der Wertpapieranalyse – Eine Darstellung und Würdigung der gesetzlichen und berufsständischen Regelungen in den Vereinigten Staaten von Amerika und der Bundesrepublik Deutschland unter Einbeziehung der europäischen Ebene, Berlin 2004.

Graham, B./Le Dodd, D. F. (2008): Security Analysis, 6th ed., New York 2008.

Graham, C. M./Cannice, M. V./Sayre, T. L. (2002): Analyzing Financial Analysts – What They Look for in Financial Reports and How They Determine Earnings' Quality, in: Journal of Management Research, 2 (2), p. 63-72.

Graham, J. R. (1999): Herding among Investment Newsletters: Theory and Evidence, in: Journal of Finance, 54 (1), p. 237-268.

Greene, W. H. (2003): Econometric Analysis, 5. ed., Upper Saddle River, NJ 2003.

Greenwald, A. G. (1976): Within-Subjects Designs: To Use or Not To Use?, in: Psychological Bulletin, 83 (2), p. 314-320.

Griffin, D./Tversky, A. (1992): The Weighing of Evidence and the Determinants of Confidence, in: Cognitive Psychology, 24 , p. 411-435.

Grochla, E. (1978): Einführung in die Organisationstheorie, Stuttgart 1978.

Große, J.-V. (2011): IFRS 13 "Fair Value Measurement" – Was sich (nicht) ändert, in: Zeitschrift für internationale und kapitalmarktorientierte Rechnungslegung, 11 (6), p. 286-296.

Grossman, S. J./Stiglitz, J. E. (1980): On the Impossibility of Informationally Efficient Markets, in: American Economic Review, 70 (3), p. 393-408.

Groysberg, B./Healy, P./Chapman, C. (2008): Buy-Side vs. Sell-Side Analysts' Earnings Forecasts, in: Financial Analysts Journal, 64 (4), p. 25-39.

Grüning, M. (2011): Publizität börsennotierter Unternehmen, Wiesbaden 2011.

H

Hagemeister, C. (2004): Bilanzierung von Sachanlagevermögen nach dem Komponentenansatz des IAS 16, Diss., Düsseldorf 2004.

Hail, L./Leuz, C. (2009): Cost of capital effects and changes in growth expectations around U.S. cross-listings, in: Journal of Financial Economics, 93 (3), p. 428-454.

Hann, R. N./Heflin, F./Subramanayam, K. R. (2007): Fair-value pension accounting, in: Journal of Accounting and Economics, 44 (3), p. 328-358.

Harris, M./Raviv, A. (1993): Differences of Opinion Make a Horse Race, in: Review of Financial Studies, 6 (3), p. 473-506.

Hart, O./Holmström, B. (1987): The Theory of Contracts, in: Bewley, T. F. (ed.): Advances in economic theory. Fifth World Congress (Economic Society Monographs No. 12), Cambridge 1987, p. 71-155.

Hax, G. (1998): Informationsintermediation durch Finanzanalysten – Eine ökonomische Analyse, Diss., Frankfurt am Main 1998.

Hayek, F. A. (1945): The Use of Knowledge in Society, in: American Economic Review, 35 (4), p. 519.

Healy, M. J./Bergquist, K. (1994): The Sales Comparison Approach and Timberland Valuation, in: Appraisal Journal, 62 (4), p. 587-595.

Henze, J. (2004): Was leisten Finanzanalysten? – Eine empirische Analyse des deutschen Aktienmarktes, Diss., 1st ed., Lohmar 2004.

Herrmann, D./Saudagaran, S. M./Thomas, W. B. (2006): The quality of fair value measures for property, plant, and equipment, in: Accounting Forum, 30 (1), p. 43-59.

Heyl, D. C. v. (1995): Noise als finanzwirtschaftliches Phänomen – Eine theoretische Untersuchung der Bedeutung von Noise am Aktienmarkt, Diss., Frankfurt am Main 1995.

Hirshleifer, D./Teoh, S. H. (2003): Limited attention, information disclosure, and financial reporting, in: Journal of Accounting and Economics, 36 (1-3), p. 337-386.

Hirshleifer, J. (1971): The Private and Social Value of Information and the Reward to Inventive Activity, in: American Economic Review, 61 (4), p. 561-574.

Hirst, D. E./Hopkins, P. E. (1998): Comprehensive Income Reporting and Analysts' Valuation Judgments, in: Journal of Accounting Research, 36 (3), p. 47-75.

Hirst, D. E./Hopkins, P. E./Wahlen, J. M. (2004): Fair Values, Income Measurement, and Bank Analysts' Risk and Valuation Judgments, in: Accounting Review, 79 (2), p. 453-472.

Hirst, D. E./Koonce, L./Simko, P. J. (1995): Investor Reactions to Financial Analysts' Research Reports, in: Journal of Accounting Research, 33 (2), p. 335-351.

Hocker, U. (2009): Die Erwartungen der Privatanleger an IR, in: Kirchhoff, K. Reiner/Piwinger, M. (eds.): Praxishandbuch Investor Relations: Das Standardwerk der Finanzkommunikation, 2nd ed., Wiesbaden 2009, p. 469-474.

Hodge, F. D. (2003): Investors' Perceptions of Earnings Quality, Auditor Independence, and the Usefulness of Audited Financial Information, in: Accounting Horizons, 17 (Supplement), p. 37-48.

Hodge, F. D./Hopkins, P. E./Pratt, J. H. (2006): Management reporting incentives and classification credibility: The effects of reporting discretion and reputation, in: Accounting, Organizations and Society, 31 (7), p. 623-634.

Hodge, F. D./Kennedy, J. J./Maines, L. A. (2004): Does Search-Facilitating Technology Improve the Transparency of Financial Reporting?, in: Accounting Review, 79 (3), p. 687-703.

Hodge, F. D./Pronk, M. (2006): The Impact of Expertise and Investment Familiarity on Investors' Use of Online Financial Report Information, in: Journal of Accounting, Auditing & Finance, 21 (3), p. 267-292.

Hoffmann, W.-D./Lüdenbach, N. (2003): Praxisprobleme der Neubewertungskonzeption nach IAS, in: Deutsches Steuerrecht, 41 (14), p. 565-569.

Hoffmann, W.-D./Lüdenbach, N. (2004): Abschreibung von Sachanlagen nach dem Komponentenansatz von IAS 16, in: Betriebs-Berater, 59 (7), p. 375-377.

Hogg, M. A./Vaughan, G. M. (2008): Social Psychology, 5th ed., Harlow, England 2008.

Holt, C. A./Laury, S. K. (2002): Risk Aversion and Incentive Effects, in: American Economic Review, 92 (5), p. 1644-1655.

Holthausen, R. W./Watts, R. L. (2001): The relevance of the value-relevance literature for financial accounting standard setting, in: Journal of Accounting and Economics, 31 (1-3), p. 3-75.

Hong, H./Kubik, J. D./Solomon, A. (2000): Security Analysts' Career Concerns and Herding of Earnings Forecasts, in: RAND Journal of Economics, 31 (1), p. 121-144.

Hooke, J. C. (1998): Security analysis on Wall Street – A comprehensive guide to today's valuation methods, New York 1998.

Hope, O.-K. (2003): Accounting Policy disclosures and Analysts' Forecasts, in: Contemporary Accounting Research, 20 (2), p. 295-321.

Hope, O.-K. (2004): Variations in the Financial Reporting Environment and Earnings Forecasting, in: Journal of International Financial Management & Accounting, 15 (1), p. 21-43.

Hopwood, W./Schaefer, T. (1989): Firm-Specific Responsiveness to Input Price Changes and the Incremental Information in Current Cost Income, in: Accounting Review, 64 (2), p. 313-328.

Horsch, A. (2005): Agency und Versicherungsintermediation, in: Horsch, A./Meinhövel, H./Paul, S. (eds.): Institutionenökonomie und Betriebswirtschaftslehre, München 2005, p. 81-99.

Horton, J./Macve, R./Serafeim, G. (2007): An experiment in "fair value" accounting? – The state of the art in research and thought leadership on accounting for life assurance in the UK and continental Europe, London 2007.

Huber, O. (1995): Das psychologische Experiment – Eine Einführung, 2nd ed., Bern 1995.

Huian, M. C. (2009): Some Aspects Regarding the Role of Fair Value Accounting During the Current Financial Crisis, Working Paper.

Huian, M. C. (2010): Impact of Current Financial Crisis on Disclosures on Financial Instruments, in: Scientific Annals of the 'Alexandru Ioan Cuza' University of Iasi, 57, p. 41-50.

Hüning, M. (2007): Kongruenzprinzip und Rechnungslegung von Sachanlagen nach IFRS, Diss., 1st ed., Lohmar 2007.

Huschke, C. (2008): Immobilienbewertung im Kontext der IFRS – Eine deduktive und empirische Untersuchung der Vorziehenswürdigkeit alternativer Heuristiken hinsichtlich Relevanz und Zuverlässigkeit bei der Fair Value-Ermittlung von Investment Properties, Diss., Wiesbaden 2008.

Hussy, W./Schreier, M./Echterhoff, G. (2010): Forschungsmethoden in Psychologie und Sozialwissenschaften für Bachelor, Berlin 2010.

Hüttner, M./Schwarting, U. (2002): Grundzüge der Marktforschung, 7th ed., München/Wien 2002.

Hwang, L.-S./Jan, C. L./Basu S. (1996): Loss Firms and Analysts' Earnings Forecast Errors, in: Journal of Financial Statement Analysis, 1 (2), p. 18-30.

I

IASB (2009): Exposure Draft Fair Value Measurement – ED FVM.

IASB (2010): Developing common fair value measurement and disclosure requirements in IFRSs and US GAAP – Comprehensive Project Summary.

IASB (2011): Accounting for available-for sale (AFS) sovereign debt – Letter to the ESMA.

J

Jaffe, J. P. (1974): Special Information and Insider Trading, in: Journal of Business, 47 (3), p. 410-428.

Jaggi, B./Jain, R. (1998): An Evaluation of Financial Analysts' Earnings Forecasts for Hong Kong Firms, in: Journal of International Financial Management & Accounting, 9 (3), p. 177-200.

Jensen, M. C. (1978): Some anomalous evidence regarding market efficiency, in: Journal of Financial Economics, 6 (2-3), p. 95-101.

Jensen, M. C./Meckling, W. H. (1976): Theory of the firm: Managerial behavior, agency costs and ownership structure, in: Journal of Financial Economics, 3 (4), p. 305-360.

Johnson, E. J./Payne, J. W./Bettman, J. R. (1988): Information displays and preference reversals, in: Organizational Behavior and Human Decision Processes, 42 (1), p. 1-21.

Jones, J. P./Stanwick, S. D. (1999): Fair Value Accounting: A Guide to Understanding the Current Standards, in: The Journal of Corporate Accounting and Finance, 11 (1), p. 103-108.

K

Kajüter, P./Bachert, K./Blaesing, D./Kleinmanns, H. (2010): Die DRS zur Lageberichterstattung auf dem Prüfstand, in: Der Betrieb, 63 (9), p. 457-465.

Kames, C. (2000): Unternehmensbewertung durch Finanzanalysten als Ausgangspunkt eines Value Based Measurement, Frankfurt am Main 2000.

Kandel, E./Pearson, N. D. (1995): Differential Interpretation of Public Signals and Trade in Speculative Markets, in: Journal of Political Economy, 103 (4), p. 831-872.

Kasper, W./Streit, M. E. (2001): Institutional economics – Social order and public policy, Cheltenham 2001.

Kay, D. A. (2005): CliffsAP Statistics, Hoboken, NJ 2005.

Kerlinger, F. N./Lee, H. B. (2000): Foundations of Behavioral Research, 3rd ed., Melbourne 2000.

Khurana, I. K./Kim, M.-S. (2003): Relative value relevance of historical cost vs. fair value: Evidence from bank holding companies, in: Journal of Accounting and Public Policy, 22 (1), p. 19-42.

Kirchhoff, K. R./Piwinger, M. (2007): Kommunikation mit Kapitalgebern: Grundlagen der Investor Relations, in: Piwinger, M./Zerfaß, A. (eds.): Handbuch Unternehmenskommunikation, Wiesbaden 2007, p. 723-740.

Klein, A./Zur, E. (2009): Entrepreneurial Shareholder Activism: Hedge Funds and Other Private Shareholders, in: Journal of Finance, 64 (1), p. 187-229.

Kornmeier, M. (2007): Wissenschaftstheorie und wissenschaftliches Arbeiten – Eine Einführung für Wirtschaftswissenschaftler, Heidelberg 2007.

Kothari, S. P./Xu Li/Short, J. E. (2009): The Effect of Disclosures by Management, Analysts, and Business Press on Cost of Capital, Return Volatility, and Analyst Forecasts: A Study Using Content Analysis, in: Accounting Review, 84 (5), p. 1639-1670.

Kretschmann, J. (1990): Die Diffusion des kritischen Rationalismus in der Betriebswirtschaftslehre, Stuttgart 1990.

Kumarasiri, J./Fisher, R. (2011): Auditors' Perceptions of Fair-Value Accounting: Developing Country Evidence, in: International Journal of Auditing, 15 (1), p. 66-87.

Küting, K./Dawo, S. (2003): Anwendungsfälle der fair value-Bewertung bei nicht finanziellen Vermögenswerten im Rahmen der International Financial Reporting Standards (IFRS), in: Zeitschrift für internationale und kapitalmarktorientierte Rechnungslegung, 3 (5), p. 228-241.

Küting, K./Kaiser, T. (2010): Fair Value-Accounting – Zu komplex für den Kapitalmarkt?, in: Corporate Finance biz, 1 (6), p. 375-386.

Küting, K./Reuter, M. (2008): Abbildung von eigenen Anteilen nach dem Entwurf des BilMoG – Auswirkungen in der Bilanzierungs- und Bilanzanalysepraxis, in: Betriebs-Berater, 63 (13), p. 658-662.

Küting, K./Reuter, M. (2009): Neubewertungsrücklagen als Konsequenz einer (erfolgs-neutralen) Fair Value-Bewertung – Untersuchung dieser IFRS-spezifischen Eigen-kapitalposten und ihrer fragwürdigen Bedeutung in der Bilanzierungspraxis, in: Zeit-schrift für internationale und kapitalmarktorientierte Rechnungslegung, 9 (3), p. 172-181.

Küting, K./Trappmann, H./Ranker, D. (2007): Gegenüberstellung der Bewertungs-konzeption von beizulegendem Wert und Fair Value im Sachanlagevermögen, in: Der Betrieb, 60 (32), p. 1709-1716.

L

La Porta, R./Lopez-de-Silanes, F./Shleifer, A./Vishny, R. W. (1998): Law and Finance, in: Journal of Political Economy, 106 (6), p. 1113-1155.

Lachmann, M./Wöhrmann, A./Wömpener, A. (2010): Investorenreaktionen auf die Fair Value-Bilanzierung von Verbindlichkeiten nach IFRS – eine experimentelle Un-tersuchung, in: Zeitschrift für Betriebswirtschaft, 80 (11), p. 1179-1206.

Laffont, J.-J./Maskin, E. S. (1990): The Efficient Market Hypothesis and Insider Trad-ing on the Stock Market, in: The Journal of Political Economy, 98 (1), p. 70-93.

Landsman, W. R. (2007): Is fair value accounting information relevant and reliable? Evidence from capital market research, in: Accounting & Business Research (Special Issue), p. 19-30.

Lang, M. H./Lins, K. V./Miller, D. P. (2003): ADRs, Analysts, and Accuracy: Does Cross Listing in the United States Improve a Firm's Information Environment and In-crease Market Value?, in: Journal of Accounting Research, 41 (2), p. 317-345.

Lang, M. H./Lins, K. V./Miller, D. P. (2004): Concentrated control, analyst following, and valuation: do analysts matter most when investors are protected least?, in: Journal of Accounting Research, 42 (3), p. 589-625.

Lang, M. H./Lundholm, R. J. (1996): Corporate Disclosure Policy and Analyst Behav-ior, in: Accounting Review, 71 (4), p. 467-492.

Larson, R. K./Street, D. L. (2004): Convergence with IFRS in an expanding Europe: progress and obstacles identified by large accounting firms' survey, in: Journal of Inter-national Accounting, Auditing and Taxation, 13 (2), p. 89-119.

Laser, J. (1995): Marktpsychologie und Börsentrends – Der Börsenzyklus unter psychologischen Aspekten, in: Schmielewski, F. (ed.): Am Puls der Märkte. Moderne und bewährte Methoden der Kursdiagnostik, Frankfurt 1995, p. 9-30.

Laux, C./Leuz, C. (2009): The crisis of fair-value accounting: Making sense of the recent debate, in: Accounting, Organizations and Society, 34 (6-7), p. 826-834.

Laux, C./Leuz, C. (2010): Did Fair-Value Accounting Contribute to the Financial Crisis?, in: Journal of Economic Perspectives, 24 (1), p. 93-118.

Leland, H. E./Pyle, D. H. (1977): Informational Asymmetries, Financial Structure, and Financial Intermediation, in: Journal of Finance, 32 (2), p. 371-387.

Leone, A. J./Wu, J. S. (2007): What Does it Take to Become a Superstar? Evidence from Institutional Investor Rankings of Financial Analysts, Simon School of Business Working Paper.

Levine, C. B./Hughes, J. S. (2005): Management compensation and earnings-based covenants as signaling devices in credit markets, in: Journal of Corporate Finance, 11 (5), p. 832-850.

Levitt, A. (1998): The Importance of High Quality Accounting Standards, in: Accounting Horizons, 12 (1), p. 79-82.

Libby, R./Bloomfield, R./Nelson, M. W. (2002): Experimental research in financial accounting, in: Accounting, Organizations and Society, 27 (8), p. 775-810.

Libby, R./Nelson, M. W./Hunton, J. E. (2006): Recognition v. Disclosure, Auditor Tolerance for Misstatement, and the Reliability of Stock-Compensation and Lease Information, in: Journal of Accounting Research, 44 (3), p. 533-560.

Lin, H.-w./McNichols, M. F. (1998): Underwriting relationships, analysts' earnings forecasts and investment recommendations, in: Journal of Accounting and Economics, 25 (1), p. 101-127.

Lingnau, V. (1995): Kritischer Rationalismus und Betriebswirtschaftslehre, in: Wirtschaftswissenschaftliches Studium, 24 (3), p. 124-129.

Lintner, J. (1965): The Valuation of Risk Assets and the Selection of Risky Investments in Stock Portfolios and Capital Budgets, in: Review of Economics & Statistics, 47 (1), p. 13-37.

Liu, P./Smith, S. D./Syed, A. A. (1990): Stock Price Reactions to The Wall Street Journal's Securities Recommendations, in: Journal of Financial and Quantitative Analysis, 25 (3), p. 399-410.

Lobo, G. J./Song, I.-M. (1989): The Incremental Information in SFAS No. 33 Income Disclosures over Historical Cost Income and Its Cash and Accrual Components, in: Accounting Review, 64 (2), p. 329-343.

Löw, E./Antonakopoulos, N./Weiland, T. (2007): SFAS 157 und das IASB Discussion Paper "Fair Value Measurements", in: Die Wirtschaftsprüfung, 60 (17), p. 730-740.

Lüdenbach, N./Freiberg, J. (2006): Zweifelhafter Objektivierungsbeitrag des Fair Value Measurements-Projekts für die IFRS-Bilanz, in: Zeitschrift für internationale und kapitalmarktorientierte Rechnungslegung, 6 (7/8), p. 437-445.

Lüßmann, L.-G. (2004): Unternehmenskontrolle, Kapitalmärkte und Fair Value Accounting, Diss., Sternenfels 2004.

Lys, T./Soo, L. G. (1995): Analysts' Forecast Precision as a Response to Competition, in: Journal of Accounting, Auditing & Finance, 10 (4), p. 751-765.

M

MacKinlay, C. A. (1997): Event Studies in Economics and Finance, in: Journal of Economic Literature, 35 (1), p. 13-39.

Magnan, M./Thornton, D. (2010): FVA: smoke & MIRRORS?, in: CA Magazine, 143 (2), p. 18-25.

Magnan, M. L. (2009): Fair Value Accounting and the Financial Crisis: Messenger or Contributor?, in: Accounting Perspectives, 8 (3), p. 189-213.

Mahoney, P. G. (2006): The Common Law and Economic Growth: Hayek Might Be Right, in: Fox, M. B./Heller, M. A. (eds.): Corporate Governance Lessons from Transition Economy Reforms, New Jersey 2006, p. 84-109.

Maines, L. A./McDaniel, L. S. (2000): Effects of Comprehensive-Income Characteristics on Nonprofessional Investors' Judgments: The Role of Financial-Statement Presentation Format, in: Accounting Review, 75 (2), p. 179-207.

Mande, V./Kwak, W. (1996): Do Japanese Analysts Overreact or Underreact to Earnings Announcements?, in: Abacus, 32 (1), p. 81.

Martin, D. W. (2000): Doing Psychology Experiments, 5th ed., Belmont, CA 2000.

May, A. (1991): Zum Stand der empirischen Forschung über Informationsverarbeitung am Aktienmarkt – Ein Überblick, in: Zeitschrift für betriebswirtschaftliche Forschung, 43 (4), p. 313-335.

McConnell, P. (2010): Response to 'Fair value accounting, financial economics and the transformation of reliability', in: Accounting & Business Research, 40 (3), p. 211-213.

McEwen, R. A./Mazza, C. R./Hunton, J. E. (2008): Effects of Managerial Discretion in Fair Value Accounting Regulation and Motivational Incentives to "Go Along" with Management on Analysts' Expectations and Judgments, in: Journal of Behavioral Finance, 9 (4), p. 240-251.

Menkhoff, L./Schmeling, M./Schmidt, U. (2010): Overconfidence, Experience, and Professionalism: An Experimental Study, Working Paper.

Menorca, E. S. (1993): Hotel Valuations: the Income Capitalisation Approach, in: Journal of Property Valuation and Investment, 11 (3), p. 211-216.

Mesa Graziano, C. de (2006): What Do Users Of Private Company Financial Statements Want?, in: Financial Executive, 22 (4), p. 44-47.

Meyer, B. D. (1995): Natural and Quasi-Experiments in Economics, in: Journal of Business & Economic Statistics, 13 (2), p. 151-161.

Michaelsen, L. (2001): Informationsintermediation für Privatanleger am Aktienmarkt unter besonderer Berücksichtigung des neuen Marktes, Diss, Lohmar 2001.

Michalkiewicz, C. (2003): Aktienanalysten – Feinde oder Verbündete im Rahmen des Investor Marketing?, in: Ebel, B./Hofer, M. B. (eds.): Investor Marketing. Aktionäre erfolgreich gewinnen, Investoren langfristig binden, Börsenkurse nachhaltig steigern, 1st ed., Wiesbaden 2003, p. 115-129.

Mihaela, L. (2008): Regarding the Users of Financial Statements and their Information Needs, in: Studies and Scientific Researches – Economic Edition (13), p. 49-55.

Mirza, A. A./Holt, G. J./Orrell, M. (2006): Wiley IFRS – International Financial Reporting Standards: Workbook and Guide, Hoboken, NJ 2006.

Möller, H. P./Hüfner, B. (2002): Empirische Forschung, in: Küpper, H.-U./Wagenhofer, A. (eds.): Handwörterbuch Unternehmensrechnung und Controlling, 4th ed., Stuttgart 2002, col. 351-359.

Morck, R./Shleifer, A./Vishny, R. W. (1988): Management ownership and market valuation: An empirical analysis – The Distribution of Power Among Corporate Managers, Shareholders, and Directors, in: Journal of Financial Economics, 20 (1/2), p. 293-315.

Moxter, A. (1982): Betriebswirtschaftliche Gewinnermittlung, Tübingen 1982.

Mozes, H. A. (2002): The Value Relevance of Financial Institutions' Fair Value Disclosures: A Study in the Difficulty of Linking Unrealized Gains and Losses to Equity Values, in: Abacus, 38 (1), p. 1-15.

Mühlbradt, F. W. (1978): Chancen und Risiken der Aktienanlage, Köln 1978.

Mujkanovic, R. (2002): Fair Value im Financial Statement nach International Accounting Standards, Stuttgart 2002.

Mujkanovic, R./Raatz, P. (2008): Der Component Approach nach IAS 16 im HGB-Abschluss?, in: Zeitschrift für internationale und kapitalmarktorientierte Rechnungslegung, 8 (4), p. 245-250.

Muller, K. A./Riedl, E. J. (2002): External Monitoring of Property Appraisal Estimates and Information Asymmetry, in: Journal of Accounting Research, 40 (3), p. 865-881.

Muller, K. A./Riedl, E. J./Sellhorn, T. (2011): Mandatory Fair Value Accounting and Information Asymmetry: Evidence from the European Real Estate Industry, in: Management Science, 57 (6), p. 1138-1153.

Müller, D. (2009): Moderatoren und Mediatoren in Regressionen, in: Albers, S./Klapper, D./Konradt, U./Walter, A./Wolf, J. (eds.): Methodik der empirischen Forschung, 3rd ed., Wiesbaden 2009, p. 238-252.

Mullins, D. W., JR. (1982): Does the capital asset pricing model work?, in: Harvard Business Review, 60 (1), p. 105.

N

Naumann, K.-P. (2006): Das Spannungsverhältnis zwischen Relevanz und Verlässlichkeit in der Rechnungslegung – Ein Beitrag zur Fortentwicklung von HGB und IFRS, in: Krawitz, N. (ed.): Rechnungslegung nach internationalen Grundsätzen, Wiesbaden 2006, p. 43-76.

Nelson, K. K. (1996): Fair Value Accounting for Commercial Banks: An Empirical Analysis of SFAS No. 107, in: Accounting Review, 71 (2), p. 161-182.

Nissim, D. (2003): Reliability of Banks' Fair Value Disclosure for Loans, in: Review of Quantitative Finance and Accounting, 20 (4), p. 355-384.

Nix, P. (2000): Die Zielgruppen von Investor Relations, in: Deutscher Investor-Relations-Kreis (ed.): Investor Relations. Professionelle Kapitalmarktkommunikation, Wiesbaden 2000, p. 35-43.

Nobes, C./Parker, R. (2004): Comparative International Accounting, 8th ed., Harlow 2004.

O

O'Brien, P. C. (1990): Forecast Accuracy of Individual Analysts in Nine Industries, in: Journal of Accounting Research, 28 (2), p. 286-304.

O'Brien, P. C./Bhushan, R. (1990): Analyst Following and Institutional Holding, in: Journal of Accounting Research, 28 (Supplement 1990), p. 55-76.

Olbrich, M. (2003): Zur Bilanzierung von als Finanzinvestition gehaltene Immobilien nach IAS 40, in: Betriebswirtschaftliche Forschung und Praxis, 55 (3), p. 346-357.

Oppermann, H. R. B./Booysen, S. F./Binnekade, C. S./Oberholster, J. G. I. (2008): Accounting Standards in brief, Cape Town 2008.

P

Pagourtzi, E./Assimakopoulos, V./Hatzichristos, T./French, N. (2003): Real estate appraisal: a review of valuation methods, in: Journal of Property Investment & Finance, 21 (4), p. 383-401.

Park, C. W./Stice, E. K. (2000): Analyst Forecasting Ability and the Stock Price Reaction to Forecast Revisions, in: Review of Accounting Studies, 5 (3), p. 259-272.

Parker, J. E. (1975): Testing Comparability and Objectivity of Exit Value Accounting, in: Accounting Review, 50 (3), p. 512-524.

Patton, A. J./Timmermann, A. (2010): Why do forecasters disagree? Lessons from the term structure of cross-sectional dispersion, in: Journal of Monetary Economics, 57 (7), p. 803-820.

Peek, E. (2005): The influence of accounting changes on financial analysts' forecast accuracy and forecasting superiority: Evidence from the Netherlands, in: European Accounting Review, 14 (2), p. 261-295.

Pellens, B./Fülbier, R. U./Gassen, J./Sellhorn, T. (2011): Internationale Rechnungslegung – IFRS 1 bis 9, IAS 1 bis 41, IFRIC-Interpretationen, Standardentwürfe, 8th ed., Stuttgart 2011.

Peng, S./Bewley, K. (2010): Adaptability to fair value accounting in an emerging economy, in: Accounting, Auditing & Accountability Journal, 23 (8), p. 982-1011.

Penman, S. H. (2007a): Financial reporting quality: is fair value a plus or a minus?, in: Accounting & Business Research (Special Issue), p. 33-43.

Penman, S. H. (2007b): Financial statement analysis and security valuation, Boston 2007.

Perridon, L./Steiner, M. (2009): Finanzwirtschaft der Unternehmung, 15th ed., München 2009.

Petroni, K. R./Wahlen, J. M. (1995): Fair Values of Equity and Debt Securities and Share Prices of Property-liability Insurers, in: Journal of Risk & Insurance, 62 (4), p. 719-737.

Pietzsch, L. (2004): Bestimmungsfaktoren der Analysten-Coverage – Eine empirische Analyse für den deutschen Kapitalmarkt, Diss., Bad Soden am Taunus 2004.

Pike, R./Meerjanssen, J./Chadwick, L. (1993): The Appraisal of Ordinary Shares by Investment Analysts in the UK and Germany, in: Accounting & Business Research, 23 (92), p. 489-499.

Piotroski, J. D./Srinivasan, S. (2008): Regulation and Bonding: The Sarbanes-Oxley Act and the Flow of International Listings, in: Journal of Accounting Research, 46 (2), p. 383-425.

Plantin, G./Sapra, H./Shin, H. S. (2004): Fair Value Reporting Standards and Market Volatility, in: Shin, H. Song (ed.): Derivatives Accounting and Risk Management. Key Concepts and the Impact of IAS 39, London 2004, p. 145-156.

Popper, K. R. (1935): Logik der Forschung – Zur Erkenntnistheorie der modernen Naturwissenschaft, Wien 1935.

Popper, K. R. (2002): The logic of scientific discovery, London 2002.

Porák, V./Achleitner, A.-K./Fieseler, C./Groth, T. (2007): Finanzkommunikation – Die Grundlagen der Investor Relations, in: Schmid, B./Lyczek, B. (eds.): Unternehmenskommunikation. Kommunikationsmanagement aus Sicht der Unternehmensführung, 1st ed., Wiesbaden 2007, p. 257-283.

Poser, H. (2006): Wissenschaftstheorie – Eine philosophische Einführung, Stuttgart 2006.

Pozen, R. C. (2009): Is It Fair to Blame Fair Value Accounting for the Financial Crisis?, in: Harvard Business Review, 87 (11), p. 85-92.

Previts, G. J./Bricker, R. J./Robinson, T. R./Young, S. J. (1994): A Content Analysis of Sell-Side Financial Analyst Company Reports, in: Accounting Horizons, 8 (2), p. 55-70.

Pring, M. J. (1980): Technical analysis explained – An illustrated guide for the investor, New York 1980.

Q

Quagli, A./Avallone, F. (2010): Fair Value or Cost Model? Drivers of Choice for IAS 40 in Real Estate Industry, in: European Accounting Review, 19 (3), p. 461-494.

R

Rack, O./Christophersen (2009): Experimente, in: Albers, S./Klapper, D./Konradt, U./Walter, A./Wolf, J. (eds.): Methodik der empirischen Forschung, 3rd ed., Wiesbaden 2009, p. 17-32.

Raffée, H./Abel, B. (1979): Wissenschaftstheoretische Grundfragen der Wirtschaftswissenschaften, München 1979.

Ramakrishnan, R. T. S./Thakor, A. V. (1984): Information Reliability and a Theory of Financial Intermediation, in: Review of Economic Studies, 51 (166), p. 415.

Ramanna, K. **(2008):** The implications of unverifiable fair-value accounting: Evidence from the political economy of goodwill accounting, in: Journal of Accounting and Economics, 45 (2-3), p. 253-281.

Ramanna, K./Watts, R. L. **(2007):** Evidence on the Effects of Unverifiable Fair-Value Accounting, Working Paper 08-014.

Ramnath, S./Rock, S./Shane, P. **(2008):** The financial analyst forecasting literature: A taxonomy with suggestions for further research, in: International Journal of Forecasting, 24 (1), p. 34-75.

Ranker, D. **(2006):** Immobilienbewertung nach HGB und IFRS – Auslegung, Konzeption und Einzelfragen der Bilanzierung des Anlagevermögens, Diss., Berlin 2006.

Regan, P. J. **(1980):** The Effect of Society Presentations on Stock Prices, in: Financial Analysts Journal, 36 (3), p. 14-39.

Regan, P. J. **(1993):** Analyst, Analyze Thyself, in: Financial Analysts Journal, 49 (4), p. 10.

Richard, J. **(2004):** The Secret Past of Fair Value: Lessons from History Applied to the French Case, in: Accounting in Europe, 1 (1), p. 95-107.

Richter, R./Furubotn, E. G. **(2003):** Neue Institutionenökonomik – Eine Einführung und kritische Würdigung, Tübingen 2003.

Robinson, D./Burton, D. **(2004):** Discretion in Financial Reporting: The Voluntary Adoption of Fair Value Accounting for Employee Stock Options, in: Accounting Horizons, 18 (2), p. 97-108.

Röckemann, C. **(1995):** Börsendienste und Anlegerverhalten – Ein empirischer Beitrag zum noise trading, Diss., Wiesbaden 1995.

Roll, R. **(1984):** Orange Juice and Weather, in: The American Economic Review, 74 (5), p. 861-880.

Rosenbaum, P. R./Rubin, D. B. **(1983):** The central role of the propensity score in observational studies for causal effects, in: Biometrika, 70 (1), p. 41-55.

Roulstone, D. T. **(2003):** Analyst Following and Market Liquidity, in: Contemporary Accounting Research, 20 (3), p. 551-578.

Rubin, D. B. **(1973):** Matching to Remove Bias in Observational Studies, in: Biometrics, 29 (1), p. 159-183.

S

Sami, H./Schwartz, B. N. (1992): Alternative Pension Liability Disclosure and the Effect on Credit Evaluation: An Experiment, in: Behavioral Research in Accounting, 4 (3), p. 49-62.

Sanbonmatsu, D. M./Kardes, F. R./Posavac, S. S./Houghton, D. C. (1997): Contextual Influences on Judgment Based on Limited Information, in: Organizational Behavior and Human Decision Processes, 69 (3), p. 251-264.

Sapusek, A. (1998): Informationseffizienz auf Kapitalmärkten – Konzepte und empirische Ergebnisse, Wiesbaden 1998.

Sarris, V. (1990): Methodologische Grundlagen der Experimentalpsychologie: Erkenntnisgewinnung und Methodik der experimentellen Psychologie, München 1990.

Scharfstein, D. S./Stein, J. C. (1990): Herd Behavior and Investment, in: American Economic Review, 80 (3), p. 465-479.

Schildbach, T. (1998): Zeitwertbilanzierung in USA und nach IAS, in: Betriebswirtschaftliche Forschung und Praxis, 50 (5), p. 580-592.

Schipper, K. (1991): Commentary on Analysts' Forecasts, in: Accounting Horizons, 5 (4), p. 105-121.

Schipper, K. (2005): The introduction of International Accounting Standards in Europe: Implications for international convergence, in: European Accounting Review, 14 (1), p. 101-126.

Schipper, K. (2007): Required Disclosures in Financial Reports, in: Accounting Review, 82 (2), p. 301-326.

Schmidt, M./Seidel, T. (2006): Planmäßige Abschreibungen im Rahmen der Neubewertung des Sachanlagevermögens gemäß IAS 16: Fehlende Systematik und Verstoß gegen das Kongruenzprinzip, in: Betriebs-Berater, 61 (11), p. 596-602.

Schmidt, R. H. (1981): Ein neo-institutionalistischer Ansatz der Finanzierungstheorie, in: Rühli, E. (ed.): Unternehmensführung aus finanz- und bankwirtschaftlicher Sicht, Stuttgart 1981, p. 135-154.

Schmidt, R. H. (1982): Rechnungslegung als Informationsproduktion auf nahezu effizienten Kapitalmärkten, in: Schmalenbachs Zeitschrift für betriebswirtschaftliche Forschung, 34 , p. 728-748.

Schmidt, R. H./Terberger, E. (2006): Grundzüge der Investitions- und Finanzierungstheorie, 4th ed., Wiesbaden 2006.

Schneider, D. (1995): Betriebswirtschaftslehre Band 1: Grundlagen, München/Wien 1995.

Scholtens, L. J. R. (1993): On the Foundations of Financial Intermediation: A Review of the Literature, in: Kredit und Kapital, 26 (1), p. 112-141.

Schroeder, R. G./Clark, M. (1998): Accounting Theory – Text and readings, 6th ed., New York 1998.

Schroeder, R. G./Clark, M. W./Cathey, J. M. (2008): Financial Accounting Theory and Analysis – Text and Cases, New York 2008.

Schurz, G. (2006): Einführung in die Wissenschaftstheorie, Darmstadt 2006.

Scott, M. C. (2005): Achieving fair value – How companies can better manage their relationships with investors, Chichester 2005.

Shadish, W. R./Cook, T. D./Campbell, D. T. (2002): Experimental and Quasi-Experimental Designs for Generalized Causal Inference, Boston, Mass. 2002.

Sharpe, I. G./Walker, R. G. (1975): Asset Revaluations and Stock Market Prices, in: Journal of Accounting Research, 13 (2), p. 293-310.

Sharpe, W. F. (1964): Capital Asset Prices: A Theory of Market Equilibrium Under Conditions of Risk, in: Journal of Finance, 19 (3), p. 425-442.

Shiller, R. J. (1984): Stock Prices and Social Dynamics, in: Brookings Papers on Economic Activity (2), p. 457-498.

Shim, E./Larkin, J. M. (1998): Towards Relevancy in Financial Reporting: Mark-to-Market Accounting, in: Journal of Applied Business Research, 14 (2), p. 33-42.

Siegel, A. F. (2012): Practical business statistics, 6th ed., Boston 2012.

Simko, P. J. (1999): Financial Instrument Fair Values and Nonfinancial Firms, in: Journal of Accounting, Auditing & Finance, 14 (3), p. 247-274.

Skogsvik, K. (1990): Current Cost Accounting Ratios as Predictors of Business Failure: The Swedish Case, in: Journal of Business Finance & Accounting, 17 (1), p. 137-160.

Smith, M. (2003): Research Methods in Accounting, London 2003.

Song, C. J./Thomas, W. B./Han Yi (2010): Value Relevance of FAS No. 157 Fair Value Hierarchy Information and the Impact of Corporate Governance Mechanisms, in: Accounting Review, 85 (4), p. 1375-1410.

Spector, S. (2009): Fair Value Measurement: An IASB project aimed at clarifying the definition of fair value, in: CGA Magazine, 43 (6), p. 52-53.

Spector, S. (2010): IFRS 9: Financial Instruments – A closer look at upcoming IASB changes, in: CGA Magazine, 44 (2), p 36-37.

Spence, M. (1973): Job Market Signaling, in: The Quarterly Journal of Economics, 87 (3), p. 355-374.

Stangor, C. (2011): Research Methods for the Behavioral Sciences, 4th ed., Australia, Belmont CA 2011.

Stanzel, M. (2007): Qualität des Aktienresearchs von Finanzanalysten – Eine theoretische und empirische Untersuchung der Gewinnprognosen und Aktienempfehlungen am deutschen Kapitalmarkt, Wiesbaden 2007.

Steiner, M./Bruns, C. (2002): Wertpapiermanagement – Professionelle Wertpapieranalyse und Portfoliostrukturierung, 8th ed., Stuttgart 2002.

Steiner, P./Uhlir, H. (2001): Wertpapieranalyse – Mit 28 Tabellen und 52 Beispielen, Heidelberg 2001.

Sterzel, J. (2011): Bewertungs- und Entscheidungsrelevanz der Humankapital-berichterstattung – Eine experimentelle Analyse aus der Perspektive privater Anleger, Wiesbaden 2011.

Stickel, S. E. (1995): The Anatomy of the Performance of Buy and Sell Recommendations, in: Financial Analysts Journal, 51 (5), p. 25-39.

Stier, W. (1999): Empirische Forschungsmethoden, 2nd ed., Berlin 1999.

Stiglitz, J. E. (1975): The Theory of "Screening", Education, and the Distribution of Income, in: American Economic Review, 65 (3), p. 283-300.

Strausz, R. (1997): Delegation of Monitoring in a Principal-Agent Relationship, in: Review of Economic Studies, 64 (3), p. 337-357.

Stubenrath, M. (2001): Kommunikation auf internationalen Kapitalmärkten – Eine informationsökonomische Analyse unter besonderer Berücksichtigung international heterogener Jahresabschlüsse, Diss., Lohmar 2001.

Süchting, J. (1995): Finanzmanagement – Theorie und Politik der Unternehmensfinanzierung, Wiesbaden 1995.

Sundaram, S./Ogden, W. A., JR./Walker, M. C. (1993): Wealth Effects of Corporate Presentations to the New York Society of Security Analysts, in: Financial Analysts Journal, 49 (2), p. 88-89.

T

Tanski, J. S. (2005): Sachanlagen nach IFRS – Bewertung, Bilanzierung und Berichterstattung, München 2005.

Thinggaard, F. (1996): Mark-to-market accounting, hedge accounting or historical cost accounting for derivative financial instruments? A survey of financial analysts in Denmark, in: European Accounting Review, 5 (1), p. 57-75.

Thomas, J. E./Wilson, B. M. (2005): The Indemnity Principle: Evolution from a Financial to a Functional Paradigm, in: Journal of Risk Management & Insurance, 10 (30), p. 1-16.

Tiemann, K. (1997): Investor Relations – Bedeutung für neu am Kapitalmarkt eingeführte Publikumsgesellschaften, Diss., Wiesbaden 1997.

Tinic, S. M. (1990): A Perspective on the Stock Market's Fixation on Accounting Numbers, in: Accounting Review, 65 (4), p. 781-796.

Trueman, B. (1994): Analyst forecasts and herding behavior, in: Review of Financial Studies, 7 (1), p. 97-124.

U

Ulrich, P./Hill, W. (1976a): Wissenschaftstheoretische Grundlagen der Betriebswirtschaftslehre (Teil I), in: Wirtschaftswissenschaftliches Studium, 5 (7), p. 304-309.

Ulrich, P./Hill, W. (1976b): Wissenschaftstheoretische Grundlagen der Betriebswirtschaftslehre (Teil II), in: Wirtschaftswissenschaftliches Studium, 5 (8), p. 345-350.

V

Vanstraelen, A./Zarzeski, M. T./Robb, S. W. G. (2003): Corporate Nonfinancial Disclosure Practices and Financial Analyst Forecast Ability Across Three European Countries, in: Journal of International Financial Management & Accounting, 14 (3), p. 249-278.

Venkatachalam, M. (1996): Value-relevance of banks' derivatives disclosures, in: Journal of Accounting and Economics, 22 (1-3), p. 327-355.

Ventolo, W. L./Williams, M. R. (2001): Fundamentals of Real Estate Appraisal, 8th ed., Chicago IL 2001.

Vergoossen, R. G. A. (1993): The use and perceived importance of annual reports by investment analysts in the Netherlands, in: European Accounting Review, 2 (2), p. 219-243.

Verse, D. A. (2006): Der Gleichbehandlungsgrundsatz im Recht der Kapitalgesellschaften, Tübingen 2006.

Viger, C./Belzile, R./Anandarajan, A. A. (2008): Disclosure versus Recognition of Stock Option Compensation: Effect on the Credit Decisions of Loan Officers, in: Behavioral Research in Accounting, 20 (1), p. 93-113.

Vollmer, R. (2008): Rechnungslegung auf informationseffizienten Kapitalmärkten, Wiesbaden 2008.

Vorstius, S. (2004): Wertrelevanz von Jahresabschlussdaten – Eine theoretische und empirische Betrachtung von Wertrelevanz im Zeitverlauf in Deutschland, Wiesbaden 2004.

W

Wagenhofer, A. (1990): Informationspolitik im Jahresabschluß – Freiwillige Informationen und strategische Bilanzanalyse, Heidelberg 1990.

Wahlen, J. M. (1994): The Nature of Information in Commercial Bank Loan Loss Disclosures, in: Accounting Review, 69 (3), p. 455-478.

Wallace, M. (2006): The Problem with Current Accounting: A Critique of SFAS 115 and SFAS 133 Using an Equity-Indexed Annuity Example, in: North American Actuarial Journal, 10 (1), p. 11-29.

Wallace, M. (2009): Is Fair-Value Accounting Responsible for the Financial Crisis?, in: Bank Accounting & Finance, 22 (1), p. 9-18.

Wang, X. (2010): Performance analysis for public and nonprofit organizations, Sudbury, Mass. 2010.

Watrin, C./Strohm, C. (2006): Principles-Based Accounting Standards – Paradigmenwechsel der US-Rechnungslegung?, in: Zeitschrift für internationale und kapitalmarktorientierte Rechnungslegung, 6 (2), p. 123-127.

Watrin, C./Strohm, C./Struffert, R. (2006): The Joint Business Combinations Project – IFRS 3 and the Project's Impact on Convergence with U.S. GAAP, in: CPA Journal, 76 (1), p. 22-25.

Watts, R. L. (2006): What has the invisible hand achieved?, in: Accounting & Business Research, 36 (International Accounting Policy Forum), p. 51-61.

Weber, M. (2006): Die Haftung des Analysten für fehlerhafte Wertpapieranalysen, Diss., 1st ed., Lohmar 2006.

Webster, M./Sell, J. (2007): Laboratory Experiments in the Social Sciences, Amsterdam 2007.

Whittington, G. (2008): Fair Value and the IASB/FASB Conceptual Framework Project: An Alternative View, in: Abacus, 44 (2), p. 139-168.

Wichels, D. (2002): Gestaltung der Kapitalmarktkommunikation mit Finanzanalysten – Eine empirische Untersuchung zum Informationsbedarf von Finanzanalysten in der Automobilindustrie, Diss., 1st ed., Wiesbaden 2002.

Wier, H. A. (2009): Fair Value or Conservatism: The Case of the Gold Industry, in: Contemporary Accounting Research, 26 (4), p. 1207-1233.

Williams, T. P. (2004): Base Adjusting in the Sales Comparison Approach, in: Appraisal Journal, 72 (2), p. 155-162.

Winchel, J. L. (2008): An Examination of Persuasive Financial Communications, University of Texas at Austin 2008.

Without Author (2011): Differences-in-Differences and A Brief Introduction to Panel Data, available at: http://econ.lse.ac.uk/~amanning/courses/ec406/ec406_DinDPanel.pdf, last revised 05.12.2011.

Wobbe, C. (2008): IFRS: Sachanlagen und Leasing: Ansatz-, Bewertungs- und Ausweismöglichkeiten, Berlin 2008.

Wohlgemuth, M./Radde, J. (2000): Der Bewertungsmaßstab "Anschaffungskosten" nach HGB und IAS – Darstellung der Besonderheiten und kritische Gegenüberstellung, in: Die Wirtschaftsprüfung, 53 (18), p. 903-911.

Womack, K. L. (1996): Do Brokerage Analysts' Recommendations Have Investment Value?, in: Journal of Finance, 51 (1), p. 137-167.

Wooldridge, J. M. (2009): Introductory econometrics – A modern approach, 4th ed., Mason, Ohio 2009.

Y

Yu, M. (2010): Analyst forecast properties, analyst following and governance disclosures: A global perspective, in: Journal of International Accounting, Auditing and Taxation, 19 (1), p. 1-15.

Z

Zaugg, D./Krämer, C./Meyer, T. (2009): Bilanzierung von Renditeliegenschaften im Bau – Stand der Umsetzung in der Praxis?, in: Zeitschrift für Internationale Rechnungslegung, 4 (12), p. 531-538.

Zülch, H. (2003): Die Bilanzierung von Investment Properties nach IAS 40, Diss., Düsseldorf 2003.

Zülch, H./Gebhardt, R. (2007): SFAS 157 und IASB Discussion Paper – aktuelle Entwicklungen auf dem Gebiet der Fair-Value-Bewertung, in: Betriebs-Berater, 62 (3), p. 147-152.

Münsteraner Schriften zur Internationalen Unternehmensrechnung

Herausgegeben von Peter Kajüter

www.peterlang.de